PRIESTS OF PROSPERITY

A volume in the series
Cornell Studies in Money
edited by Eric Helleiner and Jonathan Kirshner

A list of titles in this series is available at
www.cornellpress.cornell.edu

PRIESTS OF PROSPERITY

How Central Bankers Transformed the
Postcommunist World

Juliet Johnson

CORNELL UNIVERSITY PRESS **ITHACA AND LONDON**

First published 2016 by Cornell University Press
First paperback printing 2019

Library of Congress Cataloging-in-Publication Data

Johnson, Juliet, 1968– author.
  Priests of prosperity : how central bankers transformed the postcommunist world / Juliet Johnson.
    pages cm
  Includes bibliographical references and index.
  ISBN 978-1-5017-0022-4 (cloth)
  ISBN 978-1-5017-4682-6 (pbk.)
  1. Banks and banking, Central—Former Soviet republics. 2. Banks and banking, Central—Former communist countries. 3. Former Soviet republics—Economic policy. 4. Former communist countries—Economic policy. 5. Post-communism—Economic aspects. I. Title.
  HG3126 .J65 2016
  332.1′1—dc23   2015034169

Contents

Preface

Ulan Sarbanov never planned to become a central banker. But while working in Russia in 1993, the bright young economist from Kyrgyzstan received a summons from his country's Supreme Council. Would he return home to take a position at the National Bank of the Kyrgyz Republic (NBKR)? The NBKR, until recently a mere branch office of the Soviet central bank, had few qualified staff members and faced comprehensive restructuring. Sarbanov agreed, and as an NBKR economist worked to help his new country successfully introduce its own currency, the som. Then, in 1998, the Russian financial crisis hit neighboring Kyrgyzstan hard. In the resulting government shake-up, Sarbanov agreed to become deputy minister of finance. Shortly after Sarbanov had moved to the Finance Ministry, Kyrgyz president Askar Akayev called Sarbanov to his office. Sarbanov, mystified and somewhat awed by the prospect of meeting the president, found himself in a two-hour conversation with Akayev in which the president warned him of the corrupting influence of "big money." Akayev then told him that in one hour, Sarbanov would be introduced as the next governor of the NBKR. At that time, Sarbanov was thirty-one years old.[1]

Soviet-era central banks played a lowly role in the region's command economies, serving as accountants and cash cows for governments and state-owned enterprises. After the fall of the Berlin Wall, thousands of central bankers in East Central Europe, the Balkans, and the former Soviet Union found themselves in positions not unlike Ulan Sarbanov's. Fresh out of university or with practical experience only in the financial systems of planned economies, these men and women faced the daunting task of completely reshaping—and in some cases creating from scratch—central banks capable of controlling inflation, managing payment systems, and regulating unruly new commercial banks. As if that were not enough, most also needed to shepherd central banking laws through their legislatures and introduce new currencies to replace their old Soviet-era monies. The challenge seemed overwhelming. Yet by the mid-1990s, the postcommunist region boasted the world's most legally independent central banks. Even more astonishing, by the turn of the twenty-first century all but the most repressive postcommunist states had reasonably professional and technically proficient

---

1. Author's interview with Ulan Sarbanov, governor of the National Bank of the Kyrgyz Republic, Bishkek, Kyrgyzstan, June 2001.

central banks, as well as central bankers who had adopted prevailing international norms.

How and why did this remarkable transformation occur? Conventional wisdom holds that it happened because of the need to attract foreign investors, coercion by powerful states, or the desire to imitate Western institutions. Although each explanation contains its grain of truth, none is adequate. International incentives, pressures, and ideas may have inspired postcommunist states, but incentives, pressures, and ideas alone could not rapidly craft complex institutions or create expertise where it did not previously exist.

Instead, I argue that the transnational central banking community actively guided the transformation of postcommunist central banks. As communist regimes began collapsing in 1989, influential central bankers in the advanced industrial democracies and their allies in the International Monetary Fund (IMF) came face to face with the unprecedented opportunity to introduce their own central banking model to a region where the existing economic order had been delegitimized and where leaders sought new ways to organize and stabilize their countries' financial systems. This central banking community devoted millions of dollars and hours to lobbying, training, and technical assistance in the postcommunist world. Experienced central bankers introduced their new postcommunist colleagues to the community, persuaded them to adopt the community's principles and practices, and led hands-on efforts to help them develop the tools of modern central banking. This deliberate effort is critical to understanding postcommunist central bank development, and indeed processes of financial globalization more broadly. Central bankers like Ulan Sarbanov worked hard to transform their institutions, but crucially, they did not labor alone.

Postcommunist central bankers could not have wished for better partners. The transnational central banking community had reached a new peak of cohesiveness and influence in the 1990s. Its cohesiveness came from its shared principles and practices, its unique professional culture, its extensive transnational infrastructure, and its relative insularity. By this time central bankers had widely embraced the twin operating principles of price stability and political independence, as well as a range of complementary practices based on these principles. Central bankers shared a quasi-religious professional culture demanding fluency in both English and economics. They met and worked together through organizations such as the IMF, the Bank for International Settlements (BIS), and eventually the European Central Bank (ECB). Their close relationships, legal autonomy, and seemingly arcane expertise created a highly insular community. The community exemplified what I will call a wormhole network, a narrowly bounded identity group whose close internal connections transcend geographic distance. Taken together, these characteristics meant that central bankers often had more in common with their professional compatriots abroad than with other government officials in their own countries.

The community's international influence stemmed in part from this cohesiveness and drew on substantial ideational, material, and organizational resources. The community held a monopoly on recognized central banking expertise in the advanced industrial democracies. It possessed extensive financial means, plentiful personnel, and the support of powerful states. It had previously developed training and technical assistance programs and had worked together across borders to deliver them. Although the community's efforts dovetailed with the broader promotion of Washington Consensus free-market economic ideas, institutions, and practices to the postcommunist world, no other reform proposal had such powerful, organized promoters or such a universally accepted model as did the independent central bank focused on price stability. The confluence of this single compelling concept, a cohesive and influential international community devoted to promoting it, and the collapse of Soviet-era economic institutions opened a window of opportunity for transplanting the community's central banking model into the postcommunist world.

Such transplantation takes place in three stages: choice, transformation, and internalization. Choice refers to the initial governmental decision to enshrine central bank independence into law, transformation refers to the change process within the central bank itself, and internalization refers to embedding the transformed central bank into its broader domestic environment. In the choice stage, postcommunist governments all passed legislation granting greater political independence to their central banks. While the transnational central banking community played an important role as lobbyists and inspiration in this stage, the governments making this choice were indeed driven primarily by a desire to emulate Western-ness, bolster their sovereignty, and attract foreign capital. Most studies examining the spread of Western-style central banking to the postcommunist world focus on this initial choice.

The transnational central banking community came into its own in the transformation stage. It developed a simplified and flexible "export model" of central bank principles and practices, it had significant access to postcommunist central bankers, and it gave relatively consistent, intensive advice and assistance to postcommunist central banks (the sole exception, albeit a crucial one, was in the area of banking supervision). The community provided social and material incentives for postcommunist central bankers to accept its model and mind-set as well.

West Europeans played the most important role in this transformation campaign, although central bankers from other advanced industrial democracies also participated intensively. West Europeans took the lead in solidifying institutional connections among central banks in the advanced industrial democracies, in codifying international central banking standards, and in promoting central bank independence and the pursuit of price stability (principles that had first acquired international legitimacy through the Deutsche Bundesbank). West European central banks and West Europeans in the IMF and BIS organized and carried out much of the training and technical assistance programs for postcommunist central bankers. Western Europe also hosted the community's two most influential new training centers, the Bank of England's Centre for Central Banking Studies and the Joint Vienna Institute. Moreover, the attraction and requirements of European Union membership—with its monetary policies and institutions designed by West European central bankers—helped to deepen central bank transformation in aspiring and new-member states.

In the end, with the help of the transnational central banking community most postcommunist central banks and bankers adopted the community's core principles and practices. This remarkably successful transformation stands in sharp contrast to the results of most other international institution-building programs in the postcommunist world.[2] But on a deeper level, we must examine the meaning of success. There is no denying that newly influential, more professional, and more technically skilled central banks benefited postcommunist states. Without the active guidance of the transnational central banking community, creating such institutions would have taken far more time and effort, and with far less certain results. But relying too heavily on the core principles of political independence and price stability led the community to commit two sins in the transformation stage, one of commission and one of omission.

The sin of commission was overemphasizing independence when simplifying the central banking model for export. Many postcommunist central bankers embraced a caricatured understanding of central bank independence as a result. Zealous central bankers at times refused to cooperate with their governments and finance ministries to such an extent that monetary and fiscal policies pulled strongly in opposing directions, often to the detriment of economic stability and ultimately central bank independence itself. The emphasis on central bank independence in uncertain, unstable transitional environments also implicitly made postcommunist central bankers responsible for economic outcomes not truly under their control.

The sin of omission was the relative neglect of banking supervision. Established central bankers preferred to focus on price stability and monetary policy, and unlike in other realms did not share common views on how (or even whether) central banks should oversee commercial ones. As a result, advice and

---

2. Wedel 1998, Cooley 2000, Mendelson 2001, Henderson 2002, Barnes 2006, Bosin 2012.

assistance in banking supervision—and in pursuing financial stability more broadly—proved inconsistent, inadequate, and badly coordinated. Systemic financial crises in 1997–98 and then, more dramatically, in 2007–8 revealed the consequences of poorly regulated financial sectors and forced central bankers and governments worldwide to reconsider the prevailing intellectual consensus that central banks should narrowly focus on pursuing price stability.

These issues and more revealed themselves in the internalization stage of the transplantation process. While the transnational central banking community successfully worked to transform postcommunist central banks, it could do little to help embed them into their own societies. Established and postcommunist central bankers mutually reinforced the community's shared principles and practices through regular, intensive interactions—what I call the wormhole effect—making them virtual colleagues rather than distant foreign officials. But postcommunist politicians, commercial bankers, and publics were left out of this socialization process. Therefore, rather than embracing the central bankers' worldview, many governments that had initially supported independent central banks as symbols of national sovereignty and international respectability later balked at the concrete implications of tighter monetary policies and financial-sector regulation.

In fact, the very speed and effectiveness of the central bank transformation campaign could ironically hinder its long-term sustainability. The pace of change within central banks often outstripped that of other complementary government and economic institutions. Underdeveloped domestic financial markets responded unevenly to central bank signals, rendering monetary policies less effective. Many governments blamed their central banks for banking and currency crises, and repeatedly challenged their policies and independence. In the face of such threats, postcommunist central bankers turned to their international allies for assistance. When that help was effective, it exacerbated the wormhole effect; postcommunist central bankers' links with the transnational community strengthened while domestic critics came to see their central banks not as symbols of sovereignty but as agents of globalization. When that help was ineffective, many postcommunist central bankers, particularly more orthodox ones, lost influence domestically and their central banks grew less independent in practice.

As Ulan Sarbanov discovered, central bank transformation under especially inauspicious conditions could provide government officials a convenient scapegoat for political and economic disasters of their own making. In September 2005, after the fall of the Akayev government, Sarbanov found himself accused of corruption and placed under house arrest. One influential voice in the central banking community wrote at the time that "Ulan Sarbanov is an outstanding, modernizing central banker who has done his best to bring 'best practice' in central banking systems and techniques to the Central Bank of the Kyrgyz Republic and to his country . . . the world's central bankers should come to Sarbanov's assistance."[3] Politics, however, won out in the end. Although eventually acquitted of all charges, Sarbanov was forced to step down as NBKR governor. By the time of the 2007–8 global financial crisis, the NBKR was the world's most independent central bank in law and yet highly compromised in practice. After further political upheaval in 2010 the new NBKR governor asked Sarbanov to return as his advisor, but much time and energy had been lost.

This book draws on over 160 interviews in seventeen countries conducted primarily between February 2000 and August 2014 with central bankers, international assistance providers, policy makers, and commercial bankers in the postcommunist region, Western Europe, and North America to tell the story of the campaign to transplant a widely embraced international model of central banking to the postcommunist world. While I reflect on experiences from across the region, I engage in closer examinations of central bank development in five countries: Hungary, the Czech and Slovak Republics, Russia, and Kyrgyzstan. These countries, taken together, represented the range of postcommunist central banks to which the transnational central banking community had early and regular access.

Hungary began the postcommunist era with a distinct head start. Its hybrid goulash communism meant that it had already joined the IMF and had significant exposure to Western economic ideas and practices by 1989. When Czechoslovakia broke up in 1993, the Czech National Bank walked away with the governor and headquarters staff of the State Bank of Czechoslovakia, its facilities in Prague, and the lion's share of the country's best-educated economists. The National Bank of Slovakia, by contrast, had to be created almost entirely from scratch and under initially difficult political conditions. Yet the Slovaks largely caught up with and in certain respects later even surpassed their Czech brethren. Russia's great-power heritage, vast size, and complex economy presented a unique challenge. Although open to international contact, the Central Bank of the Russian Federation (Bank of Russia) insisted on engaging the transnational central banking community on its own terms and as an equal. Finally, Kyrgyzstan was the poorest and most financially isolated postcommunist state to open itself fully to the transnational central banking community.

Chapter 1 explains why and how central bankers in the advanced industrial democracies formed a cohesive community championing price stability and political independence in the 1990s. Chapter 2 examines the art of transplantation, taking

---

3. Quoted in "Sarbanov Should Be Supported," *Central Banking*, September 12, 2005, http://subscription.centralbanknews.com/item.asp?itemid=22990.

an innovation from one context and introducing it into another. It describes both the community's export model of central banking and the three stages of the transplantation process. Subsequent chapters place empirical meat on these theoretical bones, discussing each stage of central bank transplantation in the postcommunist world and moving from the collapse of communism to the global financial crisis of 2007–8. Chapter 3 focuses on postcommunist governments' initial choice to adopt legislation granting independence to their central banks, examining both the universal embrace of such legislation and the specific cases of Hungary, Czechoslovakia and its successor states, the Soviet Union/Russia, and Kyrgyzstan. Chapter 4 presents an overview of the transformation stage. It describes the coordination and evolution of the transnational central banking community's training and technical assistance programs and explores the campaign's overall effects in postcommunist states. Chapter 5 analyzes the Hungarian, Czech, and Slovak central banks in depth, charting their extensive transformations and surprising difficulties with internalization in the context of the European integration process. Chapter 6 moves to less hospitable soil, that of Russia and Kyrgyzstan. It explores the intensive transformation of the Bank of Russia and the NBKR, and then demonstrates how increasingly authoritarian and economically challenging domestic circumstances repeatedly undermined them. Chapter 7 views the entire transplantation experience through the lens of the global financial crisis, which fundamentally challenged the central banking model that the transnational community had just spent two decades intensively promoting to the postcommunist world.

While the intellectual and political ground is shifting for central banks everywhere, the institutional legacies of that initial moment of euphoric unity remain. For postcommunist countries the legacies lay within their central banks' norms, practices, and organizational structures, as well as in legal codes and constitutions that reflected the central banking model of the 1990s. For the world as a whole, the international financial system that supported this model—a system in which the postcommunist world became deeply intertwined—still stands, albeit shakily, as a monument to this once near-universally compelling vision of monetary order.

Notes on Nomenclature

I include diacriticals in Czech, Hungarian, and Slovak names appearing in the text. In the notes and bibliography I list names as presented in the original source material, whether with or without diacriticals.

Translations of quotations and references from Hungarian are by Dóra Piroska, translations from Czech are by the author or Victor Gomez, and translations from Russian are by the author or Baktygul Aliev.

I use the Modified Library of Congress system for Russian transliterations, with exceptions for well-known figures with names commonly spelled otherwise in English such as Yeltsin, Akayev, or Nazarbayev.

When referring to individual central banks I use the full name and the acronym that the bank itself prefers in its English-language materials. Therefore, for example, I refer to the Magyar Nemzeti Bank (MNB), but the Czech National Bank (CNB). The Bank of Russia has used multiple names and acronyms in the past, but seems to have settled on Central Bank of the Russian Federation (Bank of Russia), so I have adopted that usage. Similarly, I refer to a bank's leader by the English title the bank itself uses, such as governor, director, president, or chairman. When I refer to central bank leaders collectively or when a central bank's own naming practice is inconsistent over time I use governor as the default term.

With the exception of central bank governors and selected others whose personal biographies are key to the narrative, I have redacted the names and specific professional titles of interviewees. Most interviewees consented to be recorded; for others, I took detailed handwritten notes and transcribed them afterwards. Interviews took place primarily in English, but also in Russian and French. I retain the recordings, notes, and transcripts. I conducted all interviews personally with the exception of the April 2006 interviews at the Banque de France (by Jessica Fortin) and the August 2007 follow-up interview with Ulan Sarbanov (by Baktygul Aliev). I conducted the June 2014 interviews in conjunction with Cornel Ban and Len Seabrooke.

PRIESTS OF PROSPERITY

E PLURIBUS UNUM

"The community of central bankers transcends every political form of government."

—Senior vice president, Federal Reserve Bank of New York (2001)

The Hungarian central banker leaned in. He had something important to tell me. In mixed groups, he said, you can always spot the central bankers. "How? By their club ties and secret handshakes?" I asked jokingly. He laughed and replied that central bankers "use the same language, have the same culture. I mean, sometimes it's strange how central bankers think."[1] In conversation after conversation, central bankers from postcommunist countries told me that their compatriots around the world shared a bond, a unique set of concerns and priorities, and a similar way of thinking and acting. As newcomers to this community, they were particularly attuned to its norms and practices. Established central bankers, though more sensitive to the distinctions among individual personalities and institutions, concurred that central bankers had much in common.

Indeed, by the late 1980s central bankers across the advanced industrial democracies had come to form a cohesive transnational community. Its core institutional members included national central banks such as the Bank of England, the Deutsche Bundesbank, and the US Federal Reserve, as well as the Basel-based Bank for International Settlements and key departments within the International Monetary Fund. The subsequent establishment of the European Monetary Institute and its successor the European Central Bank, created through the joint efforts of West European central bankers, further consolidated this community. While central bankers had worked together on many occasions in decades past, they

---

1. Author's interview with a senior official in the Economics and Research Department of the Magyar Nemzeti Bank, Budapest, Hungary, March 2000.

achieved a qualitatively new level of collaboration in the 1990s. Convergences in economic theory and practice, technological advances easing international communications and travel, central bankers' increasing autonomy from their national governments, and the challenges of financial globalization all conspired to bring central bankers together intellectually and professionally as never before.

This community shared two key operational principles. Most fundamentally, central bankers came to agree that a central bank's primary task should be to maintain a low and stable inflation rate, which they referred to as price stability. Moreover, because policies aimed at achieving price stability could be politically contentious, central bankers further agreed that they needed significant independence from their governments in order to do their jobs properly. The community regularly celebrated and promoted these principles in multiple forums around the world. As a high-level IMF and former US Federal Reserve official told post-Soviet central bankers in 1994:

> Since the 1980s, there has been a convergence in thinking with respect to two ideas about central banking: first, that a central bank's main mission should be to pursue and maintain price stability as the best strategy for sustainable economic growth; and second, that to achieve its main objective, a central bank should be independent from political influences.[2]

Central bankers generally agreed that if independent central banks successfully pursued price stability, growth and employment would follow. Economic results seemed to prove the worth of the two principles, as the progressively wider adoption of laws guaranteeing central bank independence and central bank policies focused on price stability in the late 1980s and 1990s coincided with an era of low, stable inflation and steady output growth in the advanced industrial democracies. Even the US Federal Reserve, which had an unusual and politically sacrosanct dual legal mandate to pursue both price stability and maximum employment, in practice privileged its price stability objective during this period.[3] Central bankers

---

2. IMF deputy managing director Richard Erb, quoted in Zulu et al. 1994, 131.

3. As Vice President of the Federal Reserve Bank of St. Louis Daniel Thornton wrote, during this era "there appeared to be nearly unanimous agreement among [Federal Open Market] Committee members that price stability was the primary goal of policy, not for its own sake but because by pursuing this goal, policy makers simultaneously achieved the goal of maximum sustainable economic growth and consequently, maximum sustainable employment. Hence, the FOMC appears to believe it could achieve the employment aspect of [the] dual mandate by its price stability objective" (120–21). See Thornton 2012. Other central bankers took note of this as well. For example Athanasios Orphanides, MIT professor and governor of the Cypriot central bank from 2007 through 2012, said: "One might ask, how was policy practiced in the United States during the Volcker-Greenspan era, from 1979 on, a period that was very successful in achieving price stability. The answer is that looking back, both Chairmen Volcker and Greenspan effectively interpreted the legal mandate of the Fed as if it put price stability first. That is, the Fed was implicitly acting as an inflation targeting central bank." Orphanides 2013, 8.

called the halcyon years before the 2007–8 global financial crisis the Great Moderation, in capital letters. The Great Moderation raised central bankers' self-confidence
and governments' confidence in their central banks. This general agreement on
basic principles provided a powerful intellectual platform from which central bankers could work together and advance their shared interests.

At that same historical juncture, the Berlin Wall fell and the Soviet Union
imploded—and a moment of consensus met a window of opportunity. Central
banking as it had evolved in the Soviet bloc was unsuitable for managing market
economies and would need to adapt to the changing circumstances. The members of the transnational central banking community thus set out collectively and
individually to help the postcommunist countries create central banks molded
in their own image: independent, technocratic, respected anti-inflation warriors.

The Transnational Central Banking Community

Who were these "established central bankers"? The transnational central banking
community comprised far more than a handful of celebrity governors, although
one might not know it through reading popular accounts of central banking.
Although leadership and personalities are incontrovertibly important, like any
bureaucracy central banks have large professional staffs whose collective efforts
and expertise matter in policy formulation and implementation. Central bank
governors set the tone and general directions for their banks, but it is the staff
who develop the models, organize the data, crunch the numbers, arrange the
meetings, analyze the possibilities, and write the reports on which day-to-day
decisions and operations rest. Most important for our purposes, the expert staff
design and implement central bank training and technical assistance programs.
Governors may give grand speeches about central banks sharing knowledge and
practices with each other, but they would be the first to admit that dedicated
staff members did the real hands-on work. Therefore, understanding the community's character requires acknowledging the norms, practices, and hierarchies
that extended within and across central banks and their close institutional allies,
from the governors on down.

In doing so I focus on the four interlocking characteristics that made the
central banking community unusually cohesive at this historical juncture:
its widely shared principles and practices, its unique professional culture, its
transnational infrastructure, and its relative insulation from outsiders. These
characteristics yielded a particular kind of transnational community, one that
interacted, learned, and disseminated knowledge through what I call a *wormhole network*.

Wormhole

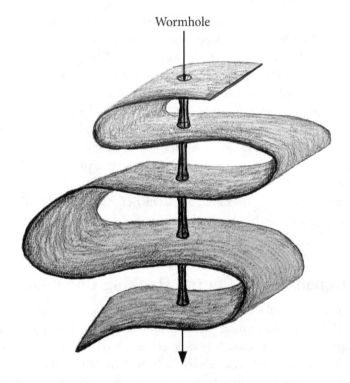

FIGURE 1.1   Artist's rendition of a wormhole. J. E. Theibert 2014.

In physics, a wormhole (or more formally, an Einstein-Rosen bridge) is a shortcut between two distant points in space-time, making otherwise faraway places immediately accessible to one another. Imagine drawing dots on either end of a piece of paper; normal travel between the two would require traversing the distance across the paper, but by folding the paper in half the dots meet instantly on top of one another. In essence, a wormhole is a bend forming a tunnel in space-time. I use the metaphorical phrase wormhole network to refer to interconnected "tunnels" of intense transnational interaction and cooperation among similar institutions and actors physically located in multiple countries—in this case, central banks and bankers.[4] Figure 1.1 illustrates a wormhole cutting through folds in space-time from what would otherwise be distant points to form such a tunnel.

---

4. In doing so, I echo Sheppard's (2002) use of the wormhole metaphor to describe the flexible geography of a globalized world. The transnational central banking community further confirms Djelic and Quack's insight that "territory and physical proximity are . . . neither necessary nor defining components of the concept of community" (Djelic and Quack 2010, 11).

Wormhole networks became possible in the digital age with the rise of sophisticated electronic communications technology and routinized international travel. A wormhole network entails constant transnational interaction, socialization, and ideological reinforcement within the network, but is thickly bounded to restrict access by outsiders. It is composed of individuals with similar professional training, worldviews, and work practices who interact regularly and cooperatively in formal and informal ways, maintain and create institutions to facilitate and reinforce this interaction, and share a distinct community identity that transcends state boundaries and is reflected in a shared mission, specialized discourse, and self-referential interaction pattern. The wormhole must be opened, purposefully maintained, and naturalized through extensive and focused community effort.

Figure 1.1 helps to visualize the simultaneously close yet internally hierarchical nature of the network. The most powerful and prestigious community members are metaphorically located at the entrance to the wormhole, while as one progresses further through it one finds the newer, follower, slightly more heterodox, and otherwise less core members. In that sense, there is a certain distance and differentiation within the community. Yet those distances pale beside the greater distance between the community members and outsiders. This has important governance ramifications. The socialization and communication across a wormhole network reinforces internal ties and encourages community members to feel closer to their transnational peers than to noncommunity actors within their own countries. That is, by enabling and privileging close transnational connections, a wormhole network simultaneously de-emphasizes or even degrades national ties. It is thus exceptionally well suited for facilitating community mobilization and for rapidly transmitting information and ideas within the network, but can make it more difficult for community members to interact effectively with nonmembers or to acknowledge and learn from conflicting views originating from outside the network. As a wormhole network, the transnational central banking community was both closely connected internally and relatively insulated externally. This represented a source of strength in its efforts to integrate postcommunist central bankers into the network, but a potential liability when the global financial crisis later challenged the community's fundamental principles and practices.

Principles and Practices

The community shared the interdependent principles of price stability and central bank independence, which in turn generated a range of corollary beliefs

and practices.[5] Price stability meant maintaining a stable and low rate of inflation, typically as measured by the consumer price index. As the BIS's Claudio
Borio put it in a retrospective on the Great Moderation era, "the prevailing pre-
crisis consensus had gravitated towards a 'narrow' view of central banking, heavily focused on price stability and supported by a belief in the self-equilibrating
properties of the economy."[6] Independence, in turn, allowed central bankers to
credibly commit to pursuing price stability because it would prevent politicians
from manipulating the money supply to boost their political fortunes.[7] Delegating authority over monetary policy to technocrats allowed a government to tie
its own hands for the greater economic good. In practice, granting independence
to a central bank meant passing legislation to shield its officials, budgets, and
decision-making processes from overt political interference. This legal independence was intended to give central bankers the freedom to make potentially painful policy decisions without fear of immediate retribution.

Three corollaries evolved from these core principles. First, public expectations
mattered. In order for a central bank to achieve price stability, the public had to
believe that the central bank possessed the tools and the freedom to restrain inflation. In other words, central bank actions had to be credible in order to be effective. Alan Blinder, former vice chairman of the US Federal Reserve Board of Governors, found in his 1999 survey of eighty-four central bank governors that they
deemed "credibility" to be "of the utmost importance" for a central bank.[8] Credibility ideally required effective communication, a simple and clear price stability mandate, an independent central bank, and well-calibrated monetary policy
instruments. Second, central bankers saw no long-run tradeoff between inflation
and either unemployment or output. This consensus emerged from academic
research in macroeconomics and underpinned central bankers' justification for
their narrow focus on price stability. Finally, central bankers came to believe that
they should not use monetary policy to preemptively address asset price bubbles.
The value of assets such as housing, equities, and gold not only rose and fell in
a natural cycle, they argued, but monetary policy represented a poor tool with

---

5. For detailed expressions of these principles and corollaries, see for example Goodfriend 2007,
Issing 2012, Mishkin 2007, Bean et al. 2010.

6. Borio 2011.

7. Rogoff 1985, Alesina and Summers 1993, Fratianni et al. 1997, Bernhard 2002, among many
others. Giving a political twist to this argument, Boylan 1998 framed the question in terms of dis-
tributive conflicts between left and right, finding that the departing authoritarian government in
Chile created a legally independent central bank in order to restrict the policy choices of the incoming
democratic regime.

8. Blinder 1999. On a five-point scale ranging from "unimportant" (1) to "of the utmost importance" (5), central bank governors rated credibility at 4.83. No central banker gave a response below 4.
Similarly, the central bankers rated independence as key to maintaining credibility, with a value of 4.51.

which to moderate that cycle. Attempting to "lean" on such bubbles would only detract from a central bank's ability to pursue its core mandate, stabilizing consumer prices. This view was at the heart of the so-called Jackson Hole consensus, named after the legendary annual conference hosted by the Federal Reserve Bank of Kansas City in Jackson Hole, Wyoming.[9]

Several "best practices" emerged from these principles and corollaries. Most notable was the rise of inflation targeting as a method of credibly committing to price stability.[10] An inflation-targeting central bank publicly states that it aims to use monetary policy to achieve and maintain a predetermined inflation rate over a set term. Inflation targets became popular because they were easy to explain and represented a concrete commitment to pursue a specific definition of price stability. The European Central Bank's informal inflation target of "below, but close to, two percent" reflected a community norm. After New Zealand adopted the first formal inflation targeting policy in 1989, many other central banks followed its lead, including the central banks of Australia, Canada, Israel, South Korea, Sweden, Switzerland, and the United Kingdom. All had inflation targets set at 3 percent per year or less.[11] The US Federal Reserve later found itself under a two-term governor, Ben Bernanke, whose academic research had strongly advocated inflation targeting. Many more central banks adopted what became known as flexible inflation targeting, in which the bank's policy making took into account both the nominal rate of inflation and the extent to which the economy was operating at full capacity (the "output gap").

Inflation targeting was the policy child of central bankers' twin beliefs in the importance of price stability and of framing public expectations. Other key practices emerging from these views included increasing the transparency of central bank activities (for example, by publishing regular inflation reports), using New Keynesian rational expectations models—mathematical models with certain built-in assumptions about how economies work—to forecast inflation rates, and referencing the Taylor Rule in policy making (as inflation rises, so should

---

9. For its genesis, see Alan Greenspan's opening remarks at the 2002 Symposium sponsored by the Federal Reserve Bank of Kansas City on "Rethinking Stabilization Policy," in Jackson Hole, August 29–31.

10. Bernanke and Mishkin 1997, Blinder 1998, Marcussen 1998, Kirshner 2003.

11. For a detailed examination of inflation targeting practice, see Hammond 2012. By the time the global financial crisis hit in 2007–8, twenty-six central banks had become formal inflation targeters (twenty-nine if one counts Finland, Spain, and Slovakia, which were inflation targeters before they adopted the euro). Of these, nineteen had inflation targets of three percent or less. Variation exists on who sets the inflation target (the central bank alone, the central bank in combination with the government, or—most unusual—the government alone), but in every case the central banks had operational autonomy in deciding how to meet the target.

interest rates)[12]. Central bankers actively debated with each other over the details and did not employ these practices mechanistically, but they did rely heavily on them as important tools and touchstones. The ever-dwindling number of central banks that had not taken on such practices usually either aspired to them or at minimum recognized alternatives as deviations from the community norm.

This community worldview had clear policy implications beyond central banking.[13] Central bankers concerned about inflation typically exhorted their governments to exercise fiscal restraint in support of the price stability imperative, because without complementary fiscal policies, conservative monetary policies could not achieve their ends. Community members worked hard to educate their governments and publics on this score. As finance journalists Deane and Pringle noted, "For the most part, central bankers think that if they keep repeating that inflation is addictive, that price stability promotes long-term growth in jobs, this will become the accepted wisdom."[14] More broadly, the community believed that states should remain relatively open to international financial markets, that the underlying causes of financial crises were poor policy choices by individual governments, and thus that central banks must protect their independence and turn their community's worldview into global common knowledge as a means to preserve the international monetary order.[15]

Professional Culture

Central bankers shared a professional culture that actively reinforced their principles, practices, and sense of community. They at times compared themselves to a sacred order, speaking of their community as a religion or a special priesthood, referring to their work as requiring trust and an air of infallibility, or describing the act of becoming a central banker as "taking the veil." More prosaically, as two insiders observed:

> Central bankers often congratulate each other at their frequent international gatherings on how remarkably well they get on together . . . They believe they think the same way and have the same reactions in the face of a rather hostile, uncomprehending non-central banker world. There

---

12. Taylor 2000.

13. See Marcussen (1998) for a more extensive discussion of central bankers' shared state-level beliefs.

14. Deane and Pringle 1995, 23.

15. For example, see Goodman 1989, Helleiner 1994, Evans 1997. Rodney Hall gives this argument even greater emphasis, stating that the "success of this emerging global system of multilevel monetary governance relies on policy convergence as 'best practice' as defined by epistemic communities of monetary economists and central bankers" (Hall 2008, 7).

is a distinct sense of a central bankers' club, bound together by a common psyche that seems to transcend differences in history, functions, degrees of independence, size, or importance.[16]

Indeed, central bankers felt themselves to be a misunderstood and underappreciated club of similarly minded individuals working in a special kind of institution. As former Federal Reserve chairman Paul Volcker observed, central bankers "are almost uniquely able to deal with each other on a basis of close understanding and frankness" because of their common "experience, tenure, and training."[17] Central banking is a distinct profession with a relatively small number of worldwide practitioners, and this distinctiveness and manageable size facilitated the development of close ties and a community culture. So too did its social status as a well-paid, white-collar profession dominated by highly educated men and widely viewed as meritocratic, technocratic, and important.[18] Central bankers built their community's legitimacy by presenting themselves as seers who could be trusted to conduct the complex, arcane, and delicate task of guiding monetary policy.

This professional central banking culture required facility in two common languages, English and economics. This powerful combination allowed central bankers to speak to and understand each other with relative ease and clarity. With rare exceptions, by the 1990s people holding high-level staff positions in the central banks of the advanced industrial democracies spoke English proficiently.[19] The major central banking journals and working papers were published in English, international conferences and meetings took place in English, and the international financial institutions' working language was English. The European Monetary Institute and then the European Central Bank conducted their day-to-day operations in English. Central bank websites and publications appeared in both English and the home language. Job advertisements for central banks usually required English proficiency as a condition of employment.[20]

---

16. Davies and Green 2010, 270.

17. Cited in Helleiner 1994, 200.

18. Even by 2008, only ten of approximately 160 central bank governors worldwide were women (Davies and Green 2010). In Adolph's broader sample of nearly six hundred monetary policy makers serving from 1950 to 2000, fully 95 percent were men (Adolph 2013). Not surprisingly, more women tend to appear as one moves down the central banking community hierarchy both internally and cross-nationally. For historical reasons postcommunist central banks are outliers in this regard, with a higher proportion of women than one would otherwise expect.

19. As an additional note, in my years of interviewing officials from central banks in the advanced industrial democracies, not once did I require a translator. On several occasions I observed meetings or courses taking place in English in which none of the participants had English as his or her native language. Basic English proficiency is assumed within the core of the community.

20. For example, see the Deutsche Bundesbank's careers page at www.bundesbank.de/Navigation/EN/Bundesbank/Career/Entry_options/entry_options.html.

The language of economics was ubiquitous as well. This language included macroeconomic terms and concepts, economic data and statistics, and the formal modeling of economic arguments and relationships. The community's shared professional culture owed much to the academic discipline of economics, and the rise in university economics backgrounds among central bankers from the 1990s on has been well documented.[21] Central bankers regularly invited like-minded academic economists to their conferences and conducted research with them. The Swiss National Bank (SNB) and the *Journal of Monetary Economics* have held an annual conference for central bank researchers and academics at the SNB's Gerzensee study center since the 1990s, for example, and academics increasingly appeared on the speakers' list at Jackson Hole.[22]

But focusing strictly on community members' academic backgrounds and connections would miss the broader point, which is that making a persuasive case for a particular policy decision and being taken seriously within the central banking community required great facility in the language of economics regardless of how that facility was acquired.[23] Economics PhDs naturally had a certain advantage and played a key role in setting and continually raising that standard, but central bankers' ongoing organized training, everyday practice, and common professional referents such as specialized journals and working papers all contributed to building and reinforcing high-level economics as a community *lingua franca*.[24] As Fourcade points out, the formalized language of economics transcended linguistic barriers, assumed cross-national validity, and positioned economics as an objective science, all characteristics that facilitated its diffusion internationally.[25] Speaking "economist" both simplified communication across this transnational central banking community and marginalized those less well versed in economic theory.

The professional status hierarchies of the community both emerged from and reinforced its beliefs, practices, and prejudices. This was a community centered in Western Europe and North America, with important but more peripheral institutional members in countries such as Australia, Chile, India, Israel, Japan, New Zealand, and South Korea. Top officials of the BIS, ECB, and IMF enjoyed high

---

21. Simmons 2006, Adolph 2013, Singleton 2010, Davies and Green 2010, Axilrod 2011.

22. Tsingou et al. 2015.

23. Neil Irwin (2013) in *The Alchemists* provides a telling illustration: Mervyn King, the former governor of the Bank of England, so privileged "theoretical rigor" that when even an academic economist on the bank's Monetary Policy Council made arguments "based on the messy realities of the world"—arguments about the unfolding financial crisis that eventually proved correct—others within the bank found him unpersuasive because he was not offering "hard evidence."

24. See also Momani (2005) on IMF recruitment practices that led to a staff with relative homogeneity in its views and demographic characteristics (education, gender, and origin).

25. Fourcade 2006.

status because of their affiliation with these peak community institutions. Within national central banks, the departments engaged in monetary policy, analysis, and research generally held the highest status; these departments, in turn, tended to have the greatest concentrations of academically trained economists as well as the individuals most adept at speaking both of central banking's dominant languages. The central bankers in these departments had on balance the strongest international connections as well, and served as community leaders and gate-keepers. A central bank's internal hierarchy generally flowed downward from the systemic and strategic toward the specific and hands-on, with banking supervision departments and their relatives near the bottom of the operational food chain. Unlike the general intellectual agreement surrounding monetary policy and many other aspects of central bank practice, the community remained far from unified on how banking supervision should be carried out and whether or not central banks should even be responsible for it in the first place. The community of the time also tended to regard supervision as messy, detailed, and less important to the central bank mission than conducting monetary policy. Central bankers' main macroeconomic models excluded financial sector variables. Many central banks did not supervise commercial banks themselves or shared supervisory responsibilities with other agencies. As a result, the central banking community privileged its monetary policy-making role while often treating supervision with relative neglect or even disdain. This prejudice later proved to be the community's Achilles' heel.

Transnational Infrastructure

Central bankers possessed a well-developed transnational infrastructure that facilitated the interaction, knowledge transfer, and cooperation necessary for building and maintaining a professional community. The Bank for International Settlements, the European Central Bank, and the International Monetary Fund regularly brought national central bankers together to discuss policy, share research, and set standards. Although founded in 1930, the BIS significantly increased its coordination activities in the late 1980s and 1990s. By 2014 the BIS had sixty member banks, employed staff from fifty-four countries, and held events in which over five thousand central bank officials from around the world participated annually.[26] The traditional central bank governors' meetings held every two months at the BIS headquarters in Basel were famous for their

---

26. See www.bis.org.

intimacy, secrecy, and fine food and drink. The ECB for its part organized standing governance and working groups for central bankers within the Eurosystem.

The transnational central banking community's IMF headquarters was the Central Banking Department and its successors, the Monetary and Exchange Affairs (MAE) Department, the Monetary and Financial Systems (MFS) Department (MFS), and most recently the Monetary and Capital Markets (MCM) Department.[27] Department directors and staff typically had professional backgrounds in national central banks. Justin B. Zulu, the Central Banking/MAE department director from 1984 until 1995, had formerly served as governor of the National Bank of Zambia and had a US economics PhD.[28] Stefan Ingves, MAE director from 1999 to 2005, had been deputy director of the Sveriges Riksbank (the Swedish central bank) from 1994 to 1998. He left the MAE in 2006 to become Sveriges Riksbank director and was succeeded by Bank of Spain governor Jaime Caruana, who then himself left in 2009 to become managing director of the BIS. Caruana's replacement, José Viñals, had been deputy governor of the Bank of Spain. The department conducted its central bank technical assistance missions with personnel seconded from member-state central banks as well; in fact, such missions typically included more "borrowed" central bankers than IMF staff. More broadly, many national central bankers served as their country's IMF representatives, became IMF resident representatives in other countries, advised on short-term IMF missions of all kinds, and trained at the IMF Institute in Washington, DC. Although powerful member states influenced high-level IMF policy decisions (e.g., regarding lending), like the national central banks IMF staff enjoyed significant technocratic autonomy in designing and implementing training and technical assistance programs.

Central bankers participated in specialized meetings, workshops, and conferences at these transnational institutions, in national central banks, and elsewhere, with the Jackson Hole retreat an annual highlight. Community members conducted research with each other and regularly arranged personnel exchanges and consultations. Many full-time BIS, IMF, and ECB staff started (or later ended) their careers at national central banks. Cash and technology greased the wheels of this intensely interactive network, allowing community members to reach each other at a moment's notice or to fly around the world for a two-day meeting.

Beyond informal community building and ideational reinforcement, this transnational infrastructure allowed central bankers to codify many shared

---

27. For a brief history see the IMF archives web entry on the department's evolution at http://archivescatalog.imf.org/detail.aspx?parentpriref=110065237.

28. Zulu's successor, the Spaniard Manual Guitián, had a PhD in economics from the University of Chicago and both started and ended his career at the IMF. He had served as MAE deputy director since 1991.

policy beliefs into formal standards intended for wider application. The IMF began more regularly publishing booklets, reports, and papers outlining what it considered to be best practice in central banking and how central banks could introduce these practices.[29] The Bank of England's Centre for Central Banking Studies authored a series of introductory handbooks on core central bank practices. The West European central banks and later the ECB successfully pushed to impose tight standards on prospective EU accession states, requiring them to adopt laws guaranteeing central bank independence and to eventually adopt the euro. Adopting the euro, in turn, required states to fulfill the Maastricht criteria, which included maintaining a low rate of inflation. The BIS Committee on Payment and Settlement Systems, established in 1990 by the G10 central bank governors, set out core principles for managing payment and settlement systems and evaluated country practices through its "Red Book" reference serial. The IMF, in cooperation with the BIS, introduced a "Code of Good Practices on Transparency in Monetary and Financial Policies" in 1999. The IMF later assessed countries' adherence to these practices through the voluntary Financial Sector Assessment Program. Other relevant community guidelines promoted international accounting standards, capital adequacy standards for commercial banks, special data dissemination standards for macroeconomic statistics, and more.

Insulation

Finally, the transnational central banking community was relatively insulated from outsiders, especially considering its power over the international financial system and national economies. This is not to say that central bankers were immune to influence from other domestic and international actors—far from it. However, the community possessed several insulating characteristics that differentiated it from most other transnational groups. Most obviously, the national central banks generally enjoyed an independent legal status above and beyond that of other government institutions, giving them greater freedom to operate. Indeed, in the 1990s countries around the world granted extensive and unprecedented legal independence to their central banks.[30] It was also a financially well off and thus relatively self-sufficient community; after all, its core members could print money and typically had significant control over their own budgets and salaries. This community had high barriers to entry as well, as central banking required specialized knowledge and skills. Specialization and status meant that

---

29. For a key example regarding inflation targeting adoption, see Schaechter et al. 2000.
30. McNamara 2002, Marcussen 2005.

the community did not necessarily look outward for new ideas beyond a limited circle of academic economists and financial-sector specialists; that is, it looked to others who spoke the community's languages and shared its worldview.

The outside world for its part generally respected and even reinforced this boundary at the time by accepting central banking as a technocratic and difficult pursuit best left to highly trained experts. As Hall has observed, "The modern faith of science and the self-consciously 'scientific' artifice constructed around modern economics, to the extent that people buy into the new faith, ensures that monetary economists who staff modern, contemporary central banks enjoy the status of high priests of the secular, scientific revolution."[31] Books about central bankers emerging from the global financial crisis bore titles such as *Secrets of the Temple*, *The Alchemists*, *Lords of Finance*, and *In Fed We Trust*, reflecting the legacy of this elevation and distancing; *Priests of Prosperity* follows in this tradition. A *Financial Times* conference panel on "Central banks and their Jedi mind tricks" in some seriousness compared ECB president Mario Draghi to Yoda.[32] This combination of public awe, trust, and ignorance regarding central banking gave the community significant latitude to conduct its core activities with minimal questioning and contestation from outside the narrow world of finance.

The Rise of the Central Bankers

The intellectual consensus and policy community developed together, over many years, and not without great difficulties. In fact, the community's guiding principles of price stability and central bank independence, taken for granted in the 1990s, were quite controversial among central bankers not long before.[33] One high-ranking BIS official remarked to me that he did not know what the post-communist central banks would have done if the Wall had fallen ten years earlier, before Western central bankers had come to this consensus.[34] Two IMF staffers (one a former Croatian central bank governor) concurred, pointing out that:

---

31. Hall 2008, 171.

32. Tom Bowker, "Mario Draghi Can 'Use the Force' in Central Banking 'Confidence Trick'," *Central Banking*, July 4, 2014.

33. Johnson 1998.

34. Author's interview with a senior official of the Bank for International Settlements, Basel, Switzerland, May 2000. Cukierman et al. (2002) made a similar observation in regards to legal central bank independence: "Our feeling is that, had central bank reform in the transition economies taken place during the 1980s rather than the 1990s, the level of CBI embodied in the new laws would have been significantly lower."

The timing of the efforts to transform [Central and East European] countries was fortunate in that a new consensus had recently been achieved in the developed market economies on many aspects of the design of monetary systems. These include the desirability of stable money, full currency convertibility, central bank autonomy, indirect instruments of monetary policy, and policy transparency. As a result, the transition countries were able to reinstall much improved legal and regulatory systems by adopting much of the best of current wisdom. The CEE countries have been able to develop modern systems in ten years that took established market economies centuries to develop.[35]

The rise of this consensus was intimately connected with that of the community itself. Changing international ideas about monetary policy, states' domestic interests in promoting monetary sovereignty and economic growth, proselytizing central bankers in Western Europe and North America, and the move toward European monetary union (EMU) combined to foster, over time, a transnational central banking community that was extensive, powerful, organized, and more united in its economic views.

The Interwar Years

Central banks first began to proliferate beyond Western Europe and the United States in the interwar period, in the wake of the collapse of the prewar monetary order. While influential British and American central bankers traveled the globe promoting liberal economic ideas, many governments desired to strengthen their identities as autonomous nations and establish firm control over their own economies.[36] These trends converged to produce a worldwide boom in central banks. The energetic Bank of England governor Montagu Norman successfully used the British-led financial committee of the League of Nations to press for central bank creation in those states receiving League assistance. Famously, Norman refused to visit countries that had yet to introduce central banks. He and his associates had a hand in creating ten new central banks from 1923–35 in countries such as Austria and New Zealand. US Federal Reserve governor Benjamin Strong and Princeton economics professor Edwin Kemmerer played parallel advisory roles on the other side of the Atlantic, as six Latin American countries founded central banks with US assistance in the 1920s. Norman, with Strong's contribution, had

---

35. Coats and Skreb 2001, 265–66.
36. See especially Helleiner 2003, Meyer 1970, Holtfrerich et al. 1999.

also formulated a statement on General Principles of Central Banking in 1921 intended for wide dissemination and adoption that extolled the need for central bank cooperation and independence.[37] In many cases assistance went far beyond simple advice, with British or US advisors serving on the boards or staffs of the new central banks.

These early central bank missionaries promoted a "sound money" philosophy based in classic liberal thought that stressed monopoly note issue and central bank independence as the best way to (re)introduce the gold standard and protect domestic economies from potentially spendthrift governments. At its root lay an inherent mistrust of popularly elected governments, which the central bankers feared might pander to the masses through unsustainable spending rather than guarding the value of their currencies. Moreover, as Helleiner demonstrates, Norman and Strong intended these newly established central banks to provide a fresh channel of international influence for the United States and the United Kingdom.[38] The role of these so-called money doctors has at times been overemphasized, as the countries involved had their own reasons for wanting to create independent central banks—reasons that sometimes contradicted the philosophy of the advisors, such as counteracting the influence of foreign banks. Nevertheless, the advisors' efforts laid the groundwork for the establishment of the transnational central banking community. Not only did they spread central banking practices and ideas, but they also established durable lines of communication among central bankers around the world.

Just as important, this era saw the creation of the Bank for International Settlements, the first international organization promoting central bank cooperation. Norman and other leading European central bankers played a key role in the BIS's founding in 1930. Although ostensibly designed to handle German reparations after World War I, its objectives (as described in Article 3 of the BIS statutes) have always been broader:

> The objects of the bank are: to promote the cooperation of central banks and to provide additional facilities for international financial operations; and to act as trustee or agent in regard to international financial settlements entrusted to it under agreements with the parties concerned.

Although German reparations payments ceased in 1931 and Bretton Woods delegates (led by US Treasury secretary Henry Morgenthau) tried to eliminate the

---

37. Sayers 1976.
38. Helleiner 2003.

"pro-German" BIS in 1944, it survived and thrived over the years as a coordina-tor and talking shop for central bankers. Although central bank cooperation, agreement, and effectiveness fell immediately after the BIS's creation because of the Great Depression of the 1930s, this crisis impressed on the BIS the need to institutionalize central bank cooperation in order to stave off future catastrophes in the increasingly volatile international financial system.

The BIS's Annual Report of 1935 stressed the importance of regular consulta-tions and the development of shared objectives among central bankers, and the BIS in subsequent years took a series of steps to turn that proclamation into real-ity. The BIS took the lead in developing the European Payments Union in 1950 and became the leading organizational expert on payment and clearing systems. It provided the forum for negotiating the secretive Gold Pool agreement of the 1960s, in which central bank governors intervened—unsuccessfully in the end—to maintain the price of gold in the face of US balance of payments weaknesses. This same systemic crisis led to the creation of the influential Group of Ten (G10) central bank governors in 1963, which has met regularly in Basel under BIS aus-pices ever since. These affairs became legendary among financiers and conspiracy theorists alike: "the gatherings begin with dinner on Sunday evening . . . What they discuss over the Cognac and cigars is their affair, they say, and there are few leaks."[39] Moreover, until the European Monetary Institute's founding in 1994, the BIS provided the primary forum for negotiations on European monetary cooperation. The BIS thus became the "central bankers' bank," combining its coordinating role with special expertise on payment systems, financial sector supervision, and statistical monitoring.

Keynesianism and Bretton Woods

The Great Depression had a visceral impact on economic thinking, as many policy makers abandoned their hands-off, classical liberal philosophies in favor of the embedded liberalism of British treasury secretary John Maynard Keynes. Outlined in Keynes's 1936 *General Theory of Employment, Interest, and Money*, Keynesianism promoted activist monetary policies and counter-cyclical fiscal policies to advance the goal of full employment. Implementing this philosophy required central banks to privilege employment over inflation fighting and to work closely with their governments rather than operating at arms' length.

---

39. Deane and Pringle 1995, 11.

The rise of Keynesianism led to an ideological split between the US Federal Reserve and the Bank of England, one that fundamentally affected their respective international advisory roles. The US Federal Reserve—and particularly Robert Triffin, the Belgian-born chief of the Latin American section—began promoting a Keynes-inspired economic program to its assistance partners.[40] Radically different from US advice in the 1920s, this approach focused on insulating domestic economies from external shocks and encouraging employment and growth. It also acknowledged that central banks in developing countries might need to lend to their own governments and even to the public on occasion, due to weak domestic financial markets. These ideas dovetailed neatly with the emerging philosophy of import substitution industrialization among Latin American economists and policy makers. First implemented in Paraguay in 1943–45 at the request of the Paraguayan government, consultations with US central bankers helped to spread central banking institutions based on this vision to ten countries in Latin America, Africa, Asia, and the Middle East in the 1940s and early 1950s.

The Bank of England, by contrast, retained its orthodox economic philosophy and actively discouraged its newly independent former colonies from adopting the "Paraguayan plan." Initially it even advised them against creating their own central banks, fearing that these institutions would fall victim to the prevailing ideas of the day and pursue inflationary developmental policies. The Bank of England also hoped to preserve the sterling area in order to wield monetary influence in its former colonial realm, so it encouraged former colonies to maintain simplified currency board arrangements and the existing colonial monetary unions.[41] Most countries ignored this British advice, however, and turned to the United States, the IMF, and the World Bank for support. Governments in Ceylon, Ethiopia, and Saudi Arabia went out of their way to recruit US advisors rather than British because they preferred the US policy approach. The British therefore switched tactics and encouraged the creation of central banks, but ones that would pursue orthodox monetary policies. This effort met with greater success, and as a result, central banks in former British colonies tended to have more conservative charters than those established with US assistance during this time. This phenomenon of "dueling advisors" demonstrates that although central bankers in the 1990s shared a basic philosophy and worked together to promote it abroad, this had not always been the case historically.

Keynesian ideas dominated at the 1944 Bretton Woods conference, where the economic eminences of the day (including Keynes himself) installed the postwar

---

40. These two paragraphs are based on Helleiner 2003.

41. The French took an even stronger stance, and used a combination of adaptation and coercion to maintain the two CFA franc monetary zones.

system of pegged exchange rates and created the IMF and the World Bank. Like the BIS in the interwar years, the IMF's founding represented this era's most significant organizational step in the construction of the transnational central banking community. The IMF was originally intended to assist its members in resolving balance of payments issues and maintaining the postwar exchange rate system. No longer would countries be tempted to resort to beggar-thy-neighbor policies when faced with temporary balance of payments difficulties. Instead, they could draw on IMF reserves until their economies had regained equilibrium. The IMF quickly developed a certain level of autonomy from its member states due to its technical expertise, specialized mandate, agenda-setting power, and control over its own budget.[42] Unlike most other international organizations, IMF members contributed only when they first joined. As a result, the IMF did not depend on current members for its operating funds.

As no theoretical approach yet explained why balance of payments difficulties arose and how they could best be resolved, IMF staffers devised their own. By 1957 this had developed into the Polak model, named after its creator, IMF economist Jacques Polak. The Polak model saw domestic deficit spending as the cause of balance of payments issues, and a reduction in both government spending and credit expansion as the cure. In short, it identified the problems and solutions as lying within the domestic economy rather than in external or systemic factors. This simple model "has proved remarkably influential and durable. Ever since its inception in the 1950s, it has performed a key role in the analysis that builds up to the conditionality of IMF borrowing."[43]

The IMF began using its models and statistics as tools with which to persuade member states to follow its recommendations.[44] Starting in the 1950s it sent missions to each member state at least once per year, making policy suggestions and demanding data. National central bankers played key roles in staffing IMF missions and as IMF counterparts in adjustment programs. The IMF introduced both lending conditionality and technical assistance in the late 1950s and early 1960s as it began to work with the developing world. In 1964 it formalized these efforts by creating the Central Banking Service (which became the Central Banking Department in 1980), the Fiscal Affairs Department (FAD), and the IMF Institute. The IMF Institute, a training center attached to IMF headquarters in Washington, DC, focused on teaching "financial programming" (IMF modeling techniques) to central bank and finance

---

42. Barnett and Finnemore 2004, Woods 2006.
43. Mahadeva and Sinclair 2002.
44. Barnett and Finnemore 2004.

ministry staffers in member states. By 1986, the IMF Institute had already trained over five thousand officials from 149 countries.[45] The CBS/CBD and FAD provided technical assistance to member states. The Central Banking Service, for example, initially worked to help new African states develop their central banks and economic expertise. The IMF's technical assistance mission grew gradually over time in parallel with the IMF's expanded membership and mandate. By 1970 the IMF provided about 70 person-years of technical assistance annually. This went up to about 100 person-years by 1980. Zaire received the most IMF technical assistance (at 40 person-years) in the 1980s, followed closely by Yemen and Botswana. IMF technical assistance hit its pre-Soviet-collapse peak during the debt crisis in 1983–85, at an average of 130 total person-years annually.[46]

The IMF's macroeconomic views fit nicely with the belt-tightening monetarist ideas that gained increasing prominence among Western central bankers in the 1970s, views reinforced by the IMF's experience with the international debt crisis in the 1980s.[47] This ideational convergence between the IMF and the national central banks would mutually enhance their international power and legitimacy.

Monetarism and the Creation of the Euro

By the 1960s the Bretton Woods exchange rate system had begun to falter. Increasing economic interdependence combined with rising US deficit spending and a growing trade imbalance all diminished confidence in the US dollar's role as the lynchpin of the system. After several multilateral reform attempts, in August 1971 US president Richard Nixon unilaterally declared that the US dollar would no longer be directly convertible into gold. Although currencies were revalued in an attempt to save the exchange rate system, even the adjusted rates could not be sustained, and in early 1973 the system collapsed. The end of Bretton Woods helped lay the foundation for two events that would further enhance central bank influence, cooperation, and consensus: the rise of monetarism and the creation of the euro.

---

45. International Monetary Fund, *Annual Report 1986*, 71.

46. Boughton 2001.

47. Although some believe that the convergence of views between central bankers and IMF staffers occurred because both groups trained as academic economists in a handful of leading North American universities, this argument does not stand up to scrutiny. While IMF staffers were primarily macroeconomists educated in North American universities, national central bankers had more diverse backgrounds and were typically educated in their home countries (with Latin American central bankers the important exception). See Adolph 2004.

In the new world of floating exchange rates, central banks no longer had to focus their efforts on maintaining their currencies' values relative to a predetermined standard. Therefore, when Keynesian policies became discredited in the 1970s as Europe and the United States faced the unanticipated problem of stagflation (simultaneously rising inflation and unemployment), countries could choose from a wider range of policy options. After extensive debate both the United States and Germany adopted monetarism as their new economic philosophy, one designed to work under floating exchange rates. Monetarism holds that central banks should control inflation by steering policy to meet a specific monetary target. Unlike Keynesianism, monetarism views monetary and fiscal policy as relatively disconnected, allowing central banks to pursue monetary targets aimed at achieving price stability even without complementary fiscal policies. Therefore, a country can control inflation while still running significant budget deficits. The German Bundesbank embraced monetarism immediately after the collapse of Bretton Woods in 1973, and its stunning success in bringing down inflation and reviving the German economy solidified the Bundesbank's independence and prestige both domestically and abroad. The US Federal Reserve came later and more expediently to monetarism, but with equally startling effects. In fact, Deane and Pringle date the rise in central bank prominence to this US decision:

> If any single time or place is to be chosen for this decisive change, it is 1979 in Belgrade. It was there that Paul Volcker abruptly left a meeting of the International Monetary Fund to return home to do something about inflation. The domestic action taken against inflation in the United States from that time onwards ... did more for central banks' reputations than anything else before or since—although it had the dismaying international consequence of precipitating the third-world debt crisis.[48]

As implemented in Germany and the United States, this philosophy implied the preeminence of price stability in central bank policy making and the importance of central bank independence in carrying it out.[49] Even though the popularity of monetary targeting itself had faded by the late 1980s in the wake of the debt crisis and massive US budget deficits, the perceived importance of price stability and central bank independence on both sides of the Atlantic remained. Central bankers, policy makers, and the IMF all came to believe that the key to successful macroeconomic management was controlling inflation and restraining fiscal

---

48. Deane and Pringle 1994.

49. As Johnson (1998) notes, this is particularly ironic considering that leading US monetarists such as Milton Friedman did not support central bank independence. They believed that central bank bureaucrats, left to their own devices, would not support adopting monetary targets.

policy, a system best preserved by enhancing central bank independence. Increasing international financial integration reinforced these principles and practices, as financial market players came to view central bank independence as a credible signal of a country's commitment to stable macroeconomic policies.[50]

For West European central bankers, the intense cooperation involved in establishing the European Union and the euro zone further institutionalized these shared principles. The Bundesbank's success in combating inflation in the 1970s and its subsequent prestige among European central bankers and policy makers meant that it had a significant advantage in attempting to craft the new European monetary institutions in its own image.[51] The European Monetary System was introduced in 1979 at the height of the Bundesbank's policy successes, so its emulation of the "German model" was hardly surprising. Moreover, European central bankers knew each other well because of their long cooperation in the BIS. They hammered out agreements on European monetary cooperation among themselves at their regular meetings, which they then promoted to their respective governments. As a result, by the time EMU became a realistic goal European elites had already accepted their central bankers' views on macroeconomic policy making and there was no serious debate over these principles.[52] European policy makers thus chose central bankers to form the core of the Delors Commission that set the ground rules for monetary union, and Bundesbank representatives proved to be its most influential members.

EMU and subsequently the euro and the ECB further institutionalized the focus on price stability and central bank independence that had underpinned the Bundesbank's earlier success, but this time for the whole European Union.[53] The European central bankers also succeeded in mandating these principles for prospective new members. Central bank independence became a requirement for EU membership with the 1993 Maastricht Treaty, while conservative monetary and fiscal policies became a requirement for joining the monetary union.

In short, by the late 1980s West European and North American central bankers had come to share a unified set of principles and practices, had significant organizational capacity, and enjoyed unprecedented support from their governments. The collapse of the Soviet bloc occurred at an auspicious time for this community, as it had reached an international consensus on the appropriate institutional framework for central banking and stood ready to facilitate post-communist states' transitions from their command economies.

---

50. Dyson et al. 1995.
51. McNamara 1998, Marcussen 2000.
52. Marcussen 2000.
53. Even long-time holdout Great Britain eventually succumbed to the growing international consensus, granting independence to the Bank of England in 1997.

Knowledge and Power

Shared expertise and ideas alone, of course, cannot win the day. Power relationships fundamentally affect the ability of a transnational policy community to successfully spread its message and model. The stronger the community's perceived legitimacy, unity, and influence among the most powerful states in the international system, the more likely it is to find its target audience receptive to its suggestions.

Political scientists first viewed the influence of international expert networks through the lens of the epistemic community, defined as a group with a unified set of principles and causal beliefs as well as a shared policy enterprise.[54] They used the term to describe transnational groups of scientists, experts, or technocrats that came together in order to influence government policies through persuasion and activism, particularly in issue areas such as environmental politics, disarmament, and human rights.[55] Such communities derived their influence from their acknowledged expertise, persuasive skills, and organizational abilities. Epistemic communities relied on moral shaming and suasion to challenge the status quo among powerful governments and implicitly did so in normatively desirable ways. For example, epistemic communities mounted educational campaigns to persuade governments to clean up the Mediterranean Sea, to disavow landmines, and to adopt "rules of war" such as the Geneva Convention. By the 1990s many had identified West European central bankers as such an epistemic community as well, citing their successful promotion of central bank independence and price stability in the creation of European monetary institutions.[56]

Scholars emphasized epistemic communities' persuasive as opposed to coercive power, and usually focused on how they shared information and enhanced communication across similarly situated groups within the advanced industrial

---

54. Haas 1992.

55. Adler 1992, Haas 1992, Adler and Haas 1992, Finnemore 1996, Keck and Sikkink 1998, Evangelista 1999, True and Mintrom 2001. Keck and Sikkink differentiate between epistemic communities and what they call transnational advocacy networks: "a transnational advocacy network includes those relevant actors working internationally on an issue, who are bound together by shared values, a common discourse, and dense exchanges of information and services." Keck and Sikkink argue that unlike transnational advocacy networks, epistemic communities are motivated in part by professional norms.

56. Dyson et al. 1995, Verdun 1998, Marcussen 2000, Andrews 2003, Kaelberer 2003. Although suggesting that central bankers were becoming "increasingly like" an epistemic community, Kapstein (1992) argued that central bankers had not yet formed an epistemic community at that point because the British and US cooperation leading to the 1988 Basel Accord on international capital adequacy standards was motivated more by political considerations than by "collective technical knowledge." By focusing on international banking regulation, however, Kapstein hit upon the one important issue-area in which central bankers had not developed consensual knowledge and practices. As I discuss throughout the book, banking supervision and regulation remained an outlier.

democracies.[57] Even studies that did cross the north-south divide often paid minimal attention to structural power relationships that could empower or disempower particular communities.[58] But the line between coercion and persuasion can be slippery. Persuasion always takes place in a specific structural context, one in which the relationship between the policy community and the target may not be equal. More recent work has explicitly recognized that transnational communities wield power through normalizing their preferred practices.[59] What needs more emphasis, however, is how transnational policy communities' motives and capabilities, embedded within a particular structural context, combine to influence the behavior of others.

Established central bankers and their governments had powerful motives to spread their institutional model to the postcommunist world, motives rooted in their position in the international financial system. Once the postcommunist states began to open their economies, ensuring systemic stability demanded transnational cooperation and standard setting.[60] As the Bundesbank wrote in justifying its technical assistance programs, "Events have shown time and again that currency crises can be exacerbated considerably by unstable national financial systems. Measures to strengthen emerging economies' financial systems are therefore of utmost importance."[61] A high-level Joint Vienna Institute official echoed these concerns, noting that the interconnectedness of trade and financial relationships meant that it was in central banks' best interest to train other central bankers.[62] One top-ranking IMF staffer put it more bluntly: "We don't do [training and technical assistance] out of pure altruism. We want people on the other side of the table who can argue with us, who can be real interlocutors on our level. That way they can understand the program and own the program."[63] More prosaically, certain smaller European countries invited newly postcommunist states to join their IMF constituencies in order to protect their voting rights, leading to closer relationships between their central banks.[64]

Just as important, the established central bankers sought to promote the social expansion of the transnational community. They believed deeply in the

---

57. Rogers 1995.

58. Keck and Sikkink 1998, x.

59. Adler 2008, Adler and Pouliot 2011.

60. Borio et al. 2008.

61. Deutsche Bundesbank, *Annual Report 1998*, 112.

62. Author's interview with a senior official of the Joint Vienna Institute, Vienna, May 2006.

63. Author's interview with a senior official of the International Monetary Fund, Washington, DC, February 2007.

64. Author's interview with a senior official of the National Bank of Belgium, London, UK, November 2007. He noted that "We [worked with them closely] in part because we wanted to help them, in part because we wanted them to agree with us."

superiority of their principles and practices, and as we will see in the coming chapters felt a moral obligation to share them. The IMF's John Odling-Smee spoke for the transnational community in saying that, "we are involved [in technical assistance] because our central banks believe it is important to support the establishment of strong new members of the family of central banks ... we are part of one central bank family with many shared concerns."[65] Community members had kinship with and sympathy for their colleagues in the postcommunist world. An influential community member remarked to me that once the postcommunist transformation began, it was a "normal desire" for the established central bankers to assist their newest compatriots.[66] As Gill Hammond of the Centre for Central Banking Studies observed:

> At the start of the 1990s, there was significant demand from central banks in former communist countries for assistance in setting up central banking operations in evolving market economies. The Bank of England saw this as a unique opportunity to help with a transfer of knowledge to these countries and at the same time, to foster a mutually supportive network of central banks worldwide. This recognized the fact that central banks are unique institutions in each country and, while there is no common set of functions that central banks carry out, there is a huge amount of common ground between them and strong mutual benefit to be gained from sharing knowledge and experience. The CCBS was established to deliver these twin objectives of sharing knowledge and building relationships.[67]

Community also meant the existence of friendly rivalry among the established central banks to see which of them could do more, do better, and work harder to provide assistance. Peer pressure, as well as competition to assist the most important or interesting postcommunist central banks, spurred the community to greater efforts.

Central bankers and their intellectual allies had far more resources to draw on in this campaign—and thus could wield potentially far greater power—than the average scientific or activist-based policy community. Although the central bankers' training and technical assistance efforts focused primarily on persuasion and socialization, this took place within global and national contexts that

---

65. Quoted in Zulu et al. 1994, 141 and 143.
66. Author's interview with a senior official of the Magyar Nemzeti Bank and the IMF, Budapest, Hungary, May 2000.
67. Gill Hammond, "The Centre for Central Banking Studies," *Summer 2006 Quarterly Bulletin*, Bank of England.

enabled, privileged, and validated their efforts. The transnational central banking community's core members possessed both political legitimacy (as government institutions) and political autonomy (as independent central banks). The community had consensual, widely legitimate principles and practices as well as the means necessary to disseminate them. Therefore, while international assistance to the postcommunist world in other areas took a few years to get up and running, central bank assistance programs could begin immediately, in many cases before the actual fall of the communist regimes.

Such multifaceted structural power placed the established central bankers in a hierarchical relationship with the postcommunist central bankers that they advised. The role of structural power in manufacturing consensus and consent—that is, in crafting worldviews—should caution us against understanding postcommunist economic transformation as in any way natural, inevitable, or agentless.[68] Transnational communities anchored in powerful states can better work to legitimate and spread their principles and practices. As those in other countries are introduced to the community, they are more likely to be absorbed into it than to change or challenge it, often accepting its basic worldview and attempting to replicate its practices at home.[69] As Strang and Soule observed, "Adopters [of new practices] may be influenced strongly by prestigious, central actors in ways that are not reciprocated . . . Lower ranking community members aspire to be like prestigious others."[70] Although the established central bankers often took great care to treat postcommunist central bankers as partners rather than students, inevitably much of the information flow and advice taking was one-way rather than a mutual learning and adaptation process, especially at the beginning.

Why did this matter for postcommunist central bank development? First, it emphasizes that the intellectual basis for the transnational central banking community's work had already been laid by the time communist governments began to fall. Postcommunist states heard little meaningful counter-discourse on central banking either from within the community itself or from the leading Western governments. The community had a widely legitimate, near-hegemonic message that many key elites in postcommunist states were prepared to accept.[71] Second,

---

68. For example, Gill (1996) points out that seeing financial globalization as "civilizing" and as "akin to forces of nature" both reifies the market and makes the dominance of this viewpoint seem inevitable.

69. Cox 1983.

70. Strang and Soule 1998, 274.

71. In Simmons's (2001) parlance, central banking is a case where the dominant center would experience "significant negative externalities" if emulation did not occur and the target states had "high incentives to emulate" the center, resulting in "market harmonization with institutional assistance."

it meant that the primary impetus for undertaking this transformation came less out of postcommunist states' domestic debates and conditions than from the external, powerful force of these internationally approved ideas and their central bank proponents. Third, it meant that the international consensus and activist transnational community would enable central bank transformation to progress more quickly than change in other postcommunist institutions. Finally, it meant that many postcommunist governments would reflexively pass legislation granting independence to their central banks without fully understanding the potential domestic economic and political consequences of doing so, both positive and negative.

In sum, although Western governments, academic experts, international institutions, and nongovernmental organizations clamored to advise postcommunist states on subjects ranging from party building to privatization to rediscovering religion, the transnational central banking community had unparalleled advantages in its particular campaign to transform central banking. Possessing a broad consensus about how central banks should work, the community gave unusually consistent advice. Building on its existing organization and resources, the community had the ability to mount extensive and increasingly coordinated training and technical assistance efforts. Offering an attractive, internationally accepted set of ideas and practices, the community's central banking model promised sovereign legitimacy to postcommunist governments as well as prestige and independence to postcommunist central bankers. Highly educated and working in small, specialized institutions, the established and the postcommunist central bankers could interact intensively as potential colleagues. If any postcommunist international assistance program could succeed in transforming Soviet-era institutions, it would be this one.

TRANSPLANTATION

"Central banking functions in transition economies . . . have been completely transformed from socialist monobanking systems to modern, independent central banks, which is a remarkable achievement."

—IMF economist Warren Coats and Croatian National Bank governor Marko Škreb (2001)

Transplantation is the art of moving ideas, policies, institutions, and practices from one environment to another. It refers to the entire process, from selection of the transplant to its transfer through its taking root. It likewise engages both diffusion and convergence, examining how innovations spread and under what circumstances they take recognizably similar shape in multiple places.[1] Transplantation has several key attributes. First, the transplant itself is *complex.* Like relocating a flower with its interdependent roots, stem, leaves, petals, and seeds, transplantation rarely involves transferring a single idea or isolated practice elsewhere. Rather, a transplant is a distinct yet organically intertwined package of ideas, policies, practices, and/or institutions. Second, the process is *active.* Institutions do not move themselves, and as Thomas Risse famously observed, "ideas do not float freely."[2] Identifiable actors conduct the transplantation, and their choices, motivations, skills, and influence affect the process and the outcome. Third, the process can be *flexible.* Innovations may be transplanted whole and unchanged, but are more commonly grafted onto existing institutions, hybridized, or pruned back (simplified for export), and can be transplanted as

---

1. It is important to distinguish policy transfer/diffusion ("the process that leads to the pattern of adoption") from convergence ("a significant increase in policy similarity across countries"). See Gilardi 2012, 454.

2. Risse-Kappen 1994.

either seedlings or mature plants.[3] This flexibility often involves tradeoffs and compromises. For example, seedlings—smaller, less involved transplants—may take root more easily and resist transplant shock, but mature transplants may be initially stronger and more attractive.

The outcome, too, is *context dependent*. A transplant's survival and development depends on myriad factors related to the skill of the transplanters and the environment's quality and compatibility. To extend the botanical metaphor, has a shade plant been placed in the sun? Do other plants challenge or crowd out the transplant? Does the transplant require symbiotes such as pollinator bees (or in our case, complementary institutions) to survive, and if so do they already exist or can they be introduced to the new environment? Is the transplant vulnerable to scavengers or foot traffic? Do important actors in the new locale view the transplant as a rose to be cultivated or as an invasive weed to be plucked? Such factors will affect the extent to which the transplant puts down solid roots and the ways in which it develops. In the end, transplants across various contexts may look slightly different and grow at varying rates, yet still be recognizable as the same species now present in places it had not before existed.

The collapse of communism presented the transnational central banking community and postcommunist states with a daunting transplantation challenge. Central banks in command and market economies were alike in name only. Communist-era central banks were designed for administrative and accounting purposes. They were subordinate to the government, fully integrated with the rest of the banking system (hence their name, monobanks), and disbursed state funds to enterprises and individuals. They had little or no control over monetary policy; indeed, monetary policy as it is commonly understood did not exist in the command economy. When governments needed more money, the central bank would issue it. Nonconvertible currencies, separate cash and noncash monetary circuits, centrally administered prices, and a shortage economy kept inflation repressed and enforced savings. Payment systems were slow and typically paper-based, as the command economy required nothing more elaborate. Without true commercial banks, banking supervision was unnecessary. These central banks were primarily tools with which to fulfill state planning targets. Communist-era central bankers, too, had different educations, experiences, and mind-sets than their counterparts in developed market economies. Staff typically did not have extensive backgrounds in economics, and positions within these banks held

---

3. Stone (2012) refers to this as policy translation, the process by and the extent to which innovations are adapted to fit local conditions.

little prestige and paid poorly. Two IMF resident representatives reflecting on their early advising experiences observed that, "where Western economists see the orderly function of markets solving economic problems, many local officials see instability, disorder, and even chaos. And it scares them."[4] In retrospect, those local officials had a point.

The postcommunist central banks faced varying initial conditions. Starting points ranged from Hungary's long experience with quasi-market "goulash communism" in the heart of Europe to the daunting political and economic environment in Central Asia. The central banks in dissolved federations had the added challenge of introducing new currencies in the midst of radical economic transformation, a region-wide economic depression, and in some cases civil war. The new central banks in Slovakia, the former Yugoslav republics (except Serbia), and the non-Russian former Soviet republics had previously been subordinate branches of their monobanks, with correspondingly less expertise and responsibility. While pro-Western and pro-market sentiment abounded in East Central Europe and the Baltics after 1989, the trade journal *Central Banking* flatly noted in 1992 that "the environment is extremely hostile for central banks" in most post-Soviet states.[5] Russia, as always, presented would-be reformers with unique challenges as the Bank of Russia confronted the legacy of over seventy years of a homegrown command economy.

The transnational central banking community sought to work with postcommunist officials to transplant its own model of central banking into this diverse and complex landscape. This chapter introduces the transplantation process. The initial section describes the transplant itself, that flexible complex of principles, practices, and institutions that comprised the "model" central bank. I then briefly explore alternative explanations for the spread of this central banking model across the postcommunist world, demonstrating the limitations of approaches based on earlier understandings of diffusion and policy transfer. The rest of the chapter describes the three stages of the transplantation process. The first stage, *choice*, concerns the initial decision to conduct a transplant. The second stage, *transformation*, concerns the active installation of the transplant. The third stage, *internalization*, concerns the sustainability of the transplant. Each stage gives rise to a different question: Why was the initial decision to borrow an outside model made? How and how effectively was the transformation conducted? To what extent does the domestic environment accept, reinforce, and deepen the changes that have taken place?

---

4. Allen and Haas 2001.
5. "The New Central Banks in the Republics of the Former U.S.S.R." 1991–92.

The Very Model of a Modern Central Bank

The transnational central banking community built its export model of central banking on the basis of the shared principles and practices described in the previous chapter. The model envisioned independent central banks focused on achieving and maintaining price stability. Yet such transplantation required a range of complementary central banking policies, practices, and institutions, which together comprised the transplant model. First, central bank legislation to acknowledge the central banks' new status and tasks would have to be introduced. International norms prescribed legal protections for central bank independence, a formal mandate to protect price or currency stability, and a range of other measures delimiting the relationships among the government, central bank, and commercial banks.

Second, postcommunist central banks needed the capability to conduct monetary policy, which entailed developing indirect policy instruments such as open-market operations, reserve requirements, and central bank lending facilities as well as economic models for policy making and forecasting.[6] Conducting monetary policy also demanded the capacity to deal with foreign exchange operations, current account convertibility, and, in some cases, new currencies. The model monetary policy regime typically began with easier-to-administer fixed or managed exchange-rate regimes and then made a gradual move toward best-practice inflation targeting.

Third, postcommunist central banks would need better payment systems. Command-era payment systems took days or weeks to clear even a relatively small number of financial transactions by market standards. Since 1980, the international standard had been a real-time gross settlement system (RTGS), a highly sophisticated payments infrastructure that processes same-day payments among financial institutions. The export model identified RTGS systems as best practice but recognized the utility of implementing intermediate steps along the way to that final goal.

Fourth, postcommunist central banks would either have to develop the capacity to supervise commercial banks themselves or their governments would need to create and staff separate agencies responsible for supervision. International standards called on supervisors to enforce Basel capital adequacy standards for commercial banks and to carry out regular inspections to ensure that commercial bankers conducted themselves according to the law.

---

6. Four small postcommunist states (Estonia 1992, Lithuania 1994, Bulgaria 1997, and Bosnia-Herzegovina 1997) adopted currency boards to establish credibility more rapidly and avert the need to develop these tools quickly, but for most countries this was not an option.

Finally, the central banks would need to institute transparency practices and a system of internal audit, both in order to effectively monitor their own activities and to establish credibility and accountability. This would demand, among other measures, that the central banks adopt international accounting standards (later called international financial reporting standards) rather than the idiosyncratic accounting systems employed in the past.

All of this, in turn, would require massive recruiting, training, and retraining of postcommunist central bankers. For transplantation to succeed, the central bankers had to acquire both the technical expertise to carry out these new tasks as well as the transnational community's "central banking" mind-set. To work with and ultimately join the transnational community, postcommunist central bankers would need to become conversant in both English and economics. Price stability and central bank independence would need to become the driving professional principles behind their work.

This was a simplified model, designed for export. Community members recognized the diversity among the established central banks—institutions that had evolved eclectically over decades and in some cases centuries, and which often had complex relationships with their own governments not fully captured in the formal concept of central bank independence. However, the basic model they promoted in the postcommunist world represented more of an ideal, a progressive distillation of the consensus views and best practices as held by the transnational central banking community of the 1990s. Simplifying, codifying, and generalizing the model made it progressively more portable and thus more powerful.

It was also, within the parameters of the central banking consensus, a flexible model. While the various community members all sought to transplant the basic model to the postcommunist world, the details of the content and the process could and did differ among them. The IMF, for example, leaned more toward a one-size-fits-all approach laced with conditionality, while the national central banks leaned more toward adaptation and promotion of their own self-perceived areas of strength. The model itself developed over time as well, moving from implicitly shared knowledge and practices to a more explicit set of prescriptions and standards. The model as used in practice also tended to emphasize areas of consensus while de-emphasizing areas in which disagreements remained. For this reason, while the community acknowledged the need to develop banking supervision, the broad disagreements on how or even whether central banks should do it led to community members downplaying this area at first in their training and technical assistance efforts.

How Did the Model Spread?

I argue that the transnational central banking community took the lead in transplanting this model into the postcommunist world and that this occurred through a complex, multilayered process. However, earlier explanations exist that each reflect one of the four major diffusion mechanisms: learning, competition, coercion, and socialization.[7] The first suggested that domestic politicians in postcommunist states adopted this model after individually and rationally learning from successful international experiences with independent central banking elsewhere. The second focused on the pressures of international market competition. The third blamed coercive conditionality imposed by powerful states and international financial institutions. The last emphasized the power of ideas, suggesting that the neoliberal zeitgeist led to broad emulation of this central banking model after the fall of communism.

Though each explanation has its strengths, none satisfactorily accounted for both the radical transformation of postcommunist central banks and the domestic difficulties and divergence that they later experienced. These approaches focused primarily on explaining the initial decision to adopt central bank independence while neglecting the deeper and longer institutional transformation process, underemphasized the hands-on role of international actors in building and defending these central banks, and often paid too little attention to how the different diffusion mechanisms interacted with one another. My argument builds on this earlier research by emphasizing the interacting influences of socialization and coercion throughout the transplantation process, as well as the active transmission rather than the passive diffusion of the central banking model.

Learning

Many economists believe that objective domestic economic imperatives drive governments to create independent central banks committed to achieving price stability. Both economic theory and international practice had demonstrated that delegating authority to an independent central bank led to improved inflation performance. From this perspective, postcommunist governments faced with inflationary conditions simply learned from the experience of other countries and took the approach that made the best economic sense. As Gabor further notes, Western economists assumed that hidden inflationary forces plagued all newly postcommunist countries and required independent, conservative central

---

7. Graham et al. (2013) distilled 104 scholarly terms for diffusion down to these four main mechanisms.

banks to fight them.[8] The rapid spread of independent central banks in the post-communist world thus represented autonomous, individual decisions by multiple governments faced with similar crises at similar times.

Although intuitively attractive, this argument's internal logic relies on two controversial assumptions. First, advocates believe that independent central banks can reduce inflation at a lower societal cost—that is, with fewer negative effects on employment and output—than can dependent ones, simply because people trust independent central banks to do what they say they will do. This credibility should then lead to quick adjustments in market expectations and wage demands in response to central bank policies. However, much evidence indicates that central bank independence either has no effect or actually raises the societal costs of disinflationary policies.[9] This occurs because independent central bankers are so concerned with preserving their reputations as credible inflation fighters that they can adopt overly tight monetary policies. As Joseph Stiglitz has observed, "I was repeatedly struck by how [central bankers] who ... worried more about inflation and less about unemployment, also more frequently saw inflation lurking around the corner."[10] Second, despite the widespread assumption that low inflation is necessarily good for the economy, even sympathetic economists find little connection between central bank independence and economic growth.[11] Steadily moderate levels of inflation (up to 20 percent annually) do not necessarily retard economic growth and may help to maintain higher employment levels.[12] Neither does evidence indicate that such moderate inflations tend to blossom into unquestionably damaging hyperinflations.

The empirical case for central bank independence suffers further when one moves beyond the realm of the advanced industrial democracies.[13] Studies have failed to find a robust link between central bank independence and low inflation in developing and transition countries.[14] In transition countries, Cukierman and

---

8. Gabor 2012.

9. Blinder 1999, Down 2004, Kissmer and Wagner 2004.

10. Stiglitz 1998, 217.

11. Alesina and Summers 1993.

12. Barro 1995, Kirshner 2003.

13. Although statistical evidence finds a relationship between independence and inflation in advanced industrial democracies, many scholars believe that even this connection is spurious, arguing that domestic cultures supporting low inflation, conservative commercial financial sectors, and other related variables better explain it. Posen 1995, Campillo and Miron 1997, Hayo 1998, Hayo and Hefeker 2002, McNamara 2002.

14. Cukierman 1992, Maxfield 1994. An exception is Loungani and Sheets (1997). However, Kissmer and Wagner (2004) point out that this study looked only at inflation in a single year (1995) and most of the central banking statutes had only recently been enacted, calling its robustness into question. When Cukierman et al. (2002) reran the analysis with their indices and broader time periods, the relationship disappeared.

colleagues, as well as Maliszewski, found that central bank independence was tied to lower inflation rates only once the country had achieved high and sustained levels of economic liberalization.[15] Arnone et al. found that while central bank independence may contribute to lower inflation rates in transition countries at the margins, other factors are far more important determinants of inflation.[16]

In light of the evidence, rather than seeing the rapid creation of independent central banks as an economic imperative, postcommunist states' shallow financial markets, intense economic transformations, and urgent need for policy coordination among multiple political and economic actors arguably could have militated against it. Moreover, postcommunist states entered the transition period under different initial conditions, including in inflation levels and regime types. Yet, as we will see, even authoritarian postcommunist states with no immediate inflation problems passed legislation granting independence to their central banks. It thus makes more sense to view independent central banking as a somewhat surprising institutional choice from an autonomous learning perspective.[17] The simultaneous and rapid introduction of independent central banks across the postcommunist world strongly suggests that international influences overwhelmed domestic considerations in the initial phases of central bank reform.

Competition

Rooted in the globalization literature, competition-based explanations suggest that postcommunist states created independent central banks in order to signal their creditworthiness to private international investors and financial markets.[18] Exposed to market pressures for the first time, governments raced to compete with one other to gain access to international trade and financial markets. As above, this explanation focuses on the choice to introduce legal central bank independence rather than on postcommunist central bank development more broadly.

Competition and the desire to demonstrate credibility certainly played an important role in convincing postcommunist policy makers to create independent central banks, but it is an unlikely candidate for prime mover in the central

---

15. Maliszewski 2000, Cukierman et al. 2002.
16. Arnone et al. 2007.
17. Grabel 2003, McNamara 2002.
18. For example, see Maxfield 1997 and Carruthers et al. 2001. On the broader theme of financial globalization reducing domestic economic flexibility, see Wriston 1992, Kahler 1992, Stallings 1992, and Strange 1986.

bank transplantation process. If international market pressures were responsible, we would expect the postcommunist states most dependent on international trade and finance to rush to create independent central banks while those
less dependent would lag far behind or adopt different models entirely. Instead,
postcommunist governments nearly all granted significant independence to their
central banks within a few years, with little regard to their reliance on international markets. Competitive pressures may have influenced the relative legal sta-
tuses of postcommunist central banks, but cannot explain the general and rapid
decisions to grant high levels of independence in the first place.

This explanation also overstates the importance of central bank independence
as a signal to international markets. When attractive investment opportunities
appeared in a postcommunist state (for example, high-yielding treasury bills,
profitable companies on the auction block, or potential partnerships in exploit-
ing natural resources such as oil and gas), international capital flowed in regardless of the status or competence of the central bank. Conversely, in the absence of
such opportunities even an internationally lauded central bank could not spur
investment, as countries like Kyrgyzstan discovered to their chagrin. Independent central banks were simply one of many signals sent to international financial markets in the postcommunist world; at best, they marginally influenced
investment decisions.

Coercion

The third approach argues that political and economic coercion from hegemonic states and international financial institutions forced postcommunist
governments to reform their economic institutions and policies.[19] Coercion
explanations focus on purposeful material pressures to make postcommunist
states transform their central banks according to a prescribed model. The United
States is usually the prime mover in such explanations, using the IMF and other
institutions to push neoliberal reforms down the throats of financially strapped
postcommunist countries through coercive conditionality.

Coercion did play an important role in postcommunist central bank development, although not as much and not in the same way as such explanations
posited. In terms of agency, West European central bankers and West Europeans
in the IMF most vigorously organized and pursued postcommunist central bank
reform. The European Union and IMF did employ coercive conditionality measures to promote independent central banks in the postcommunist world, and

---

19. Kapstein 1994, Pauly 1997, Simmons 2001.

these measures swayed government opinion, particularly regarding legal independence.[20]

However, coercion represents an incomplete explanation. Coercion works through pressuring high government officials to adopt reforms. If this were the main driver of change, we would have observed postcommunist governments in the lead, demanding that their central bankers concede to IMF or EU desires. Instead, the opposite dynamic proved more common, with postcommunist central bankers often pressuring their governments to toe the line and in many cases adopting reforms far beyond those that the IMF or EU required.[21] Moreover, my interviewees in the transnational central banking community continually emphasized that postcommunist central bankers adopted aspects of the Western model only after they themselves understood and came to agree with them. Postcommunist central bankers likewise rarely reported making internationally demanded changes against their wills or under duress. As one IMF official observed, "You can't force these banks to change. You have to change them through persuasion, arguments about best practices, peer pressure, and the importance of keeping up with their buddies. You can try to force change, but unless they wish to do it, they won't do it, or will do it only on paper. It's far from simply coercion."[22] Coercion can prod, but it cannot persuade. Like the competition approach, coercion arguments help to explain why many postcommunist governments supported legislation granting independence to their central banks or conceded to central bank actions when they might have preferred not to do so, but cannot explain the transformation processes within the central banks themselves.

Socialization

The final set of explanations focuses on the role of socialization in transferring international ideas and practices from one state to another. Socialization (also called emulation) approaches argue that prestige and persuasion convince states to adopt ideas and behaviors mirroring internationally accepted norms and

---

20. On the role of the EU in promoting institutional change in postcommunist states more broadly, see, for example, Kopstein and Reilly 2000, Kurtz 2002, Jacoby 2004, and Vachudova 2005. It is important to note that Western European central bankers (particularly the Bundesbank) were instrumental in promoting central bank independence as an EU membership requirement in the first place, so even in this case EU coercion is a manifestation of central bankers' prior ideational influence. See Marcussen 1998, McNamara 1998, and Dyson and Featherstone 1999.

21. In addition, as Randall Stone (2002) demonstrates, the IMF has failed to carry through on its threats so many times in the most strategically important postcommunist states that its conditionality often lacks credibility.

22. Author's interview with a senior IMF official, Washington, DC, November 2001.

practices. Socially constructed beliefs ultimately determine interests, rather than the other way around.[23] Institutional isomorphism, the phenomenon through which institutions become more similar around the world, occurs when follower states successively mimic dominant, prestigious world-cultural models.[24] For example, McNamara argued that the US-promoted culture of international neo-liberalism encouraged isomorphism among central banks in emerging economies as they sought to "legitimize their own efforts at reform."[25] Others such as Bockman and Eyal contended that East European economists like Poland's Leszek Balcerowicz had internalized neoliberal ideas through participation in transnational economics networks during the communist era, so that when the Soviet system fell, they advocated for and implemented these reforms at home.[26] Epstein's in-depth comparative study of four postcommunist states found that when new elites faced uncertainty over policy choice, they adopted central bank independence not for reasons of efficiency or necessity but because of its international advocates' credibility.[27] More broadly, postcommunist governments could introduce independent central banks as important symbols of national sovereignty.[28]

This focus on socialization captured a vital dynamic that other theories missed, and makes the rapid, enthusiastic, and widespread central bank reforms of the 1990s more explicable. But it still did not engage with the full transplantation process.[29] Indeed, such studies focused almost exclusively on the initial choice to create legally independent central banks. But choosing independence was only the first step in a lengthy process. Policy makers in even the most advantaged postcommunist states did not possess the knowledge or wherewithal to rapidly transform their command-era central banks without sustained assistance from outside. Moreover, some postcommunist policy makers and central bankers—such as Russia's top central banker Viktor Gerashchenko—initially held ideas inimical to those of the transnational central banking community and actively put them into practice. Although a few influential individuals in postcommu-

---

23. For example, constructivists in international political economy often emphasize the role of a hegemonic state or states in exporting the economic ideologies underpinning such institutions. See Hirschman 1989, Loriaux 1997.

24. See Meyer et al. (1997) on world society for a fundamental statement of this approach. On "imitation" see e.g., Jacoby (2001), other early and similar approaches use terms such as lesson-drawing (e.g., Rose 2002) or learning (e.g., Hall 1993).

25. McNamara 2002.

26. Bockman and Eyal 2002.

27. Epstein 2008. See also our co-authored comparison of central bank independence and euro adoption in Poland, the Czech Republic, Slovakia, and Romania (Epstein and Johnson 2010).

28. Marcussen 2005.

29. This is a common critique of diffusion and convergence studies in general. Risse-Kappen 1994, Checkel 2001, True and Mintrom 2001, Stone 2012, Graham et al. 2013.

nist states had adopted free-market ideas in the late communist era, they could not persuade and train entire cadres of central bankers, transform central bank capabilities from top to bottom, and convince postcommunist governments to support these central banks on their own.

For these reasons, my explanation emphasizes the transnational central banking community's expensive, concerted, hands-on efforts to remold postcommunist central banks in its own image. The community combined technical assistance designed to transform postcommunist central bank infrastructures with training designed to give postcommunist central bankers the skills to use their new tools and to foster a central banking culture. As one Hungarian central banker observed a decade later, these efforts came to play a "tremendous role in changing the financial culture of the country."[30]

Transplantation

Transplantation takes place in a dynamic three-stage process: choice, transformation, and internalization. Choice permits transformation to occur, while the transplant's actions, fit, and perceived effectiveness determine to what extent it will become accepted at home and further evolve. A state must work through all three stages in "domesticating" a foreign model. Each stage places different combinations of actors and diffusion mechanisms at the fore.

Choice

Governments, not central banks, have the power to adopt legislation on central bank independence. The factors most strongly affecting a government's decision on when to introduce an outside model are crisis, international legitimacy, and external incentives. A political or economic crisis can both kick-start the search for foreign models and create the opportunity for international and domestic proponents of a model to present it as a solution to the crisis situation. The deeper and more fundamental the crisis, the more likely the government is to adopt a foreign transplant rapidly and without extensive debate.

As socialization-oriented studies have shown, the international legitimacy of both the model and the policy community promoting it play a central role as well. If systemically influential states and neighboring states employ a particular

30. Author's interview with a senior official in the Human Resources Department of the Magyar Nemzeti Bank, Budapest, Hungary, February 2000.

institutional model, its perceived legitimacy rises. This accounts for the S-curve pattern of diffusion, when a model spreads rapidly among similarly situated neighboring states before new adoptions taper off.[31] At the same time, the more internationally respected, hegemonic, and resource-laden the international actors promoting the transplant, the more attractive the transplant may seem to a prospective new adopter. When a powerful transnational policy community presents an internationally lauded foreign model as a solution to a state in crisis, it invites especially uncritical imitation.[32]

External incentives often go hand-in-hand with international legitimacy. Indeed, Pollilo and Guillen's study of seventy-one countries found precisely that coercive, normative, and mimetic pressures worked together to spread central bank independence around the world.[33] Indirect incentives include expectations that adopting the new institution will send a desirable signal to other states or to international markets, while direct incentives include coercive conditionality and payoffs from external actors and institutions pushing adoption.

In the postcommunist world, adopting legislation to create independent central banks with narrow policy mandates strongly fulfilled all of these conditions. In terms of crisis, postcommunist leaders recognized that their previous economic model had run its course, and were therefore unusually open to seeking alternatives.[34] Command-era central banks needed new mandates and capabilities to function within chaotic yet increasingly market-oriented environments.

At the same time, an influential transnational community presented a clear alternative—the independent, conservative central bank—as a technocratic solution to this serious political and economic problem. The international legitimacy of both the model and the policy community promoting it led postcommunist governments to view legally independent central banks as markers of sovereignty and guarantors of international resource flows. Moreover, postcommunist governments understood that the United States, the IMF, and the EU looked favorably on central bank independence.

In introducing independent central banks, governments thus conformed to international expectations rather than responding to specific domestic demands.[35] Making the initial choice to create independent central banks required

---

31. Weyland 2006.

32. As Weyland (2006) argues, policy makers typically employ bounded rationality—the cognitive heuristics of availability, representativeness, and anchoring—in making decisions to import foreign models even in the absence of crisis. With the increased stakes and time pressure of a systemic crisis, decision makers will be even more likely to resort to such "inferential shortcuts."

33. Polillo and Guillen 2005.

34. Offe 1997.

35. McNamara 2002, Marcussen 2005.

little effort. Only heads of state and legislatures needed to be convinced to pass the requisite laws. Most countries already had a few well-placed proponents of the model, and in the early postcommunist years few other domestic actors in most countries had the knowledge or interest to contest it. During this phase the transnational central banking community served as an agenda setter and lobby-ist, often working with postcommunist central bank governors to persuade their governments to pass new central banking legislation.

With every diffusion mechanism pointing powerfully in the same direction, international influences overwhelmed differences in initial conditions and the postcommunist region soon led the entire world in legislating central bank inde-pendence. By the mid-1990s virtually every postcommunist government had granted significant legal independence to its central bank.[36]

Transformation

How, though, to move from legislating central bank independence to transform-ing postcommunist central banks? It is at this stage that a transnational policy community may actively promote its principles and practices. While occasionally the aim is to build an entirely new institution, more commonly the task involves institutional conversion—the transformation of an existing institution to reflect a new model.[37] A transnational community's ability to influence the direction and extent of transformation depends primarily on three factors: its access, the consistency and intensity of its efforts, and the social and material incentives for those in the target institution to follow its lead.

Before all else, transnational policy communities need access in order to influence transformation. While seemingly an obvious point, Iain Johnston observes that many studies wrongly "assume that agents at the systemic level have relatively unobstructed access to states and substate actors from which to diffuse new normative understandings."[38] Access is never automatic, and must be negotiated. The transnational central banking community had access to post-communist central bankers in all but the most politically closed postcommu-nist states. In those few postcommunist states and in those particular moments where the community's access to the central bank was regularly denied or restricted, transformation lagged.

---

36. Cukierman et al. 2002.
37. Thelen 2003.
38. Johnston 2001.

The consistency and intensity of the policy community's advice facilitates institutional transformation in a variety of ways. The more that disparate members of a policy community hold a consistent, unified conception of the model that they are transmitting, the easier it will be for them to work together to recreate that model elsewhere and the more difficult it will be for those in the institution undergoing conversion to imagine alternatives. Beyond general agreement and coordination within the policy community, another element that facilitates consistency is a simplification of the message; a cleaning up and "packaging" for export. Given a reasonably consistent model, an intensive transformation campaign to disseminate that model—one relying on numerous advisors, institutions, and transmission methods, and directly and repeatedly reaching a high proportion of individuals in the target organization—will achieve greater results.

With the important exception of banking supervision, the transnational central banking community excelled in the consistency and intensity of its efforts. The community possessed unifying principles and practices, promoted a simplified yet flexible model of the independent central bank for export, and developed an organizational infrastructure ensuring that its members presented relatively consistent, coordinated advice. It used these resources to mount an intense and sustained campaign to transfer its ideas and practices to postcommunist central banks. Change occurred most easily in areas where professional central bank advisors dominated and gave consistent advice, and where fewer and higher-status central bankers needed training. The more varied the donors and messages involved, and the more numerous and lower-status the relevant postcommunist central bankers, the more difficult the transformation. Monetary policy and banking supervision, the two most politically charged central bank tasks, fell on the higher and lower ends of this spectrum, respectively.

The most important incentives at play in the transformation stage are those that the transnational policy community can offer to people working within the target organization, especially to the leadership. These incentives can be both social and material, although for deep transformation to occur material incentives are not enough. Persuasion and social influence ultimately encourage those in the target organization to embrace, adapt, and defend the transplant model.[39] Policy community members can collectively grant status and membership to newcomers who accept their model, while excluding or denigrating those who fail to conform. Persuasion occurs when the newcomer develops a relationship of trust with the promoter and recognizes him or her as an authority. This is more

---

39. Johnston (2001) defines social influence as "a class of microprocesses that elicit pro-norm behavior through the distribution of social rewards and punishments."

likely to occur when the promoter and newcomer share personal and organizational characteristics.

As an internationally legitimate, high-status, autonomous, exclusive, and organized group, the transnational central banking community had strong social and persuasive leverage to bring to bear on postcommunist central bankers. The community promised postcommunist central bankers political independence, control over their budgets, better salaries, and higher status. It treated them as knowledgeable professionals, and offered them international travel, training, and membership in an influential, cohesive transnational community. The nature of central banks—particularly their relatively small, spatially centralized, and highly educated staffs—eased the way. The postcommunist central bankers represented a small group with an ostensibly technocratic mission and newfound legal autonomy, making it relatively easy and desirable for them to engage intensively with the transnational central banking community.

Conditional norms may come into play as well, facilitating the socialization process. Herrera defines a conditional norm as one that specifies the appropriate action "for certain types of actors or under certain conditions rather than for all members of the group at all times."[40] Her research convincingly demonstrates that as Russia began its economic transition, Soviet-era statisticians embraced the international System of National Accounts (SNA) because they had previously accepted it as the appropriate standard for a market economy. Once Russia itself became a market economy, the statisticians wanted to use the market-appropriate SNA. In short, Russian statisticians adopting the SNA had to change only their previous practices, not their underlying beliefs. While not quite so clear-cut for central bankers, certainly many felt that the new economic conditions made it appropriate to move toward different, market-oriented principles and practices.

Although the transnational central banking community's efforts led to remarkable transformation across the postcommunist world, certain characteristics of the individual central banks affected the shape, speed, and extent of convergence with the transplant model. Chief among these were leadership and resources. Central banks are small, hierarchical organizations in which governors play an unusually important role. If a central bank's governor embraced the transplant model and the transnational community, it accelerated the process within the bank as a whole. Human and financial resources mattered as well. If the central bank began its transformation with at least some personnel conversant in English

---

40. Herrera 2010.

and economics, if it had access to high-quality young recruits from local and international universities, if it had a lean staff and organizational structure, and if it had the financial resources to hire and retain the best people, the transnational central banking community's training and technical assistance efforts had a stronger, more concentrated base to build on and could be cumulative.

This stage of the process led not only to the transformation of postcommunist central banks, but also to the expansion of the transnational central banking community. Within a decade, most postcommunist states had technically proficient central banks and central bankers who had adopted prevailing international norms. In addition, as the more advanced postcommunist central bankers became incorporated into the transnational community they began to take active roles in advising other central bankers domestically, regionally, and internationally, blurring the initially sharp lines between "Western teachers" and "Eastern students."

Internalization

Internalization is the process through which initially foreign models become embedded and taken for granted domestically.[41] Internalization requires that, at minimum, most domestic elites tolerate the transplant's existence on its own terms, even though they may occasionally disagree with its particular actions. For full internalization to take place, domestic actors must come to see the transplant as no longer foreign at all, but rather as a necessary, everyday part of the domestic scene.

In the internalization stage, underlying domestic political and economic conditions naturally come to the fore. As Beissinger has pointed out, models initially diffuse to the most hospitable and receptive environments, only gradually working their way toward less and less fertile ground.[42] The adopters at the margins will, not surprisingly, have the most difficulty internalizing the new transplants. Beyond the importance of initial conditions, however, three other factors loom large in internalization: asynchronous transformation, two-track diffusion, and policy learning.

Asynchronous transformation acknowledges institutional codependence. Initial conditions matter, but so does the pace of change in other institutions that must support and work with the transplant, especially under conditions of systemic crisis. To return to the botanical metaphor, if a transplant is placed in an environment rife with parasites or without bees to pollinate it, it will not thrive.

---

41. Finnemore and Sikkink 1998.
42. Beissinger 2007.

When interdependent institutions are transformed at significantly different speeds or in incompatible ways, it can generate unexpected and undesirable consequences.

The concept of two-track diffusion recognizes that domestic actors inside and outside of the target institution may have different motivations and levels of engagement in the transplantation process. In our case, the extension of the transnational central banking community's wormhole network to the postcommunist central banks exacerbated these differences, with important ramifications for internalization. The postcommunist central bankers experienced an intensive socialization process guided by the transnational community, paralleled by a shallower, more incentive-driven process outside of the central banks.[43] Postcommunist central bankers embraced the logic of appropriateness, but other domestic actors often responded to the logic of consequences. Both logics could dominate at the same time but in different places, one inside the central banks and the other outside them. Although the word "diffusion" typically evokes an image of an entire country or geographic region taking on a foreign borrowing—states become democratic,[44] adopt liberal economic ideas,[45] and so forth—this obscures the spatially limited and nuanced nature of most diffusion processes. As Helleiner recognizes, "economic globalization ... must be located in specific spatial contexts in order to understand its significance."[46] The spread of the central banking model in postcommunist states occurred in a more spatially nuanced way than measures showing widespread adoption of central bank independence would indicate.

Finally, once transformation has begun in earnest, policy makers who may have initially chosen to introduce the new model without significant reflection or understanding then start to learn about its concrete political and economic effects first hand. While sometimes this facilitates the internalization process, in other instances influential elites may not like what they have learned.[47] Under such circumstances, the long-term viability of the transplant is threatened. This does not necessarily mean that the transplant will not survive, but its proponents may need to draw on external resources, champions, and justifications (such as conditionality agreements) to defend it. It also invites policy makers to attempt to square the circle through mock compliance, preserving the outward appearance of the model for external consumption while undermining its core functions in practice.[48]

---

43. Johnson 2006.
44. Kopstein and Reilly 2000.
45. Simmons and Elkins 2004.
46. Helleiner 1997.
47. Gilardi et al. 2009.
48. Walter 2008.

Internalization of the central banking model required building a strong, reliable base of domestic support for postcommunist central banks undergoing Western-oriented transformation. As postcommunist central bankers became better trained, more experienced, and more technically capable, one might have expected their credibility and support among domestic politicians, commercial bankers, and the public to grow. Instead, in many cases the opposite happened. Postcommunist central bankers regularly came under attack and their independence was often challenged and undermined. Difficult economic starting points, asynchronous transformation, two-track diffusion, and elite learning all contributed to this outcome.

Postcommunist central bankers' new policy tools often faltered both because of difficult initial conditions—particularly in the post-Soviet states—and because the pace of central bank transformation outstripped that of most other government and economic institutions. In North America and Western Europe, supporting legal and market institutions had predated independent central banks. In the postcommunist world, the situation was reversed. As one Czech central banker admitted to me in 2000, "Traditional theoretical concepts just don't work very well yet. . . . Ten years just isn't enough data on which to build models."[49] Facing significant uncertainty, shallow financial markets, weak tax bases, and corrupt and inexperienced judiciaries, central bankers' monetary policies were often ineffective and their regulatory efforts undermined. Ironically, the relatively rapid transformation of postcommunist central banks at times undercut its sustainability, as other government agencies were unable to provide the necessary fiscal and judicial support for central bank policies. Most postcommunist countries experienced serious financial crises, and central bank independence provided only limited protection from inflation. Many postcommunist politicians drew negative lessons from crisis experiences, finding their touted independent central banks unable to fulfill their stated missions.

The two-track diffusion process drove a deeper wedge between postcommunist central bankers and those in other domestic institutions. The central bankers had entered the transnational community's wormhole network. The community worked hard to integrate them, encouraging them to adopt its principles and practices, embrace its culture, participate in its events, and implicitly to replicate its insularity. But while postcommunist central bankers themselves became relatively well integrated into the transnational community—sharing ideas, attending regular meetings, and communicating so intensively that it significantly

---

49. Author's interview with an official in the Real Economy Division of the Czech National Bank, Prague, Czech Republic, May 2000.

reduced the practical "distance" among them—other domestic actors did not and could not share in this experience. As a result, postcommunist central bankers often grew to have more in common with central bankers abroad than with other political and economic actors in their own countries. This proved to be a double-edged sword when postcommunist central bankers found themselves embattled politically. When faced with a domestic backlash, postcommunist central bankers' ideals and community spirit often encouraged them to openly defy their governments and lean on their international networks for support rather than to learn to work with their opponents, short-circuiting the internalization process. The simplified export model exacerbated the problem; while established central bankers understood independence as a nuanced and contextual concept, the community had not always presented it that way to postcommunist central bankers, nor had the postcommunist central bankers necessarily appreciated the nuance.

As time went on, postcommunist politicians also came to better understand the economic and political trade-offs involved in conservative monetary policy and stricter financial supervision. Some politicians, particularly but not uniformly on the left, found central bank actions too constraining to suit their policy goals. As postcommunist governments and politicians grew increasingly confident in their own judgment, they also became less willing to accept at face value the claims of outside advisors and their own central bankers. Postcommunist publics and commercial financial sectors had exhibited little intrinsic demand for conservative, independent central banks. Independent central banks did not appear as a direct response to inflation, nor did domestic commercial bankers lobby for central bank independence as had happened in the advanced industrial democracies.

As domestic actors learned more about how their central banks operated in practice, external incentives and coercion often became key to preserving the central banks' authority. Where these incentives weakened—either because sovereignty, funds, and legitimacy had been obtained, or because governments ceased to care about them—domestic support for the central banks could wane as well. The central banks' legal independence and stability mandates made them useful political scapegoats in economic downturns, often undermining their domestic legitimacy and credibility. As several former Soviet republics became less democratic and more nationalistic over time, their political leaders had less interest in supporting independent monetary authorities championed by foreign democratic states. Many commercial bankers also became bitter adversaries of their own central banks. In one extreme case, a disgruntled Russian banker hired hit men to assassinate the Bank of Russia's well-known regulatory head Andrei Kozlov. The most politically savvy postcommunist central bank governors like

Romania's long-serving Mugur Isărescu could often deflect such challenges through strategic networking, tactical compromise, a reputation for integrity, and financial support for public works and culture, but the desire and ability to do so represented the exception rather than the rule.

Transplant models rarely come through intact, even under the best of circumstances. An analysis of postcommunist central banking shows an important reason why: it is a multi-stage process rather than a single event. Embracing a new model, transforming institutions to conform to it, and internalizing the transplant within society each occur through different mechanisms and require different conditions and tools. Not only is each stage difficult to work through, but asynchronous transformation and two-track diffusion can mean that early successes actually derail later ones. The following chapters explore the transplantation of the central banking model to the postcommunist world in detail, from choosing central bank independence through the transnational community's transformation campaign to the challenges of internalization.

CHOOSING INDEPENDENCE

"I hear, but I do not listen."

—European Central Bank president Wim Duisenberg (2001)

With these infamous words refusing European leaders' increasingly desperate requests that he cut interest rates in 2001, ECB president Wim Duisenberg publicly affirmed the principle of central bank independence. By the mid-1990s, every single postcommunist government had passed legislation granting significant independence to its central bank (see table 3.1).[1] In fact, a strong majority granted their central banks greater independence than the central banks of the advanced industrial democracies had enjoyed in the 1980s. About one-third gave their central banks more legal independence than the Deutsche Bundesbank, previously considered the gold standard. Nor was this top third merely the "usual suspects" in East Central Europe—it included states as diverse as the Czech Republic, Armenia, Moldova, and Kazakhstan. Legislating central bank independence does not mean that a government will necessarily respect its own laws in practice, but it does indicate that postcommunist governments found value in passing these laws.

The ubiquitous embrace of central bank independence differed markedly from the divergent laws postcommunist governments adopted in other realms. Privatization laws allowed for methods ranging from voucher auctions to sales and varied significantly in their treatment of potential foreign investors, while

---

1. Cukierman et al. 2002. Similarly, Maxfield (1997) found that the average level of statutory central bank independence in fourteen postcommunist states from 1990 through 1994 (using the coding method from Cukierman et al. 1992) was .45, comparable to Western Europe's .46 ranking.

TABLE 3.1 Postcommunist central bank independence in the 1990s

COUNTRY	CB LAW YEAR	LVAW	LVES	LVESX
Albania	1992	0.51	0.47	0.49
Armenia	1993	0.3	0.6	0.34
	1996	0.85	1	0.9
Azerbaijan	1992	0.22	NA	0.42
	1996	0.24	NA	0.37
Belarus	1992	0.73	0.75	0.67
Bulgaria	1991	0.55	NA	0.65
Croatia	1992	0.44	0.6	0.49
Czech Republic	1991	0.73	0.96	0.73
Estonia	1993	0.78	0.96	0.58
Georgia	1995	0.73	0.68	0.62
Hungary	1991	0.67	0.79	0.61
Kazakhstan	1993	0.32	0.63	0.56
	1995	0.44	0.92	0.79
Kyrgyzstan	1992	0.52	0.55	0.55
Latvia	1992	0.49	0.96	0.73
Lithuania	1991	0.28	0.37	0.25
	1996	0.78	0.96	0.58
Macedonia	1995	0.41	0.68	0.55
Moldova	1991	0.38	0.84	0.54
	1995	0.73	0.96	0.94
Mongolia	1991	0.43	0.96	0.61
	1996	0.55	0.92	0.68
Poland	1991	0.46	0.49	0.32
	1997	0.89	0.92	0.95
Romania	1991	0.34	0.51	0.32
Russia	1990	0.43	0.47	0.41
	1995	0.49	0.47	0.38
Slovak Republic	1992	0.62	0.92	0.73
Slovenia	1991	0.63	0.72	0.52
Tajikistan	1993	0.36	NA	0.29
Turkmenistan	1992	0.26	0.25	0.19
Ukraine	1991	0.42	NA	NA
Uzbekistan	1992	0.41	NA	0.71
	1995	0.56	0.92	0.92
Average (for those with two)		0.51	0.73	0.57
First law		0.36	0.62	0.46
Second law		0.62	0.88	0.72

Country (1980s)	LVAW	LVES
Germany	0.69	0.87
Switzerland	0.64	0.4
United States	0.48	0.16
Canada	0.45	0.25
Australia	0.36	0.29
UK	0.27	0.04
New Zealand	0.24	0.08
Japan	0.18	0.27
Norway	0.17	0.21

Source: Adapted from Cukierman et al. (2002), tables 1 and 2. *NB:* Cukierman et al. did not include all 1990s postcommunist central banking laws and significant amendments.

Notes: LVES is a narrow index measuring only the most important aspects of central bank independence: the allocation of authority for monetary policy, the conflict resolution procedures, and the degree of focus on price stability. LVESX includes the LVES measures plus a weighted average taking into account legal limitations on central bank lending to the government. LVAW is a broader aggregate index measuring 16 weighted features, including the LVESX measures plus the term of office and appointment/dismissal procedures for the governor and board members. The closer to 1, the more independent the central bank.

NA means not enough information was available to construct the index.

some countries passed little or no privatization legislation at all. Postcommunist countries experimented with different electoral systems and introduced both presidential and parliamentary regimes. While countries like Czechoslovakia instituted sweeping lustration laws to remove former communist officials from the civil service, others such as Russia ignored the issue entirely. Some countries passed new laws protecting minority rights, while others denied minority groups rights that they had previously enjoyed under the communist regime. Foreign advisors made recommendations to postcommunist states in all of these areas and more, but with little consistency in policy prescriptions or legal outcomes. In short, legislation enshrining central bank independence represents a significant outlier in postcommunist legal development. Postcommunist countries all made similar choices, at least on paper, to shield their monetary authorities from the political process in some way. Why?

Political and economic uncertainty as well as the international consensus favoring independent central banks gave postcommunist states multiple motives to pass such legislation. Postcommunist countries initially adopted their central banking laws in the early 1990s as part of the worldwide wave of pro-independence laws. Powerful states, international investors, and above all the transnational central banking community all promoted independent central banks, and as a result, postcommunist governments came to view their central banks as markers of sovereignty and guarantors of international resource flows. Postcommunist governments that hoped to join the European Union, that worked most closely with the IMF, and that had new democratic leaders and previous experience with the transnational central banking community tended to grant their central banks the highest levels of legal independence. But even postcommunist governments with less welcoming initial conditions and domestic political dynamics chose to pass legislation increasing the independence of their central banks in the face of these multiple and overwhelming international influences.

The Choice

Central bank independence is somewhat of a misnomer, as no domestic economic institution can be completely free from politics. If central bankers ignore all political sentiment they risk losing their independent status. Transparency guidelines also bind most independent central banks, requiring them to report on their activities to an elected legislature, to publish the minutes of their board meetings, or to otherwise justify their decisions and performance. Nevertheless, laws granting central banks extensive decision making and financial autonomy from elected authorities can significantly shield central bankers from the political process.

Most research on postcommunist central banking has focused tightly on legal independence: how to measure it, why it has become so prevalent, and what effects it has. More broadly, economists birthed an entire cottage industry to measure central bank independence.[2] They generally agreed that three key measures indicated the highest level of legal independence: if the law mandates price stability as the main goal of monetary policy, if it prohibits central bank lending to the government, and if it allows the central bank to choose its policy rates and tools without government interference (e.g., government representatives on the central bank's board).[3] Other common measures deem a central bank more politically independent if its governor enjoys a term of at least six to eight years, if its board members hold lengthy terms not synchronized with the electoral cycle, if the appointment process is clear and relatively apolitical, if the governor and board members must possess particular professional qualifications, and if the governor and board members may not simultaneously hold other posts. A central bank is considered more economically independent if it controls its own budget and salaries, if it does not conduct banking supervision, and if it possesses a wide range of monetary policy instruments. The underlying presumption is the more independence the better, because more independent central banks can more credibly pursue price stability.

Postcommunist governments—not their central bankers—had the ultimate power to choose central bank independence.[4] Understanding their choices involves answering two separate questions. First, why did postcommunist governments all pass laws increasing the independence of their central banks in the early 1990s? Second, why did some governments choose higher levels of legal independence than others—higher even than the Bundesbank? Both the international

---

2. The pioneering studies measuring legal central bank independence were Cukierman et al. 1992 and Grilli et al. 1991. Key studies comparing central bank independence in transition states before the global financial crisis included Siklos 1994, Loungani and Sheets 1997, Radzyner and Riesinger 1997, Elgie 1998, Lybek 1999, Dvorsky 2000, Hochreiter and Kowalski 2000, Mahadeva and Sterne 2000, Maliszewski 2000, Berger et al. 2001, Neyapti 2001, Cukierman et al. 2002, and Arnone et al. 2007. All found a high level of legal central bank independence in the postcommunist world, both in absolute terms and in comparison to other regions. For example, Arnone et al. (2007) wrote that, "Central banks of countries in transition have reached CBA [central bank autonomy] scores that are comparable with, and sometimes even higher than, CBA in the advanced economies." Mahadeva and Sterne (2000) also noted this result in their survey of ninety-four central banks, finding that industrialized and transitional states both had high degrees of *de jure* independence, with developing states lagging considerably behind.

3. Arnone et al. 2007.

4. The only example of internationally imposed postcommunist central bank independence occurred in Bosnia-Herzegovina. Article VII of the November 1995 Dayton peace agreement guaranteed the central bank's independence and required that its first governor be a foreigner. A central banker from New Zealand, Peter Nicholl, served for five years as its first governor.

consensus and the uncertainty of the transition explain the rapid initial choice of central bank independence across the postcommunist states. This consensus encouraged postcommunist governments seeking quick solutions to new problems to introduce the international model primarily because of its symbolic and ready-made qualities. By contrast, direct international influences (both persuasive and coercive) and differing domestic conditions better explain the variance in degree of legal independence that emerged among postcommunist states.[5]

Only emulation in the face of uncertainty can explain why postcommunist states granted significant legal independence to their central banks so rapidly, most in 1990–92. The majority adopted their first central banking laws before applying for IMF membership, so IMF loan conditionality cannot explain it. Just two countries, Hungary and Bulgaria, had signed IMF standby agreements before passing their first laws and only two more, Albania and Romania, signed their first standby agreements within a year of doing so. EU conditionality cannot explain it either, because at this point the EU had yet to ratify the Maastricht Treaty requiring central bank independence for member states. Small, resource-poor countries and large, resource-rich ones alike passed these laws. Countries experiencing high inflation and those as yet without serious inflation problems passed these laws, as did those in every postcommunist region, from East Central Europe to Central Asia.[6] It happened in both newly Western-oriented democracies like Poland and inward-looking autocracies led by Soviet-era elites like Uzbekistan. The only condition that stopped postcommunist governments from immediately adopting laws on central bank independence was civil war—in rump Yugoslavia and Tajikistan—and at that only temporarily.

The international model resonated in the postcommunist world because of the collapse of communist-era political and economic institutions. The two pillars of the system—the Communist Party and the command economy—had lost integrity and legitimacy. As the previous order came into question, economic relationships shifted and a scramble to gain control over material resources ensued. Government officials, enterprise directors, and entrepreneurs of various sorts began to formally and informally appropriate state property. Currencies often became unstable, and in many countries dollarization, arrears, and barter began to proliferate. Trade relationships faltered badly as

---

5. Epstein (2008) similarly emphasizes varying domestic openness to international influences (what she refers to as the "social context" of reform) in explaining differences in both legal and actual central bank independence in postcommunist states.

6. Cukierman et al. (2002) found that inflation did not significantly affect legal independence levels in the postcommunist world. Both Quaglia (2005) and Marcussen (2005) pointed out that legal central bank independence and inflation are not closely related in the rest of the world, either.

well, as countries found their traditional Soviet bloc partners often unwilling to or incapable of maintaining previous ties. Faced with the daunting task of managing an inherently unruly and uncertain economic transformation, new postcommunist governments avidly sought help and shortcuts. As King notes, "ideas are most important during periods of uncertainty or in complex and technical issue areas. These situations obscure the distributional effects of a given institutional arrangement or policy choice, making it difficult for interest groups to identify where their interests lie."[7] Command-era central banks needed new mandates and capabilities to function within the chaotic yet increasingly market-oriented environment. Under these circumstances, it made perfect sense to borrow legislation from elsewhere. For example, Hungary, Poland, and Czechoslovakia modeled their central bank legislation after the German law on the Bundesbank, while Slovenia borrowed from both the Austrian and German laws.

Given the international consensus, postcommunist countries chose to adopt central bank independence in pursuit of international legitimacy and national sovereignty regardless of its fit with domestic conditions.[8] As Marcussen observed, "sometimes states simply adopt a certain organizational structure such as a central bank because the act in itself will classify the state as being modern and developed and thereby a legitimate actor in world society."[9] By adopting this legislation, governments conformed to international expectations and models. For example, many postcommunist governments passed laws limiting central bank participation in the primary securities market before they had begun to issue government securities in the first place. Many laws also limited central bank financing of the government well before it was realistically possible to do so in practice, given underdeveloped or nonexistent securities markets and taxation bureaucracies. Therefore:

> The spread of central bank independence should be seen as a fundamentally social and political phenomenon, rooted in the logic of organisational mimicry and global norms of neoliberal governance. Organisational models are diffused across borders through the perceptions and actions of people seeking to replicate others' success and legitimise their own efforts at reform by borrowing rules from other settings, even if these rules are materially inappropriate to their local needs.[10]

---

7. King 2005.
8. McNamara 2002, Grabel 2003, Marcussen 2005, Quaglia 2005.
9. Marcussen 2005.
10. McNamara 2002.

The postcommunist choice for central bank independence represented more than a desperate grab at a ready-made solution to restore economic order. The international consensus meant that postcommunist governments believed that this choice would yield greater international resources and legitimacy. Once central bank independence came to be considered best practice among the advanced industrial democracies, postcommunist governments hoped that passing such legislation would serve as a cheap yet effective signal leading to increased foreign investment and support from international financial institutions. Although this initial choice did not significantly affect foreign resource flows to postcommunist states, the more important fact is that postcommunist governments believed that it might. International advisors reinforced this belief, emphasizing that independent central banks indicated to the outside world that a country was serious about reform.

More fundamentally, postcommunist leaders' desire for their states to be taken seriously, to be considered legitimate members of the international system, meant adopting institutional forms characteristic of high-status independent states. In 1990, former US Federal Reserve governor Paul Volcker kicked off a conference on central banking in emerging markets by wondering aloud why postcommunist leaders had become so enamored of independent central banks. He pointed out that socialist economies historically had a good record on inflation and that under the wrong circumstances, central banks could become engines of inflation rather than the reverse. Given this, he said, "it seems to me . . . the reason that there is so much talk about central banking is that it is very much tied up with ideas of sovereignty, of autonomy, of discretion, and of economic policy making."[11] Most postcommunist countries had not experienced meaningful sovereignty for years, if ever.

For their part, postcommunist central bankers embraced the conflation of national sovereignty with "sovereignty" for their institutions. For example, the governors of the three Baltic central banks met in August 1990 to declare support for "the idea that the central banks should be independent of USSR banks, as well as of their own governments."[12] Adopting central bank independence often represented a deeper identity claim as well, especially in East Central Europe and the Baltics. In the 1980s and early 1990s, many leaders and citizens viewed Western societies as prosperous, free, and worthy of emulation. By borrowing Western economic practices, they both affirmed a desire to grow wealthy

---

11. Quoted in Federal Reserve Bank of Kansas City 1990.

12. "Baltic Central Bank Leaders Urge Independence," Vilnius Domestic Service, August 28, 1990, translated in FBIS-SOV 90-168, August 29, 1990, 65.

through engagement with the West and rejected their previous, enforced identification with the Soviet Union. Even key Russian leaders strongly identified with the West in the early 1990s.

Uncertainty and the international consensus explain why postcommunist states introduced laws on central bank independence. However, it does not explain why some created more legally independent central banks than others or why some later enhanced their initial legislation while others did not. For this, more direct international influences and differing domestic conditions were at play. Governments revising their central banking laws soon after adopting their initial laws almost always increased the independence of their central banks.[13] As a result, countries with back-to-back reforms on average had higher levels of central bank independence by the late 1990s than those with only one round of legislation. Governments revising their legislation often did so because of direct international influences, both coercive and persuasive. By 1993 Central and East European countries knew that EU membership would require a very high level of central bank independence and the front-runner accession states began to modify their legislation accordingly. The IMF also made its lending agreements conditional on promises to carry out liberalizing reforms such as revising central banking laws.[14]

However, these international pressures were not simply commands to postcommunist governments to "free your central banks!" Transnational community members provided extensive technical assistance in drafting and commenting on central bank legislation. During this process they spent hundreds of hours not only suggesting text and revisions, but also explaining the reasons behind their proposals to postcommunist government officials, politicians, and central bankers. During this process international advisors had ample opportunity to persuade their postcommunist interlocutors of the wisdom of their approach, and the consensus on the key legislative elements necessary to strengthen central bank independence contributed greatly to their credibility. Just as important, domestic supporters could also invoke these external pressures and use the advisors' carefully crafted arguments to bolster their own positions. When politicians or nascent interest groups questioned such legislation, the financial, intellectual, and moral support of international actors could tip the scales in favor of its domestic proponents. Epstein, for example, convincingly shows how such

---

13. Cukierman et al. 1992.

14. Confirming this relationship, Polillo and Guillen (2005) found that independence levels were highly correlated with IMF loan dependence. IMF conditionality often did not have its broader intended effects on postcommunist governments, however, as experiences in Ukraine and Russia demonstrated. Stone 2002, Epstein 2008.

a transnational coalition between international financial institutions and the National Bank of Poland succeeded in defeating a legal challenge to central bank independence by a newly elected coalition government of communist successor parties in 1994.[15]

Domestic factors mattered as well, although not those typically mentioned in the literature on central bank independence. Neither party bargains, supportive lobbying by the financial sector, nor opposition from trade unions or exporters played important roles.[16] Nascent party systems, economic uncertainty, and the larger issues of sovereignty, identity, and foreign investment meant that the predictable patterns of political jockeying typical of advanced industrial democracies were largely absent. Postcommunist commercial banks if anything usually argued against independent central banks, as they feared more stringent regulation of their often dubious activities. Rather, two other domestic factors loomed large: whether or not the transition empowered new political leaders, and the extent of pre-1989 exposure to Western economic ideas and institutions.

By new leadership I mean leaders and parties coming to power who had not held important decision-making authority beforehand. This mattered for four reasons. First, inexperienced political leaders had less stake in and knowledge of the existing system, and thus were more likely to embrace foreign models and advisors. Second, as former outsiders they entered office with a public mandate to overhaul the government. Third, some of these new leaders had been former dissidents supported morally and on occasion financially by Western governments. As a result, they often welcomed reform models and suggestions from the West. Finally, new leaders meant new economic advisory teams, and so a political transition could empower pro-market economists who had been marginalized under the previous regime. New leadership helped foster enhanced central banking legislation in countries such as Czechoslovakia, Estonia, and Kyrgyzstan, while communist-era leaders' continuing hold on power in places like Azerbaijan, Romania, Ukraine, and Kazakhstan meant that relatively less legislative change could occur. For example, Romania's first postcommunist leaders, former members of dictator Nicolae Ceaușescu's inner circle, were more concerned with reconsolidating their power than with impressing and working with outsiders. Only with the election of the opposition Democratic Convention of Romania in 1996 did an enhancement of Romania's

---

15. Epstein 2008, Epstein and Johnson 2009.

16. On the argument that politicians strengthen central bank independence to defuse party conflicts over monetary policy, see Bernhard 2002. On the argument that unions and exporters will oppose central bank independence, see Frieden and Rogowski 1998, Bearce 2003. On the argument that governments adopt central bank independence in response to lobbying pressures from the commercial financial sector, see Posen 1995.

central banking law become possible.[17] Similarly, in a reverse direction unusual for this decade, when Bulgaria's former communists returned to power in 1993 they undermined the Bulgarian National Bank and in 1996 passed a short-lived law weakening its independence.[18]

In addition, individuals in some postcommunist countries, most notably in East Central Europe, had earlier exposure to and connections with Western economic networks and institutions. Bockman and Eyal have argued that dense transnational economic networks crossing the Iron Curtain explain the rapid adoption of neoliberal reforms in East Central Europe.[19] Many other East European and a few Soviet economists not actively involved in these networks had traveled abroad and had read works by Western scholars such as Samuelson and Friedman in the 1980s. As a result, such economists often (although not always) became early advocates of the Western central banking model. Where new post-communist political leaders came to power they often brought these economists into their governments and central banks. In such cases, the empowered economists joined forces with the transnational central banking community to help promote its central banking model in their countries. This further demonstrates the power of the international consensus, because Western free marketeers like Milton Friedman, Friedrich Hayek, and Margaret Thatcher—favorites of postcommunist radical reformers—had in their time expressed deep reservations about central bank independence. Only in the late 1980s did instituting central bank independence come to be considered a conservative, neoliberal choice.

Central Bank Independence in Authoritarian States

Although postcommunist governments all chose to adopt legislation giving significant independence to their central banks, for such independence to be meaningful domestically governments must respect it in practice. It makes little sense to talk about central bank independence in consolidated authoritarian states, as by definition such states do not adhere to the rule of law.[20] Genuine conflict between an authoritarian government and a central bank cannot be resolved in the central

---

17. Epstein 2008. For a defense of Romanian central bank independence in the early 1990s, see Cerna et al. 1999.

18. The Bulgarian Socialist Party's uncontrolled fiscal profligacy led to financial collapse and new elections in 1997, after which the victorious opposition not only restored the BNB's independence but also instituted a currency board to shore up Bulgaria's international credibility. See Ganev 2007.

19. Bockman and Eyal 2002. See also Greskovits (1998) on Hungary.

20. Abdelal 2001.

bank's favor, and indeed will rarely ever arise publicly. Central bank independence is a feature of democratic polities designed to mitigate a specific deficiency of democratic systems—politicians' temptation to spend freely before elections.

My analysis thus concentrates primarily on the twenty-one postcommunist states that experienced political liberalization during the 1990s rather than on those that were clearly authoritarian at the time: Azerbaijan, Belarus, Kazakhstan, Tajikistan, Turkmenistan, Uzbekistan, and Yugoslavia/Serbia. Serbia subsequently experienced both political liberalization and central bank transformation, but the others remained consolidated authoritarian regimes. Although no postcommunist government fully respected its central bank's independence, the more politically open states gave their central banks greater potential to develop along international lines. By contrast, legal central bank independence under authoritarian governments did not necessarily have such ramifications. Central bank governors' tenures in authoritarian postcommunist states are revealing in this regard. Throughout the 1990s, all but Kazakhstan's central bank demonstrated either unusually stable leadership (Azerbaijan, Tajikistan, Turkmenistan, and Uzbekistan) or numerous changes in leadership (Belarus and Serbia), reflecting in both instances their governors' subordinate status.[21]

This raises the question of why authoritarian states would introduce legal central bank independence in the first place. Elsewhere, most famously in Chile, authoritarian leaders who expected to lose power through political liberalization granted independence to their central banks in order to tie the hands of their anticipated successors.[22] But in the authoritarian postcommunist states, leaders did not expect to lose power and usually preferred to retain control over central bank policies. Instead, path dependence, sovereignty aspirations, and international legitimacy concerns drove post-Soviet authoritarian states to adopt such legislation. These states modeled their initial central bank laws after the USSR's 1990 Law on the Gosbank, which in turn had drawn on Western models. As one Russian scholar observed, at that time "everyone wanted to have their own central banks, embassies, did not want to pay taxes into the state coffers."[23] Passing central

---

21. Later Belarus and Turkmenistan changed positions, with pliant Belarussian governor Petr Prokopovich serving from 1998 through 2008, while from 1999 on several Turkmen governors were fired for alleged abuse of power. For example, in May 2006 Turkmen dictator Saparmurat Niyazov fired his central bank governor on national television, saying that, "I cannot trust him with state money. Let him go and work as a common teacher." Niyazov had telegraphed the move two weeks before, saying that of five previous central bank governors, "four are already in jail and one is on the run." See "Turkmenistan's Central Bank Chief Sacked," Central Banking, May 15, 2006.

22. Boylan 2001.

23. Aleksey Podberezkin, quoted in Ol'ga Solomonova, "Kto razvalil Sovetskii soiuz? [Who Destroyed the Soviet Union?]," Trud, 46, March 17, 2006.

banking legislation was also a cheap signal to international financial institutions and investors, since the laws in practice could not restrain authoritarian leaders.

The post-Soviet authoritarian states did differ in one respect, though, and that is in the amount of access that they granted to the transnational central banking community in the 1990s. Central bankers in Turkmenistan and Uzbekistan had little exposure to the community due to the closed nature of their regimes. But in Kazakhstan and Belarus (and to a lesser extent, Azerbaijan and Tajikistan), central bankers did participate in international training and technical assistance programs. Belarus's central bankers engaged with the community early on, before President Aleksandr Lukashenka consolidated his authoritarian regime in the mid-1990s, and managed to maintain some of these ties afterward. An IMF official once remarked to me that Belarussian central bankers told him they would "be ready" if and when the regime opened up.

Kazakhstan was an even more interesting case. President Nursultan Nazarbayev ruled as an authoritarian leader, yet encouraged his central bankers to take advantage of outside advice and contacts. This fit with the Kazakh elite's legitimation strategy. As Schatz explains, the Kazakh leadership could not rest its initial claims to legitimacy on ethnicity, economic performance, history, or democratic freedoms, so it turned to international engagement and recognition to justify its rule. He notes that, "international actors, in turn, used this access to soften Kazakhstan's authoritarianism, while they enjoyed no equivalent access in Uzbekistan and Turkmenistan."[24] Like the Belarussian central bank staff, Kazakh central bankers enthusiastically engaged with the community when given the opportunity. Although central bank transformation remained more limited in authoritarian regimes, when international contact occurred the institutions responded. In short, access is key. Such access in effect opened the wormhole between the postcommunist central banks and the transnational central banking community, allowing intellectual, professional, and institutional connections to grow and strengthen among them.

Separate Pathways, One Choice

Examination of the initial choice processes in Hungary, Czechoslovakia, Russia, and Kyrgyzstan demonstrates concretely how postcommunist governments converged on legal central bank independence from different starting places and through internationally mediated mechanisms. Hungary began its political

---

24. Schatz 2006.

transition having already partially liberalized its economy, meaning that its politicians, economists, and central bankers understood Western central banking better
than those in other postcommunist states. This led to a process of independence
by negotiation. Political parties actively debated the details of the new central
banking legislation, with transnational community members serving as both lobbyists and consultants. In Czechoslovakia, by contrast, prevailing pro-market sentiment without much practical experience yielded independence by consensus, as
no major political or economic actors raised objections to a strong law.

Russia experienced the most complicated process, as its government introduced legal central bank independence in two phases. The Russian Soviet Federated Socialist Republic (RSFSR) adopted its first law in 1990 while still part of the
USSR, as an assertion of economic sovereignty against the central Soviet state.
The post-Soviet government of the Russian Federation then adopted a second,
more detailed law in 1995 in the face of deep divisions between the president and
parliament, neither of which wanted the other to control the central bank. The
transnational central banking community played an active role in supporting
and commenting on the draft legislation, with many of their line-by-line suggestions reflected in the final 1995 law. Finally, Kyrgyzstan's government, with little
theoretical and no practical market experience, passed its legislation on the rec-
ommendation of international actors without meaningful parliamentary debate.
Across the board, the international consensus on central bank independence, the
external incentives to adopt it, and the atmosphere of deep domestic economic
uncertainty ultimately made such legislation the preferred policy choice of these
disparate postcommunist governments.

Hungary: Independence through Negotiation

Economist Kálmán Mizsei observed that "1989 was much less of a threshold in
Hungary than elsewhere."[25] By that point Hungary had already undergone three
decades of gradual economic reform, so Hungarian politicians, economists, and
central bankers began the political transition with more market-oriented experience and Western contacts than other postcommunist states.[26] Hungary also had

---

25. Mizsei 1993.

26. As the influential Hungarian economists Werner Riecke (who held several top positions at the
MNB) and László Antal wrote, "These events are extremely important, because all participants in the
economy . . . were able at least partially to acquire the capabilities and knowledge that are needed to
run a market economy . . . Hungary was thus able to avoid the paradoxical situation—which indeed
occurred in all other transforming economies—that all the newly created institutions formally fulfill
the legal requirements of a market economy, but the behavior of the economic actors and the attitude
of the whole system are driven by the past." Riecke and Antal 1993.

a comparatively well-developed party system by the time of its first free elections in March 1990. Although all parties agreed on the need to rejoin Europe, the various players had a greater understanding of what central bank independence might mean in practice than did politicians elsewhere in the postcommunist world. As a result, while the new Hungarian government quickly agreed to draft a law on central bank independence, key details of the legislation proved controversial. But the Magyar Nemzeti Bank (MNB) and international advisors worked together to write the strong 1991 Act on the Magyar Nemzeti Bank and to persuade parliament to pass it, in the end making only a few concessions to opponents.

Hungary had long been a Western-oriented brick in the Soviet bloc. The Hungarian uprising of 1956 sparked the Warsaw Pact's first invasion to repress political openness in a member state. Hungary's party leaders learned that although the Soviet Union would not tolerate political deviance, it might allow economic tinkering. Hungary's communist government under János Kádár introduced the so-called New Economic Mechanism (NEM) in 1968, a program that brought market elements to the centrally planned economy. This evolved over time into a system with private entrepreneurs, small-scale private agriculture, partially liberalized prices and trade, and a rudimentary supporting legal framework. Hungary joined the IMF in May 1982 and began borrowing from Western banks, accumulating a sizeable sovereign debt. Hungarians thus were already partially integrated into the global capitalist economy by the time that the Soviet bloc imploded.

The NEM and its aftermath not only partially liberalized the economy, but the economics profession as well. László Csaba notes that Hungarian economists participated in the International Economic Association in the 1970s and 1980s, that János Kornai was elected president of both the Econometric Society in 1978 and the European Economic Association in 1987, and that the Budapest University of Economics dropped "Karl Marx" from its name and introduced standard micro and macroeconomics courses in 1986.[27] Hungarian economists also led a vigorous debate in journal articles and the press on accelerating economic reform, a debate that laid the groundwork for changes in policy in the 1980s.[28] As two IMF regional specialists observed, "At the start of the transition, Hungary had more sophisticated economists than anywhere else in the Soviet bloc."[29] These economists had developed diverse ideas about the proper pace and nature of reform, with some pushing for rapid change and others supporting a more gradual move toward international standards.

---

27. Csaba 2002.
28. Berend 1990.
29. Allen and Haas 2001.

The ruling Hungarian Socialist Workers' Party broke the state-controlled monobank into a central bank and commercial banks in 1987, earlier than the other East Central European states.[30] As the Party's control over the political system began to break down, the MNB gained significant informal autonomy to address inflation and deal with Hungary's growing external debt burden. After the March 1990 elections this informal autonomy continued, supported by a friendly agreement between new MNB governor György Surányi and the prime minister, Hungarian Democratic Forum leader József Antall.[31] Meanwhile, the MNB and its international advisors had already begun drafting a new central banking law in late 1989. From the beginning the MNB wanted a strong law based on that of the Bundesbank, and they used the close Hungarian-German connection to help justify it.

The international community played two roles in crafting the 1991 Act on the Magyar Nemzeti Bank: as legitimizing symbol and model, and as legislative consultants and lobbyists. The draft law was closely modeled on the Bundesbank's, and top MNB officials consistently invoked the example of the Bundesbank in their public statements defending the legislation.[32] They referred to the Bundesbank's recognized, respected strength and effectiveness, arguing that Hungary should have a law just as good as the German one.[33] MNB leaders also consulted closely with IMF officials and West European central bankers in drafting the law. The MNB relied especially on IMF resident representative György Szapáry, Alexandre Lamfalussy at the BIS, and European central bank governors such as the Bank of Italy's Guido Carli, the Banque de France's Jacques de Larosière, and the Bundesbank's Karl Otto Pöhl. Surányi reported that he repeatedly discussed tricky

---

30. According to Mihály Kupa, former Finance Minister, the government did so in response to IMF pressures. Interview with Mihály Kupa, "Setting a Bad Example," HVG.hu, January 24, 2007, http://hvg.hu/english/20070124_kupa_mihaly_eng.aspx.

31. Gedeon 1997, Karádi 1999. See also "A törvényjavaslat függetlenséget garantál Surányi György nyilatkozata az MTI-nek [The proposed Act guarantees independence declared György Surányi to MTI]," *Világgazdaság*, September 28, 1991. Surányi had previously led the Ministry of Finance's Financial Research Institute and then—after being fired in 1986 for his too-radical economic proposals—was a finance professor at the Budapest University of Economics.

32. For example, see MNB managing director Rezső Nyers Jr. in "Biztos középút: A magyar jegybank jövője [The Certain Middle Ground: The Future of the Central Bank]," *Magyar Hírlap*, October 13, 1989; MNB governor Ferenc Bartha in Judit Rédei, "Az MNB számvetése [An assessment by MNB]," *Magyarország*, April 6, 1990, 14/90, 35; and MNB governor György Surányi in Ilona Kocsis, "Önállósodási törekvések: Interjú az MNB elnökével [Aspiration for Independence: Interview with the governor of the MNB]," *Magyar Hírlap*, December 11, 1990.

33. The MNB also often referred to its long European history, invoking its founding after World War I. Both Bank of England Governor Montagu Norman and the Financial Committee of the League of Nations played a key role in the MNB's establishment in April 1924, which occurred as part of a League of Nations stabilization program. Bácskai 1997, Szapáry 1997.

legislative issues with his fellow governors, stating that they were "extremely helpful in designing the central bank act at that time."[34] He was also impressed by their personal autonomy and their consensual views. Since West European central bank governors were embroiled in similar domestic discussions about central bank independence and the future European Central Bank at the time, these conversations were more than merely academic. In fact, the Italian and French governments granted legal independence to their central banks only in 1993, two years after the Hungarians.

BIS general manager Alexandre Lamfalussy, Hungarian by birth, played a critical role in persuading Hungarian politicians to support central bank independence. Lamfalussy, who would later become a key architect of the ECB and president of the European Monetary Institute, had a high reputation among Hungarian politicians and in particular with Prime Minister Antall. Lamfalussy discussed the need for strong legislation in Hungary with politicians in both public and private forums. Surányi gave him personal credit for successfully educating lawmakers about what central banks do and why legal independence and conservative monetary policy were so important for Hungary.[35] The highlight was his appearance at a meeting of the parliamentary committee responsible for finalizing the law in August 1991, where he assured policy makers that the draft law met international standards as written and should not be watered down.[36]

The MNB needed this international support to get the Act passed, as it faced vocal opposition from within the ruling HDF party and from the Ministry of Finance. Debate on the Act lasted well over a year, from the time the new government came to power in March 1990 to the Act's passage in October 1991. Prominent HDF deputies such as Iván Szabó and István Csurka were loath to cede economic power to the MNB. The Ministry of Finance, for its part, wanted to preserve its ability to borrow from the MNB at will. HDF deputies proposed several amendments to weaken the draft law, suggesting everything from limiting the governor's term to four years to fully subordinating the MNB to the parliament. In September 1991, near the end of formal debate on the bill, Szabó made one last attempt to undermine it by proposing over fifty amendments.[37] Surányi, his top deputies, and his international supporters managed to squelch the opposition both by defending the importance of central bank independence and by

---

34. Author's interview with MNB governor György Surányi, Budapest, Hungary, March 2000.

35. Ibid.

36. "Nemzetközi szintű banktörvények: Országgyűlési bizottságok ülései [Bank laws according to international standards: Meetings of the parliamentary committees]," *Népszabadság*, August 30, 1991.

37. "Független marad az MNB [The MNB remains independent]," *Napi Világgazdaság*, October 22, 1991, 5. Surányi reportedly threatened to resign if the amendments were passed.

assuring politicians that independence did not mean that the MNB would refuse to cooperate with the government.[38] On the contrary, the MNB would "perform like a good football referee, in the sense that nobody should notice that it is on the field."[39] Surányi personally assured parliament that in any future dispute between the MNB and parliament, parliament's views would take precedence.[40]

As a result, the MNB had to compromise on only two main questions: who would nominate the governor and vice governors, and whether or not the MNB could finance the budget deficit. Although the MNB preferred that its top leaders be nominated by the president and confirmed by parliament, the Act gave nomination power to the prime minister instead.[41] This allayed parliament's fears of creating an uncontrollable central bank. The budget deficit question proved most contentious. Although the MNB wanted the Act to immediately limit its financing to no more than 3 percent of the annual budget, politicians such as Szabó and László Békési (the vice president of the parliamentary budget committee) expressed skepticism that doing so would be feasible given the country's difficult economic circumstances.[42] In the end, the Act allowed unlimited MNB budget financing in 1992, 5 percent in 1993, 4 percent in 1994, and 3 percent thereafter.[43] In every other respect, however, the Act closely mirrored the Bundesbank law and gave the MNB significant independence. The MNB would set and conduct its own monetary policy, the governor would have a six-year term, and the MNB was mandated to maintain internal and external currency stability. As Surányi observed, "the proposed Act found a balance between independence and cooperation between the government and the central bank . . . The six parties in

---

38. See, for example, Judit Rédei, "Az MNB számvetése [An assessment by MNB]," *Magyarország*, April 6, 1990, 14/90, 35; Péter Lovász, "Nem vagyunk túl a válság nehezén: Interjú a Magyar Nemzeti Bank elnökével [We are still not over the most difficult part of the crisis: Interview with the governor of the National Bank of Hungary]," *Népszava*, August 30, 1990, 5; and Péter Lovász, "Összhangban az európai fejlődéssel: A jegybank önálló: Beszélgetés Tarafás Imre MNB-elnökhelyettessel [In harmony with the European development: The Central Bank is independent: Interview with Imre Tarafás, vice governor of the MNB]," *Népszava*, July 17, 1991, 5.

39. Interview with Sándor Czirják, MNB vice governor. Károly Csabai, "Az MNB nem pumpál pénzt a gazdaságba [The MNB is not pumping money into the economy]," *Népszabadság*, August 22, 1990.

40. Ilona Kocsis, "Önállósodási törekvések: Interjú az MNB elnökével [Aspiration for Independence: Interview with the president of the MNB]," *Magyar Hírlap*, December 11, 1990. Surányi also pointed out that if parliament forced the MNB to carry out a policy it opposed, the MNB would not be responsible for the consequences.

41. The Act also put equal numbers of MNB officials and external members on the central bank's council.

42. "Mint púpos gyerek a prés alatt [A slow transformation]," *Világgazdaság*, October 19, 1990.

43. Ágnes Gyenis, "Célegyenesben a jegybanktörvény: Az MNB megvívta harcát [The Act on the Central Bank is at the finish line: The MNB has fought its fights]," *Napi Világgazdaság*, May 25, 1991.

the Parliament continue to agree on the necessity of the autonomy of the central bank."[44]

Parliament approved the Act in October 1991 with 68 percent voting in favor, a figure that would have been even higher if the Alliance of Free Democrats had not voted against it to protest the last-minute modifications weakening the law.[45] The Act came into force as of December 1, 1991, and Surányi ceded his governorship to HDF Minister of Industry Péter Ákos Bod. Although parliament proved incapable of meeting the agreed-on budget financing limits, the 1991 Act set a legal foundation for central bank independence in Hungary, independence that was strengthened in 1996 in order to move closer to EU requirements. As we will see later, over the next several years international influences encouraged Hungarian politicians to continue increasing the MNB's legal independence even as they grew more suspicious of the MNB's policies.

Czechoslovakia: Independence through Consensus

Czechoslovak policy makers turned to the international community to transform their central banking laws as well. The November 1989 Velvet Revolution initiated a sharp break with the previous regime, bringing to power individuals with a strong commitment to political democracy and economic liberalization. These leaders embraced the Western central banking model and looked to international institutions to legitimize and assist their efforts to transform the State Bank of Czechoslovakia (SBCS). Beyond this small circle, however, few domestic actors held strong opinions about central bank independence and its ramifications were not widely understood. Therefore, its international legitimacy made passing the initial legislation relatively uncontroversial.

Unlike Hungary, Czechoslovakia did not experience significant economic openness before 1989. The Soviet crackdown following the 1968 Prague Spring had a chilling effect not only on policy experimentation, but also on the economics profession. As Czech National Bank (CNB) governor Zdeněk Tůma observed with only slight exaggeration in 2004:

> We have almost forgotten that 15 years ago there were not any Czechs nor Slovaks educated in modern economics or business . . . Nobody— with one exception—was allowed to study abroad since the 1960s. When my friend Martin Kupka returned from Geneva in 1989 from his

---

44. "A törvényjavaslat függetlenséget garantál Surányi György nyilatkozata az MTI-nek [The proposed Act guarantees independence declared György Surányi to MTI]," *Világgazdaság*, September 28, 1991.

45. Gedeon 1997.

studies, he brought the textbook on macroeconomics by Dornbusch and Fischer. He told me: "We should translate it into Czech." . . . Later on, we translated the textbook on corporate finance by Brealey and Myers. In other words, we started from scratch.[46]

In the political purges after 1968, many Czechoslovak economists lost their jobs and the government banned translations of key Western economic treatises.[47] Numerous economists went into exile in the West as well, taking positions in universities, research institutes, and international financial institutions. Within Czechoslovakia, non-Party economists found themselves barred from university teaching, publication, and travel outside the Soviet bloc. Only in the 1980s did pockets of economic dissent begin to appear in places such as the Economics Institute at the Czechoslovak Academy of Sciences, the SBCS, and the Czechoslovak Economic Society. The Institute of Forecasting at the Czechoslovak Academy of Sciences brought together many reform-oriented economists, including future Czech prime ministers Václav Klaus and Miloš Zeman as well as several future Czech central bankers. This group had access to certain Western journals, Russian translations of Western economic literature, and select authors translated into Czech such as Samuelson and Arrow.[48] When the 1989 Velvet Revolution occurred, only this small group had been significantly exposed to Western economic ideas. This group had a domestic monopoly on market economic expertise and a faith in its principles untempered by practice.

More important, these economists ascended to political power in postcommunist Czechoslovakia. The communist regime in Czechoslovakia collapsed quickly. Student demonstrations kicked off the Velvet Revolution on November 17, 1989, and eleven days later the Communist Party of Czechoslovakia announced that it would cede power. With the agreement of Civic Forum—the umbrella group of opposition leaders informally led by dissident Václav Havel—outgoing Party boss Gustáv Husák appointed a temporary successor government on December 10. Prague Spring leader Alexander Dubček was elected speaker of the reformed parliament on December 28 and Havel assumed the Czechoslovak presidency on December 29. Civic Forum and its Slovak counterpart, Public Against Violence, dominated the first free elections held in June 1990. Václav Klaus participated actively in the transition, becoming Minister of Finance after the Velvet Revolution and head of Civic Forum in October 1990. His political influence and the country's need for a radical economic overhaul brought his economic circle

---

46. Zdeněk Tůma, speech at CMC Graduation, School of Business, December 4, 2004, Prague. www.cnb.cz/www.cnb.cz/en/conferences/speeches/tuma_cmcgraduation04122004.html.

47. Havel 1992.

48. Turnovec 2002.

to power. As Jiří Jonáš notes, "there was thus a direct relationship between the results of earlier theoretical discussions and the formulation of the new strategy for economic reform."[49] Although the economists sparred over certain details of the reform program, all agreed on the need for macroeconomic stabilization, price and trade liberalization, and fundamental banking reform.

The communist government had passed a new central banking law just a few days before the Velvet Revolution, one that came into force on January 1, 1990. This law split the monobank into a central bank (the SBCS) and commercial banks and gave the SBCS responsibility for ensuring currency stability, but it did not give the SBCS policy-making or budgetary autonomy. The empowered economists, led by new SBCS governor Josef Tošovský (appointed in January 1990), quickly set out to rectify the situation with the help of the transnational central banking community. International advisors did not need to persuade their interlocutors of the model's desirability or legitimacy. Rather, the transnational central banking community worked together with the SBCS and political leaders to craft a strong central bank law in 1990–91, one modeled heavily on the Bundesbank's law.[50]

Czechoslovakia joined the IMF and World Bank in September 1990, facilitating this cooperation. Drábek notes that "from virtually zero contacts before 1989, Czechoslovakia was inundated with International Monetary Fund and World Bank missions," and that "there was virtually a complete meeting of minds [with the IMF] in the design of the stabilization program."[51] The Czechoslovak government and the IMF concluded a Structural Adjustment Loan agreement in December 1990 that included the government's promise to introduce new banking laws in parliament. The IMF and the government could conclude such a detailed agreement primarily because the government had already begun to implement its recommendations. The IMF agreement gave an international stamp of approval to these policies and eased Czechoslovakia's access to international financial markets.[52]

As a result, unlike in Hungary, the new Czechoslovak central banking law met with little parliamentary opposition. The only hesitation came from the Slovak side. Although Czechs and Slovaks agreed on the need for central bank independence, some sovereignty-minded Slovaks futilely argued that the SBCS should be organized on a federal basis like the US Federal Reserve.[53] On December 20, 1991,

---

49. Jonáš 1993. Jonáš was a member of this circle who left Czechoslovakia to work at the International Monetary Fund.

50. Mataj and Vojtíšek 1992, Czech National Bank 2003.

51. Drábek 1995.

52. Czech National Bank 2003.

53. Dědek 1996. Dědek (a top Czech central banker) argued that the Bundesbank's high credibility won the day for the Czech preferences; the precedent of a unitary SBCS and the dominance of Czech economists in the government no doubt had some influence as well. The Slovak side lost a similar argument on federalizing the SBCS in 1968. Hlavatý and Zelinka 2003.

the Act on the Czechoslovak State Bank passed unanimously on the Czech side of parliament and overwhelmingly on the Slovak side.[54] It took effect on February 1, 1992. The law established an independent central bank and made currency stability the SBCS's primary aim. In contrast to the Hungarian law, it also gave the president appointment power over the governor and board members. It did permit the SBCS to finance up to 5 percent of the budget deficit, but unlike in Hungary this measure was not controversial. The SBCS, the government, and the IMF all supported conservative monetary and fiscal policies, so they did not feel the need to immediately impose a tighter legal limit to restrain the government. As a leading Czech economist noted, "passage of the Act in this form confirms how rapidly a political consensus has been achieved regarding the positive significance of central bank independence on currency stability in this country."[55]

While the Act and policy consensus put the SBCS's independence on a solid footing, in subsequent months clashes over political and economic sovereignty between Slovak and Czech politicians brought its unified existence into question. In the June 1992 Slovak elections, Vladimír Mečiar and his Movement for a Democratic Slovakia came to power. Mečiar, who had been Slovak prime minister representing Public Against Violence from June 1990 until April 1991, campaigned on a platform of granting Slovakia more autonomy within the federation and easing the pace of economic transformation. Meanwhile, Václav Klaus's staunchly unitarist and pro-rapid reform Civic Democratic Party, a remnant of the Civic Forum, won the June 1992 Czech elections. The two sides clashed immediately. After brief, halfhearted negotiations, Klaus and Mečiar agreed on July 23 to split Czechoslovakia in two as of December 31, 1992, a decision subsequently ratified by both parliaments but not put to a popular vote. The Czech and Slovak sides each began to draft legislation to create two independent central banks, the Czech from SBCS headquarters in Prague and the Slovak from the SBCS branch in Bratislava.

The Czech side took the opportunity to enshrine central bank independence into the new Constitution of the Czech Republic, passed on December 16, 1992. The Czech parliament passed the Act on the Czech National Bank one day later, based on the previous Act on the SBCS. This legislation further institutionalized the CNB's independence and transferred the rights and duties of the SBCS to the CNB.[56] Josef Tošovský stayed on as the governor of the CNB, making the

---

54. On the Czech side of parliament there were fifty-eight yeas, no nays, and four absences; on the Slovak side there were forty-six yeas, twelve nays, and two absences. Pospíšil 1996.

55. Pospíšil 1997.

56. 1993 Constitution of the Czech Republic, Chapter 6, Article 68.

transition from SBCS to CNB nearly seamless. The Slovak parliament passed the Act on the National Bank of Slovakia (NBS) one month earlier, on November 18. The Slovak Act mirrored the original SBCS law as well, granting the NBS independence and charging it with the pursuit of currency stability. The NBS's establishment represented a cherished symbol of sovereignty for the Slovak political leadership. Indeed, rather than acknowledging the Act on the NBS as a near-twin of the previous Czechoslovak law, Slovak observers cited German, Swiss, and Austrian legislation as its inspirations.[57] The legal foundations laid by the Act on the SBCS and the Act on the NBS helped to preserve the NBS's policy-making autonomy during the 1990s, despite the Mečiar government's economic heterodoxy and Slovakia's pariah-state status in Europe at the time.

Russia: Independence through Conflict

The Russian government introduced the Bank of Russia's legal independence in the 1990 Law on the Central Bank of the RSFSR (Bank of Russia), enhanced it in the Russian Constitution of December 1993, and further institutionalized it in the April 1995 revised Law on the Central Bank of the Russian Federation (Bank of Russia). But the Bank of Russia did not gain legal independence in the same orderly fashion as the MNB and the SBCS—far from it. Rather, the Russian Republic's government founded the Bank of Russia and adopted its 1990 legislation during a bitter sovereignty battle with the central Soviet government during the waning days of the USSR. In the Bank of Russia's first post-Soviet years, conflict between President Boris Yeltsin's government and the Russian parliament kept the Bank of Russia independent, supported by the IMF (Russia joined the Fund in June 1992). Only in 1994 were political conditions stable enough to begin drafting a revised Russian central banking law with international assistance. The resulting 1995 law more fully enshrined central bank independence in Russia, despite a parliament, government, financial sector, and even a few central bankers who often did not agree with or understand the stability mandate that justified this independence internationally. As Tompson aptly observed in 1998, "External lenders have played a key role in sustaining central bank independence in the absence of any strong societal coalition in favor of it."[58]

Soviet leader Mikhail Gorbachev's introduction of perestroika (restructuring) in 1987 was the USSR's first meaningful flirtation with market economics since Lenin's New Economic Policy of the early 1920s. Unlike in Central and Eastern

---

57. Kollar 1998, Sobek 2003.
58. Tompson 1998a.

Europe where many had considered the command economy a Soviet imposition, in the USSR the command economy was all almost anyone had ever known. With but a few important exceptions, Soviet economists had little exposure to Western economic ideas and practices. In Russia, the heart of the Soviet state, homegrown economic theories, departments, institutes, and journals inspired by Marxism-Leninism held sway. As the economist Yevgenii Yasin observed, "the theoretical framework of the 1987 reform was fashioned by the most progressive Soviet academic economists out of the stock of ideas which they had accumulated over the twenty years of Brezhnev's rule under strong ideological pressure and in isolation from the main currents of Western economics. It could not have been otherwise."[59] Gorbachev's economic advisors did not intend to create a Western-style market economy, and instead looked to Hungary's New Economic Mechanism and to Chinese economic reforms as potential models.[60] Soviet economic officials were so intellectually ill-prepared for change that beginning in 1989, as it became clear that perestroika could not salvage the system, the Socioeconomic Department of the Communist Party's Central Committee sent many officials "abroad on a quest to learn about the market experience."[61]

Nevertheless, a few Western-oriented economists did emerge in the late Soviet period, and their influence grew as both the Soviet and the Russian governments became increasingly dissatisfied with the disastrously poor performance of the perestroika-era economy. Neither Gorbachev nor Yeltsin understood market economics, particularly banking and finance, so as the system began collapsing they reached out to those with such expertise.[62] These included economists such as Yasin, Grigorii Yavlinskii, Yegor Gaidar, and Boris Fedorov. Fedorov, who would play a key role in crafting both the 1990 and 1995 Russian central banking laws, became a relative expert in Western finance while working at the State Bank of the USSR (Gosbank) in the 1980s. In his memoirs, he wrote that, "my economic outlook in great part was formed under the influence of the Quarterly Bulletin of the Bank of England—one of the most professional banks in the world."[63] Fedorov, Gaidar, and their compatriots were further impressed by the design and initial successes of Polish finance minister Leszek Balcerowicz's "shock therapy" plan for economic transformation in 1990.[64] When Yeltsin brought these economists

59. Yasin 1998a.

60. Abalkin 1987.

61. Belik 1998. According to department head Yurii Belik, they visited countries such as Sweden, France, Germany, Belgium, Finland, Japan, and the United States, and they discussed economic reform issues with the IMF, WB, OECD, EEC, and academic experts.

62. Prostiakov 1998, "The Politics of Central Banking in East Europe" 1991–92, Matiukhin 1993.

63. Fedorov 1999.

64. Yasin 1998b.

into his government, they became the leading advocates for monetary and fiscal conservatism in the early 1990s.

Soviet central bank reform began with a Council of Ministers decree in July 1987 creating a two-tiered banking system. As of January 1, 1988, Gosbank USSR became the central bank, while five specialized banks (or *spetsbanki*) would serve different sectors of the Soviet economy.[65] The USSR Supreme Soviet appointed Viktor Gerashchenko, a former executive of Vneshekonombank USSR (the Bank for Foreign Economic Affairs), to head Gosbank in August 1989. Despite Gerashchenko's best efforts, as the barely controlled Soviet economic decentralization progressed Gosbank had an increasingly difficult time managing the spetsbanki and maintaining monetary sovereignty over the fifteen Soviet republics. Estonia created its own central bank in January 1990, followed by Lithuania in February. The Russian Republic's bid for control, however, proved the real threat to Gosbank. After the election of the Russian Congress of People's Deputies in March 1990 and Yeltsin's ascension as its head, the Russian Republic declared its sovereignty on June 12, 1990. Soon afterward the Russian Supreme Soviet adopted a resolution calling for the creation of an independent Central Bank of Russia and declared the spetsbanki on Russian territory to be Russian property.[66]

Over Gerashchenko's bitter protests, the newly appointed Bank of Russia governor Georgii Matiukhin, an academic economist, managed to take over the Russian Republic's main Gosbank branch.[67] The Bank of Russia then began to pick the Soviet banking system apart bit by bit, persuading individual Russian spetsbank branches to re-register as independent commercial banks under its jurisdiction. Influential Russian banker Garegin Tosunian remembered this time as "a political moment . . . [Gosbank and the Bank of Russia] competed with each other . . . so banks had the opportunity to choose—if I prefer the instructions

---

65. The Council of Ministers resolution that created the spetsbanki, "O sovershenstvovanii na povyshenie effektivnosti ekonomiki [On the improvement of the increasing effectiveness of the economy]," was introduced on July 17, 1987, as a part of a package of ten decrees (collectively titled "O korennoi perestroike [On the roots of perestroika]") that supplemented the 1987 Law on State Enterprises. See Tosunian 1995.

66. "O gosudarstvennom banke RSFSR i bankakh na territorii respubliki [On the State Bank of the RSFSR and the banks on the territory of the Republic]," decree of the Supreme Soviet of the RSFSR, July 13, 1990.

67. Matiukhin 1993. Speaker of the Supreme Soviet Ruslan Khasbulatov chose Matiukhin, whom he had met at the Plekhanov Institute. For more detail on the war of the banks, see Johnson 2000. Although at this point he did not anticipate the Soviet break-up, Matiukhin did expect the Bank of Russia to wrest control of the Republic's monetary system from Gosbank and at some point perhaps issue a separate Russian currency. Sergei Panasenko, "Predsedatel' Tsentral'nogo Banka RSFSR Georgii Matiukhin: My gotovy k finansovoi nezavisimosti [Chairman of the Central Bank of the RSFSR Georgii Matiukhin: We are ready for financial independence]." *Rossiiskaia gazeta*, December 23, 1990.

of Gosbank, I will place myself under its jurisdiction. If I prefer the instructions of the Central Bank, then I will choose it . . . It was complete chaos."[68] This dual power culminated in the Soviet and Russian parliaments passing conflicting central banking laws within days of each other in December 1990.

The Law on the Gosbank adopted by the USSR Supreme Soviet ostensibly created a Federal Reserve-style system with Gosbank USSR at the center. Gerashchenko had pushed for this law earlier, and his influential support ensured the law's smooth passage. As he stated, "if we are going to make our banking system a two-tier one, as is the case throughout the world, we need first of all a law on the main bank: the USSR State Bank as the only one which has the right to perform currency and credit emission."[69] The law made Gosbank accountable to the USSR Supreme Soviet and independent of the executive and administration.[70] For the first time in Soviet history it also set limits on Gosbank funding of the Ministry of Finance, a radical change.[71]

The Russian law, on the other hand, granted independence to the Bank of Russia without acknowledging any Soviet central authority.[72] Yeltsin's advisor Boris Fedorov drafted the law with Western standards in mind. Although modified from his original version, the resulting law made the Bank of Russia independent of the government and accountable to parliament, limited Bank of Russia lending to the Ministry of Finance to six months, gave the governor a five-year term, allowed the president to nominate the governor and the parliament to confirm, and ensured that all board members came from within the Bank of Russia itself. As Fedorov remembers it, Bank of Russia governor Georgii Matiukhin and Supreme Soviet speaker Ruslan Khasbulatov pushed the law through an uncomprehending parliament "in record time . . . Matiukhin laid the foundation for our Central Bank and its independence."[73] This Russian legislation, drawn up in haste to strike a blow against the Soviet Union, formalized the independent Bank of Russia as a symbol of Russian sovereignty.

---

68. Author's interview with Technobank president Garegin Tosunian, Moscow, Russia, July 1995.

69. Ivan Zhagel interview with Viktor Gerashchenko, chairman of the board of Gosbank, *Izvestiia*, June 26, 1990. Translated as "Gosbank Head Claims Changes Needed in Banking," FBIS-SOV-90-129, July 5, 1990.

70. S. Chugaev, "On the Eve of the Congress—*Izvestiia* Parliamentary Correspondent Reports from the Kremlin," *Izvestiia*, December 12, 1990, 1–2, translated in *Current Digest of the Soviet Press* 42, no. 50 (1990).

71. Barkovskii 1998.

72. The law only mentions the USSR twice, both times in the context of allowing the Bank of Russia to join with other central banks from the Soviet republics if it so chose. Law of the Russian Soviet Federated Socialist Republic "O tsentral'nom banke RSFSR (Banke Rossii) [On the Central Bank of the RSFSR (Bank of Russia)]," December 2, 1990.

73. Fedorov 1999.

The Bank of Russia and Gosbank continued to operate in parallel until the failed coup attempt of August 1991 assured the Soviet Union's demise. On August 23, Yeltsin ordered the USSR Council of Ministers to complete the transfer of Soviet-level organizations on Russian territory to the Russian state by the end of the year.[74] Freed of the need to coordinate with Gorbachev, Gaidar and Yeltsin prepared to introduce radical economic reform in Russia at the beginning of 1992 and the Russian Supreme Soviet granted them temporary powers to conduct economic policy by decree. Gaidar and Yeltsin went too far, however, when they tried to subordinate the Bank of Russia to executive control by decree in November 1991. The Bank of Russia protested vehemently, and the Supreme Soviet unanimously blocked the attempt.[75] One Bank of Russia official defended the bank's independence with reference to external influences, noting that:

> When foreign investors and representatives come here, first and foremost they demand the stability of the bank . . . the handing over of the bank to the presidential structure would naturally strengthen the president's power, but I doubt that it would strengthen the reliability and stability of the banking system from the point of view of confidence in it on the part of foreign partners.[76]

Foreshadowing the president and parliament's later conflicts, neither side wanted to cede control of such an important institution to the other, and international norms, investors, and advisors assured them that they should not do so.

On December 20, 1991, Gosbank was abolished and the Bank of Russia took over the rest of its Russia-based resources.[77] However, other Soviet successor states still used the ruble as currency and their central banks could directly issue ruble-denominated credits, making it nearly impossible for the Bank of Russia to control the money supply. When the Russian government's price liberalization and macroeconomic stabilization program faltered within weeks of its January inception, the Bank of Russia came under heavy fire from both the Yeltsin administration and the Russian Supreme Soviet. Beyond the confounding effects of the ruble zone, the fundamental problem was a lack of agreement among the Russian government, parliament, and central bank on the proper course and speed

---

74. The Russian government appointed Andrei Zverov, the Russian Republic's deputy minister of finance, as temporary director of Gosbank, although Gerashchenko refused to leave his post and did not submit his resignation until December 26.

75. Gaidar 1999.

76. Interview with Vladimir Rassakov, deputy chairman of the Bank of Russia, on the *Parliamentary Herald* television program, December 2, 1991, translated in FBIS-SOV 91-235, December 6, 1991, 60–62.

77. Barkovskii 1998.

of reforms, exacerbated by the painful unanticipated consequences of Russia's initial "shock therapy" attempt.

This conflict preserved the Bank of Russia's independence despite the protestations of the government that it was under parliament's sway and vice-versa, but at the cost of uncoordinated and contradictory policy making.[78] The Bank of Russia's power in the triad increased when an embarrassing financial scandal forced Matiukhin from office and Gaidar chose influential and well-connected former Gosbank governor Viktor Gerashchenko to replace him. The conflict led to a string of initiatives by both president and parliament to further formalize the Bank of Russia's independence, even as each tried and usually failed to undermine the Bank of Russia regarding specific policies. This battle gave the Bank of Russia wide latitude to implement its own preferred policies until Yeltsin forcefully disbanded the Supreme Soviet in October 1993.

Immediately afterward, Yeltsin passed a decree subordinating the Bank of Russia to the executive until elections for a new lower house of parliament, the State Duma, could be held in December. Although Gerashchenko had supported the Supreme Soviet in its battle with Yeltsin, Yeltsin reappointed him as Bank of Russia governor after he agreed to abide by the presidential decree.[79] The December 1993 elections restored the Bank of Russia's legal independence, as anti-Yeltsin forces won a plurality in the State Duma and Russia's new constitution, written by Yeltsin's team, came into effect. The constitution guaranteed the Bank of Russia's independence, declared its main goal to be protecting the stability of the ruble, and gave the president the power to appoint the Bank of Russia governor with the Duma's confirmation.[80] Yeltsin's team and its IMF advisors supported the Western central banking model enough in theory to enshrine the Bank of Russia's legal independence in the constitution despite their deep suspicions of the Bank's work in practice. Boris Fedorov in particular had a strong personal antipathy toward Gerashchenko and his policies.

The 1995 Law on the Central Bank of the Russian Federation, Russia's first post-Soviet central banking law, reflected this combination of Fedorov's mistrust, Gerashchenko's defense of central bank independence, the Yeltsin team's commitment to Western ideals, and the influence of international advisors. Fedorov had been elected to the State Duma in December 1993 and drafted the law in early 1994 in his capacity as head of the Duma subcommittee on monetary and financial policy. He stated that "I wrote it in a month, drawing in much

---

78. Tompson 1998a, Gaidar 1999, Johnson 2000.

79. Oleg Roganov, "Tsentrobank gotov finansirovat' prezidenta [The Central Bank is ready to finance the president]," *Kommersant*, September 23, 1993.

80. Articles 75 and 83 of the Constitution of the Russian Federation, ratified December 12, 1993.

practical material and experience from different countries of the world."[81] Gerashchenko, although cautioning that the law should "pay attention to Russian specifics rather than blindly copying foreign legal acts," fully supported a new law that would flesh out the Bank of Russia's powers as enshrined in the constitution.[82] Equally important, transnational central banking community members provided detailed commentary on the draft law, with many of their suggestions finding their way into the final document.

Two sets of joint commentaries from Federal Reserve Bank of New York president Gerald Corrigan's Russian-American Bankers Forum and the New York-based Financial Services Volunteer Corps illustrate the dynamic at work.[83] They directed their comments on the first draft in May 1994 to Fedorov, at his request, and on a revised draft in October 1994 to Gerashchenko, at his request. Numerous important suggestions made in response to the first draft were incorporated into the revised version, including tightening the language on the Bank of Russia's objectives, defining what "accountability" to parliament meant, removing a section allowing the governor to be dismissed for "inappropriate performance," defining monetary policy instruments, forbidding direct financing of the budget deficit or purchase of securities on the primary market, and making the Bank of Russia the sole agent of monetary policy, among many others. The revised draft also removed, at the Americans' suggestion, a Fedorov-inspired clause allowing the Minister of Finance to suspend Bank of Russia decisions for up to seven days. Two of their main suggestions on the revised draft then appeared in the final version: removing a clause allowing the Bank of Russia to grant secured credit to the Ministry of Finance for up to three months, and removing another allowing the Duma to dismiss the governor if it disapproved of the bank's annual report. In short, the efforts of these international advisors markedly strengthened the Bank of Russia's legal independence.

The major conflict between the bank and the parliament over the draft law dealt with the role of outsiders in policy making. The first draft, reflecting Fedorov and his colleagues' preferences, gave policy-making control to a monetary policy council composed primarily of outsiders due to Fedorov's distrust of Gerashchenko. The Bank of Russia vehemently protested, and international

---

81. Fedorov 1999.

82. Gerashchenko 1994.

83. Financial Services Volunteer Corps and Russian-American Bankers Forum, "Comments on the Draft 'Law on the Central Bank of the Russian Federation' (May 1994)" and "Comments on the Draft 'Federal Law on the Central Bank of the Russian Federation (October 1994)" (mimeos). The Russians did reject a few of the recommendations, most notably the suggestion to grant greater policy-making influence to the Bank of Russia's territorial branches in emulation of the US Federal Reserve.

advisors recommended giving it at least a majority of one on the council.[84] The revised draft reflected the bank's preferences, giving authority to a board composed entirely of Bank of Russia officials. Fedorov formally objected, arguing that outsiders be given voting membership on the board.[85] The final version represented a compromise, leaving policy-making authority with the bank-constituted board but also creating an advisory National Banking Council composed of outside representatives.[86] During the process Fedorov called on Bank of Russia officials to testify to parliament, Gerashchenko worked hard to convince Duma deputies to accept the finalized law, and both invoked IMF demands as a justification for passing it.[87] Although the upper house of parliament rejected the bill for giving too much independence to the Bank of Russia, the State Duma overrode the rejection and Yeltsin signed the bill on April 15, 1995.[88] The resulting law reduced the governor's term to four years from five, but in every other way strengthened the Bank of Russia's legal independence and gave it a firmer foundation for its operations.[89]

Kyrgyzstan: Independence by Recommendation

Kyrgyzstan took a surprisingly straightforward path to legislating central bank independence. As a small, poor Soviet republic highly dependent economically and politically on Russia, Kyrgyzstan's Soviet-era government preferred to preserve the USSR and the unified Soviet monetary system. It followed the Soviet

---

84. For example, Bank of Russia deputy governor Aleksandr Khandruev argued that the council would undermine the Bank of Russia's independence and insisted on empowering it with "purely consultative duties" (quoted in Nikita Kirichenko and Elena Makovskaia, "Tsentrobank ne khochet, chtoby ego opekali [The Central Bank doesn't want a guardian]." *Kommersant—Vlast'*, May 24, 1994). The Bank of Russia representative to the subcommittee on monetary and credit policy was the only one who did not approve of the draft at the subcommittee's May meeting. See Fedorov's "Poiasnitel'naia zapiska [Explanatory Notes]" appended to the revised draft as distributed for discussion by the State Duma on July 20, 1994 (mimeo).

85. Boris Fedorov, "Poiasnitel'naia zapiska [Explanatory Notes]" appended to the revised draft as distributed for discussion by the State Duma on July 20, 1994 (mimeo).

86. Law of the Russian Federation "O vnesenii izmenenii i dopolnenii v Zakon RSFSR 'O tsentral'nom banke RSFSR (Banke Rossii)' [On the Introduction of Changes and Additions to the Law of the RSFSR 'On the Central Bank of the RSFSR (Bank of Russia)']," April 12, 1995.

87. Tompson 1998a, Fedorov 1999.

88. Aleksandr Lin'kov, "Strasti vokrug Tsentrobanka [Passion concerning the Central Bank]," *Rossiiskaia gazeta*, March 22, 1995.

89. Tompson 1998a, Stoliarenko 1999, Mikhail Zadornov, "Chego zhdat' ot novykh zakonov o bankakh? [What to expect from the new banking laws?]," *Biznes i banki*, 1, 1995. Although Cukierman et al. (2002) ranked this law as giving the Bank of Russia slightly less independence than the 1990 law, this is due to coding error. For example, they code the 1995 law as permitting the Bank of Russia to buy government securities on the primary market, when in fact the legislation forbids it.

government's lead on economic policy until systemic disintegration made it impossible to do so. Once the Soviet breakup became inevitable, Kyrgyz leaders looked to international assistance to help support and restructure the failing economy. As a result, the first Kyrgyz central bank law in June 1991 reflected the 1990 Soviet law, while the second in December 1992 reflected IMF advice. Since both legislated central bank independence, the National Bank of the Kyrgyz Republic (NBKR) started its existence with a relatively firm and uncontested legal status.

Kyrgyzstan in the late 1980s had no previous experience with economic reform save the perestroika-era directives that trickled down from Moscow, and had little homegrown economics tradition either. One Kyrgyz central banker lamented to me in 2001 that Western economics literature had only begun regularly appearing in the local libraries two years earlier, and asked, "Can you really study [economics] from the internet?" Moreover, the most educated and internationally networked segment of the Kyrgyz population—ethnic Russians—left Kyrgyzstan in droves after 1989, falling from an initial population of almost one million to only two hundred thousand five years later.[90] As perestroika progressed, though, a few Kyrgyz were exposed to Western economic thought in Moscow. One was physicist and future Kyrgyz president Askar Akayev. Akayev was elected to the USSR Congress of People's Deputies in 1989 and became a member of the USSR Supreme Soviet's economic reform committee. He wrote in his memoir that to perform his work on the committee in 1989–90 he had to teach himself market economics, reading Schumpeter, Hayek, Erhard, Keynes, and Friedman.[91] At this point he became sold on the need for radical reform. Akayev also mentioned that he met regularly with international advisors, often from the IMF, after he became Kyrgyz president in October 1991 and that these advisors fundamentally shaped his views on economic transformation. Akayev's memoir quoted extensively from Schumpter and Hayek, railed against the evils of inflation, and spoke admiringly of the radical reform policies of Poland's Balcerowicz and Russia's Gaidar.

Akayev's attraction to radical reform had both intellectual and instrumental components. The only new post-Soviet leader in Central Asia, Akayev claimed legitimacy to rule based on adopting Western-oriented political and economic reforms.[92] The Kyrgyz leadership also realized that Kyrgyzstan would need extensive outside assistance to transform its underdeveloped, resource-poor economy

---

90. Olcott 1996, 88.
91. Akayev 2001.
92. Schatz 2009.

in the absence of continued Russian support.[93] Akayev promoted Kyrgyzstan as the "Asian Switzerland," opening it up to international finance, advice, and trade while undertaking the most radical economic reforms in the region. As Olcott astutely observes, "President Akayev's strategy was designed to make potential investors emotionally committed to assisting this struggling democracy in a part of the world dominated by despots."[94]

Kyrgyzstan thus chose central bank independence in an atmosphere of extreme uncertainty and enforced political and economic change. The Kyrgyz Supreme Soviet approved the Soviet republic's first central banking law in June 1991, the second-to-last Central Asian republic to do so. This law, passed without controversy, was modeled after the December 1990 USSR Law on the Gosbank and positioned the NBKR as a cog in the larger Soviet central banking system. In doing so, the Kyrgyz Supreme Soviet borrowed the relatively progressive character of the original Gosbank law. As Gosbank chairman Gerashchenko had pointed out, the Law on the Gosbank conformed in great part to international standards. A leading Austrian central banker confirmed in 1991 that, "the function of the central bank according to the Law on the Gosbank appears to contain the main features of a western central bank."[95] The Kyrgyz law gave the monetary authorities independence from the executive and made them accountable to parliament, as well as charged them with defending currency stability. The NBKR governor and board would enjoy five-year terms, and the parliament would set an annual limit on central bank credit to the government.[96]

After the failure of the August 1991 coup attempt in Moscow, Kyrgyzstan declared independence from the USSR and undertook radical economic reform measures in parallel with Russia's. It liberalized most prices, reduced wages and subsidies, and introduced a privatization program. Like Russia it suffered high inflation and falling output in 1992, made worse on the smaller country by the collapse of interstate trade.[97] In desperate need of advice and financing, Kyrgyzstan applied for IMF membership in January 1992 and became a member in May, kicking off extensive IMF participation in Kyrgyz economic reform. This included detailed assistance in drafting a new, post-independence central bank law, passed by the Kyrgyz parliament in December 1992. On the IMF's recommendations, the law strengthened the NBKR's independence, gave it control over

---

93. Anderson 1999.
94. Olcott 1996.
95. Poenisch 1991.
96. World Bank 1993.
97. Pomfret 1995.

Kyrgyz gold and currency reserves, placed tight limits on central bank financing of the government, and enhanced the NBKR's bank supervisory powers.[98] Parliament presented no objection to the new legislation. Not only did it not understand the law's potential implications, but IMF funding also appeared to depend on its passage.

Kyrgyzstan—with intensive IMF aid—successfully left the ruble zone and introduced its own currency, the som, in May 1993. Once Kyrgyzstan separated its monetary system from Russia's, the NBKR could use its legal power to conduct Kyrgyz monetary policy. NBKR officials subsequently invoked this law often to defend their independence before parliament and the unruly Kyrgyz financial sector.[99] With extensive additional international advice and assistance, the NBKR strengthened its statutory independence further in the amendments to the law "On the National Bank of the Kyrgyz Republic" passed in 1997.[100] Among other measures, this new legislation forbade the NBKR from lending to the government, lengthened the governor's term to seven years, gave the NBKR sole responsibility for making monetary policy, and reinforced price stability as the NBKR's key objective.

From Choice to Transformation

Hungary, the Czech and Slovak Republics, Russia, and Kyrgyzstan all adopted legislation granting independence to their central banks from separate starting points and through separate paths, drawn together by the attraction of the Western central banking model and its transnational proponents. Whether achieved through negotiation, consensus, conflict, or recommendation, choosing central bank independence promised postcommunist governments recognition of their sovereignty, international approval, and material rewards. Legislating central bank independence had a snowball effect in the postcommunist world, with

---

98. Odling-Smee 1993; L. Tsyplakova, "Dva etazha sistemy [A Two-Tier System]," *Slovo Kyrgyzstana*, August 25, 1994.

99. For example, see M. Abakirov, "Na perestroechnom puti [On the path to perestroika]," *Slovo Kyrgyzstana*, August 11, 1994; Marat Sultanov, "Doklad predsedatelia Natsional'nogo Banka Kyrgyzskoi Respubliki M. Sultanova na zasedanii sobraniia narodnykh predstavitelei Zhogorku Kenesha 29 noiabria 1995 Goda [Report of the Chairman of the National Bank of the Kyrgyz Republic M. Sultanov on the Meeting of the Assembly of People's Representatives of the Jorgorku Kenesh, 29 November 1995]," *Bankovskii vestnik*, December 1995.

100. "O reforme finansovogo i bankovskogo sektora v Kyrgyzskoi Respublike [On the reform of the financial and banking sector in the Kyrgyz Republic]," *Bankovskii vestnik*, December 1996; "Iasnee zakon—vyshe nadezhnost' [Clearer law—higher reliability]," *Slovo Kyrgyzstana*, December 12, 1996.

one country's adoption making the others more likely to do so as well. In all of these cases, governments chose to introduce and strengthen central bank independence throughout the 1990s in response to international sentiment, advice, and pressures. While postcommunist governments had significant ideational and material incentives to adopt central bank independence, the transnational central banking community worked actively with postcommunist central bankers to frame these incentives in the best possible light and to persuade governments to make this fateful choice.

But legislation was only the first step, one that confirmed postcommunist governments' initial commitment to independent central banking. This commitment was based on economic beliefs and international advice but untested in postcommunist practice. While governments passed laws granting independence to their central banks, the central bankers had to learn how to perform their difficult, fundamentally altered tasks. The transnational central banking community responded with an array of training and technical assistance programs designed to transfer the Western central banking model to the postcommunist world and to integrate the postcommunist central bankers into its community. The transformation campaign had begun.

THE TRANSFORMATION CAMPAIGN

"If you are willing to join the club, you will be supported."

—Magyar Nemzeti Bank governor György Surányi (2000)

While the transnational central banking community encouraged postcommunist governments to adopt legislation granting independence to their central banks, it came into its own with the campaign to transform the beliefs and practices of post-communist central bankers. The community had the motivation and ability to mount a relatively consistent, intensive assistance campaign, supported and legitimized by the most powerful governments in the world. Driven by a desire to preserve international financial stability and to draw new members into the community, established central bankers individually and collectively deployed their extensive organizational, human, and material resources to develop training and technical assistance programs for the postcommunist central banks. Postcommunist central bankers overwhelmingly welcomed this assistance because of the community's international status and model, the challenge of managing the complex postcommunist economic environment, and the social and material incentives for joining the community.

Although West Europeans were most heavily involved, the entire transnational community participated in the transformation campaign. The IMF, BIS, and later the ECB provided organizational resources, training, and technical assistance. At least twenty-five national central banks, primarily from the advanced industrial democracies, designed and participated in multilateral and bilateral training and technical assistance efforts. This included all of the established European central banks, from Portugal to Finland; the Commonwealth central banks of the United Kingdom, Canada, Australia, and New Zealand; plus the central banks of the United States, Israel, Iceland, Japan, and more. Central bankers and banking supervisors provided additional support through organizations like the US Financial

Services Volunteer Corps and the US Treasury; through technical assistance programs funded by the EU and the United States Agency for International Development (USAID); through aid subcontractors such as Barents; and through West European commercial banks and bankers' associations.

This chapter concentrates on the first decade of transformation when donors and recipients worked hardest to transplant the international central banking model into postcommunist soil, but follows the ebbs and flows of the campaign through its rediscovery of banking supervision after 1998 and up until the existential challenge of the global financial crisis. The nature, quality, and organization of assistance evolved over time, as both the donors and the recipients gained knowledge and experience. Although recipient central banks asked for extensive assistance from the start, the donors' programs gradually became more explicitly demand-driven because the recipients grew more confident in assessing their own needs and capabilities, as well as the strengths and weaknesses of the various donors and programs. As postcommunist central bankers grew more fluent in economics, training courses became shorter and more focused, dealing with more advanced subjects. As they grew more fluent in English, fewer courses and materials were offered with Russian translation. Training relationships became more collaborative. Donors began to specialize more in the types of aid they provided and the countries in which they focused their efforts. Programs in Central and Eastern Europe became more EU-oriented, and the most advanced postcommunist countries began to provide assistance to others. In former Soviet states the campaign became more focused on especially difficult tasks and most authoritarian states greatly limited their participation.[1] As the organizational capacity of the transnational central banking community to deliver training and technical assistance increased, the need for formal coordination decreased as the postcommunist central bankers became increasingly integrated into the informal—and thus more flexible and responsive—transnational central banking network.

Overall, the transformation campaign bore remarkable fruit. Where the transnational central banking community enjoyed sustained access, postcommunist central bankers usually adopted its core ideas and practices. The formal and informal interactions between established central bankers and their postcommunist counterparts built and reinforced their institutional and interpersonal ties through the distance-defying wormhole effect. The ready supply of relatively consistent, well-packaged assistance and heavy demand for it made central bank transformation faster than other postcommunist institutional changes. Within a decade of the

---

1. In interviews conducted from 2001 through 2006, officials from five donor institutions independently singled out Belarus, Uzbekistan, and Turkmenistan as "hopeless" cases for assistance due to overwhelming political interference in central bank operations.

fall of the Berlin Wall, most central bankers in the postcommunist world had come to think and act much like those in the advanced industrial democracies.

Organizing the Assistance

Assistance began on an ad hoc basis in the 1980s as community members offered help and as requests poured in from nearly and newly postcommunist central banks and their governments in Central and Eastern Europe. It quickly became clear that the size of the task demanded greater organization in order to minimize duplication and ensure that all postcommunist central banks were adequately served. Technical assistance especially required coordination given the wide variety of potential donors, needs, and delivery methods. One IMF official admitted that donor central banks initially "cherry picked" their recipients and tasks for technical assistance.[2] Another European central banker confirmed this, observing: "there's actually competition among donors to assist places like Slovenia, a small, excellent bank."[3] Less high-profile central banking assistance tasks could fall through the cracks as well, as initially occurred with banking supervision. On the recipient side many postcommunist central banks asked multiple established ones to provide similar assistance programs, leading to wasted and at times competitive efforts. As a result, the BIS and the IMF stepped in to organize the assistance effort for the national central banks. True to their natures and often working in concert with one another, the collegial BIS served primarily as a forum for making contacts and centralizing information while the prescriptive IMF actively assigned and implemented many assistance tasks. Later the European Central Bank played a more prominent role in the organization efforts, especially in East Central Europe and the Balkans.

Organizational preparation took place at a series of high-profile meetings and conferences in 1990 and 1991. The G10 meetings of central bankers and finance ministers in 1990 gave the BIS a formal mandate to coordinate central banking aid efforts to Central and Eastern Europe.[4] In August 1990 the Federal Reserve Bank of Kansas City's annual Jackson Hole conference focused on "Central Banking Issues in Emerging Market-Oriented Economies," with Western participants including US Federal Reserve Board chairman Alan Greenspan and former chairman Paul Volcker, top officials of the central banks of Canada, England,

---

2. Author's interview with a senior IMF official, Washington, DC, November 2001.

3. Author's interview with a senior official responsible for technical assistance in the Österreichische Nationalbank, Vienna, Austria, May 2000.

4. The Group of Ten includes eleven countries (Belgium, Canada, France, Germany, Italy, Japan, the Netherlands, Sweden, Switzerland, the United Kingdom, and the United States) that consult on economic matters.

Switzerland, France, Belgium, and Germany, and high-ranking staff from the IMF. Participants from the region included the governors or deputy governors of the central banks of Poland, Bulgaria, Yugoslavia, the USSR, Romania, Hungary, and Czechoslovakia—in other words, every transition state of the moment except Albania and Mongolia.[5] The BIS convened its first donor meeting of the G10 central banks plus Austria in early 1991, and subsequently held joint meetings for donors and recipients every six months.

The BIS meetings initially covered only Central and Eastern Europe, but after the Soviet breakup the BIS held separate twice-yearly meetings for the former Soviet Union as well.[6] These gatherings, dubbed the Coordinators for Technical Assistance and Training meetings, brought together the aid coordinators for the donor and recipient central banks (typically the heads of a special department or sub-department in the donor central banks and the heads of human resource departments in the recipient central banks). Through these meetings the central bankers reviewed and revised their technical assistance and training programs by giving presentations on their activities, evaluating trends in assistance, and exchanging assistance offers and requests. The BIS served as a natural host for these meetings given its status as a long-standing forum for formal and informal cooperation among central bankers.[7] At the initial meetings the recipients were hesitant to talk to the donors and channeled their requests and concerns through the BIS staff, but the donors and recipients quickly got to know each other and began to arrange assistance directly. As technical coordination became more routinized over time and as the postcommunist central bankers became more integrated into the community the meetings occurred less frequently, with the final meeting held in Basel in July 2008.

The BIS also created and maintained a database on assistance efforts, gathering information from both donor and recipient central banks. The BIS started collecting data for Central and Eastern Europe in 1991 and extended it to the former Soviet Union in 1992. Each database entry included information on the donor, the recipient, the type of assistance program (training, technical assistance, resident advisor, etc.), the general topic, and its date and length. Although the database suffered from inconsistencies and was not comprehensive, it presented a general picture of central bank aid flows to the region. Most important, it allowed central bank donors and recipients to see who was providing what

5. See Federal Reserve Bank of Kansas City 1990.

6. The BIS included the Baltic states in their Central and East European (CEE) Group, while the IMF included them in their European II group at the time (with the other former Soviet republics). The BIS held its CEE meetings in English and the FSU meetings in simultaneous Russian translation.

7. Crockett 1997.

kinds of assistance, enabling efforts to resist duplication and cover more areas. One official emphasized that the BIS maintained the database purely for information purposes, stating that, "we at the BIS never attempted to say to any central bank that you should do this, [or that] you're the third Central Bank providing technical assistance for payments. That's up to you."[8] The database proved especially useful in the early years when central banks simultaneously requested assistance on the same topics from several potential donors.

More broadly, the G10 asked the IMF and World Bank to "take the lead in assisting the transition economies . . . Although there was little precedent for an effort of this type, a professional consensus developed rapidly. The transition countries needed both macroeconomic stabilization and massive structural reform."[9] Apart from training through the Joint Vienna Institute and the IMF Institute (discussed below), the IMF organized its transformation campaign for central banks primarily through the technical assistance unit of its central bank-focused department. The Central Banking Department began organizing technical assistance to the region in 1989–90 when it arranged for staff from six national central banks to work with the National Bank of Poland. It expanded this coordinating role the following year, sending technical assistance teams recruited from fourteen different national central banks to the State Bank of Czechoslovakia, the National Bank of Romania, and the Bulgarian National Bank.[10]

In 1992 the IMF began focusing on the central banks of the former Soviet Union. Under a G7 mandate, the newly renamed Monetary and Exchange Affairs (MAE) Department worked to coordinate the efforts of twenty-three national central banks to provide intensive, targeted technical assistance to the former Soviet central banks.[11] These efforts started with an organizational meeting in St. Petersburg, Russia, that gave rise to the so-called Matrix (table 4.1). The Matrix identified ten substantive areas of assistance (e.g., accounting and internal audit, monetary analysis and research) and assigned a particular national central bank or banks to assist each country in each area. Although national central banks varied in their adherence to the Matrix and some objected to its rigid structure, the Matrix framed much of the IMF-coordinated technical assistance to central banks of the former Soviet Union in subsequent years.

The MAE reinforced its organizational efforts by hosting twice-yearly assistance meetings for the former Soviet Union at the BIS in parallel with the BIS's own coordination meetings through 1998. The MAE meetings brought its large

---

8. Author's interview with a senior official in the Monetary and Economic Department of the Bank for International Settlements, Basel, Switzerland, May 2000.

9. Fischer 2004.

10. *IMF Annual Reports*, 1991 and 1992.

11. Zulu et al. 1994.

TABLE 4.1 IMF/MAE technical assistance program to the former Soviet Union

COUNTRY	CENTRAL BANK ACCOUNTING AND INTERNAL AUDIT	BANKING SUPERVISION AND REGULATION	BALANCE OF PAYMENTS ANALYSIS AND RESEARCH	FOREIGN EXCHANGE OPERATIONS, REGULATIONS, RESERVE MANAGEMENT, AND MARKET DEVELOPMENT	MONETARY OPERATIONS AND MONEY MARKET DEVELOPMENT	MONETARY ANALYSIS AND RESEARCH	ORGANIZATION AND MANAGEMENT STRUCTURE	PAYMENT, CLEARING, AND SETTLEMENT SYSTEM	PUBLIC DEBT MANAGEMENT AND GOVERNMENT SECURITIES MARKET	INTRODUCTION OF NEW CURRENCY
Armenia	New Zealand	USA	Israel	France	Portugal	Israel	MAE	Netherlands	Portugal	MAE
Azerbaijan	Austria	France	Turkey	Japan	Italy	Turkey	Norway	USA	UK	MAE
Belarus	Denmark	Netherlands	Ireland	Germany	UK	Finland	USA	Austria	Israel	MAE
Estonia	Denmark/Sweden	Iceland	Finland	Sweden	Finland	Finland	Finland	Finland	Finland	MAE
Georgia	Australia	USA	Canada	Italy	New Zealand	Germany	Germany	Netherlands	New Zealand	MAE
Kazakhstan	France	UK	Italy	Belgium	USA	Canada	USA	Japan	USA	MAE
Kyrgyz Republic	France	UK	Italy	Switzerland	USA	Canada	Netherlands	Japan	USA	MAE
Latvia	Finland	Sweden/Canada	Norway	Denmark	Norway	Norway	Finland	Norway	Norway	MAE
Lithuania	MAE	MAE	Norway	Finland	Norway	Norway	MAE	Norway	MAE	MAE
Moldova	New Zealand	USA	Israel	France	Portugal	Israel	MAE	Australia	Portugal	MAE
Russian Federation	Austria	France	Canada	Japan	Italy	Germany/USA	Norway	Task Force	UK	MAE
Tajikistan	Canada	Turkey	Netherlands	Denmark	Turkey	Netherlands	Ireland	France	MAE	MAE
Turkmenistan	Australia	USA	Turkey	Italy	Turkey	Turkey	Germany	Australia	Turkey	MAE
Ukraine	Denmark	Netherlands	Ireland	Germany	UK	Finland	Netherlands	Australia	Israel	MAE
Uzbekistan	Canada	Turkey	Netherlands	Turkey	Turkey	Netherlands	Ireland	France	MAE	MAE

Source: Zulu et al. 1994.

group of donors together with the vice governors of the recipient central banks, and included both joint sessions and sessions for the donors alone. The MAE and Bank of Russia also held a joint meeting in St. Petersburg in April 1994 to evaluate the initial assistance efforts in the former Soviet Union. As the IMF's report after the final coordination meeting in May 1998 observed, "The expertise and staff resources devoted to providing this assistance have been considerable—about 166 staff years to date. Of this total, experts from the cooperating central banks contributed an impressive four-fifths of the total, or 94 staff-years, with the remainder of the 22 staff years coming from the IMF."[12] In short, the MAE organized the assistance but established central bankers from IMF member states carried most of it out. These numbers represented only six years of technical assistance, assistance only to the former Soviet central banks, and only the technical assistance provided under this specific mandate; when combined with the training and technical assistance provided elsewhere and by the rest of the community, the massive effort involved becomes apparent.

Finally, after its establishment in 1998 the ECB gradually began coordinating more and more of the Eurosystem's training and technical assistance efforts. While these efforts focused primarily on Central and Eastern Europe, the ECB also coordinated a few key programs for former Soviet states, most notably a major 2003–5 program to improve banking supervision in Russia. An ECB official observed that this "assistance started without our being conscious of it," as a natural part of its leading role in the Eurosystem.[13] One of the first efforts involved organizing an extensive 1999 report on payment systems development in would-be accession countries. To produce the analysis, the ECB Payment Systems Division assigned two Eurosystem counterparts to each of the eleven participating countries; for example, the National Bank of Slovakia worked with the Bundesbank and the National Bank of Belgium.[14] In November 1999, the ECB and the Bank of Finland organized a high-level policy seminar on central banking issues in the twelve prospective accession countries, laying the groundwork for systematic multilateral cooperation preparing the central banks to meet accession requirements.[15] By June 2000, the ECB had over one hundred separate events, projects, and initiatives planned for the following month alone. As the ECB's assistance coordinators told me at the time, "We have a specific goal to achieve—integration into

12. Knight et al. 1999.

13. Author's interview with a senior European Relations official of the European Central Bank, Frankfurt, Germany, June 2000.

14. Holicka 1999.

15. European Central Bank 2000.

our system . . . We don't want to replace what already exists with the national central banks. We're complementary, more focused . . . By simply directing activities we can contribute a lot."[16]

As several postcommunist states moved toward EU accession in 2004 and 2007, the ECB's aid coordination efforts became more intensive and focused. The ECB worked to harmonize the relevant accession-country legislation with the EU's *acquis communautaire*, to improve central bank operations, to upgrade payment and settlement systems to EU standards, and to harmonize statistics and IT infrastructure and applications. As with the IMF, the ECB staff itself did not provide most of the aid; rather, the national central banks provided the personnel while the ECB coordinated the projects. One ECB official observed that EU accession requirements had created a "benign environment" for transformation by setting a clear, consistent agenda.[17] Over time the ECB gradually took over the role that the BIS and IMF had earlier served for the EU accession countries, reinforcing and deepening the transformation process. As an Austrian central banker said to me in May 2006:

> If I were writing your book, I'd put the emphasis on EU projects, which have increased in importance especially for central banks—they do large, long-term projects now that are much more significant than short-term IMF missions. This is the best kind of technical assistance model—the EU funds it, the ECB coordinates it, and experts from the national central banks do the advising. In this way several central banks can cooperate—we would have liked to do more before, but it was hard because we're so small.[18]

This quote describes what former ECB president Willem Duisenberg called the Eurosystem approach. Introducing the ambitious project to revamp Russian banking supervision, Duisenberg stated: "The project will be coordinated by an ECB team . . . The national central banks as well as the non-central bank supervisory authorities of the United Kingdom, Finland and Sweden will provide the experts for the planned courses and seminars, most of which will take place in Moscow at the [Bank of Russia] premises. Study visits of [Bank of Russia] experts

---

16. Author's interview with two senior European Relations officials of the European Central Bank, Frankfurt, Germany, June 2000.

17. Author's interview with a key member of the European Central Bank assistance team, Frankfurt, Germany, May 2007.

18. Author's interview with a senior official responsible for technical assistance in the Österreichische Nationalbank, Vienna, Austria, June 2006.

to EU countries will also be organized."[19] The ECB saw its role in these assistance efforts as an ongoing one. Even after several postcommunist countries joined the EU, the ECB continued to coordinate projects for nonsystem central banks, especially in the Balkans, Russia, and Ukraine.

The organizational efforts of the IMF, BIS, and ECB enhanced the national central banks' ability to provide consistent, intensive, and timely training and technical assistance to postcommunist central bankers. Within and beyond this framework, the community worked toward transplanting its central banking model into the postcommunist world.

The Donors and Their Programs

Technical assistance programs focused on developing the organization, infrastructure, and practices of the central banks. They came in the form of short-term missions (often IMF-sponsored) and long-term advisors ("resident experts") sent to work with individual central banks. The most intensive technical assistance efforts took place in the early 1990s, as postcommunist central banks built capabilities to conduct open market operations, operate payment systems, and carry out other vital central banking tasks.

Training efforts included founding new educational centers designed to teach specialized central banking skills, conducting in-house training seminars either at the donor or at the recipient central banks, and accepting postcommunist central bankers for residential internships. The Bank of England founded the Centre for Central Banking Studies (CCBS) in 1990 to conduct training and coordinate the bank's technical assistance. In 1992 the IMF, BIS, Österreichische Nationalbank (OeNB), and three other international organizations teamed up to create the Joint Vienna Institute (JVI), intended to train postcommunist officials in banking and finance. The Banque de France created its International Banking and Finance Institute in 1997, while the Bundesbank founded its Center for Technical Central Bank Cooperation (Zentrum für Technische Zentralbank-Kooperation, or TZK) in 2005 to formalize its extensive training and technical assistance programs. Established training centers such as the IMF Institute in Washington, DC, and the Swiss National Bank's study center in Gerzensee also

---

19. Introductory statement by Willem Duisenberg on the occasion of the signing of the TACIS "Central Bank Training" contract and of a Protocol between the European Central Bank, the Delegation of the European Commission in Russia and the Bank of Russia, Moscow, October 13, 2003. Available at www.ecb.europa.eu/press/pressconf/2003/html/is031013.en.html. For the final book publication, see Olsen 2005.

trained numerous postcommunist central bankers. Many national central banks provided training and internships on a less formal basis as well. For example, from 1992 through 1999 the Bundesbank conducted over two hundred training seminars abroad and sponsored approximately one thousand short-term study visits and seminars in Germany, while the US Federal Reserve Bank of Kansas City continually hosted a small, rotating group of postcommunist central bankers for six-month internships.

These training efforts reached both across and deep within postcommunist central banks. According to data from the CCBS and the JVI, personnel from every postcommunist central bank participated in at least one of their training sessions.[20] Table 4.2 shows the number of Hungarian and Kyrgyz central bankers who participated in training courses from 1996 through 1999, an intensive development period for both banks. Well over three hundred central bankers from each country took foreign training programs during these four years alone, representing a substantial proportion of their staffs.[21] In addition, the transnational central banking community assisted many postcommunist central banks in developing their own domestic training centers. These training programs not only aimed to pass on the knowledge necessary to run a central bank according to international standards, but to enmesh postcommunist central bankers within the transnational central banking network.

The donor institutions paid for most of this assistance themselves. Not only did they provide staff time, but they often covered salaries, travel, and accommodation expenses as well. When national central bankers participated in IMF missions, the IMF paid their expenses. The training centers typically covered room, board, and tuition for postcommunist participants, although the participants' own central banks often funded their travel to and from the courses. The EU's PHARE and TACIS programs provided financing for a number of central bank assistance programs in the postcommunist world; for example, TACIS funded the Eurosystem projects to restructure Russian banking supervision.[22] The CCBS

---

20. Participant home-country information kindly provided to the author by the CCBS in 2001 and 2006, and by the JVI in 2006 and 2014.

21. Some Hungarian and Kyrgyz central bankers took more than one course during that period of time.

22. PHARE was created at the June 1989 G24 meeting, and stands for Poland and Hungary Assistance Reconstruction Economic program; it quickly expanded to the other CEE states, and then to the Baltic states in 1991. TACIS was created in 1991 and stands for Technical Assistance for the Commonwealth of Independent States. The TACIS program covered the former FSU countries save the Baltics (it also covered Mongolia from 1991 through 2003). Central banking assistance comprised a small part of the PHARE and TACIS programs, which were the EU's primary assistance vehicles for the postcommunist states.

TABLE 4.2 MNB and NBKR participants in training seminars abroad, 1996–1999*

	MAGYAR NEMZETI BANK			NATIONAL BANK OF THE KYRGYZ REPUBLIC		
	MONETARY POLICY	FINANCIAL SYSTEM	OTHER	MONETARY POLICY	FINANCIAL SYSTEM	OTHER
Bank of England (CCBS)	27	21	11	24	14	13
Banque de France	21	8	27	14	11	21
Deutsche Bundesbank	20	5	27	8	18	41
Banca d'Italia	8	10	8	1	6	1
Swiss National Bank	9	3	0	10	1	1
Other Central Banks	19	18	15	7	7	8
Joint Vienna Institute	13	17	22	44	35	23
Other Institutes	15	1	13	25	20	30
Totals:	132	83	123	133	112	138

Sources: Departments of Human Resources, Magyar Nemzeti Bank and National Bank of the Kyrgyz Republic. Although staff levels fluctuated, on average the MNB had about 1,000 employees and the NBKR about 400 employees at their respective headquarters in Budapest and Bishkek during this period.

Notes: Monetary Policy includes courses on monetary policy, economic modeling, foreign exchange, government debt, and statistics. *Financial System* includes courses on banking supervision, payment systems, financial markets, money laundering, and cash management. *Other* includes courses on internal audit, accounting, human resources, security, legal issues, the European Union, and others.

*Excluding language training

received supplementary support from PHARE, TACIS, and the British Government's Know-How Fund.[23] Especially at first, though, the national central banks preferred to use EU funding programs only on long-term projects and only when absolutely necessary. EU application and reporting requirements were notoriously complicated and time-consuming, the approval process was slow, and the funding often arrived so late that the "funded" activity had already been completed. After the ECB became involved in coordination, the national central banks' capacity to use PHARE and TACIS funding grew. USAID also funded a variety of technical assistance programs for postcommunist central banks, especially for improving banking supervision. It was the primary funder for the Financial Services Volunteer Corps, providing the FSVC with millions in grant support for its programs in the postcommunist world.

So many institutions and individuals from the transnational central banking community provided so much training and technical assistance to postcommunist central banks that it would be impossible to cover it all in a single book. Instead, I take a closer look below at the work of five representative institutions: two national central banks (the Bank of England and the Bundesbank), an

23. Fleming and Cole 1995.

international organization (the IMF), a consortium (the JVI), and a US nongovernmental organization (the FSVC). The analysis demonstrates how their programs differed from yet complemented one another, and how, taken as a whole, the community's transformation campaign arguably represented the most concentrated and comprehensive foreign aid effort in the postcommunist world.

The Bank of England

The Bank of England provided training and technical assistance through its Centre for Central Banking Studies. The bank founded the CCBS in 1990 primarily to provide assistance to central banks in postcommunist states. As long-time staffer and eventual director Gill Hammond wrote, "The Bank of England saw a unique opportunity to help with a transfer of knowledge to these countries and, at the same time, to foster a mutually supportive network of central banks worldwide."[24] It held its first three seminars for postcommunist central bankers in late 1990 and held six more in 1991. By 1995 the CCBS regularly conducted between twenty and twenty-five on-site courses per year and a similar number abroad.[25] From 1990 through 2005 the CCBS had trained almost six thousand postcommunist central bankers—nearly as many as the JVI during that same period—and over fifteen thousand central bankers in total (table 4.6). Its peak years for training postcommunist central bankers were 1993–96, with approximately six hundred per year. By 1998, central bankers from postcommunist countries represented less than half of those taking CCBS courses as the CCBS expanded its mandate globally.

CCBS courses focused on topics such as monetary policy, payment systems, economic modeling, and government debt management. They became more specialized over time, with general courses on central banking and personnel training replaced by topical seminars and expert forums by the end of the 1990s. The CCBS diversified its courses on monetary policy and operations to focus on more specialized areas, and stopped offering courses in Russian translation once students' English-language abilities improved. As technical skill levels rose, the CCBS also began holding intensive collaborative research workshops for more advanced postcommunist central bankers in 1998, after which the CCBS conducted two or three of these workshops per year. At these workshops, participating central bankers spent one week discussing a key topic (e.g., Transmission

---

24. Gill Hammond, "The Centre for Central Banking Studies," *Bank of England Quarterly Bulletin* (Summer 2006): 190–95.
25. Ibid.

Mechanisms and Monetary Policy Implementation), followed by three-month projects in London that produced a series of related research papers (some published subsequently as edited volumes). In 2004, the CCBS introduced annual specialist seminars for central bank chief economic officers, a high-profile event still going strong over a decade later.

The CCBS considered itself to be a long-term service provider to the community and kept in touch with former participants via a newsletter and e-mail. The newsletter revealed the personal as well as professional connections forged during these courses. The first issue contained a poem written by a Russian participant in a November 1992 CCBS course in St. Petersburg, as well as a photo of participants in a June 1992 Hungarian CCBS course dressed in bathing suits and standing in Lake Balaton. The summer 1999 edition featured a wonderful story worth quoting at length, entitled "Inflation Targeters Take a Beating (at Football)":

> Gloomy voices demanded changes to the "operational framework" after the Inflation Targeters of the Czech National Bank, Bank of England, and National Bank of Poland suffered a humiliating 13–3 defeat at the hands of the combined forces of the Money and Exchange Rate Targeters of Hungary, Slovenia, and Slovakia . . . It was the penultimate evening of a Workshop on Intermediate Policy Targets run jointly by the National Bank of Hungary and the Bank of England. . . . Gabriel Sterne [blamed] his team's poor stamina on [the CCBS's Lavan] Mahadeva's late night modeling binges. It is claimed that Mahadeva woke up Czech modeler Emil Stavrev at 2:30am the previous morning with shrieks of "I've got the Czech model to solve in rational expectations mode!" Indeed, Mahadeva and Stavrev were seen blatantly flaunting their model in a seminar shortly before kick off.[26]

This levity and after-hours environment should not be mistaken for a lack of rigor. One staffer opined that the CCBS offered more challenging courses than did the IMF Institute, even the Institute's so-called capstone courses.[27] The CCBS, unlike the JVI, did not cover participants' travel and accommodation costs, which some suggested contributed to a greater seriousness of purpose.[28] When

---

26. Gabriel Sterne, "Inflation Targeters Take a Beating (at Football)," *CCBS News* 12 (Summer 1999), 5.

27. Author's interview with a senior CCBS official at the Bank of England, London, UK, April 2001.

28. Grants from the EU and the British Know-How Fund administered through the CCBS sometimes covered these costs for post-communist participants, especially early on. The courses themselves were free.

I observed a CCBS Financial Management course in 2001 students around the table actively participated, and cues printed on the back of their name plates reminded them that "success depends on you," "say what you think," "confine your remarks to the subject under discussion," "as a courtesy to others, be punctual," and "appreciate the other person's point of view," among others. The CCBS staff chose participants carefully, looking for those most suitable (e.g., "why bring someone from a currency board country to a course on monetary policy?"), with strong English-language abilities, and from diverse countries. They also sanctioned the occasional participant who skipped classes, was disruptive, or seemed to be in London primarily to shop.

The CCBS over time became increasingly identified as a research institution as well. To support its training efforts, the CCBS published free, downloadable Handbooks in Central Banking to explain basic concepts to new central bankers in an accessible way. The first handbook, *Introduction to Monetary Policy*, appeared in 1996. By 2006 the series included twenty-five titles; by 2015 the regular series had reached Handbook #33, plus additional Technical Handbooks on economic modeling.[29] As demand for assistance rose, in 1999 the CCBS added a complementary Lecture Series as well. CCBS staff and CCBS workshops produced sixteen books and dozens of articles on topics such as payment systems, monetary policy, and the future of central banking.

The CCBS also carried out technical assistance, although this comprised a smaller part of its efforts. It primarily coordinated the Bank of England's staff contributions to IMF missions. When CCBS and other bank staff went on bilateral technical assistance missions, these were almost always short-term and based on a request from the recipient central bank. The CCBS arranged on average thirty to fifty short-term, tailored informational visits to the Bank of England each year for small groups of senior central bankers. On occasion, however, the CCBS engaged in more intensive technical assistance. Most notably, the CCBS's Simon Gray spent four months in Iraq in 2003 helping to set up its new central bank and introduce the new Iraqi currency.[30] This reflected the increasingly global reach of the CCBS since its creation in 1990. Although initially designed primarily to assist postcommunist states, within a decade it provided extensive training to central bankers around the world.

---

29. Centre for Central Banking Studies, "Prospectus 2001"; Centre for Central Banking Studies website, 2006 and 2014. Available at www.bankofengland.co.uk/education/Pages/ccbs/publications.aspx.

30. Gray and Nell 2005, Hammond, "The Centre for Central Banking Studies." The US Treasury under deputy treasury secretary John Taylor (of the Taylor Rule, temporarily on leave from Stanford) led the Iraqi financial reconstruction. Taylor 2007.

The Deutsche Bundesbank

Like the CCBS, the Bundesbank concentrated primarily on bilateral aid projects and provided extensive assistance throughout the postcommunist transformation process. It differed, however, in both the content and range of its assistance. Whereas the Bank of England founded the CCBS as an educational and research institution early on, the Bundesbank primarily provided technical assistance and seminars tailored to specific requests. In addition, although the Bundesbank did expand its geographic reach over time, it remained concentrated on assisting the postcommunist central banks.

In 1992 the Bundesbank conducted just 34 technical assistance and training projects, with 270 participants. Yet over the period 1992–2000, it conducted over 200 training seminars abroad with around 6,000 participants; about 1,000 study visits and seminars in Germany with over 5,000 participants; and devoted over 7,000 person-days (or 27 person-years) to consulting assignments.[31] Its activities continued to increase over time; the Bundesbank conducted over 300 assistance activities in 2005 alone, with a total of just over 3,000 participants from almost eighty countries.[32] These numbers stayed relatively steady in subsequent years and maintained a primary focus on the postcommunist world. The Bundesbank covered the costs of accommodation, per diem, and health insurance for its Frankfurt-based seminars, while participants made their own travel arrangements. In the case of external seminars and technical assistance, the Bundesbank paid the travel costs for its personnel while the recipient central bank arranged room and board.

Although the Bundesbank had a long tradition of providing ad hoc bilateral assistance to other central banks (beginning in Africa), its programs became much more extensive and organized due to the demand from the postcommunist world. In 1991 it restructured the Technical Central Bank Cooperation unit

---

31. Deutsche Bundesbank, "Technical Central Bank Cooperation," mimeo, June 1, 2001.

32. Deutsche Bundesbank, Center for Technical Central Bank Cooperation (Zentrum für Technische Zentralbank-Kooperation) website, www.bundesbank.de/Redaktion/EN/Standardartikel/Bundesbank/Technical_Central_Bank_Cooperation/technical_central_bank_cooperation.html. The single exception was 2001: "In 2001 the Technical Central Bank Cooperation Division organised 160 training initiatives, involving a total of more than 1,800 foreign central bank staff. This means that for the first time since 1992 there was a fall in the number of activities from the previous year; in 2000 some two thousand foreign central bank staff members had taken part in 189 training activities in Germany and abroad. This reflects the additional internal pressure caused by the introduction of the euro banknotes and coins. In 2001 the sustained high international demand for the Bundesbank's technical central bank cooperation services could therefore not be met in full. The euro banknotes and coins have now been successfully introduced and an increase in technical central bank cooperation activities can therefore be expected during 2002." Deutsche Bundesbank, *2001 Annual Report*, 176.

within its Foreign Department, and in 1994 created a separate Technical Central Bank Cooperation Division. Its first postcommunist seminar was an eight-week course on central banking in Prague in 1992 for the Czech National Bank. As the Bundesbank's coordinator for technical assistance recalled in 2000, "they asked us to do it—our system is totally demand driven. We'll do any subject they ask for, even monetary policy, though we no longer carry out monetary policy ourselves."[33] The Bundesbank continued to conduct these so-called specialized seminars (a cross between training and technical assistance) on requested topics both in Germany and abroad. Demand was heaviest for monetary policy, payment systems, banking supervision, and accounting and internal audit.

Due to overwhelming requests for particular topics, in the mid-1990s the Bundesbank began offering monthly "standard seminars" for central bankers in Germany. Although the Bundesbank gave the seminars in German for the first two years, after staffers noticed that the same few people kept participating they switched to English to reach a wider audience. Once the switch was made, the demand for participation regularly exceeded the supply of places. In early 2000 the Bundesbank added a program for EU accession states, offering seminars on EU-related issues such as law and payment systems. The Bundesbank occasionally sent lecturers to BIS and IMF training programs as well.

Just as important, the Bundesbank sent numerous staffers on technical assistance projects abroad and arranged thousands of short- and long-term study visits to the Bundesbank. With its sixteen thousand staff members at the time, the Bundesbank could nearly always find appropriate experts to participate in technical assistance projects and study visits. The coordinator emphasized that during the study visits "We don't tell these banks how to restructure. Rather, their personnel find themselves in the Bundesbank, see how we operate, and realize that some areas of their own banks aren't so productive. Then, they make the changes on their own. So they don't get direct advice from us—we can only talk to them about our own experiences."

From 1992 through 1996, over 70 percent of the Bundesbank's assistance went to postcommunist states, with 26 percent going to Central and Eastern Europe and 45 percent to the former Soviet Union.[34] In the late 1990s the focus shifted even more heavily eastwards. In 1997, for example, requests for cooperation from the Caucasus and Central Asia increased significantly. About half of those

---

33. Author's interview with a senior official in charge of technical central bank cooperation at the Deutsche Bundesbank, Frankfurt, Germany, June 2000.

34. Deutsche Bundesbank, "The Bundesbank's Technical Central Bank Cooperation with Countries in Transition," *Monthly Report*, April 1997, 47–52.

participating in the Bundesbank's cooperation programs that year came from Russia, Ukraine, Poland, and Kyrgyzstan.[35] As the coordinator noted, as of 2000, "broken down by person-hours of assistance, we've given the most to Russia and Ukraine. Russians, in particular, need to be here on the job in order to see how things work. There was a short period after the [1998] crisis when Russians stopped visiting the Bundesbank, but last autumn they started coming back again." From 1992 through 1999 Russians participated in the most Bundesbank seminars, while Ukraine absorbed the most person-days of technical consultations (over 1,200).

This former Soviet-centric pattern persisted, but the Bundesbank increased its cooperation with Central and Eastern Europe again as EU accession approached. In 2004 the Bundesbank added EU-financed, ECB-organized twinning projects to its assistance repertoire, aimed at facilitating new EU members' entry into the euro zone.[36] It participated in a large twinning project with the Czech National Bank on financial stability, and in smaller ones in Turkey, Ukraine, and the Balkans. In July 2005 the Bundesbank founded the Center for Technical Central Bank Cooperation (TZK). The TZK's first director, Jürgen Sterlepper, had spent years advising the Russian and Ukrainian central banks, and married a Georgian central banker. With twenty-five staff members and reporting directly to the Bundesbank's vice governor, the TZK further institutionalized and intensified the Bundesbank's training and technical assistance programming. As the TZK leadership observed at an October 2010 Bundesbank conference celebrating twenty years of technical central bank cooperation:

> [D]espite unresolved political and structural problems, which still persist in many countries, and unavoidable hindrances in some cases, major progress has been achieved in setting up modern central banks thanks to technical central bank cooperation. In many cases, cooperation with the Bundesbank has, at least indirectly, stepped up the pressure to adopt modern central banking acts and pursue stability-oriented monetary and financial market policies thus contributing to "exporting" our "central bank philosophy" to other countries. In many developing nations, EMEs and transition countries, the central bank has now become the most modern and sometimes also most reliable institution in public administration.[37]

---

35. Deutsche Bundesbank, *1997 Annual Report*.

36. Author's interview with a senior official in the Center for Technical Central Bank Cooperation of the Deutsche Bundesbank, Frankfurt, Germany, May 2007.

37. Jürgen Sterlepper and Martin Dinkelborg, 2010, "20 Years of Technical Central Bank Cooperation at the Deutsche Bundesbank," www.bundesbank.de/Redaktion/EN/Downloads/Press/Current_Issues/20_years_of_technical_central_bank_cooperation_tcbc_at_the_deutsche_bundesbank.pdf%3F__blob%3DpublicationFile.

In keeping with Bundesbank tradition, this philosophy included reminding other central bankers not to forget about monetary aggregates when conducting monetary policy.[38] Demonstrating the ongoing nature of transformation, in FY 2012–13 the TZK provided twenty-seven bilateral assistance missions reaching 341 postcommunist central bankers, in addition to a twinning project for Serbia carried out in partnership with the Czech National Bank, joint activities with the ECB and other training centers, and the regular courses held at its own facilities.[39] Throughout the transformation period, the Bundesbank was the leading source of bilateral technical assistance for the postcommunist world.

The International Monetary Fund

While the IMF's postcommunist lending programs and loan conditionality received a great deal of attention, both positive and negative, the IMF's training and technical assistance programs—programs that did as much or more to transform postcommunist states than their more high-profile companions—received relatively little press. As former IMF director Stanley Fischer once pointed out, "The IMF devotes more than twice as many staff resources to surveillance and technical assistance, taken together, as it does to the operation of its lending programs."[40] In the 1990s, the IMF rapidly upgraded its assistance provision capacity. Criticized in the past for not sufficiently emphasizing central banking and its proper relationship to governments, the IMF from the start "decided to link advice on central bank instruments and techniques with broader policy advice" in working with the postcommunist states.[41] The IMF estimated that it provided nearly two hundred person-years of technical assistance for postcommunist financial-sector development (primarily to central banks) between 1989 and 1999.[42]

The Monetary and Exchange Affairs Department provided the majority of this technical assistance, with contributions from the Fiscal Affairs and the Statistics Departments. The MAE focused on monetary and exchange rate policy, payment systems reform, legal reform, internal audit, and, later, banking supervision. The

38. Author's interview with a senior official in the Center for Technical Central Bank Cooperation of the Deutsche Bundesbank, Frankfurt, Germany, May 2007.

39. Center for Technical Central Bank Cooperation annual report 2012/13, www.bundesbank. de/Redaktion/EN/Downloads/Bundesbank/TCBC/annual_report_2012_2013.pdf?_blob= publicationFile.

40. Fischer 2004.

41. "The Politics of Central Banking in East Europe" 1991–92.

42. International Monetary Fund 2000.

IMF also assigned resident representatives to many postcommunist states, with offices often located within the central banks themselves. From these vantage points, the resident representatives had ideal positions from which to give day-to-day advice on central banking operations and policy.

The MAE organized its technical assistance in concert with the recipient countries, often based on conversations at the Basel meetings. The MAE would conduct a "pre-visit" to prepare an initial assessment of the central bank's needs, the IMF's regional management teams and Washington staff would review it, and the mission chiefs would discuss the review and send a final version to senior management for approval. If approved, the assessment went to the country authorities and the two sides would develop a schedule for assistance provision. IMF-organized expert teams went to participating postcommunist central banks two or three times per year on average in the 1990s, and wrote lengthy, detailed reports that were, in the words of one IMF official, "like bricks."[43] The MAE organized numerous external training workshops as well, usually engaging four IMF staffers and four national central bank experts to lead each workshop.[44]

Table 4.3 breaks down by country the IMF's astounding 345.2 total person-years of technical assistance to the postcommunist world from 1990–2000, the bulk of it dedicated to the financial sector. It reveals the IMF's strong focus on the former Soviet states, particularly Russia and Ukraine, as well as on countries with more difficult initial conditions. IMF technical assistance declined after the 1990s, especially to Ukraine, Georgia, Tajikistan, Azerbaijan, and the Baltic states. Where the MAE previously sent two to three missions per year, afterward it typically sent perhaps one mission plus individual experts on an as-needed basis. The IMF noted that, "A more active role by other TA providers, particularly the European Union, is an important cause of this decline."[45] The 1997–98 Asian/Russian financial crisis also reoriented the IMF's interest toward providing financial sector surveillance through its new Financial Sector Assessment Program (FSAP). The FSAP's voluntary Financial System Stability Assessment reports gauged individual countries' financial sector stability and development. The MAE was renamed the Monetary and Financial Systems Department in 2003 with a formally expanded mandate to include financial system surveillance. While technical assistance remained an important endeavor for the department, it began to take a back seat to the surveillance function in the postcommunist world. In total,

---

43. Author's interview with a senior IMF official, Washington, DC, November 2001.
44. IMF Institute 1994–95.
45. Independent Evaluation Office 2005.

TABLE 4.3   IMF technical assistance to postcommunist countries, 1990–2000

COUNTRY		STAFF YEARS
Russian Federation		38.7
Baltic countries		22.8
Estonia	5.8	
Latvia	5.8	
Lithuania	11.2	
Other Central and Eastern European countries		
Former Soviet Union		61.0
Belarus	13.3	
Moldova	13.6	
Ukraine	34.2	
Pre-1990 IMF members		23.9
Hungary	3.4	
Poland	13.7	
Romania	6.7	
Yugoslavia and successors		32.1
Bosnia and Herzegovina	11.5	
Croatia	7.5	
FR Yugoslavia (Serbia and Montenegro)	3.3	
FYR Macedonia	9.4	
Slovenia	0.4	
Other European countries		47.9
Albania	23.4	
Bulgaria	17.3	
Czechoslovakia	1.7	
Czech Republic	3.1	
Slovak Republic	2.4	
Caucasus region		45.0
Armenia	11.9	
Azerbaijan	12.3	
Georgia	20.8	
Central Asia		73.8
Kazakhstan	14.8	
Kyrgyz Republic	14.6	
Mongolia	17.6	
Tajikistan	10.3	
Turkmenistan	10.1	
Uzbekistan	6.4	
Total staff-years		345.2
Percentage of total IMF technical assistance		22.2

Source: Boughton 2012, from IMF staff calculations.

the IMF provided 530 person-years of technical assistance to postcommunist states in the twenty-five years after the fall of the Wall.[46]

In addition, over one thousand postcommunist central bankers took training courses at the IMF Institute in Washington, DC, between 1989 and 2006.[47]

---

46. Roaf et al. 2014.
47. PATS System, IMF Institute, 2006.

Participant numbers became significant only after 1995 because the Institute's courses demanded fluency in English and economics. The IMF Institute was established in 1964 to provide training in economic management and expanded its course offerings during the 1990s to meet the new demand. Its expert-level courses meant that postcommunist central bankers could learn side-by-side with central bankers from other regions, as the courses permitted only one participant per country and emphasized team projects. The IMF Institute also organized special seminars for senior postcommunist officials in an effort to develop more broad-based support for macroeconomic reforms. For example, it organized a 1995 seminar on macroeconomic and financial policies in Bangkok for high-level officials from the five Central Asian states. According to the Institute, the seminar "gave participants an opportunity to observe a booming market economy and to meet with senior staff of the Bank of Thailand to be briefed on the operations of the Central Bank in a market economy."[48] But the IMF's most significant training contribution came through its participation in the Joint Vienna Institute (JVI), a training center designed specifically for the postcommunist world.

The Joint Vienna Institute

The IMF, BIS, World Bank, OECD, European Bank for Reconstruction and Development, and the Austrian authorities (the OeNB and the Ministry of Finance) jointly organized the JVI in September 1992 "in order to offer courses for officials of the central banks and of the economic and financial authorities of the countries whose economies were formerly subject to central planning."[49] Each sponsoring organization taught its own specialized courses at the JVI, each lasting from a few days to several weeks. During the first year, as one donor put it, "there was nothing joint about it—each organization simply came in and did their courses." But in late 1992 representatives from the sponsoring organizations met with a facilitator outside Oxford and put together the "comprehensive course." This course included a cohesive range of topics relevant to transition economies; each sponsoring organization taught the segment related to its area of expertise. These comprehensive courses initially lasted five to six months, preceded by lengthy introductory courses in several postcommunist cities. As skill levels rose the partners redesigned the comprehensive course to become a fourteen-week course in Applied Economic Policy.

Figure 4.1 shows the number of central bankers trained in JVI courses annually from 1992 through 2013. In total, postcommunist central bankers took well

---

48. IMF Institute 1994–95.
49. Joint Vienna Institute, "Program 2000."

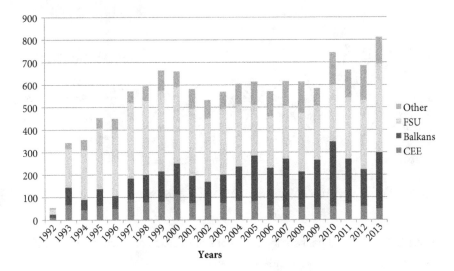

FIGURE 4.1   Central bankers in JVI courses, 1992–2013.

Source: Derived from Joint Vienna Institute database, 2006 and 2014.

over ten thousand JVI courses. Considering that most postcommunist central banks had around four hundred to six hundred staff members at their head-quarters (from governors to accountants to security guards), this represented a significant proportion of the "trainable" population. Because JVI courses were typically pitched at a more introductory level, postcommunist central banks tended to use them for newer staff and participation skewed toward the for-mer Soviet Union and the Balkans. Looking at participation from our five case countries (figure 4.2) emphasizes this for Hungary, where multiple interviewees told me that by the mid-1990s all but the rawest recruits on the MNB staff had moved beyond the JVI level. On the flip side, focus groups with central bankers in Macedonia and Kosovo in 2014 confirmed that both central banks still sent most of their operational staff members to the JVI regularly.[50]

The initial idea for the JVI came from the OeNB, which sought to institution-alize postcommunist central bank training after its positive experiences organiz-ing an earlier series of retreats for central bankers. The OeNB convinced the IMF and the other sponsoring organizations that it would be a good idea, and after negotiations all signed an agreement to establish the JVI.[51] The JVI was

---

50. Focus groups conducted by the author, Cornel Ban, and Leonard Seabrooke with officials of the National Bank of the Republic of Macedonia and the Central Bank of the Republic of Kosovo, in Skopje, FYR Macedonia and Pristina, Kosovo, June 2014.

51. Author's interview with a senior official of the Joint Vienna Institute, Vienna, Austria, May 2006.

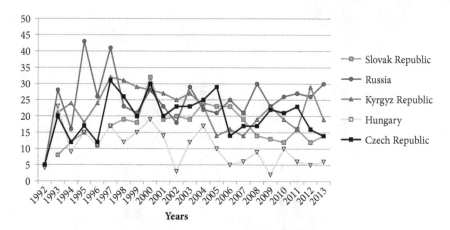

FIGURE 4.2   Central bankers in JVI courses from case countries, 1992–2013.

Source: Derived from Joint Vienna Institute database, 2006 and 2014.

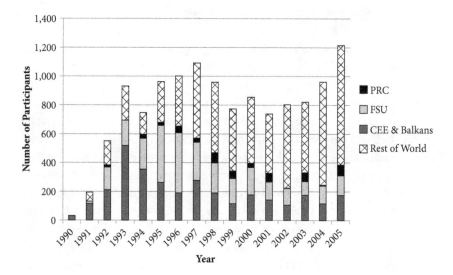

FIGURE 4.3   CCBS course participants, 1990–2005.

Source: Derived from CCBS database, 2000, 2005, and 2006.

originally located in the Austrian Customs Training School building, which had spare capacity after Austria joined the EU and the demand for border guards and customs officials declined. The JVI hit rough spots at the beginning, as the lengthy courses too often did not gel well or saw graduates take their new skills to international organizations or the private sector instead of remaining in central banks and finance ministries. The introduction of shorter and more specialized courses, as well as more careful screening of participants, did much to resolve these issues.

The JVI itself had a small, largely administrative staff, with the participating institutions sending experts to teach individual courses in their areas of specialty (e.g., the IMF on macroeconomic issues or the BIS on payment systems). The JVI provided free housing for participants and charged no tuition. Most of the sponsoring organizations paid the travel costs and other expenses for participants in their courses. In addition to financial support from the founding institutions, the JVI received contributions from the EU and from individual European central banks and government agencies.

In May 2000 I sat in on a session of a core JVI course, one on Macroeconomic Analysis and Policy given by IMF Institute staff. The thirty participants included central bankers from throughout the postcommunist world, as well as China and Myanmar. Although none of the instructors or students were native English speakers, the course was given in English. The JVI provided simultaneous Russian translation via earphone, which seven participants from the former Soviet Union used. After class, one instructor told me that his lectures "aim for the middle" because of the disparity in knowledge among participants. At the culmination of this course, students participated in a simulation in which they designed and presented programs on how to stabilize the Ukrainian economy. The instructor observed that in these simulations the class always acted like an IMF mission would, balancing budgets through cuts in expenditures and increases in tax revenues, and wondered ironically why these same officials appeared not to listen as closely when IMF missions recommended similar measures to their home countries.

The JVI's founders initially viewed it as a bridge institution to train officials until postcommunist universities could retool their economics departments.[52] They created the JVI with a sunset clause and planned to close it down by August 2004. In light of the strong continued demand for training, however, in 2002 the sponsoring organizations made the JVI a permanent training institute and provided it with new, high-quality facilities in central Vienna. The motivation and professionalism of the students continued to rise, the selection process became more rigorous, and the student base continued to trend eastward, especially toward Russia and Central Asia. From its origins as a small training center living on borrowed time, the JVI became firmly institutionalized in the heart of Europe and its success inspired the IMF to found several similar regional training centers around the world.

---

52. Author's interview with a senior official of the Joint Vienna Institute, Vienna, Austria, May 2006.

The Financial Services Volunteer Corps

While the preceding cases emphasized the more multilateral, public European approach to assistance, the FSVC exemplified the US public-private partnership approach. The FSVC, a nongovernmental organization devoted to providing financial-sector technical assistance, "was established in response to the historic events that took place in Central Europe and the former Soviet Union during the late 1980s and early 1990s."[53] Former US secretary of state and Federal Reserve Bank of New York president Cyrus Vance joined former US deputy secretary of state and Goldman Sachs co-chairman John Whitehead to found the FSVC in 1990 at the request of then-president George H. W. Bush. They quickly formed an informal alliance with the then-president of the Federal Reserve Bank of New York Gerald Corrigan, who had a special interest in Russian assistance and who himself founded the Russian-American Bankers Forum in 1992. In 1993, Vance recruited Federal Reserve Bank of New York senior vice president J. Andrew Spindler to serve as the FSVC's executive director. This group's high-level connections allowed the FSVC to build an extensive volunteer contingent from the US Federal Reserve banks, the Federal Deposit Insurance Corporation, the Treasury Department, the Office of the Comptroller of the Currency, and other primarily US-based financial institutions and service providers. The FSVC's key financial donors were USAID and the US State Department, while the organizations providing volunteers contributed their staff members' time. The FSVC itself grew from a small staff of under ten in the early 1990s to an organization with headquarters in New York and field offices in multiple countries.

According to the FSVC, from its founding in 1990 through 2005 "more than 7,000 experts from the financial, legal and regulatory communities have taken part in more than 1,400 FSVC missions, reaching nearly 30,000 counterparts in thirty developing and transition countries."[54] By 2015, this number had reached over 8,500 experts, 2,700 missions, and 35,000 counterparts in over thirty-five countries; the FSVC had received about $90 million in total funding and estimated that it had provided over $210 million in assistance.[55] Of that amount, about half went toward central banking activities such as developing monetary policy instruments, payment systems, banking supervision capabilities, and central banking legislation. In 2005, for example, the FSVC devoted exactly eighty of its 160 technical assistance projects to central banking and payments issues.[56] While

---

53. Financial Services Volunteer Corps, summary brochure, 2001.

54. Financial Services Volunteer Corps, www.fsvc.org/about/whoweare.html (as of August 2006).

55. Financial Services Volunteer Corps, www.fsvc.org/node/33.

56. Financial Services Volunteer Corps, Quarterly Report, Fourth Quarter 2005.

the vast majority of its projects in the 1990s focused on postcommunist states, as transformation progressed its activities expanded and re-oriented more toward Asia, Africa, and the Middle East.

The FSVC's work was almost entirely demand-driven and short-term. The FSVC typically sent experts to recipient countries for one-week visits, a necessity given its volunteer basis. In addition, the FSVC carried out many consulting activities (such as commenting on central bank draft legislation) from abroad. The FSVC kept a database of practitioner-volunteers expert in various issues, and often sent volunteers on missions to the same country and/or on the same topic multiple times. For example, from 1995 through 1999 the FSVC carried out 221 projects in Russia with 258 volunteers, 35 percent of whom performed two or more assignments.[57]

Although not the largest player in central banking assistance to the postcommunist world, the FSVC complemented the international organizations and national central banks in a number of ways. First, the FSVC's extensive network of specialists meant that it could often respond more quickly to highly specific technical assistance requests. Second, because the FSVC worked through volunteers, the recipients generally trusted that they had no direct conflict of interest or broader institutional agenda to promote. Recipients usually felt this objectivity and trust with the national central banks as well, but sometimes less so with the IMF, EU, or paid consultants. The FSVC emphasized that it did not push US-oriented solutions, and if it felt it was not in the best position to provide advice it would use its community contacts to direct the recipient elsewhere. For example, in the mid-1990s Belarus requested assistance with its settlement system. The FSVC recognized that the US experience would be less relevant for such a small country and contacted the National Bank of Switzerland instead, arranging to provide the needed assistance through Zurich. The FSVC volunteers often worked side by side with advisors from other national central banks and international organizations on tasks such as payment systems development, especially in complex countries such as Russia. Like that of other community members, the FSVC's workload increased every year, reaching new regions and including more projects. After the global financial crisis it increased its focus on financial regulation, supervision, and risk management, leading major new projects in Russia and Albania. Given the decentralized nature of the US Federal Reserve and financial regulatory sector in comparison to those of other advanced industrial democracies, the FSVC played an important coordination role befitting a US political culture inclined toward public-private cooperation and volunteerism.

---

57. CARANA Corporation, *Evaluation of the Financial Services Volunteer Corps (FSVC) Project in Russia*, prepared for USAID, February 29, 2000.

The Rewards of Membership

Central bankers across the postcommunist world received significant social and material rewards from embracing the transnational central banking community. The community offered them concrete, internationally accepted and tested ways to approach their complicated new jobs. The established central bankers approached the postcommunist central bankers as colleagues and professionals, saying in effect "here is what we do every day, here is how we do it, here is why we do it. We would like to help you to do it in your country as well." This technocratic approach appealed to the educated—and often quite young—economists, mathematicians, and accountants in postcommunist central banks. The community encouraged and enabled postcommunist central bankers to travel to London, Vienna, Paris, New York, and other international cities to study central banking, to network with fellow central bankers, and to learn to identify with the central banking community.

Postcommunist central bankers emerging from a rigidly hierarchical system in which central banks had played a minor role found the principle of central bank independence especially attractive. The transnational community told postcommunist central bankers that they could legitimately demand autonomy, referring to international practice and providing international support. Central bank independence also usually implied some budgetary autonomy, often allowing central bankers to earn higher salaries than other government bureaucrats. The community also emphasized that independence and price stability went hand in hand; protecting the country from shortsighted politicians bent on inflating the domestic currency was the essential justification for independence. Therefore, it made sense for many postcommunist central bankers to begin to see themselves as technocratic guardians of macroeconomic rectitude in perpetual potential conflict with domestic politicians.

Regular interactions with the transnational central banking community reinforced these views. To give just one example, in November 1996 the CCBS and the OeNB each held separate workshops on East Central European "Monetary Policy in Transition," one in London and the other in Vienna. Central bankers from Hungary, Poland, the Czech Republic, and Slovakia wrote papers for each, with different central bankers participating in the two workshops.[58] The journal *Central Banking* published the CCBS workshop papers, with the CCBS's Glenn Hoggarth penning an overview comparing the postcommunist central banks' monetary goals, targets, and inflation rates with each other and with the Bank

---

58. The CCBS workshop included Slovenian central bankers as well.

of England.[59] The overview praised the central banks' monetary operations as "quickly approaching or already matching the best practices used amongst the Western economies." At the same time, it concluded with a warning to the post-communist central bankers that aiming for "true price stability" rather than accepting persistent moderate inflation would mean adopting floating exchange rate regimes (which all four countries eventually did).

The OeNB workshop included not only postcommunist central bankers, but Western European economists and central bankers as well. The first session focused on monetary, inflation, and exchange rate targeting in Western Europe; the second on monetary policy in EMU; and the third on developments in East Central European monetary policy.[60] For the third session, papers by Westerners sandwiched the postcommunist central bankers' contributions, with the IMF's Leslie Lipschitz writing on "Where Do We Stand with Monetary Transformation in Central and Eastern Europe?" and the BIS's Renato Filosa writing on "The Relevance of Other Countries' Experience" for postcommunist monetary policy development. José de Matos of the Banco de Portugal wrapped up the proceedings with a luncheon speech on "Recent Experience with Successful Transformation—The Case of Portugal." Like the CCBS workshop, the OeNB workshop welcomed the postcommunist central bankers as valued (though junior) colleagues, reaffirmed the international consensus, and made the path forward to full community membership clear.

More generally, the community publicly applauded postcommunist central bankers who defied political pressures to ease monetary policy and chastised those who capitulated to such requests. The relatively small size and intercon-nectedness of the community gave additional weight to these social carrots and sticks. Postcommunist central banks and bankers thus became increasingly integrated into the community's professional culture over time. The regularity with which postcommunist central bank officials subsequently joined inter-national financial institutions reflected this integration. To give a few of the more prominent examples, former Croatian governor Marko Škreb became an IMF economist, former Czech governor Josef Tošovský became chairman of the Financial Stability Institute, former Albanian governor Kristaq Luniku joined the World Bank, and both former Georgian governor Irakli Managadze and former Polish governor Hanna Gronkiewicz-Waltz went to work for the European Bank for Reconstruction and Development after their central bank tenures ended.

---

59. Hoggarth 1997.
60. Achleitner 1997.

Nearly all of my interviewees in postcommunist central banks confirmed that they felt themselves to be part of a transnational community, a view held particularly strongly by central bankers in leadership positions and in monetary policy or research-oriented divisions and one that grew more definitive with time. This community identification often transcended simply professional connections. One Slovak central banker memorably told me in 2006 that "I know that if I go to Malaysia and I lose my money, I will knock on the doors of the central bank of Malaysia and I will go to the governor or the vice governor, I will mention that I am from the National Bank of Slovakia . . . and I am sure that they will help me. They really will. There is a kind of big family."[61] Central bankers in a 2014 focus group in Kosovo said that they had "friends" in other central banks "everywhere" and would have no hesitation contacting them for advice.[62] In those few instances where interviewees did not yet feel like members of the community, they often blamed it on their own failings. For example, one Romanian central banker said that it was "our fault" that his mid-status division was not better integrated internationally, because its work remained "humble" and in "an awkward stage" compared to other central banks in Europe.[63] Tellingly, across the postcommunist world central bankers often described their closest outside colleagues as those in central banks abroad rather than in other domestic government agencies. Indeed, when asked in 2014 if they felt a greater connection to foreign central bankers than to other domestic officials, an entire Albanian central bank focus group laughed loudly and one simply said, to nods of approval, "of course!"[64]

The Scope of Transformation

Established central bankers, postcommunist central bankers, and informed outsiders concurred on the impressive overall speed and scope of postcommunist central banking transformation. In a view common among donors, one IMF official I interviewed praised postcommunist central bankers for invariably being the first in their countries to understand macroeconomic problems and observed that technical assistance succeeded more readily in central banking than in other areas.[65] Another emphasized that postcommunist central bankers quickly came

---

61. Author's interview with a senior official in the Monetary Division of the National Bank of Slovakia, Bratislava, Slovakia, May 2006.

62. Focus group conducted by author, Cornel Ban, and Leonard Seabrooke with officials from the Central Bank of the Republic of Kosovo, Pristina, Kosovo, June 2014.

63. Author's interview with a senior official of the National Bank of Romania, June 2014.

64. Focus group conducted by author, Cornel Ban, and Leonard Seabrooke with six officials from the Bank of Albania, Tirana, Albania, June 2014.

65. Author's interview with a senior IMF official, Washington, DC, November 2001.

TABLE 4.4   Beliefs of postcommunist central bankers, 2000–2001

	HUNGARY		CZECH REPUBLIC		KYRGYZSTAN	
	MODE	MEDIAN	MODE	MEDIAN	MODE	MEDIAN
Price stability should be the primary goal of the central bank	5	4	5	5	5	4
The central bank alone should determine monetary policy	5	5	5	5	5	5
Central banks should be independent from the executive	5	5	5	5	5	5
Independent central banks contribute to economic growth	4	4	4	4	4	4
Central banks should be allowed to loan money to the government	2	2	1	2	2	2
Central banks should promote employment	2	2	2	2	3	3

Notes: 5 = strongly agree, 4 = agree, 3 = neutral, 2 = disagree, and 1 = strongly disagree. Magyar Nemzeti Bank, N = 86, March 2000; Czech National Bank, N = 33, June 2000; National Bank of the Kyrgyz Republic, N = 66, May 2001.

to accept "international best practices," and believed that training and technical assistance had played the key role in this process.[66] As a Banque de France official summed up, "The world of central banking is convergent by nature."[67]

Multiple measures lend credence to these evaluations. In 2000–2001 I conducted a survey of central bankers in Hungary, the Czech Republic, and Kyrgyzstan.[68] These anonymous surveys garnered 185 total responses (a 76 percent response rate) from personnel sampled across a range of departments, ages, and tenure. One part of the survey asked respondents to react to several statements about central banking, some consistent with the Western central banking model and others not. Table 4.4 presents the results. Central bankers in all three countries expressed strong agreement with the statements "Price stability should be the primary goal of the central bank," "The central bank alone should determine monetary policy," and "Central banks should be independent from the executive," mirroring the international consensus. They also agreed with the statement "Independent central banks contribute to economic growth," reflecting a widespread belief within the central banking community, but one that empirical evidence does not clearly support.

---

66. Ibid.

67. Jessica Fortin interview with a senior assistance coordinator at the Banque de France, Paris, France, April 2006.

68. I carried out these surveys with the invaluable cooperation of the human resources departments of the MNB, CNB, and NBKR. Data files available on request.

Postcommunist central bankers strongly disagreed with the heterodox view that "Central banks should be allowed to loan money to the government."[69] Perhaps more surprisingly, they disagreed with (Hungarians and Czechs) or regarded neutrally (Kyrgyz) the statement that "Central banks should promote employment." Given high unemployment rates in many postcommunist states and the dual formal mandate of the respected US Federal Reserve, central bankers might plausibly have viewed this statement more positively. However, as discussed earlier, the transnational community's export model rejected this belief—and thus, so did most of the respondents. Across the range of surveyed beliefs, postcommunist central bankers consistently echoed the export model. These beliefs directly contradicted previous practice in command-era central banks and did not vary significantly by age or tenure at the central bank, indicating that in many cases command-era central bankers had come to share the transnational community's views on central banking best practice. Indeed, it is important to point out that although new hires were typically more flexible, many long-time central bank staff successfully made the transition from command-era central banking, not just psychologically but technically as well. As one young Czech central banker observed, "Some people can change. For example, we used to work with SPSS, and then we switched to EViews [econometric modeling software commonly used in central banks]. Many people had trouble switching over, but my predecessor, seventy-two years old, had no problem with this. He read the manual, and soon he was teaching us how to do it. It depends on the person. Some are lazy, while lots of old people are skilled and professional. Those who couldn't adapt were told to leave."[70]

The mission statements, annual reports, and public pronouncements of postcommunist central banks reflected these shared beliefs. For example, the Bank of Russia's two-volume textbook on its operations proclaimed independence and price stability as the twin pillars of effective central banking.[71] Postcommunist central bank websites contained prominent references to these principles, and central bank governors regularly defended independence and price stability in public statements both at home and abroad. Further reflecting integration

---

69. In a smaller canvassing of deputy central bank governors in the Czech Republic, Hungary, Poland, and Slovakia, Beblavy (2003) similarly found that the post-communist respondents agreed with central bankers in industrial countries on the relative importance of independent monetary goal-setting and rate-setting, price stability, and prohibitions on loans to the government.

70. Author's interview with a central banker in the Real Economy Division of the Czech National Bank, Prague, Czech Republic, May 2000.

71. Golikova and Khokhlenikova 2000.

with the international community, within a decade of the Soviet collapse central banks in all but four authoritarian postcommunist states had developed extensive English-language websites.[72]

The surveyed central bankers shared similar views about which central banks were most worthy of emulation as well. Of 135 central bankers who answered the open-ended question, "Which central bank do you consider to be the best in the world?" 48 percent said the US Federal Reserve, 26 percent said the Bundesbank, and 16 percent said the Bank of England. My interviews revealed the same pattern—postcommunist central bankers looked primarily to these three banks as models. As one Kyrgyz central banker said, "We know more about Western central banks than about central banks in the [former Soviet Union]."[73]

Postcommunist central banks also experienced significant, convergent change in technical practices. The survey asked central bankers to evaluate how their own bank measured up to "international standards" in nine key areas.[74] As table 4.5 demonstrates, Hungarian and Czech central bankers rated themselves as "very close" to meeting international standards in every area except banking supervision. Kyrgyz central bankers, who started much further behind, rated their bank as having made "a lot of progress" toward international standards in every area except banking supervision. Other research from the late 1990s came to similar conclusions. Krzak and Schubert observed of the Czech Republic, Hungary, Slovakia, Slovenia, and Poland that "all important elements of modern monetary policy are in place,"[75] while Healey and Wisniewski demonstrated extensive technical convergence across five East European central banks.[76] In another major study, the IMF measured post-Soviet central bank development

72. In 2002 only Azerbaijan, Tajikistan, Turkmenistan, and Uzbekistan did not yet have English-language versions of their websites, and by 2008 only Uzbekistan (with a site in Uzbek and Russian) and Turkmenistan (with no website at all) did not. By August 2014 even Uzbekistan (www.cbu.uz/eng) and Turkmenistan (www.cbt.tm/en/) had English-language websites, although clicking the "About Bank" button at the top of the Turkmen site led to a page that said simply "No Information."

73. Author's interview with a senior official in the Foreign Exchange Department of the National Bank of the Kyrgyz Republic, Bishkek, Kyrgyzstan, May 2001.

74. These are the same nine areas that the IMF and cooperating central banks targeted for technical assistance in the Matrix. As a side note, even though the survey did not define "international standards" in the nine areas, over a decade of interaction with the transnational central banking community meant that the respondents did not hesitate to measure their banks against such standards. The export model had become common knowledge.

75. Krzak and Schubert 1997.

76. Healey and Wisniewski 1999.

TABLE 4.5   Comparative central bank development, 2000–2001

	HUNGARY		CZECH REPUBLIC		KYRGYZSTAN	
	MODE	MEDIAN	MODE	MEDIAN	MODE	MEDIAN
Accounting systems and internal audit	4	4	3	4	3	3
Banking supervision and regulation	3	3	4	3.5	2	2.5
Foreign exchange operations	4	4	4	4	3	3
Monetary policy operations	4	4	4	4	3	3
Monetary analysis and research	4	4	4	4	3	3
Organization and management structure	4	4	4	4	3	3
Payment, clearing, and settlement	4	4	4	4	2	3
Public debt and securities management	4	4	4	4	3	3
Central banking legislation	4	4	4	4	3	3

The survey asked central bankers:

In your opinion, how does your central bank rank in the following areas?

Scale:

5 Completely meets or exceeds international standards

4 Comes very close to meeting international standards

3 Has made a lot of progress in moving towards international standards

2 Has made some progress in moving towards international standards

1 Has made no progress in moving towards international standards

Notes: Magyar Nemzeti Bank, N = 86, March 2000; Czech National Bank, N = 33, June 2000; National Bank of the Kyrgyz Republic, N = 66, May 2001.

as of mid-1997 (table 4.6). The IMF ranked the central banks overall and in seven functional areas: central bank legislation, monetary operations and debt management, foreign exchange operations, banking supervision, bank restructuring, payment systems, and central bank accounting and audit. Eight of the nine non-authoritarian states received the top overall ranking of three, signifying "substantial progress," while the other—Ukraine—received a two (signifying "moderate progress").[77] By contrast, of the six authoritarian states only Kazakhstan's central bank received a top ranking, not surprising as it was the only one to which the transnational central banking community enjoyed sustained and open access.

My interviews, survey data, and studies by other researchers uniformly indicated that the transnational central banking community's assistance qualitatively increased the speed and scope of postcommunist central bank transformation. In interview after interview, postcommunist central bankers told me that technical assistance and training programs had been vital to their work and that they developed lasting contacts with other central bankers through these experiences. For example, a Bulgarian central banker described his course at the IMF Institute as a "revelation," and explained that this training had enabled the Bulgarian

---

77. Knight et al. 1999.

TABLE 4.6 IMF-ranked progress on central bank reform in the former Soviet Union as of 1997

	CENTRAL BANK LEGISLATION	MONETARY OPERATIONS AND DEBT MANAGEMENT	FOREIGN EXCHANGE OPERATIONS	BANKING SUPERVISION	BANK RESTRUCTURING	PAYMENTS AND AUDIT SYSTEM	CENTRAL BANK ACCOUNTING	OVERALL RANKING
Armenia	III	II	III	III	III	II	III	III
Estonia	III	*	III	III	III	III	III	III
Georgia	III	II	III	III	III	II	III	III
Kyrgyz Republic	III	III	III	III	III	III	III	III
Latvia	II	III	III	III	II	III	III	III
Lithuania	III	*	III	III	III	III	III	III
Moldova	III	II	III	III	II	II	III	III
Russia	II	III	III	II	III	III	II	III
Ukraine	I	II	III	II	II	II	II	II
Authoritarian states								
Azerbaijan	II	I	II	II	II	II	III	II
Belarus	I	I	I	I	I	III	III	I
Kazakhstan	II	III	III	III	III	III	III	III
Tajikistan	II	I	I	I	I	I	I	I
Turkmenistan	II	I	I	II	I	II	II	I
Uzbekistan	II	II	I	II	II	II	II	II

Source: Adapted from Knight et al. 1999.

Rankings key: (I) = Limited Progress, (II) = Moderate Progress, (III) = Substantial Progress

* Currency board

National Bank to manage its foreign exchange reserves.[78] Statements by post-Soviet central bankers at the Joint Meetings on Central Banking Technical Assistance in St. Petersburg, Russia, in April 1994 all stressed the importance that technical assistance had already played at that early date in transforming their institutions. In his closing remarks, the Bank of Russia's Aleksandr Khandruev observed that technical assistance had:

> enabled the central banks of the recipient countries to master the art of managing the money supply, exchange rate policy, and the banking system. Technical assistance taught them to speak the language of a market-oriented economy and it gave them the sense of belonging to the international community of central banks . . . both the donors and the recipients regarded technical assistance as highly important.[79]

In terms of training, a systematic JVI assessment of its signature Applied Economic Policy program from 1993 through 2003 revealed that all forty central bankers surveyed considered the AEP to have been "important" or "very important" to their professional careers.[80] Eighty-six percent agreed that the course taught them "analytical skills that could be used to find solutions to economic problems facing [their] country" and 95 percent said that they had disseminated what they had learned to others in their central banks. My own survey results reflected this perceived value as well (table 4.7). I asked respondents to rank the usefulness of community-sponsored courses taken at home and abroad, answering the question "On a scale of 1 (not useful at all) to 5 (extremely useful), how useful were these courses to your work?" The first category included courses arranged and taught by the staff of international financial institutions and national central banks but conducted at the postcommunist central bank, usually at the bank's own training center. The second category included courses taken at the IMF Institute, the Joint Vienna Institute, and national central bank training centers such as the CCBS. Central bankers in Hungary, the Czech Republic, and Kyrgyzstan all gave the courses top rankings of four and five, and regarded courses taken abroad as having been especially valuable.[81] Moreover, in addition to the direct effects of training and technical assistance, the community regularly

---

78. Author's interview with a senior analyst in the Treasury Directorate of the Bulgarian National Bank, Vienna, Austria, May 2000.

79. Zulu et al. 1994.

80. Albegova 2006. The assessment surveyed participants and their employers from the first eleven AEP programs, including forty central bankers.

81. Postcommunist central bankers felt that courses taken abroad were typically taught at a higher level than those in their home countries, making the foreign courses more useful for the better-prepared central bankers from the relatively advanced countries.

TABLE 4.7   Perceived value of training programs, 2000–2001

	FOREIGN-TAUGHT IN-HOUSE		COURSES TAKEN ABROAD	
	MODE	MEDIAN	MODE	MEDIAN
Hungary	4	4	5	4
Czech Republic	4	4	5	4.5
Kyrgyzstan	4	4	5	5

The survey asked central bankers:

If you have participated in one or more courses [offered by the transnational central banking community], on a scale of 1 (not useful at all) to 5 (extremely useful), how useful were these courses to your work?

Notes: Magyar Nemzeti Bank, N = 86, March 2000; Czech National Bank, N = 33, June 2000; National Bank of the Kyrgyz Republic, N = 66, May 2001.

pressured and lobbied postcommunist governments on behalf of their central banks, and the central banks used community recommendations to justify their policies and development activities. As will be demonstrated in greater detail in the following two chapters, without the transnational central banking community, postcommunist central bank transformation would not have been nearly so rapid or comprehensive.

Accounting for Difference

Nevertheless, within the overall pattern of remarkable change certain kinds of central bank departments and certain central banks adopted the Western model more quickly and completely than others. In terms of competencies, transformation occurred most easily in areas that the transnational community most valued and agreed on, and where fewer and higher-status central bankers needed training. The more varied the donors and messages involved, and the more numerous and lower-status the target postcommunist central bankers, the more difficult the transformation. Monetary policy, for example, usually moved toward international standards relatively quickly. Departments focusing on monetary policy (and research, a closely related area) were the most prestigious in central banks, staffed by a small number of highly trained professionals. These central bankers studied economic indicators, devised economic models, and developed and worked with the bank's tools of monetary policy. The transnational central banking community gave top priority to assistance in this area, and IMF resident advisors, IMF missions, bilateral central bank technical assistance programs, and high-level training programs focused heavily on it. Postcommunist central bankers in monetary policy and research departments were the most likely to speak English, typically received the highest salaries among regular central banking staff, and were the most likely to have taken part in educational programs abroad. As table 4.2 demonstrated, over one-third of all foreign training courses taken by Hungarian and Kyrgyz central bankers from 1996 through 1999 directly involved monetary policy. In another example, one Czech central banker estimated that 80 percent of the bank's research division had spent at least six months studying abroad, typically in Britain or the United States.[82]

The transnational central banking community also gave focused and consistent advice in this area. Economic modeling within central banks had become a well-developed, highly technocratic skill. Central bankers agreed on the desirability of using indirect monetary policy tools, especially open-market operations, to fulfill monetary policy goals. They agreed that price stability (or currency stability in exchange-rate targeting systems) should be the primary policy goal. They agreed that exchange-rate targeting was the best interim strategy for countries just embarking on transition, while more "advanced" countries with better monetary policy tools should adopt inflation targeting.[83] As Stanley Fischer wrote, "During the 1990s, the IMF frequently recommended the adoption of inflation targeting . . . this required a great deal of preparation, including the development of inflation forecasting models in the central bank, and changes in the legal framework."[84] Assistance focused tightly on developing standard monetary policy tools and models, and training the best postcommunist central bankers how to use them. By 2009 nine postcommunist central banks had become formal inflation targeters, and as of 2015 another five had publicly announced informal inflation targets (table 4.8). Five others had joined the euro zone, thus importing the ECB's informal 2 percent target. Even the few postcommunist central banks still using other regimes typically acknowledged the desirability of moving to inflation targeting or euro adoption. Kyrgyz central bankers expressed such eagerness to adopt formal inflation targeting that the IMF had to tell them to wait, that the preconditions to make it work were not yet in place.[85] Among the inflation targeters, those with targets above 4 percent usually declared their intention to move progressively toward lower targets in future.

---

82. Author's interview with a senior official in the Research Unit of the Czech National Bank, Prague, Czech Republic, May 2000.

83. Wagner 1998. Alternately, for small countries planning to join the EU, the central banking community endorsed fixed exchange rates as interim options.

84. Fischer 2004. See also Schaechter et al. 2000.

85. IMF Country Report No. 05/47, February 2005. Kyrgyz Republic: 2004 Article IV Consultation and Request to Extend the PRGF Arrangement—Staff Report; Staff Supplement; Public Information Notice and Press Release on the Executive Board Discussion; and Statement by the Executive Director for the Kyrgyz Republic.

TABLE 4.8 Monetary policy regimes in postcommunist states, 2015

INDEPENDENT INFLATION TARGETERS			EURO ZONE		OTHER	
Formal	*Year*	*2015 Target*	*Members*	*Year*	*Exchange rate targeters*	*Year*
Czech Republic	1998	2% +/-1%	Slovenia	2007	Croatia	Euro, 2002
Poland	1998	2.5% +/-1%	Slovakia	2009	Macedonia	Euro, 2002
Hungary	2001	3% +/-1%	Estonia	2011	Kazakhstan	Crawling peg to USD; planned move to inflation targeting
Slovakia	2005	Euro in 2009	Latvia	2014		
Romania	2005	2.5% +/-1%	Lithuania	2015	*Monetary aggregate targeters*	*Year*
Serbia	2006	4% +/-1.5%	*Unilateral adoption*		Kyrgyzstan	
Armenia	2006	4% +/-1.5%	Kosovo	2002	Tajikistan	2002
Albania	2009	3% +/-1%	Montenegro	2002	Uzbekistan	2002
Georgia	2009	5%	*Euro currency board*		*Fixed exchange rate*	*Year*
			Bosnia and Herzegovina	2002	Turkmenistan	Fix to USD since 2009
Informal, target announced	*Year*	*2015 Target*	Bulgaria	2002		
Azerbaijan	2002	5-6%				
Belarus	2002	18% +/-2%				
Moldova		5% +/-1.5%				
Russia		4.5% +/-1.5%				
Ukraine		9%				

Sources: 2015 inflation targets at www.centralbanknews.info/p/inflation-targets.html; IMF Policy Paper, "Conditionality in Evolving Monetary Policy Regimes," March 5, 2013; various central bank websites.

Banking supervision, by contrast, proved the most difficult area to transform. The surveyed Czech, Hungarian, and Kyrgyz central bankers' agreement that their countries' banking supervision capabilities remained farthest from international standards reflected a region-wide phenomenon, and contradicted the IMF's earlier, overly rosy assessment of banking supervision progress in the former Soviet Union (see table 4.6). The European Bank for Reconstruction and Development rankings confirmed the correspondingly slow and uneven progress in banking sector reform, with only one postcommunist central bank—Hungary—earning a score of four (representing "significant progress" toward BIS standards) by 2000; only five countries had reached this mark by the time the global financial crisis hit in 2008.[86]

Why? First, remember that community members did not agree on whether or not central banks should be involved in supervision at all, much less on how to do it. Banking supervision systems varied widely in structure and practice across countries.[87] Central banks could be either entirely, partially, or not at all responsible for supervision. Supervisory agencies might focus strictly on banking, or have jurisdiction over securities and other financial markets as well (consolidated supervision). Supervisory agencies might be more or less independent from the government. Banking supervision and supervisors within central banks enjoyed a relatively lower status within the transnational community, and were in turn less tightly identified with it than central bankers specializing in other operational realms. No consensus existed on best practice banking regulations, restrictions, or supervisory powers when the postcommunist transition began, with the notable exception of the Basel I capital adequacy standards.[88] This began to change only with the September 1997 publication of the Basel Committee's Core Principles for Banking Supervision and the 1997 Asian financial crisis, both of which increased the community's interest in financial stability issues. As one outside consultant argued, "when USAID was getting involved in [banking supervision assistance] in 1993–94, it wasn't so 'sexy'. Nobody else really cared. Not even the Fund. You know when they got interested? When Indonesia and Korea crashed."[89] The crisis

---

86. See the EBRD Transition Report 2008. The additional countries earning a four included Croatia, Latvia, and Estonia, plus implicitly the Czech Republic, which by 2008 was no longer included in the EBRD transition rankings.

87. For a comprehensive study of banking supervision practices, see Barth et al. 2006.

88. The BIS Basel Committee on Banking Supervision promulgated the Basel capital adequacy standards (Basel I) in 1988. The core element set the minimum level of risk-weighted capital that banks should hold at a capital-assets ratio of eight percent. The Committee later significantly updated and expanded these standards with the more controversial Basel II (2004) and Basel III (2010–11) agreements.

89. Author's interview with a USAID consultant, Reston, Virginia, November 2001.

led the G7 central bank governors and finance ministers to create the Financial Stability Forum in April 1999, and the IMF and World Bank to jointly introduce the Financial Sector Assessment Program in May 1999.[90]

As a result, unlike in other central bank competencies, donor attention to banking supervision was inconsistent and dispersed as well. Although the transnational central banking community provided advice on banking supervision, the World Bank, USAID, the EU's PHARE/TACIS, various national supervisory agencies, and private-sector financial companies became even more heavily involved. Moreover, organizations such as USAID and the PHARE/TACIS program usually contracted out banking supervision projects to professional consulting agencies, which in turn sometimes subcontracted aspects of the projects to others. This diversity in donors contributed to a diversity in results. In particular, although many postcommunist banking supervisors had good experiences with advisors from the for-profit consulting agencies, others felt that the assistance was too often superficial or inappropriate, especially in the early years. At times postcommunist central bankers also questioned consultants' motives, finding the contractual, commercial relationships not as collegial or productive as the assistance they received directly from other central banks.

On the postcommunist side, banking supervisors were more numerous and typically had a lower professional status within the central bank than those in other operational departments. In some countries supervisors worked either primarily in regional branch offices of the central bank or in separate supervisory agencies lacking independence. Moreover, practically every postcommunist state experienced a banking crisis in the 1990s due to the legacy of bad loans from state-owned and formerly state-owned commercial banks, initially lax licensing and regulatory policies, and the postcommunist economic recession. Banking supervision thus became politically charged, as disciplining or shutting down problem banks invariably stepped on influential toes. Banking supervisors, already on the margins of the central banking community, often became cynical about their jobs or quit them entirely to work for the commercial banks they

---

90. The Financial Stability Forum "brings together on a regular basis national authorities responsible for financial stability in significant international financial centers, international financial institutions, sector-specific international groupings of regulators and supervisors, and committees of central bank experts. The FSF seeks to co-ordinate the efforts of these various bodies in order to promote international financial stability, improve the functioning of markets, and reduce systemic risk" (www.fsforum.org/home, as accessed in 2006). The FSAP "seeks to identify the strengths and vulnerabilities of a country's financial system; to determine how key sources of risk are being managed; to ascertain the sector's developmental and technical assistance needs; and to help prioritize policy responses" (www.imf.org/external/np/fsap/fsap.asp). In addition, the crisis contributed to the International Organization of Securities Commissions' (IOSCO) decision to adopt the Objectives and Principles of Securities Regulation (IOSCO Principles) in 1998.

had once supervised. Gerard Caprio Jr.'s 1998–99 survey on banking supervision revealed that nine of seventeen postcommunist central banks in nonauthoritarian countries reported that ex-supervisors were "frequently" employed by the banking industry, while only four reported that this happened "rarely" or "never" (in Macedonia, the Czech Republic, Latvia, and Poland).[91] Banking supervisors in the seventeen states had an average tenure of less than five years. The combination of inconsistent, underemphasized, and poorly coordinated assistance and more complex recipient issues meant that banking supervision, though improved across the postcommunist world, did not transform as uniformly or quickly as other aspects of central banking.

Variation by Central Bank

Postcommunist central banks had different starting conditions and abilities to absorb assistance. Even though central banks in all of the nonauthoritarian postcommunist states (and some authoritarian ones) made significant progress toward meeting international standards, the central banks that began the transition with head starts generally stayed ahead. Starting points ranged from the Magyar Nemzeti Bank's long quasi-market experience to the Central Asian and Caucasian central banks' creation from near-scratch and in daunting economic environments. The most challenged central banks had to exert far greater effort in order to reach international standards. The consistency and character of central bank leadership; staff background, numbers, and turnover; and in later years the clarifying carrot of EU membership mattered as well.

Established central bankers interviewed at the turn of the millennium typically singled out the Hungarian, Polish, Czech, and Slovenian central banks as especially advanced; regarded the Russian central bank as capable but hampered by politics and culture; and felt that the central banks in places like Moldova, Kyrgyzstan, and Georgia were catching up quickly but had more difficulty in meeting international standards. Given that the central banks with the most difficult starting points often also had fewer external "carrots" to reach for and greater leadership and staffing issues, the extent of the changes that did take place is doubly surprising. The World Bank's representative in Kyrgyzstan at the time argued that the National Bank of the Kyrgyz Republic deserved more credit for its transformation than the Magyar Nemzeti Bank, because given their respective starting points the NBKR had experienced a more fundamental transformation.[92]

---

91. Barth et al. 2006. The raw data were included on a CD sold with the book.
92. Author's interview with a senior official of the World Bank Resident Mission in Kyrgyzstan, Bishkek, Kyrgyzstan, June 2001.

The more challenging a central bank's starting position, the more difficulties that central bank typically faced with staff quality and turnover. Many Central and East European states had some central bank staff with previous exposure to international ideas and practices. These central banks, closer to Western Europe and with more Western-oriented educational systems, also had a relatively easier time hiring and training English speakers. Central European University (CEU), the new English-language social sciences graduate university in Budapest founded by George Soros and dedicated to bringing Western economic, political science, and sociological expertise to the postcommunist world, accelerated regional progress as well.[93] Differences in language abilities translated into differences in central bank development capabilities. While the JVI and, at times, other training centers offered certain courses in simultaneous Russian translation, the most advanced courses were offered only in English and the central banking community's key reference publications were in English. Without a good command of English, a postcommunist central banker could not be fully integrated into the transnational community.

Countries that had to create central banks from command-era regional branches or from scratch also needed to hire most of their staff in a matter of months, in contrast to the heritage central banks that could both retrain experienced staff and hire anew. On the one hand, this provided an opportunity to bring in young, open-minded, energetic staff and start fresh. But the more hiring necessary, the less selective the central banks could be. Central banks hired waves of graduates right out of university, in some cases even those without economics and/or English-language backgrounds. Under such circumstances postcommunist central banks relied even more heavily on international training courses to provide new hires with the basic tools necessary for their jobs. Central banks varied in size as well, with the larger central banks and those with branch offices facing more complicated recruitment, training, and retention issues (table 4.9). The Bank of Russia, with an immense staff spread across more than sixty far-flung branch offices, faced a uniquely difficult problem in this regard.

In addition, while all postcommunist central banks initially faced staff retention problems, central bankers in the poorer states (typically the former Soviet ones), where government positions paid relatively badly, had the greatest incentives to seek other positions after their training. One interviewee noted that JVI-trained central bankers found their skills in demand and would often move into

---

93. By the CEU's own count, thirty-two of its graduates were working in postcommunist central banks by 2014. The only post-Soviet countries well represented were Georgia and Azerbaijan (in fact, the governor of the Central Bank of the Republic of Azerbaijan was a CEU graduate).

TABLE 4.9   Central bank staff numbers (period averages)

	1991–1995	1996–2000	2001–2005
Albania	251	302	317
Armenia		334	413
Azerbaijan		729	417
Belarus	434	668	773
Bosnia and Herzegovina		171	234
Bulgaria	650	1,170	1,085
Croatia		568	584
Czech Republic*	1,547	1,548	1,461
Estonia	253	289	259
Georgia	326	363	506
Georgia*			590
Hungary*	2,521	1,526	1,104
Kazakhstan	718	854	861
Kyrgyzstan	360	414	416
Latvia	440	695	722
Lithuania	715	874	871
Macedonia		239	335
Moldova	359	495	495
Montenegro			400
Poland			1,636
Poland*		6,274	
Romania*		3,879	2,618
Russia		1,706	
Russia*		65,219	81,567
Serbia		1,000	1,156
Slovakia*	829	1,302	1,314
Slovenia	376	392	386
Tajikistan		464	536
Turkmenistan		1,076	639
Ukraine		964	999
Uzbekistan*	9,239	10,600	2,321

Sources: Data from Pringle 1994 and 2006 and Valach 2004. Staff numbers supplied by the central banks, often with years missing.

*Includes branches

international organizations or the private sector, especially in the early years.[94] An NBKR governor observed that Kyrgyzstan suffered more broadly from a psychology of "temporary people"—the best-educated and trained people often left the country.[95] In sum, the less well-paid the central bankers in comparison to the private and international sectors, the more the transnational community ended up training central bankers who then left their central banks. Turnover

---

94. Author's interview with a senior official in the Foreign Research Division of the Österreichische Nationalbank, Vienna, Austria, April 2000.

95. Author's interview with Ulan Sarbanov, governor of the National Bank of the Kyrgyz Republic, Bishkek, Kyrgyzstan, June 2001.

contributed to the language problem as well. Postcommunist central banks went to great efforts to train their staffs in English and economics. But central banks in poorer countries lost more of those whom they trained and had more difficulty finding new hires with high-level economics and English-language capabilities.

Central bank leadership could further help or hinder transformation. Successful transformation along international lines required some stability and commitment at the top. Postcommunist states with rare exceptions replaced their command-era central bank governors within a year of communism's collapse.[96] Although the first appointees worked out well in many cases, in others corruption scandals and crises led to leadership instability throughout the 1990s.[97] Without stable, consistent leadership, would-be donors had more difficulty initiating and maintaining technical assistance programs. Central bank leadership, especially the governor, set the tone for the rest of the bank. The governor's encouragement (or at least tacit consent), made it far easier to bring outside ideas and practices systematically on board. For example, when György Surányi again became head of the Magyar Nemzeti Bank in 1995, he reorganized, modernized, and downsized the bank; raised salaries; and brought top young people into the research divisions. This in turn raised the prestige and capabilities of the bank. Alternately, disengaged, politicized, patronage-based central bank leadership set the opposite tone. Especially in the early years, many postcommunist central bank governors also had to be persuaded of the value of the transnational central banking community's principles and practices. Epstein, for example, describes how Polish governor Hanna Gronkiewicz-Waltz's initially unorthodox views on monetary policy changed under international influences.[98] But when central bank governors worked as partners with the transnational central banking community, their staffs followed along.

The Power of Community

After the collapse of communism, the transnational central banking community engaged in an extensive, targeted effort to transform postcommunist central banks according to the community's flexible export model. Each community

---

96. One exception, Armenia's Isaak Isaakian, governed the central bank from 1986 through 1994. In a more complicated case, Soviet central bank head Viktor Gerashchenko (1988–91) also became the second (1992–94) and fifth (1998–2002) governor of the Bank of Russia.

97. As discussed in chapter 2, the authoritarian states represent special cases in this regard. Belarus, rump Yugoslavia (Serbia), and later Turkmenistan regularly fired governors on political grounds. In one notorious case, Belarussian central bank governor Tamara Vinnikova went missing under house arrest in 1997 after accusing the Belarussian leadership of massive misappropriation of funds. She managed to flee the country in 1999.

98. Epstein 2008.

member had a slightly different focus. The BIS served as a collegial forum and clearinghouse. The IMF organized technical assistance and trained central bankers, often in the broader context of loans and conditionality. The ECB integrated new and aspiring EU members into the European financial community. The JVI, CCBS, and other centers trained thousands of postcommunist central bankers to think, speak, and work in the transnational community's languages and practices. National central banks shared their expertise through tailored programs and assistance missions. The FSVC provided rapid-response teams for specific technical tasks. IMF and ECB assistance was more supply-driven and came with strings attached, while bilateral aid from the national central banks and the FSVC was primarily demand-driven and offered without broader obligations. Nevertheless, these diverse members of the transnational central banking community worked together to promote a basic shared model of what postcommunist central banks could and should become.

Europeans played the dominant role in organizing the transformation campaign and promoting the model. This contrasts with conventional wisdom that saw the United States as the primary promoter and enforcer of neoliberal economic reforms in the postcommunist world. It also complements Abdelal's surprising finding that Europeans rather than Americans drove the international movement for capital account liberalization in the 1990s.[99] Although US central bankers and institutions regularly provided assistance to postcommunist central banks, they did not do so on the same scale as the Europeans. Even the IMF, though influenced by its major shareholder, was governed and staffed primarily by non-Americans.[100]

The transnational central banking community's organizational skills and resources enabled it to provide more focused, concentrated, and sustained assistance than occurred in other postcommunist realms. No permanent, intensive training institutes comparable to the CCBS or JVI existed for postcommunist judges, party members, or civil society leaders. No organized transnational community promoted a single, unchallenged vision for agricultural reform, social welfare restructuring, or military reorganization. The transnational central banking community, by contrast, quietly organized the central banking equivalent of a Marshall Plan.

This process not only strengthened the postcommunist central banks, but the transnational community as well. This joint effort led to increased community

---

99. Abdelal 2007.

100. Moreover, in the most notable cases where the US government influenced the IMF's postcommunist lending policies, it asked the IMF to ease, not tighten, lending conditionality in Russia and Ukraine. Stone 2002.

membership and cooperation, the creation of new community-controlled educational institutions, and an expansion of the community's activities. On a deeper level, the experience further unified the transnational community by forcing established central bankers to explicitly define, explain, and refine their guiding principles and practices in order to teach them to postcommunist central bankers. The teaching and learning process reinforced these beliefs within the existing community and expanded their influence beyond the network's previous boundaries. In ways that its members could not have anticipated, the postcommunist transformation further empowered the transnational central banking community.

Four developments in particular stand out. First, the postcommunist transformation campaign forced central bankers to codify their ideas, standards, and practices into an exportable model. Before they could pass on their knowledge to others, they had to explicitly express and justify their mostly implicit ways of thinking and working. What did it mean to be a central banker? Why and how do we do what we do? By persuading postcommunist governments and central banks to think and behave in certain ways, they reinforced these concepts among themselves. By working together on assistance projects, they also learned more about the organization and practices of other central banks. The need to codify best practices for postcommunist central bankers contributed to the development of improved payment systems standards, banking supervision standards, and benchmarks to evaluate central and commercial banking practices.

Second, assisting postcommunist states expanded the already strong informal ties and sense of mission among established central bankers. Those West European central bankers who created the euro zone and engaged with the postcommunist world at the same time had especially intense experiences. As a European central banker observed, once central bankers had carried out their first assistance missions, they always wanted to continue: "they get socialized, excited, convinced that they're having a positive effect."[101] Indeed, central bankers participating in assistance efforts often found the work extraordinarily meaningful. In interview after interview, they told me that this work was, in the words of one former US Federal Reserve official, "the most satisfying professional experience of my life."[102] He further noted that, "The motives of the people that were providing the assistance weren't based on money. They were helping because they just wanted to help. . . . it was altruism and it was a sense of public service . . . they

---

101. Author's interview with a senior official in the Österreichische Nationalbank, Vienna, Austria, May 2006.

102. Interview with a former official of the Federal Reserve Bank of New York, New York City, December 2001.

view it as an honor to be selected and an honor to engage in this kind of public service." Another central banker observed that he came out of the experience with a much greater understanding of his own country's central bank and financial system. As one long-time advisor succinctly put it, "You get much more than you give, it sounds trite, but it's the way it is."

Third, over this period the transnational central banking community expanded its training, technical assistance, and cooperation infrastructure. The postcommunist transformation birthed new institutions such as the CCBS, JVI, and FSVC. It led to the creation of large new departments within central banks like the ECB, the Bundesbank, the Banque de France, and the Österreichische Nationalbank. It led to increased institutionalization of technical assistance provision in the IMF and the BIS. Central bank technical cooperation became far more organized, professionalized, and strategic because of the postcommunist challenge. Such infrastructure developments typically prove persistent, as the nullification of the JVI's sunset clause shows. The initially ad hoc transformation campaign became institutionalized. Once the postcommunist mission had advanced successfully, this cooperation sparked a collective desire and ability to achieve a truly global reach. Although targeted assistance to postcommunist states decreased gradually after the 1990s as these central banks became more capable, the community's overall assistance programs actually grew. The IMF, CCBS, Bundesbank, JVI, and FSVC—as well as many other national central banks not discussed here in detail—all provided substantially more training and technical assistance over the years as the transnational central banking community used the infrastructure it had developed for the postcommunist world to engage central bankers in Africa, Asia, Latin America, and the Middle East. As a result, the community's influence spread more deeply among central bankers worldwide.

The Paradox of Internalization

Yet transformation is only the middle of the transplantation process, not the end. A transplant must put down solid roots in its new environment, stretching beyond its institutional base, in order to survive and thrive. One might have expected that as postcommunist central banks grew more capable and internationally legitimate, their domestic support bases would expand as well. In exceptional cases such as Estonia, this is exactly what happened.[103] But politicians more

---

103. In tiny Estonia, the Eesti Pank (Bank of Estonia) and its currency board remained a key symbol of sovereignty, reflecting Estonia's fervent pro-EU (and anti-Russian) political culture. Greskovits 2009.

often became skeptical of the central bankers' work precisely as the central bankers themselves became increasingly socialized into the transnational community. The following chapters take a closer look at central bank transformation and internalization in Hungary, the Czech Republic, Slovakia, Russia, and Kyrgyzstan. As these explorations reveal, the very speed and scope of central bank transformation often paradoxically undermined the internalization process.

Asynchronous transformation—faster transformation in central banks than in other institutions—meant that central bankers' tools and techniques were not as effective in transitional economic environments as in established market economies. Postcommunist central bankers thus found themselves in a difficult position. On the one hand, they were legally independent and responsible for their countries' currencies. On the other, even monetary sources of inflation were often beyond their control. This made it difficult for postcommunist central bankers to create and maintain stability in their domestic financial systems. Most postcommunist countries experienced currency and/or banking crises in the 1990s, often despite the best efforts of their central banks. Such crises undermined the central banks' efforts to build domestic support and legitimacy. Postcommunist politicians, meanwhile, learned and grew more confident as the transition progressed. Financial instability, fed by asynchronous transformation, could teach politicians that independent central banks were ineffective. Conservative monetary policies and stricter financial regulation could teach them that independent central banks would challenge their fiscal policies and crack down on their political supporters. Political experience could teach them that independent central banks made ideal public scapegoats for economic problems.

Politicians were especially likely to learn such negative lessons because postcommunist governments, publics, and commercial banks had expressed little intrinsic demand for what independent central banks had to offer. The governments had created independent central banks primarily in response to external influences. However, independent central banks can operate sustainably and successfully over the long term only with a domestic societal commitment to low inflation and a belief in the central bank's technocratic expertise in delivering it.[104] Ten years after the transformation began, long-time Czech National Bank governor Josef Tošovský neatly summed up the central banks' predicament:

> In the advanced market economies, central bank independence has
> grown as the political authorities and the public have gradually become

---

104. One study of nine EU countries found that inflation levels were more closely related to public opinion about inflation than to the degree of central bank independence (Hayo 1998). Put a different way, independent central banks may only be viable "as long as the public's 'perceived consensus' about economic policies and macroeconomic outcomes is real" (Freeman 2002). For an in-depth examination, see Tognato (2012) on stability cultures and independent central banks in Europe.

aware of the advantages for the whole economy of low inflation and stable growth. . . . In general, transition economies formally embraced most of the European legal framework's elements defining the position of central banks. But the principle of central bank independence embodied in that framework has not yet been fully accepted by the public and especially by politicians. When macroeconomic imbalances accumulated, central banks often had the unpopular task of announcing the bad news. If in addition a central bank responded with an appropriate tightening of monetary policy, it fell into even greater disfavor, being blamed for the slowing of growth, increasing unemployment, and social unrest. The reaction of governments or representative bodies was to try to get them under control. This political pressure has been a fact of life for the central banks of most countries in our region. I see this as a symptom of the immaturity of the transition economies . . .[105]

My Hungarian, Czech, and Kyrgyz surveys reflected this belief (table 4.10). Most central bankers felt at best lukewarm about the knowledge of and support for their work among politicians, commercial bankers, and publics. Moreover, while Hungarian central bankers agreed that commercial bankers understood their work, this did not translate into support. At the far end, Kyrgyz central bankers actively disagreed with the statement "commercial bankers support the work of my central bank."

Therefore, it is not surprising that the central banks in all of my case-study countries—and most others as well—subsequently faced serious political attacks. Politicians and publics in numerous postcommunist countries blamed central bank policies for currency devaluations. Only the four central banks running currency boards managed to escape sustained political criticism over monetary policy, precisely because they lacked monetary policy discretion. Likewise, central bankers were often criticized both for wanting to close problem banks (before banking crises), and for not having closed problem banks fast enough (after banking crises). More prosaically, as time went on politicians became more confident about challenging central bank policies when they conflicted with government spending priorities. These challenges often went far beyond simple criticism, becoming sustained, public efforts to curtail central bank independence both legally and in practice.

Central bankers, by now socialized into the transnational community and believing in their mission and their independence, fought back. Not only did

105. Josef Tošovský, Governor of the Czech National Bank, "Ten Years On: Some Lessons from the Transition," Per Jacobsson Lecture, September 2000, Prague. Available from the CNB website at www.cnb.cz/en/public/media_service/conferences/speeches/download/mmf_per_jacobsson.pdf.

TABLE 4.10 Domestic support for central banks, 2000–2001

	HUNGARY		CZECH REPUBLIC		KYRGYZSTAN	
	MODE	MEDIAN	MODE	MEDIAN	MODE	MEDIAN
The executive supports the work of my central bank	3	3	3	3	3	3
The executive understands the work of my central bank	3	3	3	3	3	3
Commercial bankers support the work of my central bank	3	3	3	3	2	2
Commercial bankers understand the work of my central bank	4	4	3	3.5	3	3
The public supports the work of my central bank	3	3	3	3	3	3
The public understands the work of my central bank	2	2	3	3	3	3

Notes: 5 = strongly agree, 4 = agree, 3 = neutral, 2 = disagree, and 1 = strongly disagree. Magyar Nemzeti Bank, *N* = 86, March 2000; Czech National Bank, *N* = 33, June 2000; National Bank of the Kyrgyz Republic, *N* = 66, May 2001.

they respond forcefully to government challenges, but they called on their allies in the transnational central banking community for help. When the coercive and persuasive pressures that the IMF, ECB, and other community institutions could bring to bear mattered to the government, it usually backed down. This happened more commonly, although not exclusively, in the would-be EU accession states. In these cases the central banks maintained their independence, but at the cost of revealing that their key support base lay outside their own countries. Such successful challenges could exacerbate the wormhole effect, further drawing postcommunist central bank staff into the transnational community and alienating them from their domestic critics. But where international pressures failed, vulnerable postcommunist central banks often lost these challenges and became increasingly politicized, isolated, or ineffective domestically. Epstein convincingly demonstrates the effects of this failure in Ukraine, where governments unswayed by the transnational community systematically undermined and politicized the National Bank of Ukraine (NBU).[106] As one West European central banker remarked to me in frustration, the NBU was "interested in our advice at the expert level, but not at the board level. The board members are only interested in sightseeing."[107] This domestic contestation and politicization meant

---

106. Epstein 2008.
107. Author's interview with a senior West European central bank official, May 2000.

TABLE 4.11   Postcommunist central bank governors in politics, 1990–2008

GOVERNOR		POLITICAL POSITION
Albania	D. Vrioni, 1993–94	Member of Parliament, 1995–
Armenia	B. Asatryan, 1994–98	Member of Parliament, 1995–98
	T. Sargsyan, 1998–2008	Prime minister, 2008–14
Bulgaria	*I. Iskrov*, 2003–	Member of Parliament, 2001–3
Estonia	S. Kallas, 1991–95	Prime minister, 1999–2002
Georgia	N. Javakhishvili, 1994–98	Member of Parliament, 1999–2003
Kazakhstan	G. Bainazarov, 1992–93	Member of Parliament, 1994
	D. Sembayev, 1993–96	Member of Parliament, 1996–99
	O. Jandosov, 1996–98	Ak Zhol party co-leader, 2002–9
Kyrgyzstan	M. Sultanov, 1994–98	Member of Parliament, 2000–2009
		Speaker of Parliament, 2006–9
Latvia	E. Repše, 1991–2001	Prime minister, New Era leader, 2002–4
Lithuania	*V. Baldišis*, 1990–93	Member of Parliament, 1990–92
Poland	H. Gronkiewicz-Waltz, 1992–2000	Member of Parliament, 2005–6
	L. Balcerowicz, 2001–7	Freedom Union leader, 1995–2000
Romania	M. Isărescu, 1990–98; 2000–	Prime minister, 1999–2000
Russia	V. Gerashchenko, 1992–94,	Rodina cofounder, 2003
	1998–2002	Member of Parliament, 2003–4
Serbia	D. Avramović, 1994–96	Zajedno coalition leader, 1996
Slovenia	M. Gaspari, 2001–7	Major presidential candidate, 2007
Ukraine	V. Yushchenko, 1993–99	Prime minister, 1999–2001
		Our Ukraine leader, 2002–5
		President, 2005–10
	S. Tihipko, 2002–4	Labor Ukraine leader, 2000–5
		Elected to Parliament, 2000 and 2004

Notes: As of 2008, before the global financial crisis. Includes governors in electoral politics serving as president, prime minister, a political party leader, or in parliament. Does not include other ministerial positions (e.g., finance minister) or governors who ran for parliament as regular party members and lost. It also excludes Czech National Bank governor Josef Tošovský (1993–2000), who briefly served as an appointed acting prime minister in 1997–98 during a political crisis.
Italics denote those who served in politics before becoming central bank governors.

that central bank governors across the postcommunist region often found themselves drawn into electoral politics as well. At least twenty governors served as party leaders, parliamentarians, or prime ministers between 1990 and 2008, the vast majority doing so after their tenures at the central bank had ended and often having run in opposition to incumbent governments (see table 4.11). While central bankers in the advanced industrial democracies had the luxury of eschewing formal politics, the political engagement of many former central bank governors in postcommunist states reflected the challenges of the internalization process. As we will see in greater detail in the following chapters, postcommunist central bankers walked a precarious tightrope between the transnational community and their national constituencies.

THE POLITICS OF EUROPEAN INTEGRATION

"The Bank of England . . . worked together with us as a mother loves her children."

—Economist, Magyar Nemzeti Bank (2000)

Central banks in postcommunist Europe were the first to be swept into the arms of the transnational central banking community. As the old regimes fell, community members offered training and technical assistance, while the postcommunist central bankers simultaneously reached out for support. Central and East European central bankers flooded London, Frankfurt, Basel, Vienna, New York, Washington, and other community hubs. The national central banks, the IMF, and the BIS talking-shop played the leading role in the early transformation of Central and East European central banks. Although the European Union's PHARE program financed several early assistance efforts, the EU's major initial contribution was pressuring governments to increase their central banks' legal independence to meet EU standards. The European Central Bank become involved in the transformation process after its creation in 1998, at which point it undertook important efforts to harmonize central bank practices with EU requirements.

Over the course of the 1990s Central and East European central bankers became ever-more integrated into the transnational community as information flowed through the wormhole network connecting the central banks and reinforced their shared ideas and practices. Central and East European central bankers, persuaded by their constant exposure to the community's consistent, attractive, and structured model, became strong domestic proponents of central bank independence and price stability. Equally as important, technical assistance and training gave them the standard tools with which to implement their chosen policies.

At the same time, after the initial honeymoon period many Central and East European political leaders came to regret their earlier decisions to grant so much independence to their central banks. They found that the central banks' preferred monetary policies often conflicted with their domestic development plans, and that the central banks could not prevent banking and currency crises. As a result, many central banks across the region were targets of heavy government criticism and attempts, both formal and informal, to rein in their independence. These efforts typically failed, however, due in great part to perceived and actual external pressures. Chief among these were the pointed and unified critiques by high-status foreign central bankers, IMF threats to withhold funding, and EU accession requirements. As long as international approval remained valuable to Central and East European governments, their central banks grew stronger and more influential despite domestic debates over their policies and efficacy.

While this dynamic occurred throughout the region, this chapter focuses on the experiences of Hungary and of the Czech and Slovak Republics. Hungary represented the best-case scenario, the country that began in the most advantageous political and economic position. Strong leadership and well-paid, well-educated staff made the Magyar Nemzeti Bank an ideal candidate for transformation. Not surprisingly, the MNB developed rapidly with community support, particularly in terms of monetary policy and research. But I also use this "best case" to further illustrate the relative difficulty of transforming banking supervision in comparison with monetary policy. Then, in the second section, the paired case study of the Czech and Slovak central banks most clearly reveals the leveling capabilities of international assistance. Although the Czech National Bank retained the vast majority of the State Bank of Czechoslovakia's experienced staff after the country's split, with the help of the transnational central banking community the National Bank of Slovakia quickly gained ground on its richer relation.

As soon as these central banks began exercising their independence and demonstrating fallibility in the mid-1990s, disgruntled governments in all three states tried to amend their central banking laws to curtail their independence. With the timely help of the transnational central banking community, the self-confident central banks roundly thwarted these early efforts to curtail their powers. However, subsequent battles over euro adoption after EU accession in 2004 brought conflicts to a head in all three countries, as the increasingly embattled central bankers pushed for rapid euro adoption in order to commit their governments to the monetary discipline of the European Central Bank. The transnational community did not consistently support the central banks on that issue, however, leading to political defeats and curbed powers for the Hungarian and Czech national banks.

Racing Ahead: The Magyar Nemzeti Bank

The MNB took advantage of training and technical assistance programs from the moment the transition began, encouraged by leadership that considered it a priority and a political atmosphere in favor of "rejoining" Europe. IMF missions and programs helped set developmental goals through the mid-1990s, while impending EU membership played that role afterward. Technical assistance increased the MNB's capabilities in the early- and mid-1990s, and training programs throughout the decade raised staff qualifications. Long-term exchange programs, seminars, and joint research and publication with foreign central bankers had a major impact on policy and research departments, not only increasing Hungarian central bankers' technical knowledge, but reinforcing their shared ideas and practices. By the end of the 1990s, the MNB had itself begun providing assistance to other central banks in transition.

The MNB drew on technical assistance most heavily in the early and mid-1990s, especially through IMF missions. This technical assistance focused on foreign exchange operations, statistics, organization, and internal audit. For example, György Szapáry, the IMF resident representative to Hungary from 1990 through 1993, explained that an IMF mission on foreign exchange market liberalization in 1992 had led to the recommendations being implemented a few weeks later.[1] Szapáry himself represented a pivotal intellectual bridge between the MNB and the transnational central banking community. An expatriate Hungarian forced to leave the country in 1956, Szapáry left the IMF to formally join the MNB leadership in 1994. He served alternately as Advisor to the Governor or as Deputy Governor for nearly a decade, and in those capacities shaped MNB development and policies throughout this key period.

The MNB coordinated especially closely with the IMF in the early years during Hungary's stand-by lending arrangement. The IMF made loan disbursal conditional on Hungary meeting certain economic and structural benchmarks, a conditionality with teeth since the IMF cut Hungary off briefly in 1989 and again in 1993 for not fulfilling its targets. This gave the government a specific reform

---

1. Author's interview with György Szapáry, deputy governor of the Magyar Nemzeti Bank, Budapest, Hungary, May 2000.

agenda to fulfill, gave the MNB leverage in its demands for independence and resources, and gave the IMF a greater stake in Hungary's economic transformation process. The IMF resident representative set up shop in a well-appointed suite in the main MNB headquarters building, not far from the governor's office, and had daily contact with MNB staff that continued well after the last IMF lending program for Hungary expired in 1998. As my interviewees noted, although most of the IMF's recommended policies were not new concepts for the MNB staff, discussing the details with IMF technical assistance teams both sharpened their focus and made it possible to act on the recommendations. EU accession served a similar purpose later by setting performance benchmarks for the MNB. Impending EU accession encouraged the MNB to work to meet EU standards and forestalled potential domestic debate about their nature or timing.

The development of the MNB Statistics Department illustrated the effectiveness of this technical assistance and benchmarking. The MNB needed to create a sophisticated statistics department in order to gather more accurate data for economic forecasting and for IMF-required reports. When the MNB created the Statistics Department in 1994, an IMF technical assistance mission analyzed the MNB's existing practices and made detailed recommendations. This sparked MNB staff visits to the statistics departments of the Austrian, Turkish, French, and Belgian central banks, and regular consultations with European central bankers—particularly the Bundesbank—on methodology, new surveys, and new statistics. The revitalized Statistics Department continued to receive IMF advisors once or twice a year to discuss further changes, and welcomed this contact. As one statistician observed, "We follow IMF international guidelines not just because they recommend it, but because it's part of being a member of the international community."[2] By all accounts the MNB's statistics improved dramatically as a result, facilitating the development of economic models and the use of indirect tools of monetary policy.[3] In 1999 the Statistics Department began to receive technical assistance from the European Central Bank to prepare for EU accession, and had achieved harmonization with ECB requirements by 2003.[4]

Training played if anything an even more important role in the MNB's transformation. While a few select MNB economists had taken courses at the IMF Institute and the Swiss National Bank's Gerzensee center in the 1980s, between 1990 and 1999 individual MNB employees attended central banking courses abroad over eight hundred times. The National Bank of Belgium and the OeNB

---

2. Author's interview with a senior official in the Statistics Department, Magyar Nemzeti Bank, Budapest, Hungary, March 2000.

3. For example, see Statistics Department 2001.

4. *2003 Annual Report of the Magyar Nemzeti Bank.*

trained the most MNB staff in the first few years, while the Bank of England's CCBS, the Banque de France, and the Bundesbank later became the leading destinations.[5] The staff took many courses at the MNB taught by foreign experts as well. Early on the MNB also sent employees to the International Bankers' Training Center (IBTC) in Budapest, founded in 1988 to provide general financial education to Hungarian businesspeople and bankers. Although the IBTC focused primarily on training commercial bankers after the mid-1990s, there were over two thousand MNB participants in IBTC short courses between 1989 and 1994.

MNB staff especially valued the courses they took abroad, and their demand for such training was initially higher than the transnational central banking community's ability to provide it. In the mid-1990s the MNB began to prepare comprehensive lists of training and technical assistance requests to take to the regular BIS coordinators' meetings. On one such list that I saw for the year 2000, ten different MNB departments had made detailed assistance requests of specific West European central banks.[6] The Economics and Research Department led the pack with requests for consultation on eighteen separate topics, including inflation targeting, disinflation strategies, and European business cycles. Other postcommunist central banks followed the MNB's lead, and the coordinators' meetings became a negotiating forum in which the postcommunist central banks would request extensive and specific assistance, and the donor central banks would attempt to fulfill those requests. In this respect, postcommunist demand pushed the community to expand its assistance capabilities further and faster.

Human Resources

After a few initial hiccups, the MNB's internationally minded governors and its ability to attract and retain a well-educated, young staff enabled the bank to absorb this technical assistance and training. When Hungary introduced a two-tier banking system in 1987 the MNB already had some staff with Western training and experience as well as a leadership committed to bringing the bank into the transnational central banking community. Despite three instances of politically motivated turnover, governors Ferenc Bartha (1988–1990), György Surányi (1990–1991 and 1995–2001), and Péter Ákos Bod (1991–1994) provided continuity

---

5. Various *Annual Reports* and data provided by the MNB Human Resource Management Department. See also table 4.2.

6. Human Resource Management Department, "A Detailed List of the Topics National Bank of Hungary Would Like to Discuss Mainly with EU Central Banks in 2000," mimeo, Magyar Nemzeti Bank, November 1999.

inasmuch as all were economic liberals sympathetic to the internationalization of the central bank. Miklós Németh, the socialist prime minister who presided over Hungary's transformation from a one-party state, had appointed Bartha to the MNB because of Bartha's relative youth and liberal views. After the first free elections in 1990 the Antall government—like most of the first elected postcommunist governments—replaced the central bank governor. A six-party consensus approved György Surányi's appointment, in great part because of his strong national and international reputation as an economist and World Bank expert.[7] The government used Surányi's appointment to send a message to the international community that it was serious about fighting inflation and the budget deficit.

Nevertheless, the MNB hemorrhaged its most qualified staff through the late 1980s and early 1990s. From 1987 through 1991 the MNB nearly doubled its pre-1987 annual turnover rates of about 10 percent a year, reaching a peak of 21 percent in 1989.[8] As then-governor Bartha lamented in 1990, "The employees of the MNB work in constant uncertainty and political mistrust and earn much less than their counterparts at commercial banks. As a result . . . my colleagues leave the bank for better positions in commercial banks, where they do not have to debate constantly with the government, political parties, banks, enterprises and the public."[9]

After the 1991 Act on the National Bank gave the MNB increased budgetary autonomy, it was able to gradually raise staff salaries and attrition diminished. At the same time, however, the MNB lost its governor again. Prime Minister Antall used the opportunity provided by the new law to replace Surányi with a loyalist from his own ruling Hungarian Democratic Forum (HDF) party, Minister of Industry Péter Ákos Bod. Bod had fewer international connections and less financial expertise than Surányi, and admitted that he was at first skeptical of Hungary's IMF and World Bank partners. However, he soon came to see their advice as "well worth listening to," especially on macroeconomic matters, because they had lengthy experience in Hungary and understood the country's conditions.[10] The MNB changed more slowly during the Bod years than under Surányi because of Bod's lack of experience and outsider status. After the 1994 elections

---

7. Várhegyi 1996.

8. *1991 Annual Report of the Magyar Nemzeti Bank.*

9. Judit Rédei, "Az MNB számvetése [An assessment by the MNB]," *Magyarország,* April 6, 1990, 14/90, 35.

10. Quoted in Blejer and Coricelli 1995.

the new governing coalition pressured Bod to resign, and when he did so Surányi returned as MNB governor, buoyed by strong international support.[11]

Surányi's second tenure reinforced the MNB's internationalization through reorganization and a strong emphasis on training. Salaries become fully competitive with the commercial banks, in conjunction with a massive reorganization that led to the MNB-initiated firing of 357 staff members in 1995. From 1995 through 1997, the MNB staff shrank by over a thousand people (42 percent).[12] But unlike the earlier losses of better qualified, in-demand staff, in this reorganization the MNB let go its weak or redundant staff members. After this reduction, each remaining central banker could take part in more training experiences.

The MNB also concentrated on hiring young new staff members with economics backgrounds and English-language abilities. The staff's average age in January 2000 was forty, while department managers averaged forty-five and the governor himself was only forty-six.[13] The MNB also instituted foreign-language requirements for its positions, asking even security guards to learn basic English. To help staff meet these requirements the MNB introduced its own language courses, over 90 percent in English and a few others in German and French. In 1989 over two hundred MNB employees participated in these courses. When the MNB added financial incentives for language learning in 1991, the participation rate shot up to over five hundred and stayed at 350–450 students per year throughout the decade. By 1993 the MNB already claimed to have over one hundred employees with a "mastery" of English, as demonstrated by examination.[14] In 1997 the MNB instituted a more comprehensive four-year English-language program, with the aim of having half of the MNB staff reach "proficiency" within five years. The MNB staff's early emphasis on English enabled them to take advantage of the full range of international technical assistance and training programs without having to rely on translation. For example, English-speaking staff could participate in courses at the IMF Institute or take up study tours at the Federal Reserve Bank of Kansas City.

In sum, as a result of the community's assistance efforts and the MNB's leadership and personnel policies, by the late 1990s the MNB had "the best group of economic analysts in the country" (according to a Hungarian commercial

11. Várhegyi 1996.

12. *1995 Annual Report of the Magyar Nemzeti Bank* and *1997 Annual Report of the Magyar Nemzeti Bank.*

13. Author's interview with a senior official in the Human Resource Management Department, Magyar Nemzeti Bank, Budapest, Hungary, February 2000.

14. *1993 Annual Report of the Magyar Nemzeti Bank.*

banker) and could hand pick its new staff from among the top university economics graduates (according to an IMF advisor). Ironically, this also ensured that the developmental gap between monetary policy and banking supervision would emerge strongly in Hungary, because from early on Hungary had a separate banking supervision agency without the independence, resources, or international support of the MNB.

Monetary Policy

The MNB's monetary policy instruments, modeling, and research capabilities evolved quickly during the 1990s. The MNB in the 1980s had a secretive, convoluted structure, and had been accused of manipulating information about the government deficit to satisfy IMF demands and "preserve the country's creditworthiness."[15] The MNB's instruments in the late 1980s were "primitive" (in Surányi's words), it had little capacity to accurately measure inflation, credit, or other financial indicators, and its information technology was far behind the times.[16] At the same time, the MNB began in a stronger position than its fellow postcommunist central banks. It was the first to use indirect instruments of monetary policy (in 1987) and the first to use treasury bills in open-market operations.[17]

Hungary began its transition with a pegged exchange rate, and after price, trade, and interest rate liberalizations in 1989–91 the MNB aimed to achieve both price stability and external equilibrium.[18] In 1991 the MNB began to focus more on inflation reduction, after fending off a foreign exchange crisis in 1990 (thanks in part to IMF support) and after the Act on the MNB stipulated price stability as its main goal. The MNB used the pegged but adjustable exchange rate as its intermediate policy target, since uncertain money demand and transmission processes made monetary targeting unreliable.[19] The MNB relied primarily on high reserve ratios and certificates of deposit to soak up liquidity from 1990 through 1992. From 1993 on the MNB turned more toward open-market operations such as treasury bill and bond auctions (introduced in 1988 and 1993 respectively),

---

15. Tardos 1991, Csaba 1995.

16. Király 1993. As she wrote, "the Hungarian statistical system has collapsed: not only are comparable time series missing, but reliable actual descriptive data (GDP, income, consumption) are missing as well. Under these circumstances an econometric model builder is tempted to abandon hope" (138).

17. Fleming and Cole 1995.

18. MNB, "Financial Sector and Monetary Policy in Hungary 1991–1994," mimeo.

19. Neményi 1997.

repurchase agreements (repos), and foreign currency transactions; interest rate changes (especially repo rates) played the core role in monetary policy.

Hungary moved to a crawling peg exchange rate in March 1995 as part of an IMF-backed economic stabilization plan initiated by the new Socialist-led government. As a result, the MNB began to pursue price stability as its sole long-run goal and chose the nominal exchange rate as its intermediate target. Inflation initially increased under the crawling peg, but by late 1996 it had restabilized at 20–25 percent. It fell to around 10 percent by 2000, with the MNB unable to lower it further through its usual monetary policy measures. In an effort to stamp out remaining inflation, the MNB moved to an inflation-targeting regime in 2001 within a +/−15 percent exchange rate band. The MNB and government agreed on a long-term target of 2 percent, aiming to reduce inflation to meet this target by 2006.[20] The MNB announced its targets eighteen months in advance and communicated regularly through its *Quarterly Report on Inflation*, published since 1997. The OECD deemed the inflation-targeting regime to "resemble best practice."[21]

How did the MNB move from limited tools and information to formal inflation targeting in one decade? Five central bankers I interviewed who began their MNB careers in monetary policy and research-oriented departments in the early 1990s stressed the importance of intensive courses abroad and regular interaction with IMF staff and established central bankers in shaping their ideas and making their work possible during that first decade of transition. Discussing early courses she had taken at the CCBS, IMF Institute, National Bank of Belgium, and OeNB, one central banker remarked, "we didn't have any experience in this field, so it was a new situation for us, and it helped us so much."[22] Another reflected on the importance of international assistance by saying "after joining the bank we had to change our thinking—you have to change your mind, your concepts, and your language, all the institutional background has changed."[23] Yet another discussed the heavy involvement of the IMF and the Bank of England in the early years. He stated that in the early 1990s "we looked [more] to the IMF for our ideas, but now [in 2000] we look to London or Frankfurt. The ideas are still coming from abroad, because we are not confident enough to produce our own."[24] The fourth, who

---

20. Monetary and Exchange Affairs and European I Departments 2002.

21. OECD 2004.

22. Author's interview with a senior official in the Economics and Research Department, Magyar Nemzeti Bank, Budapest, Hungary, March 2000.

23. Author's interview with an analyst in the Economics and Research Department, Magyar Nemzeti Bank, Budapest, Hungary, March 2000.

24. Author's interview with an analyst in the Modeling Division of the Economics and Research Department, Magyar Nemzeti Bank, Budapest, Hungary, February 2000.

had spent time at the Bank of England, remarked on its high standards of professionalism and said that "we aspire to be like them."[25] The fifth said that he found the CCBS monetary policy seminars especially helpful: "It's useful to know what's going on in these areas. Especially in a country like this where academic communication is not very good. If you have not kept up with international events, or international communication, you are lost. These seminars give you a chance not to be stupid."[26] He also noted that he often turned to contacts at the Finnish and Swedish central banks for advice on technical matters. Later in the 1990s the EU became more involved. The central bankers especially lauded an EU-financed seminar that brought internationally renowned academic economists to Hungary to speak and work with a small number of handpicked, mostly younger MNB employees.

Such experiences helped to shape the MNB's monetary policies, tools, and research. Perhaps the most notable evolution in the MNB's thought was the changing attitude toward moderate inflation over time.[27] In the early 1990s many Hungarian central bankers and economists, including Surányi, did not regard moderate inflation as a particular problem. But by the mid-1990s MNB sentiment had turned against moderate inflation as an acceptable long-term trend. While government officials acknowledged the need to eventually lower inflation to West European levels for instrumental reasons (to meet the Maastricht criteria), MNB staff came to see moderate inflation in Hungary as undesirable in and of itself. As Surányi and Vincze wrote in 1997, it was "cruel" and "painful" for citizens.[28] At the same time, MNB staff still felt that inflation should be reduced at a gentle pace and only after structural and financial reforms, in contrast to the prevailing community view favoring rapid disinflation. Papers from a June 1997 joint IMF-MNB seminar on moderate inflation highlighted this tension. While several Hungarian participants argued in favor of gradual disinflation, the IMF officials, academic economists, and invited central bankers from Poland and Croatia all recommended rapid disinflation for Hungary. In his critical commen-

---

25. Author's interview with a senior official in the Monetary Policy Department, Magyar Nemzeti Bank, Budapest, Hungary, March 2000.

26. Author's interview with a senior official in the Economics and Research Department, Magyar Nemzeti Bank, Budapest, Hungary, March 2000.

27. Academic economists typically describe moderate inflation as rates of 15–30 percent per year, although community members tend to see the lower bound at around eight percent. The Cottarelli and Szapáry edited volume defines it loosely as "say, below 30 percent but well above the 0–2 percent range often regarded as constituting price stability in Western Europe." Cottarelli and Szapáry 1998.

28. Surányi and Vincze 1998. In their acknowledgments, Surányi and Vincze also thank four MNB officials, IMF resident representative Mark Allen, and Szapáry (with both MNB and IMF ties) for their comments on the paper.

tary on Surányi and Vincze's paper, IMF official Carlo Cottarelli said flatly that "a rapid disinflation strategy [in Hungary] is likely to be successful."[29] Within two years, the consensus community view and the example of Poland's disinflation had sold the MNB on a more rapid strategy, one that the move to inflation targeting in 2001 was designed to facilitate.

By the time the MNB adopted full inflation targeting, its strong Statistics Department and its economic modelers' international contacts allowed the MNB to implement it in a sophisticated manner. The Czechs and Poles, who began inflation targeting a few years earlier, had experienced difficulties with the off-the-shelf forecasting models they had imported from abroad. Learning from this, the MNB drew on technical assistance to develop its own model, which had "the same kind of structure but much wider parameters."[30] The ECB set forth requirements that member central banks' models had to meet, providing additional focus for the Hungarian model. The MNB sent staff abroad to see how other central banks' models worked, bought the IMF forecasting model, and participated in the ECB's forecasting working group while crafting their own model. Afterward, they demonstrated their model's advances at seminars and workshops in other central banks. The MNB Economics and Monetary Policy Department, the department responsible for monetary policy, research, and modeling, became widely known as the top central bank research group in the postcommunist region. Ironically, however, the government's expansionary fiscal policy regularly failed to support the MNB's monetary policy, resulting in exchange rate volatility that undermined the credibility of the MNB's inflation-targeting regime.[31]

Banking Supervision

While the MNB's monetary policy capabilities developed rapidly and in tune with international standards from the beginning, the same cannot be said for Hungarian banking supervision. While reforms did take place during the 1990s, supervisory capacity did not improve significantly until after 1998 when international cooperation, influence, and interest in capacity building increased.

Unlike in other postcommunist states, Hungary's central bank lost primary responsibility for supervision immediately after the establishment of the two-tiered banking system. A department in the Ministry of Finance was responsible

---

29. Cottarelli 1998.

30. Author's interview with a senior official in the Economics and Monetary Policy Department, Magyar Nemzeti Bank, Budapest, Hungary, January 2006.

31. Author's interview with a former member of the MNB Monetary Policy Council, Budapest, Hungary, June 2014.

for supervision until 1991, when the Hungarian Banking Supervisory Authority (HBSA) was created. The 1991 Act on Financial Institutions required commercial banks to meet Basel capital adequacy standards, but maintained restrictions on universal banking and did not give the HBSA sufficient authority or autonomy to effectively regulate the banking system. For several years the MNB had to carry out on-site supervision on the HBSA's behalf because the HBSA had not yet developed the ability to do so on its own, and the HBSA needed the approval of yet another body, the Banking Supervisory Committee, in order to take major decisions and to introduce and enforce regulations.[32] The HBSA, neither autonomous nor prestigious, also could not pay or train its staff in the same way as the MNB. According to Szapáry, this meant that in practice it could not do its job for several years.[33] Many of my interviewees opined that the "worst" staff from the MNB went to the HBSA, and certainly most would not have chosen to go there given the differences in working conditions. The HBSA also had difficulties because of its merger with the Capital Market Supervision authority in 1997, as they formally became one agency but maintained separate IT systems and staffs.

During the 1990s the supervisory authority was not integrated into a transnational community, as international standards were unclear and assistance was fragmented. Banking supervisors did not have access to the same kinds of training courses as the MNB, and technical assistance came primarily through short-term consultants. A high-level interviewee at the supervisory agency told me that he had participated in numerous overseas courses while previously employed at the MNB—including at the Federal Reserve Bank of Kansas City, the CCBS, and the National Bank of Belgium—but that he stopped doing so after he moved to the supervisory agency.[34] The HBSA also had a difficult relationship with USAID, a key technical assistance provider for banking supervision in the 1990s. For example, when asked about USAID, one HBSA interviewee expressed mixed feelings about the agency's experience. On the one hand, he lauded the experienced banking supervisors sent by Barents on a long-term USAID contract to help them develop on-site supervision capabilities. On the other, he deemed a "disaster" another USAID advisor sent to advise them on off-site surveillance "who only knew theory," saying that the sole concrete outcome of this project was translating a US manual into Hungarian.[35] For their part, USAID officials

---

32. Borish, et al. 1996.

33. Szapáry 2002.

34. Author's interview with a senior official of the Hungarian Banking and Capital Market Supervision authority, Budapest, Hungary, March 2000.

35. Ibid.

felt that the Hungarians often did not really want their help. As a result, during the 1990s the HBSA made little progress in adopting even emerging international practices regarding risk assessment.[36]

The ramifications of this lack of capability and autonomy became clear during the 1998 Postabank scandal, when multi-million dollar financial misdeeds at one of the country's largest banks forced a state bailout and takeover. Although the HBSA had previously known about Postabank's problems, it did nothing to sanction the bank or to help resolve them. HBSA officials claimed to have been hamstrung because they had insufficient authority to take action, but the Hungarian government thought differently and fired the HBSA's director and deputy director. An OECD report found that the HBSA had indeed had enough authority to act, but simply chose not to do so.[37] A senior official in the caretaker Postabank administration agreed, observing that "the head of supervision . . . never wanted any conflict, he never wanted to make decisions, and he found excuses in the text of the law."[38] He further opined that most HBSA staff supervisors were "truly incompetent" and yet were charged with supervising large banks. The OECD argued that the Postabank incident revealed the need to increase the agency's independence in order to help prevent such inaction in the future.

The Postabank scandal and the 1997 Asian financial crisis refocused both the Hungarian authorities and the international community on the need to improve Hungarian banking supervision. In 1999 Hungary overhauled its banking supervision staff in line with OECD recommendations.[39] In April 2000, after studying the experience of the Nordic countries and Britain, it introduced consolidated financial market supervision.[40] The Hungarian Financial Supervisory Authority (HFSA) gathered Banking and Capital Market Supervision, State Pension Fund Supervision, and State Insurance Supervision into one regulatory body. At the same time, Hungary agreed to become one of the first countries to undergo an IMF/World Bank Financial System Stability Assessment in 2000. This evaluation, carried out by a World Bank staffer, a Belgian banking supervisor, and an Indian central banker, analyzed Hungarian banking supervision in reference to the Basel Core Principles.[41] The FSSA recommendations subsequently became a "major reference point" for reform.[42] The European Union conducted its own

36. Piroska 2004.
37. OECD 2000.
38. Author's interview with a senior official of Postabank, Budapest, Hungary, February 2000.
39. OECD 2000.
40. Balogh 2005.
41. Monetary and Exchange Affairs and European I Departments 2002.
42. Balogh 2005.

analysis based on the FSSA, culminating in an agreement on an Action Plan for reform measures to be taken. As a result, the HFSA for the first time began issuing best practice recommendations, legislation came into force increasing the HFSA's autonomy, and HFSA staff received more comprehensive training and better pay.[43] In sum, international recommendations and assistance, EU accession pressures, and the Postabank scandal pushed the HFSA farther toward meeting existing international standards. Nevertheless, weaknesses remained in the HFSA's supervision capabilities. Although the Hungarian banking system gradually became more stable, many chalked this up to the rapid influx of West European banks into the Hungarian market rather than to the improved abilities of the supervisors.

Government Reactions to MNB Policies

The initial concerns politicians had raised over central bank independence during the debate over the 1991 Act on the Magyar Nemzeti Bank resurfaced and grew louder during the 1990s, as many Hungarian leaders criticized MNB policy decisions. From 1991 through 1994 the HDF-led government had three major clashes with the MNB, all of which the MNB lost. As we have seen, the government replaced Surányi as governor with Bod in late 1991. A MNB vice governor was fired after the MNB raised interest rates in September 1993 against the government's wishes.[44] Most notably, the parliament passed legislation in December 1993 that raised the limit for MNB financing of the budget deficit in 1994, overriding the Act on the Magyar Nemzeti Bank.

At the same time, the persistent twin deficit in the budget and the current account pushed the government into a string of unplanned currency devaluations. As one MNB banker stated, "the credibility of the exchange rate system had been completely destroyed by the middle of 1994."[45] The IMF briefly suspended its stand-by credit agreement with Hungary in response to the government's expansionary fiscal policy. One contemporary observer argued that the MNB's tense relationship with the Ministry of Finance, limited statistical capabilities, and unstable research team made it difficult for the MNB to defend itself against the government during this period.[46] As the MNB's capabilities improved and as EU accession became a more realistic possibility the MNB gained more

43. Monetary and Exchange Affairs and European I Departments 2002, Piroska 2004.
44. Csaba 1995.
45. Neményi 1997.
46. Emília Papp, "Felpuhult a jegybanki önállóság [The autonomy of the central bank is softened]," *Magyar Hírlap*, June 6, 1994.

leverage in these battles, but Hungarian politicians did not become any happier with MNB policies.

Conflict came to a head once again in the debate over the 1996 revision to the Act on the Magyar Nemzeti Bank that strengthened the MNB's independence. These revisions would not have happened without active international support. Indeed, at the start of the drafting process Prime Minister Gyula Horn opined that the revised act should weaken, not strengthen, the MNB's independence, because he felt that the government wrongly had no influence over MNB monetary policy.[47] The Hungarian Bankers' Association, the Ministry of Finance, and an influential group of academic economists also vigorously objected to the MNB's monetary policies, which they argued harmed economic growth and suffocated business development.[48] Nevertheless, the revised Act passed with support from Socialist and Fidesz MPs primarily because parliamentarians saw it as a necessary part of moving toward international and EU standards. According to Surányi, the BIS, IMF, OECD, and EU had commented on the MNB's draft law in detail and defended it to Hungarian politicians.[49] The Act decidedly strengthened the MNB's independence in terms of appointments and budget financing, bringing the law nearer to EU requirements.[50]

This revised Act helped to "lock in" central bank independence in Hungary, even as many in politics, business, and the academic community remained wary of central bank policies. Karádi argued, for example, that the 1996 Act helped to keep the pro-growth Fidesz-led coalition government elected in 1998 from changing the crawling peg system and prematurely dismissing Surányi.[51] Fidesz prime minister Viktor Orbán wanted to fire Surányi immediately after the

---

47. "MNB, a la Horn Gyula [MNB, a la Gyula Horn]," *Figyelő*, February 8, 1995, 33.

48. "A bankárok bírálják az MNB monetáris politikáját [The bankers are criticizing the monetary policy of the MNB]," *Napi Gazdaság*, January 27, 1995, 1 and 3; Emília Sebők, "Nem mindegy honnan nézzük. A nyugodtnak látszó felszín alatt jól fejlett nézetkülönbségek húzódnak [Our viewpoint does matter: Below the calm surface, there are well developed differences of opinions]," *Figyelő*, March 30, 1995, 33,34; and "Közgazdászcsoport az MNB jogállásáról szóló módosítás ellen—Bankóprés a felemelkedésért? [A group of economists oppose the change in the Act on the Central Bank—Seigniorage for advancement?" *Világgazdaság*, November 27, 1996.

49. Author's interview with György Surányi, governor of the Magyar Nemzeti Bank, Budapest, Hungary, May 2000.

50. "Függetlenedik a jegybank: A jegybanktörvény igazodik a Maastrichti elvekhez [The Central Bank will be more independent: The Act on the Central Bank adjusts to the Maastricht principles]," *Napi Gazdaság*, October 5, 1996; and Károly Bognár, "Közelebb Európához: Bodnár Zoltán, az MNB alelnöke az új jegybanktörvényről [Closer to Europe: Interview with Zoltan Bodnár, the vice governor of the MNB on the new Act on the Central Bank]," *Bank és Tőzsde*, January 31, 1997.

51. Karádi 1999.

election, but was dissuaded from doing so on the grounds that it would harm Hungary's international reputation.[52] The revised Act also helped the MNB maintain its policy independence (though not its political support) during the scandal that broke in 1999 over massive losses at CW Bank, a state-owned Viennese bank the MNB had inherited in 1990.[53] Further pro-independence, EU-conforming legal revisions were passed in June 2001 under the leadership of Zsigmond Járai, the former Finance Minister who became MNB governor after the end of Surányi's term in 2000. According to Járai, the 2001 revisions reflected the recommendations of the European Monetary Institute and consultations with the Czech National Bank, among others.[54] The 2001 Act on the Magyar Nemzeti Bank brought Hungarian central banking legislation into close conformity with the EU *acquis*. In short, while the MNB had thoroughly internalized the ideas and practices of the transnational central banking community during the 1990s, many Hungarian politicians and interest groups did not accept that central bank independence and price stability had intrinsic value. Rather, they supported these principles primarily because of external pressures, first from the IMF and later from the European Union.

Unequal Spoils: The Czech and Slovak National Banks

Divorce is never easy, especially when one partner walks away with all the goods. While the 1993 Velvet Divorce caused barely a hiccup for the new Czech National Bank (CNB), the National Bank of Slovakia (NBS) found itself forced to start almost completely from scratch in a much more difficult economic environment. The State Bank of Czechoslovakia (SBCS) had made significant progress in its initial transformation after the November 1991 Velvet Revolution, and the CNB inherited the lion's share of the SBCS's experienced personnel, financial infrastructure, and facilities. Moreover, the Slovaks immediately faced a lack of confidence in their new currency and large twin deficits, contributing to capital flight, demonetization and dollarization, and a collapse in official reserves.[55] Nevertheless,

---

52. Péter Kóczián, "Intés az őrzőkhöz [Warning to the Guardians]," *Élet és Irodalom*, January 28, 2000, 4–5. As we will see in chapter 7, such concerns failed to deter Orbán the next time he came to power.

53. Péter Szakonyi and Pál Szombathy, "Fidesz bírálat a nemzeti banknak: A kormányfő szerint 70 millilárd ráfizetést kozott az adóságállomány csere—ma tesznek feljelentést a bécsi leány ügyében [Fidesz criticizes the National Bank: According to the Prime Minister, the credit swap caused 70 billion in losses—today it will file charges in the case of the Vienna subsidiary]," *Magyar Hírlap*, September 13, 1999.

54. "The pages of independence: The parliament is debating the new Act," *Bank és Tőzsde*, April 6, 2001.

55. Georgiou 1998.

within a decade both central banks had become capable, independent institutions with well-trained staff. The transnational central banking community played an instrumental role in their rapid transformations, encouraging deeper reforms in the CNB and enabling the NBS to emerge as a modern central bank from its origins as the SBCS branch office in Bratislava.

When Czechoslovakia split up in January 1993, its central bank did as well. Internationally respected SBCS governor Josef Tošovský stayed on at the new Czech National Bank, serving as governor nearly continually during the 1990s. Named "Central Banker of the Year" by *Euromoney* magazine in 1993, community members and CNB staffers alike credited him with spearheading the CNB's Western-oriented transformation. As one Czech central banker stated, "We didn't hesitate. We knew we had to join the West . . . In the CNB, these changes are Tošovský's work. He constituted the bank as a typical Western European bank. He took the structure, methods, and technical ways of the West and put them in the CNB."[56]

The CNB had about 1,550 employees in 1993, retaining all but one person from the SBCS federal headquarters in Prague.[57] In essence, the CNB emerged from the breakup with an experienced staff that had already gone through three years' worth of international training and technical assistance. A Slovak central banker observed that, "It was practically sufficient for the Czech side to merely change its name signs, since contacts with the world, intensive training visits and professional training of the Prague staff had already begun after 1st January 1990."[58] Some of these officials were highly trained indeed. For example, in 1990–91 the SBCS advertised a special intensive three-year finance course for would-be central bankers. After receiving over two hundred applications, the SBCS selected twenty-five students based on their knowledge of math, statistics, and English to be trained by foreign specialists in Prague, England, and the United States.[59] Many rose to become high-level CNB officials over the next decade or so, including a board member and three department directors. In another case, Tošovský recruited new staff from the Czech economics university, CERGE, through a seminar he taught personally for advanced students.

The National Bank of Slovakia, on the other hand, started its preparation for independence in 1992 with the original eighty-four staff members of the SBCS's

---

56. Author's interview with an official in the Real Economy Division, Czech National Bank, Prague, Czech Republic, May 2000.

57. Czech National Bank 2003; author's interview with a deputy governor of the National Bank of Slovakia, Bratislava, Slovakia, May 2006.

58. Valach 2005.

59. International Monetary Fund 2005 and author's interview with a senior official in human resources, Czech National Bank, Prague, Czech Republic, May 2000.

Slovak branch in Bratislava, which had previously done little more than facilitate currency circulation. A hiring spree bumped these numbers up to 895 by end-1993 and 1,147 by end-1994. One of the NBS's first department heads said simply that, "we hired people from the street. The only particular was to have a university education and speak English . . . because only a few people spoke English here in the bank at the time."[60] This resulted in a very young, very inexperienced central bank staff, but one open to and excited about international ideas and practices.

As part of its baptism by fire, the NBS did much of its hiring before it even had a governor.[61] Although the Slovak central bank law required the president to nominate the governor and deputy governors, and parliament to approve them, Slovakia did not have an official president until March 1993. Once President Michal Kováč took office, a few more months of infighting passed until new NBS governor Vladimír Masár's appointment in July 1993. Before heading the committee to found the NBS in 1992, Masár had been loan department director for a Slovak commercial bank.[62] Despite these relatively humble beginnings and fears that Masár was too close to free-spending Euro-pariah prime minister Vladimír Mečiar, Masár became committed to developing the NBS according to international standards and to maintaining its independence. He served as governor until the end of his term in 1999, having gained a strong reputation for professionalism. His deputy governor Marián Jusko then replaced him, providing continuity in NBS leadership.

Both central banks placed a major emphasis on staff retention and language acquisition, enabling them to take advantage of international training and technical assistance. In contrast to the MNB, neither the CNB nor NBS could pay their staffs as well as the leading commercial banks, resulting in relatively higher turnover rates. However, both compensated for the pay differential by offering international training, regular hours, and extensive benefits. For example, the CNB had its own recreation center, day care, and doctor on site.[63] For its part, the NBS offered loans to its staff at 1 percent interest, deeply discounted accommodation in two NBS-owned hotels, and 350 staff parking spaces in jammed downtown Bratislava.[64] Both also provided language training, although the CNB did so

60. Author's interview with a deputy governor of the National Bank of Slovakia, Bratislava, Slovakia, May 2006.

61. Georgiou 1998.

62. Daniel Borský and Daniel J. Stoll, "Exclusive Interview with National Bank Governor Vladimír Masár," *Slovak Spectator*, March 13, 1997, www.spectator.sk/articles/view/8360/1/.

63. Author's interview with a senior official of the Joint Vienna Institute, Vienna, Austria, May 2006.

64. Author's interview with a senior official in the Monetary Policy Department, National Bank of Slovakia, Bratislava, Slovakia, May 2006.

more systematically than the NBS. An average of five hundred staff members per year took part in CNB language training in the 1990s, primarily English-language courses but also French and German.[65] One CNB official noted that anyone at the bank could take language classes twice per week during working hours—at several levels and with only ten to twelve students per class—while CNB managers could arrange for private language tutors.[66] The NBS, because it started from scratch, focused more on hiring young graduates who already had English skills. It also offered language training through its Institute of Banking Education.

Both central banks made heavy use of international technical assistance and training, especially in the early years. The CNB, as the heir of the SBCS, did begin the postcommunist period with a few staff familiar with central banking abroad. In the 1980s, for example, the SBCS had held seminars on econometrics and arranged some short study tours to West European central banks.[67] After the Velvet Revolution, SBCS officials embraced the opportunity to put theory into practice. As SBCS First Deputy Chairman Vladimir Valach observed, "On 1st January 1990, development became much faster. The whole top management of the new federal Central Bank changed . . . I got the chance to be at the centre of an unrepeatable process of bank reform, of the ferment of seeking new routes, approaches and mechanisms."[68]

The SBCS researchers' immediate commitment to Western-oriented transformation was evident in the pages of *Finance a úvěr* (Finance and Credit), an academic journal jointly published by the SBCS and the Ministry of Finance. Its content changed dramatically after 1989, with articles appearing in 1990–92 on radical economic reform, monetary policy in the United States, and similar topics. It had long published parallel Czech and Russian tables of contents, but switched to Czech and English in 1991. During this period the journal also introduced a regular section on Finance and Credit Abroad, published a profile of Alan Greenspan, and reprinted large portions of Frederic Mishkin's textbook *The Economics of Money, Banking, and Financial Markets*. In short, top SBCS officials committed quickly to adopting the Western central banking model. The tasks that remained were to disseminate these ideas throughout the bank, to acquire the knowledge necessary to implement them, and to build the necessary technical infrastructure. The transnational central banking community jumped in wholeheartedly to assist.

The SBCS/CNB relied heavily on the community's hundreds of technical assistance missions and training programs in the 1990s.[69] In terms of technical

---

65. Czech National Bank 2003.

66. Author's interview with a senior official in the Monetary Section, Czech National Bank, Prague, Czech Republic, May 2000.

67. Velek 1996.

68. Valach 2004.

69. Czech National Bank 2003, Tůma 2004.

assistance, it had a resident IMF advisor and welcomed regular IMF general and specialized missions. For example, several special missions in the early 1990s advised the CNB in great detail on resolving problems with its monetary and banking statistics, such as rectifying classification errors in CNB banking analyses, dealing with inconsistencies in statistics compilation between departments, and generating IMF-compatible statistics. One mission would explain to CNB staff how to carry out a task, while a follow-up mission a few months later would check on the work they had prepared.[70] Similarly, after the Czechs liberalized their capital account in 1995 they called on experts from the Bundesbank and Banque de France for assistance in monitoring capital flows.

In terms of training, SBCS/CNB staff immediately began taking part in courses and study visits in central banks around the world. These efforts were intensive in the early years, with (for example) 54 staff members attending JVI courses, 114 attending CCBS courses, and 21 attending IMF Institute courses between 1992 and 1995.[71] But the sheer scale and persistence of training is most evident in the CNB's Human Resources Department 1997 and 1999 reports on training.[72] As table 5.1 demonstrates, from 1996 through 1999 Czech central bankers took part nearly 1,500 times in community study programs in Prague or abroad, totaling almost twelve thousand days of training. One report also broke down training by department, unsurprisingly revealing that the Monetary Department had the heaviest participation in courses taken abroad. With forty staffers taking courses in 1999, the number almost doubled that of the second-place department.[73] All of this exposure to the community's export model made its mark. For example, increasing international influence on CNB thinking is evident in the citation patterns in CNB working papers during the 1990s (table 5.2). While in 1992 over half of the papers' scholarly citations referenced Czech-language sources, by 1998–99 foreign-language citations (predominantly in English) represented over 75 percent of the total.

The case of Stanislav Polák, founder of the CNB's Economic Modeling Division, further illustrates the intensity of the international integration process for the Czech central banking elite.[74] Polák joined the SBCS's monetary division in

---

70. Author's interview with a senior official in the Balance of Payments Division of the Statistics Department, Czech National Bank, Prague, Czech Republic, May 2000.

71. Data kindly provided by the JVI, CCBS, and IMF Institute.

72. The Human Resources Department said that it misplaced its pre-1997 reports on training when the department moved during the CNB's building renovation.

73. Human Resources Department, "Hodnocení vzdělávání zaměstnanců ČNB v roce 1999 [Survey of the Educational Activities of the CNB in 1999]," mimeo, Czech National Bank, May 2000.

74. Author's interview with Stanislav Polák, director of the Economic Modeling Division, Czech National Bank, Prague, Czech Republic, May 2000.

TABLE 5.1 CNB participation in international courses, 1996–1999

COURSE TYPE	NUMBER OF PARTICIPANTS				NUMBER OF STUDY DAYS			
	1996	1997	1998	1999	1996	1997	1998	1999
Foreign-taught seminars at the CNB	198	122	90	191	698	359	288	205
Courses at other central banks (e.g., CCBS)	90	92	73	108	743	640	643	540
Courses taught at the JVI and IMF Institute	19	35	20	18	229	460	272	436
Long-term study tours (e.g., at CCBS, KC Fed)	6	2	4	4	1,382	197	722	289
Other courses taken abroad (inc. FSVC and courses or trips funded by PHARE, other EU sources, Know-How Fund, etc., many at foreign central banks)	107	154	97	55	953	1,535	795	346
TOTAL	420	405	284	376	4,005	3,191	2,720	1,816

Sources: Czech National Bank Human Resources Department, "Přehled a hodnocení vzdělávání zaměstnanců ČNB v r. 1997 [Survey of the Educational Activities of the CNB in 1997]" (January 1998) and "Hodnocení vzdělávání zaměstnanců ČNB v roce 1999 [Survey of the Educational Activities of the CNB in 1999]" (May 2000), mimeos.

TABLE 5.2 Citation patterns in CNB working papers

YEAR	NUMBER OF WORKING PAPERS*	CZECH-LANGUAGE ARTICLES CITED AS % OF TOTAL**
1999	9	22.2
1998	18	23.2
1997	17	26.7
1996	16	38.2
1995	17	40.1
1994	12	37.4
1993	9	45.8
1992	3	52.0

* Excluding papers on strictly historical topics, unavailable papers, and a paper on Hungary by a visiting Hungarian economist (six papers total). The number of working papers fell temporarily after the 1998 CNB reorganization and breakup of the Institute of Economics.

** Includes only research articles

1991, after university and military service. His boss immediately sent him to a CCBS course, which he said "was interesting for me because I knew almost nothing at that time about central banking." The IMF resident representative and the biannual IMF missions had an "important influence" as well, and confirmed that, "I needed a better background for my work." He subsequently took part in a three-month IMF Institute course in Washington, DC, in 1993, and then an intensive JVI course that began in Prague and finished with six months in Vienna. But, he said, "even six months wasn't enough." Through the Fulbright Commission, he arranged to spend the 1995–96 academic year at Cornell University. During this year, "because I wanted to see real life" on the study trip, he contacted Prakash Loungani in the International Finance Division of the US Federal Reserve Board and arranged to spend two months in Washington, DC, at the Fed. Using this knowledge, he helped to create the CNB's modeling division during the bank's organizational shake-up in 1998. Polák later became the head of the CNB's External Economic Relations Division and then in 2004 the Czech Republic's representative to the IMF.

While the CNB absorbed international ideas and practices like a sponge, the NBS received even more intensive and basic technical assistance and training. As Governor Marián Jusko observed in retrospect:

> We had no monetary department, no banking supervision department, and no reserves management department . . . we had to build whole new departments from scratch . . . we lacked any credibility . . . We got help from a few central banks and from a number of international financial institutions—the IMF, the BIS, the World Bank, and the European Bank for Reconstruction and Development. We sent our young people to special seminars organized by these institutions and they sent advisors to the bank . . . I have to thank the international financial community for their help.[75]

The IMF's Monetary and Exchange Affairs Department sent its first technical assistance mission to the new NBS in December 1992, before the official breakup of Czechoslovakia. This comprehensive mission team included three MAE officials (including the director), four West European central bankers, and a West European banking supervisor. PHARE and EBRD representatives accompanied the mission as well.[76] The mission entitled its comprehensive report simply "Slovak Republic: Development of the National Bank of Slovakia." The mission gave advice on all aspects of forming the NBS, including central banking law, monetary policy, statistics, foreign exchange operations, and banking supervision. This advice went into great detail, providing specific plans of action with suggested completion dates for development tasks in several areas. The mission also proposed extensive long-term cooperation with the NBS through a resident representative as well as expert visits and further IMF missions on more specific topics.

---

75. "Interview: Marián Jusko" 2000.
76. For a discussion of PHARE's early involvement in Slovakia, see De Smet 1998.

All of my interviewees at the NBS stressed the vital role that the IMF and central bankers from Austria, Finland, Germany, the United Kingdom, and France, among others, played in getting the new institution off the ground and running smoothly.

Similarly, the NBS had to train its new staff in the fundamentals of central banking. From 1993 through 1996, NBS staff took part 8,760 times in 1,362 training courses in Slovakia and abroad—an average of about eight courses for each NBS employee.[77] One central banker hired in July 1993 said that the NBS sent "almost everybody" in the monetary policy department to the JVI to take introductory crash courses in macro and microeconomics.[78] New staff also attended many basic courses at the CCBS, the Banque de France, the National Bank of Belgium, and the Banca d'Italia. In addition, with assistance from organizations such as USAID (through KPMG Peat Marwick), the US Treasury, and PHARE, the NBS set up an Institute of Banking Education.[79] In the words of the NBS director of human resources:

> The Institute of Banking Education ... cooperates with the most important institutes of banking education in developed countries and plays an intermediary role in spreading modern and effective banking products to both employees of the NBS and to other Slovak banking and financial institutions ... we try to make information from the banking sector accessible to our employees to the extent that their professional level will be comparable to the professional level of employees in central banks in developed countries.[80]

Nevertheless, as in the MNB and the CNB, my interviewees reported that the courses they took abroad made the most impact on their thinking and practices. For example, during her first three years at the bank one new hire participated in the most intensive JVI course, five CCBS courses, and courses at the Swiss National Bank, the National Bank of Belgium, the Banque de France, and the Federal Reserve Bank of New York. As she observed, "we started from the beginning and they told us everything ... step by step we created what we have now."[81] Such intensive international training and technical assistance allowed the NBS to catch up to the more privileged CNB quickly in many respects, despite the NBS's brand-new staff and less favorable political and economic conditions.

---

77. Kralik 1998.

78. Author's interview with an official in the Monetary Policy Department, National Bank of Slovakia, Bratislava, Slovakia, May 2006.

79. Garay 1998.

80. Kralik 1998.

81. Author's interview with an official in the Monetary Policy Department, National Bank of Slovakia, Bratislava, Slovakia, May 2006.

Convergence in Monetary Policy

The realm of monetary policy best demonstrates the transnational central banking community's influence in closing the initial gap between the CNB and NBS. Like the MNB, both the CNB and the NBS had developed strong reputations for monetary policy-making expertise by the turn of the century. Both also eventually adopted inflation targeting after beginning the postcommunist period with fixed exchange rate regimes. However, they reached this outcome from different starting points and through different paths. The CNB, confident in its abilities, developed its policies based as much on emulating international practice as on targeted assistance, while the NBS relied much more heavily on intensive, direct community advice and assistance in building its monetary policy-making capabilities. The CNB adopted inflation targeting soon after the May 1997 collapse of the Czech fixed exchange-rate regime, while with the community's help the NBS took a slow and steady approach to introducing new monetary policy instruments and more technically demanding policy regimes.

The SBCS/CNB strongly emphasized research from the beginning, and its highly skilled, internationally educated research team had an ongoing and fundamental impact on Czech monetary policy making. Until 1998 research took place primarily in the Institute of Economics, a semi-autonomous CNB division that brought together the country's leading experts on monetary policy (many of whom later became CNB board members and department heads). These researchers not only regularly took part in high-level community courses and workshops but, like modeler Stanislav Polák, also had typically studied economics at Western universities for at least six months.[82] When a CNB restructuring broke up the Institute in 1998, CNB divisions fought to acquire its personnel. Research continued informally in various departments, including the monetary division, the new modeling division, and a smaller research group until the CNB established the Economic Research Department in mid-2001.[83] These CNB researchers represented the key link between the community and the rest of the bank, encouraging their colleagues not only to adopt international standards,

---

82. Author's interview with a senior researcher in the Czech National Bank, Prague, Czech Republic, March 2000.

83. The ERD had an explicitly international outlook, writing: "a special concern is the study stays by foreign experts. They would be highly desirable to cultivate our internal research environment, to generate new impulses and, in particular, to provide professional guidance in those areas where we lack our own expertise. Such areas are currently especially financial markets and financial stability. The study stay of Mr. Aleš Bulíř who joined ERD from August 2002 through July 2003 was of great help. However, this took place only thanks to specific circumstances of his sabbatical leave from the IMF." Czech National Bank 2003.

but to begin to play a role in setting them. While this contributed to the CNB's rapid development and integration into the community, it also encouraged the CNB to occasionally adopt monetary policies too ambitious for the transitional economic environment.

The SBCS/CNB leadership, Czech government, and IMF were in agreement from the beginning about the need to fundamentally restructure the economy. In fact, Czech monetary and fiscal policies were "so radical at times that they kept even the Fund staff blushing."[84] The credit policies the three parties agreed on for 1990–91 aimed to almost completely restrict the creation of additional credit in the economy.[85] As such, the question was not whether to attempt to drive inflation down rapidly, but how. The SBCS/CNB had a two-pronged strategy between 1991 and mid-1996: maintaining the koruna's exchange rate against a basket of currencies within a narrow +/-0.5 percent band, and targeting the money supply. Although the MNB had rejected monetary targeting as too difficult in the uncertain transitional environment, the CNB argued that they adopted the strategy "based on the practice in the German Bundesbank, then undoubtedly the most highly respected central monetary institution."[86] The SBCS/CNB moved rapidly to using a variety of indirect tools to conduct monetary policy, eliminating direct credit controls in 1992. The CNB also gained great confidence from its smooth introduction of the new Czech koruna in 1993, stating that "the Czech currency separation scenario became part of a set of IMF recommendations . . . [and] won [the CNB] considerable credibility in the eyes of the public."[87]

Unfortunately for the CNB, its monetary policy ran into two problems. First, as even the CNB came to admit, the money supply and the inflation rate had no clear connection to one another in the transitional environment.[88] This rendered the CNB's monetary targeting ineffective in reducing inflation, which hovered between 8 and 10 percent from 1994 through 1997. Second, the dual strategies of maintaining the fixed exchange rate and targeting the money supply were fundamentally incompatible after the Czech Republic moved to current account convertibility and liberalized capital flows.[89] As the CNB itself put it in retrospect:

---

84. Drábek 1995.
85. Hrnčíř 1992.
86. Czech National Bank 2003.
87. Ibid.
88. *1995 Annual Report of the Czech National Bank.*
89. E.g., see Brada and Kutan 1999.

This monetary policy—based on market instruments—fell ever deeper into the "sterilisation trap." The foreign exchange interventions needed to maintain the fixed rate led to sharp growth in the money supply. To mitigate the inflationary consequences of this, it was necessary to absorb (sterilise) the surplus money from the market, which stimulated growth in interest rates. The higher interest rates led in turn to growth in the interest rate differential and hence to further inflow of capital.[90]

In a sense, the Czechs were done in by their own reputation as a radically reforming emerging market. Speculative capital rushed in to take advantage of the open Czech market, confident that conservative Czech monetary and fiscal policies would protect their investments. When emerging twin deficits forced the CNB to further tighten monetary policy in order to control inflation, rising interest rates brought in even more speculative capital. Then, the coincidence of the Klaus government's collapse with the Asian financial crisis in early 1997 shook investor confidence and led to a sharp May 1997 attack on the koruna that was not easily resolved and damaged the CNB's reputation.

However, because the May 1997 crisis precluded returning to a fixed exchange-rate regime, it gave the upper hand to CNB researchers who had become enamored of the emerging international trend of inflation targeting. These researchers strongly lobbied the CNB's board to adopt inflation targeting.[91] Although the still-uncertain relationship among the money supply, interest rates, and inflation in the Czech Republic made an inflation-targeting strategy problematic, proponents argued that its importance lay not so much in meeting the precise targets as in making monetary policy increasingly transparent and predictable.[92] The CNB board consequently decided to adopt this strategy in December 1997, without even consulting the Czech government.[93] In its 1997 Article IV consultation with the Czech Republic, IMF directors expressed mixed feelings about the CNB's choice. While many approved of the strategy, others expressed concern that the Czechs had adopted inflation targeting too early in the economic devel-

---

90. Czech National Bank 2003.

91. Kreidl and Tůma 1996; Šmídková and Hrnčíř 1998.

92. For example, see Miroslav Hrnčíř, "Klady nízké inflace převažují [The advantages of low inflation predominate]," March 11, 1998 and Jiří Pospíšil, "Čistá inflace je v pozornosti měnové politiky ČNB [Core inflation is in the sights of the CNB's monetary policy]," *Hospodářské noviny*, February 10, 1998. In addition, for a spirited defense of inflation targeting by a noted Czech economist, see František Vencovský, "Kupní síla koruny se stává prioritou [The purchasing power of the koruna is becoming a priority]," *Hospodářské noviny*, March 5, 1998.

93. Czech National Bank 2003.

opment process.[94] As it turned out, the CNB regularly missed its inflation targets for the first several years. Nevertheless, the CNB continually refined its inflation-targeting strategy and took great pride in having been the first postcommunist central bank to adopt it.

Unlike the CNB, the NBS had to take a step "backwards" with its monetary policy after the Czechoslovak breakup. Economic uncertainty, lack of credibility, few knowledgeable staff, and a highly underdeveloped banking sector forced the NBS to devalue the new Slovak currency by 10 percent and—with the IMF's blessing—revert to using direct credit controls for the first few years after its creation. During late 1992 and throughout 1993, the new NBS staff got a crash course in monetary policy making. They devoured the relevant books and started analyzing Slovak economic data with outside help. As one interviewee told me, "We used the IMF manual. [The IMF representative] helped us to . . . calculate the money supply . . . The time series were zero. The first numbers were also almost zero."[95] Deputy governor Elena Kohútiková summed up the NBS's experience in this way:

> The year 1993 was an extraordinary and very risky year. A completely new institution was created in Slovakia; its success and position depended on its ability to persuade the public of its efficacy. In the area of monetary policy, we had little experience in those times, but we were helped by experts from other central banks and the IMF. They helped us to understand the basic relationships, basic projections, the principles of monetary policy making, and to know which instruments were to be applied for its implementation. This period had a unique atmosphere. There was an extraordinary spirit of fellowship, we took pleasure in every success. I remember how happy we were when the foreign exchange reserves began to increase or inflation to fall.[96]

Over the next three or four years the NBS successfully managed the fixed exchange-rate system and gradually switched over from direct to indirect monetary policy instruments. In the process, it developed a strong reputation for independence and conservative monetary policy making, often in defiance of the Mečiar government. As the IMF resident representative to Slovakia during that period observed, "It has been most impressive to me that technical expertise

---

94. International Monetary Fund, Press Release, "IMF Concludes Article IV Consultation with the Czech Republic," March 6, 1998, www.imf.org/external/np/sec/pn/1998/pn9812.htm.

95. Author's interview with an official in the Monetary Policy Department, National Bank of Slovakia, Bratislava, Slovakia, May 2006.

96. Kohutikova 2000.

as well as macroeconomic policy capacity in the NBS are matched by an exemplary pursuit of the appropriate vision and goals for a central bank."[97] Although Slovakia did not face a currency crisis like the Czech one, the same difficulties of controlling inflation while maintaining a fixed exchange rate regime and liberalizing capital flows appeared. Ironically, the Slovak situation was better than the Czech primarily because international financial markets' distrust of the Mečiar government kept Slovakia from receiving extensive capital inflows in the 1990s despite the NBS's high interest rates.

In 1998 government spending before the September parliamentary elections and devaluation rumors prompted the NBS (with the IMF's approval, but not necessarily the government's) to float the Slovak koruna in October in order to give the bank more leverage over monetary policy.[98] The NBS had been quietly preparing to do this earlier in the year, with community assistance. For example, a top official in the monetary department reported that when the NBS considered floating the koruna in 1998, he asked Jusko if it would be possible to visit the central banks of Finland and Sweden to investigate the mechanics of doing so. As he put it, "The governor looked at me and said, 'next week I'm going to the BIS for a governors' meeting, I will ask them.' The week after that, I was flying to Helsinki and Stockholm."[99] The Finnish and Swedish central banks each prepared a week-long program for him on introducing inflation targeting, managing a floating exchange rate regime, and interest-rate management.

In developing its monetary policy strategies and tools, NBS leaders continually aimed toward international standards, in particular those of the ECB.[100] The NBS conducted an implicit inflation-targeting strategy through 2004. Although NBS policy makers had often discussed moving to a formal inflation target, they and their advisors concluded that policy transmission mechanisms had still not developed enough for formal targeting.[101] In 2005, the NBS judged the time ripe to adopt a formal inflation target. It set its long-term target at 2 percent, the level of the European Central Bank. IMF and CNB staff assisted the NBS monetary department in creating the medium-term model as well as the monitoring and forecasting capabilities necessary to implement inflation targeting.[102] In choosing

---

97. Georgiou 1998.

98. "NBS Is Waiting for a New Government, Its Program and Budget," Slovenska Tlacova Agentura, October 9, 1998; and "Central Bank Expects New Government to Strengthen Slovak Currency," BBC Monitoring European—Political, October 21, 1998.

99. Author's interview with a senior official in the Monetary Policy Department, National Bank of Slovakia, Bratislava, Slovakia, May 2006.

100. For example, see Jusko 1998, 2003.

101. Nell 2004, Reľovský 2004.

102. Gavura and Reľovský 2005.

this strategy, the NBS was influenced not only by the international turn toward inflation targeting in many high-profile central banks, but by the availability of appropriate technical assistance and by the CNB's promotion of inflation target-ing to the other regional central banks.[103] This strategy proved so successful for the NBS that Slovakia quickly became a leading postcommunist candidate for euro adoption, second only to Slovenia.

Government Reactions to CNB and NBS Policies

Although both the CNB and NBS started out with significant government support, controversial monetary policies and damaging banking crises soon engendered more antagonistic government-central bank relationships. Both governments eventually attempted to reduce their central banks' independence, the Slovak gov-ernment in 1997 and the Czech government in 2000. Both central banks fought these attempts vigorously, defending their internationally legitimized principles and practices in parliament and the press. In the end, neither government suc-cessfully undermined its central bank's legal independence during these episodes, primarily because of international pressures not to do so. While IMF influence played the key role in Slovakia, EU requirements did so in the Czech Republic.

In Slovakia, tensions between the NBS and the Mečiar government heated up in late 1996 when the NBS significantly tightened monetary policy after the government approved a budget for 1997 with a planned deficit of 3.7 percent of GDP. Although the government heavily criticized the NBS and appointed a former deputy finance minister to the NBS board in response, Governor Masár remained defiant, stating, "we are not stepping aside from our monetary goals."[104] In October 1997 the government, fed up with its uncooperative central bank, proposed amending the Act on the NBS to significantly reduce its independence. Amendments included requiring parliament to approve the NBS budget, raising the limit for NBS financing of the budget deficit through treasury bill purchases from 5 to 10 percent, and raising the number of banking council members from eight to ten (of which five would be appointed on the Finance Minister's rec-ommendation). The Mečiar cabinet approved the changes over Masár's protests, doing so while the governor was away on business in Indonesia.[105]

---

103. Poland and Romania, the other two large postcommunist EU member states, also adopted inflation targeting in 1999 and 2005, respectively. Both drew heavily on the Czech experience in the process.

104. Tatiana Vacova, "Slovak Central Banker Reaffirms Tight Money Policy," *Reuters News*, March 5, 1997.

105. *CTK Business News*, "Slovak Cabinet Ignores NBS Remarks on Amendment to NBS Act," October 1, 1997.

However, the Slovak parliament still had to vote on the amendments. Masár argued that the changes could threaten the stability of the Slovak koruna and that the NBS, as the only state institution with some autonomy from the government, should not be undermined.[106] Unmoved by Masár's concerns, parliament approved the amendments on its first reading on November 12, which sent the proposal to committee for further discussion.[107] At that point, everything changed. An IMF mission to Slovakia released a report on November 13 criticizing the proposed amendments. Masár went on the offensive, downplaying his earlier domestic political arguments and instead pointing out that the IMF and international rating agencies would react negatively toward Slovakia if the proposals passed.[108] In the debate in parliament right before the vote, Masár quoted directly and at length from the scathing IMF report.[109] He also noted that entry into the European Union required central bank independence. With Slovakia dependent on IMF loans, interested in international investment, and recently rejected as a prospective first-round postcommunist EU entrant, Masár's invocation of international opinion did the trick. Although Finance Minister Sergei Kozlik countered that "many instructions passed to us by important institutions . . . are not always applicable in countries that are undergoing transition," Masár's appeal raised enough concerns among the ruling party's two smaller coalition partners to stall the process.[110] Faced with dissent, parliament postponed the final vote until December.

Furious, Mečiar stepped up his attacks on the NBS, not only criticizing its monetary policy but blaming it for inappropriate supervision of the Investment and Development Bank (which the NBS had recently placed under forced administration) and for overspending on its lavish new headquarters building downtown.[111] He painted a picture of a rogue central bank out of control, one

106. Peter Laca, "Slovak Cbank Says Draft Threatens Crown Stability," Reuters News, October 6, 1997; "Slovak Central Banker Questions Reorganization Plan," Wall Street Journal Europe, October 7, 1997, 10.

107. Peter Laca, "Slovak Parl Votes Cbank Law to Second Reading," Reuters News, November 12, 1997.

108. "Slovak NBS Governor Urges Parl't to Reject NBS Law," Reuters News, November 21, 1997; "Parliament to Decide on NBS's Autonomy Next December," CTK Business News, November 21, 1997.

109. "Central Bank Chief, Minister Clash over Law Curbing Central Bank Independence," CTK Business News, November 24, 1997.

110. Ibid.; Peter Laca, "Decision on Crucial Slovak Cen Bank Law Postponed," Reuters News, November 21, 1997.

111. "Central Bank Responsible for Bank Crisis—Premier," BBC Monitoring Service: Central Europe & Balkans, December 24, 1997. The CNB was also criticized for the amount it spent on renovating its expansive downtown Prague headquarters, costing it public support.

that needed more government oversight to restrain its worst impulses. Nevertheless, Mečiar failed to persuade his party's coalition members. The smaller parties forced another vote postponement until February 1998.[112] At the same time, the NBS confirmed it would maintain a tight monetary policy in 1998, despite government pressures.[113] The proposed changes to the Act on the NBS, so heavily promoted by the Mečiar government, finally died on the vine. The next significant amendment to the Act, passed easily in April 2001 under a more sympathetic center-right coalition government and with an eye toward EU requirements, increased the NBS's independence by simultaneously raising its supervisory powers, changing its main goal from currency stability to price stability, and forbidding the NBS from financing the budget through treasury bill purchases.[114]

Like the NBS, the CNB in its early years avidly pursued monetary policy convergence with Europe and enjoyed relatively solid political support. However, the CNB's formerly secure status came into question after the May 1997 currency crisis. The ensuing political and economic turmoil contributed to the resignation of Prime Minister Václav Klaus (head of the center-right Civic Democratic Party, ODS) and his temporary replacement by CNB governor Tošovský in December 1997.[115] Tošovský, respected in Czech and international circles as ethical and highly competent, was generally regarded as a welcome choice to briefly run the country.[116] Tošovský led a caretaker government until the newly elected minority government of Miloš Zeman and his Czech Social Democratic Party (ČSSD) took power in July 1998. However, circumstances surrounding the 1997 events turned both Klaus and Zeman against the CNB. Klaus blamed the CNB's tight monetary policy for the 1997 crisis and his own political troubles, while Zeman blamed the same restrictive CNB policies for the Czech Republic's slow post-crisis recovery.[117]

As a result, in 2000 bitter political opponents Zeman and Klaus came together to attempt to reduce the independence of the central bank. In preparing an

---

112. "Voting on Controversial Amendment to NBS Act Postponed Again," CTK Business News, December 16, 1997.

113. Peter Javurek, "Slovak Cbank Sets Up Showdown with Tight 98 Policy," Reuters News, December 18, 1997.

114. Sobek 2003.

115. It was at this moment that the CNB took the opportunity to introduce inflation targeting.

116. For example, see "Finanční trhy na zvolení Josefa Tošovského zareagovaly kladně [Financial markets react positively to the choice of Josef Tosovsky]," *Hospodářské noviny*, December 17, 1997 and Josef Pravec, "Konečně krok vpřed [Finally a step forward]," *Hospodářské noviny*, December 17, 1997.

117. Klaus 2000, Bönker 2006. For an early example of the emerging political divisions over the CNB's monetary policy, see "Rozdílné názory na krok centrální banky [Differing opinions on the central bank's step]," *Hospodářské noviny*, June 26, 1995.

amendment to the Act on the CNB, Klaus's ODS party introduced new limitations such as requiring the CNB to set the inflation target in consultation with the government and to get parliamentary approval of its budget, as well as requiring governmental approval of the president's choices for the CNB governor and board. Visually capturing the moment, the May 29 cover of the Czech economic weekly *Euro* featured a doctored photo of Tošovský wearing studded leather restraints around his neck and hands, being pulled backwards on a chain presumably held by Klaus.[118] Zeman's government accepted the ODS proposals in June 2000. The IMF, ECB, and European Commission all spoke out against the draft amendment, as did the CNB and President Václav Havel. Nevertheless, the ČSSD and ODS-dominated parliament not only passed the amendment, but later overrode Havel's veto of it. The revised Act on the CNB took effect in January 2001. It briefly seemed as if central bank independence had suffered a devastating blow in the Czech Republic.

The influence of international institutions ultimately foiled Klaus and Zeman's efforts, however, as the CNB's protected constitutional status and EU accession pressures undid the amendment's constraints on the central bank. The first strand unraveled as Zeman unwittingly went too far in his pressure on the CNB. In November 2000, Tošovský resigned from the CNB in order to direct the Financial Stability Institute in Basel, and President Havel named Zdenek Tůma as his replacement. The Zeman government appealed Tůma's appointment to the Constitutional Court, arguing that it required governmental approval. In response, the Constitutional Court not only rejected the government's petition, but declared that the provision on appointments in the revised Act on the CNB violated the CNB's independence and was thus unconstitutional. The 1993 Constitution's protections for central bank independence, inspired by international experience and advice, thus successfully shielded the CNB from the government's legal challenges seven years later. In May 2002, under pressure from the EU—which argued that the other ODS-sponsored parts of the 2000 revised Act contradicted the *acquis*—a new amendment fully restoring the CNB's previous status came into effect.

To the chagrin of many Czech politicians, academics, and businesspeople, the CNB continued to keep a tight hold on monetary policy throughout this period of political turmoil. In a survey of articles in the leading Czech financial newspaper, Adam Geršl found that every single government comment published from 1997 through 2005 that expressed dissatisfaction with the CNB wanted the CNB

---

118. "Zákon o ČNB: Pokušení prof. Václava [Law on the CNB: The temptation of Prof. Vaclav]," *Euro*, May 29, 2000.

to ease monetary policy. Other interest groups sent similar signals: the financial sector (70%), employers (100%), unions (100%), and "others" (96.5%).[119] The CNB remained unmoved. In the end, the 2002 amended Act on the Czech National Bank protected the CNB's independence, changed its primary objective to price stability, and prohibited it from providing short-term credit to the government. Like the NBS, with external support the CNB emerged from this challenge strengthened in law but embattled in practice.

The Battle for the Euro

The two-track diffusion process meant that while Hungarian, Czech, and Slovak central bankers had embraced the transnational central banking community by the time their countries joined the European Union, many other domestic political actors had grown increasingly skeptical of the central banks' mandates and practices. To counter domestic opposition, the central bankers had relied on and became accustomed to receiving broad, consistent international support. Indeed, despite regular government criticism, attempts to undermine the central banks' monetary policies and legal status foundered when a united community weighed in on their new colleagues' sides.

Given this dependence on international pressures to maintain their domestic positions, Central and East European central bankers at the turn of the millennium feared that external support would no longer carry the same weight with their governments after EU accession. In response, the central bankers lobbied to adopt the euro as soon as possible after membership. They took this position out of weakness, not strength, viewing the external constraint of euro adoption and monetary subordination to the European Central Bank as the best way to ensure stable, conservative long-term economic policies in their own countries. The resulting battle for the euro impressively demonstrated the ideological commitment of the central bankers, the weakness of their domestic support, and their reliance on international pressures to keep their governments in line. But while the postcommunist central bankers saw euro adoption as vital at the time, divisions within the transnational central banking community over euro zone expansion meant that domestic political dynamics rather than

---

119. Geršl 2006. Geršl himself was an excellent example of Czech integration into the transnational central banking community. After completing his PhD at Charles University in Prague, he started his career in the CNB in 2001, went to work for the ECB in 2004, went back to the CNB in 2005, and then moved to the JVI in 2012.

international pressures determined the outcome in the new accession states. In Hungary, the Czech Republic, and Slovakia, the MNB and CNB's failures to win this domestic battle ultimately undermined their influence, while the NBS and its allies succeeded by cleverly manipulating political circumstances to circumvent domestic opposition.

Central Bankers Embrace the Euro

According to the terms of EU accession, new member states commit to entering monetary union once they have fulfilled the Maastricht criteria and received the official blessing of current EMU members. The key Maastricht provisions include achieving a "high degree of price stability," maintaining low and sustainable government debt and deficit levels, ensuring convergent long-term interest rates, and successfully participating in ERM II, the exchange rate mechanism of the European Monetary System. The European Commission and ECB interpreted these criteria to mean inflation rates no more than 2 percent above the average of the three member states with the lowest rates, a public debt less than 60 percent of GDP, a budget deficit below 3 percent of GDP, and participation in ERM II for at least two years. ERM II committed the member state to maintain a predetermined euro exchange rate within a fluctuation band of +/-15 percent. Therefore, the earliest possible date that a May 2004 accession state could have adopted the euro would have been May 2006, assuming entry into ERM II immediately upon EU accession. Table 5.3 illustrates the Maastricht criteria convergence status of the new member states as of 2006.

Only deep mistrust of their own governments could lead central bankers in the larger new member states to advocate rapid euro adoption so strongly. Although such a move made economic sense for the smaller new member states, it carried far greater risks for the Czech Republic, Hungary, Poland, and Slovakia.[120] First, joining the euro zone would mean sacrificing the central banks' control over monetary policy. They would become appendages of the ECB, committed to carrying out ECB policies designed for the EU as a whole and not necessarily suited to their domestic economic conditions. Second, premature euro adoption carried significant economic risks. George Soros, who profited so handsomely from the ERM's collapse in 1992, warned his native country not to join ERM II too early and leave itself vulnerable to speculators.[121] Many outside experts

---

120. Johnson 2008b.

121. See Economist Intelligence Unit, "Hungary: Euro Freaks," *Business Eastern Europe*, July 28, 2003; and Adriana Arai, "Czech Ctrl Bk Downplays FX Crisis Risk in EU Newcomers," Dow Jones, April 19, 2004.

TABLE 5.3 Euro zone convergence status of new EU member states, 2006

	GDP 2006 (EUR BILLIONS)	EXCHANGE RATE REGIME (IMMEDIATELY PRE-ERM II)	ERM II MEMBER	HICP 2006 (2001–2005 AVG.)	DEFICIT AS % GDP 2006 (2003–2005 AVG.)	DEBT AS % GDP 2006 (2003–2005 AVG.)	LONG-TERM INTEREST RATES 12/06 (12/05)
Reference values	—		2 years	3.0*	-3.0	60.0	6.4**
Poland	271.5	Float	No	1.3 (2.7)	-3.9 (-5.4)	47.8 (46.6)	5.14 (5.16)
Czech Republic	114	Managed float	No	2.1 (2.0)	-2.9 (-4.4)	30.4 (30.2)	3.68 (3.61)
Romania	97.1	Managed float	No	6.6 (18.3)	-1.9 (-1.5)	12.4 (18.7)	7.42 (N/A)
Hungary	89.9	Float	No	4.0 (5.8)	-9.2 (-7.2)	66 (59.7)	6.81 (6.89)
Slovakia (1/09)	43.9	Managed float	11/2005	4.3 (5.8)	-3.4 (-2.6)	30.7 (39.3)	4.15 (3.62)
Slovenia (1/07)	29.7	Managed float	6/2004	2.3 (5.5)	1.8 (-2.2)	29.1 (27.6)	3.8 (3.69)
Bulgaria	25.1	Currency board	No	7.4 (5.5)	3.3 (1.4)	22.8 (37.6)	4.18 (N/A)
Lithuania	23.7	Currency board	6/2004	3.8 (0.9)	-0.3 (-1.1)	18.2 (19.7)	4.28 (3.79)
Latvia	16.2	Euro peg	5/2005	6.6 (4.1)	0.4 (-1.0)	10 (13.8)	4.9 (3.59)
Cyprus (1/08)	13.5	Euro peg	5/2005	2.2 (2.5)	-1.5 (-4.3)	65.3 (69.4)	4.44 (4.09)
Estonia	13.1	Currency board	6/2004	4.4 (3.5)	3.8 (1.8)	4.1 (5.0)	N/A
Malta (1/08)	5.1	Basket peg	5/2005	2.6 (2.5)	-2.6 (-5.9)	66.5 (70.9)	5.18 (4.39)

Sources: ECB Monthly Bulletin and Statistics Pocket Books; May 2007 Convergence Report (reference values, April 2006–March 2007); May 2006 Convergence Report on Slovenia (Slovenian Maastricht criteria statistics).

Notes: Boldface values met euro zone entry requirements; boldface countries had joined the euro zone by 2009. Primary statistics are 2006 averages, except for Slovenia, Cyprus, and Malta (these figures come from the relevant Convergence Reports).

* Poland (1.5), Finland (1.3), Sweden (1.6) → Average 1.5, Reference +1.5%

** Poland (5.3), Finland (3.9), Sweden (3.8) → Average 4.4, Reference +2%

believed the risks to be high because the Central and East European states had significant investment needs as well as productivity and price levels well below the EU average.[122] Potential risks included entering the euro zone with an over-valued exchange rate and the inflationary impact of euro zone entry in the wake of high productivity growth in the traded-goods sector (the Balassa-Samuelson effect).[123] Moreover, allowing more time for financial market deepening, coordinating payment systems, working with EU statistical and accounting systems, and other elements of financial sector development would improve monetary policy transmission mechanisms and allow the central banks to more effectively implement the ECB's monetary policies. These problems—especially considering the euro's own instability at the time—should have dampened the central bankers' enthusiasm.

However, the postcommunist central bankers felt that only pursuing the goal of rapid euro adoption could force their governments to restrain their fiscal policies.[124] Top CNB officials from Governor Zdeněk Tůma on down regularly chided the government for not adopting more radical fiscal reforms, stating that it threatened the Czech Republic's ability to adopt the euro in 2007.[125] Similarly, as one Hungarian central banker put it, "euro zone convergence provides a unique opportunity for accession countries to abandon macroeconomic stabilization policies that suffer from weak credibility."[126] Tellingly, the postcommunist central bankers all strongly opposed flexibility in the fiscal Maastricht criteria and in the Stability and Growth Pact (which committed euro zone members to maintain the low deficits and debt required for euro zone entry). Most dramatically, in an August 2003 interview with the *Financial Times* the governors of the Czech, Hungarian, and Polish central banks all criticized the move by France and Germany to ease the Pact's rules. The MNB's Járai stated that, "this lack of discipline ... sets a very bad example for us," while the CNB's Tůma observed that, "we must have sustainable public finances. The EU club cannot afford to forget

---

122. Krenzler and Senior Nello 1999, Dumke and Sherman 2000, Égert et al. 2003.

123. Dumke and Sherman 2000, Kenen and Meade 2004, Vintrová 2004, Watson 2004.

124. The central bankers' actions echoed earlier efforts by Italian leaders to use EMU as a *vincolo esterno* (external tie) to overcome their domestic political divisions over economic policy (Dyson and Featherstone 1996, 1999). In Italy, however, central bankers and leading politicians worked together to apply the *vincolo esterno*, and did so in a context of relatively greater domestic support for independent central banks as institutions than in Central and Eastern Europe.

125. See "Central Bank Governor Pushes 'More Radical' Public Finance Reform," Interfax Czech Republic & Slovakia Weekly Business Report, January 24, 2003; "Czech c.banker warns reform delays threaten crown," Reuters, April 24, 2003.

126. Csermely 2004.

that . . . some rules must be respected."[127] Without the external constraint of EU requirements, the central bankers feared that their governments would ignore their own calls for fiscal rectitude.

The Hungarian, Czech, and Slovak central banks therefore recommended rapid euro adoption in the lead-up to accession, emphasizing the benefits and downplaying the risks. In early May 2003 Járai stated that Hungary ought to enter ERM II in 2005 in order to maintain the possibility of adopting the euro in 2007, opining that, "early euro adoption would have overwhelming benefits for economic growth and monetary stability."[128] MNB analysts argued that Hungary and the euro zone constituted an optimal currency area, and that euro zone membership promised lower transaction costs, increased foreign trade, and lower real interest rates.[129] The CNB also suggested 2007 as the Czech Republic's target entry date, most notably in the CNB's draft Euro Accession Strategy of December 2002.[130] Vice governor Oldřich Dědek in particular made the case for fast-track euro adoption, stating that, "while the benefits are obvious, the costs are in some ways both vague and embedded in an environment that is either archaic or hypothetical . . . the Czech Republic should adopt the euro as its currency as soon after accession to the EU as possible."[131] NBS analysts conducted similar studies arguing that the benefits of early euro adoption significantly outweighed the costs.[132]

The International Dissensus

Unfortunately for the postcommunist central bankers, the international support they had come to rely on in battles with their governments was not forthcoming. The transnational central banking community and other international financial authorities not only gave inconsistent policy advice regarding the euro, but their own actions and those of the "old 15" EU members undermined the euro zone's attractiveness. As a result, international actors lacked credibility with Central and

---

127. Andreas Krosta and Tony Major, "Central Banks Urge Adherence to Pact Budget Deficit Rules," *Financial Times*, August 29, 2003.

128. "Hungary's Ctrl Bk to Propose 2005 ERM II Entry—Paper," Dow Jones International, May 26, 2003.

129. Csajbók and Csermely 2002.

130. Czech National Bank, "The Czech Republic and the Euro—Draft Accession Strategy," December 23, 2002, https://www.cnb.cz/miranda2/export/sites/www.cnb.cz/en/monetary_policy/strategic_documents/download/cr_eu_231202_en.pdf.

131. See Dědek 1998, 2002, 2004: 45. Indeed, the one Czech central bank researcher who had consistently argued against early euro adoption, Stanislava Janáčková, retired from the CNB in 2000 and began working for President Václav Klaus. Janácková 2002, Janácková and Janácek 2004.

132. Šramko 2008.

East European governments on the interrelated issues of whether, when, and how to adopt the common currency.

Not only had there already been open dissent among West European countries about the euro, ECB policy, and the Stability and Growth Pact, but the United Kingdom, Sweden, and Denmark had been notable euro opt-outs.[133] In addition, international actors sent mixed messages to Central and East Europe on adoption timing. On the one hand, the IMF, OECD, World Bank, and international investors pushed the new-member states to quickly develop euro adoption strategies with firm time commitments.[134] Some outside central bankers and economists also advocated rapid adoption or even unilateral euroization.[135] On the other hand, many other foreign experts urged great caution and lengthy postponements.[136] Most important, the ECB itself discouraged the new-member states from pursuing rapid euro adoption. ECB president Jean-Claude Trichet argued pedantically that the new-member states were akin to young but underdeveloped athletes seeking to join a "champions league" before they were fit.[137] Given ongoing French and Italian criticism of ECB policy, the inability of even Germany and France to respect the Stability and Growth Pact, and its previous problematic experience with Greece prematurely entering the euro zone, the ECB was wary of bringing in new members who might be less than fully committed or able to adhere to the rules. As a consequence, the ECB used a strict interpretation of the Maastricht criteria to delay Central and East European states' euro zone membership. Compared with Greece's noncompliance with the convergence criteria prior to membership, for example, Lithuania's exclusion from joining the euro zone in January appeared arbitrary.[138]

International actors contradicted each other regarding the mandated process of euro adoption as well. The European Commission and the ECB insisted that the new-member states meet the Maastricht criteria to the letter before accession. Others criticized the criteria as too restrictive, especially the requirement

---

133. The United Kingdom and Denmark had legal opt-outs negotiated into the Maastricht Treaty. Sweden is under obligation to join but has so far chosen not to pursue ERM II entry.

134. Bönker 2006.

135. Schoors 2002, Eichengreen 2003, Breuss et al. 2004.

136. Krenzler and Senior Nello 1999, Dumke and Sherman 2000, Égert et al. 2003, Begg 2006.

137. Jean-Claude Trichet, "Looking at EU and Euro Area Enlargement from a Central Banker's Angle: The Views of the ECB," speech delivered at the Diplomatic Institute, Sofia, February 27, 2006, www.ecb.eu/press/key/date/2006/html/sp060227.en.html.

138. Lithuania missed fulfilling the convergence criteria because its 2005 inflation rate of 2.63 percent was marginally above that year's 2.6 percent standard. The Lithuanian government particularly objected to this judgement because the benchmark inflation rate for gaining euro zone membership at that moment—set in reference to the three EU states with the lowest rates—included Sweden, not itself a euro zone member. Lithuania did not join the euro zone until January 2015.

that the fast-growing prospective euro zone members both maintain very low inflation rates and remain in the ERM II pegged exchange-rate regime for at least two years. For example, an IMF report otherwise praising the ECB argued that, "the Maastricht criteria—specifically the inflation criterion together with the exchange rate stability criterion—could be overly binding for the CECs [Central-East European countries]."[139] Moreover, in the case of euro adoption the processes of central bank internationalization and Europeanization conflicted with each other. Best practice monetary policy in the transnational central banking community called for inflation targeting. Indeed, the ECB itself was an informal inflation targeter. Entering ERM II, however, would force inflation-targeting central banks in the new-member states to adhere to a less flexible peg.

In short, Central and East European governments felt relatively little international pressure on the euro issue because of the transnational community's inconsistent advice and actions regarding the desirability, timing, and mechanisms of adoption. This lack of consistency and credibility left the door open for wide-ranging domestic debates about the euro, battles that confident domestic policy makers, central bankers, academics, and interest groups were by that time relatively well-equipped to wage. Adding fuel to the fire, even two years after EU accession most Central and East Europeans still mistakenly believed that their countries were under no legal obligation to adopt the euro.[140]

Two Early Adoption Efforts Fail

Without effective international support, the Hungarian and Czech central bankers' efforts to restrain government spending by pressing for early euro adoption met with strong resistance. Their governments did not take the central bankers' proposed adoption dates seriously and actually increased their budget deficits and public debts in the immediate run-up to EU accession. Hungary's fiscal deficit widened from 4.2 percent of GDP in 2000 to 9.2 percent by 2002, and in late 2003 was still at 5.9 percent, well above the 3 percent Maastricht limit. Public debt in Hungary was at 55.7 percent of GDP in 2000 and had crept up near 60 percent by late 2003. While the Czech Republic's public debt remained safely below the 60 percent limit, its deficit went from 4.2 percent of GDP in 2000 to 6.7 percent in 2002, and had climbed to 7 percent by late 2003. This led to increasing tensions

---

139. Schadler et al. 2005.

140. Seventy-five percent of Poles believed this, while in no country was the percentage agreeing less than 50. "Flash Eurobarometer 195: Introduction of the Euro in the New Member States, 2006," http://ec.europa.eu/public_opinion/flash/fl191_sum_en.pdf.

between the central banks and the governments, and ultimately a loss of credibility and influence for the central banks.

In Hungary, Prime Minister Péter Medgyessy and the Hungarian Socialist Party (the MSZP) ultimately preferred to promote Hungary's economic "competitiveness" rather than adopt the more conservative policies favored by the MNB. The MSZP also viewed MNB governor Járai as a political opponent, since he had been appointed by the previous Fidesz government and had once served as its finance minister. Large deviations from the fiscal and inflationary commitments in Hungary's pre-accession Economic Program led to speculative attacks on the forint in January 2003, followed by a depreciation and downward readjustment of the exchange rate band in June. In July 2003 Hungary pushed back its planned euro adoption date to January 2008.[141] Within weeks the central bank again began accusing the government of not taking its commitment seriously, and in September Járai stated that while adopting the euro in 2008 remained a feasible goal, a "fundamental change in economic policies is needed."[142] The central bank suffered another blow when the deteriorating economic situation led to the January 2004 firing of Finance Minister Csaba László, a supporter of 2008 euro adoption.

Prime Minister Medgyessy then asked the new finance minister, Tibor Draskovics, to "review" the feasibility of the planned January 2008 euro adoption date. At the review's end in May the government and finance ministry set 2010 as the new target for joining the euro zone, with the central bank reluctantly "supporting" the decision.[143] Almost immediately the central bank began criticizing the finance ministry and the government again, saying that the proposed euro convergence program was too slow to meet the new target date.[144] Leading Hungarian business associations had earlier called for Járai's resignation and for legally making competitiveness instead of price stability the central bank's primary goal; by July 2004 the government and the finance ministry had also become united in their criticism of the central bank's monetary policies.[145] One

141. "Hungary to Introduce EUR from Jan 1 2008," Dow Jones International News, July 16, 2003.

142. "Central Bank Head Járai Urges Budget Reform Ahead of EU Accession," Interfax Hungary Weekly Business Report, September 29, 2003.

143. Christopher Condon, "Hungary Sets New Euro Entry Target," *Financial Times*, May 13, 2004; "Hungary Cenbank Says Supports New Euro Entry Plan," Reuters, May 13, 2004.

144. Economist Intelligence Unit, "Country Watchlist: Hungary," *Business Eastern Europe*, June 7, 2004; Interfax Hungary Weekly Business Report, "Further HUF 100–150 Billion Budget Cuts Needed, Says Járai—Converge Program 'Realistic,'" June 17, 2004; Tomos Packer, "Finance Minister Defies Central Bank Criticism," Emerging Markets Daily News, June 30, 2004; "Renewed Tensions Emerge Between Hungary's Government and Central Bank," WMRC Daily Analysis, June 29, 2004.

145. "Munkaadói kirohanás a jegybankelnök ellen [Employers are criticizing the governor of the central bank]," *Magyar Nemzet*, June 12, 2002; Sandor Peto, "Hungary Employers Want C.bank Chief to Quit," Reuters, December 5, 2002; and "Entrepreneurs' Alliance Warns Against Rush to Euro, Criticizes Tax Regime," Interfax Hungary Weekly Business Report, November 17, 2003.

MSZP leader opined that "the central bank should take the general state of the economy more seriously into consideration when making its decisions," while Draskovics blasted the central bank for focusing on "how weak we are and how [we] will not succeed."[146]

In August 2004 Medgyessy resigned and was replaced by Socialist Ferenc Gyurcsány, kicking off another wave of public warnings and recriminations among Járai, Draskovics, and the new leadership. Attempting to bring the MNB to heel, in December 2004 the Hungarian parliament amended the Act on the Magyar Nemzeti Bank to expand the size of the MNB's monetary council from nine to thirteen members. Although Járai deemed the amendment "uncultured, against the constitution, and against Europe," four new council members personally selected by Prime Minister Gyurcsány began their terms in March 2005.[147] The campaign to force the government to support the MNB's preferred monetary and fiscal policies through early euro adoption had failed, with the MNB's domestic support reaching a new low in its wake.

Remarkably, the situation for the CNB was even worse. After the CNB presented the government with its draft plan recommending euro adoption in 2007, months of discussion followed during which the CNB regularly criticized the government for badly missing its fiscal deficit targets and not taking the Maastricht criteria seriously.[148] President Václav Klaus, a long-time opponent of the central bank, hit back by criticizing the CNB's inflation targeting as "fiction" and stating that it would be "unwise" to adopt the euro.[149] In September 2003 the CNB and government agreed on a revised euro adoption strategy with an expected entry date of 2009–10, representing a significant loss for the central bank.[150] CNB governor Tůma skipped a subsequent cabinet meeting in which the new plan was to be discussed.[151]

Even this agreement proved unsustainable, and tensions grew as the government continued to spend in excess of the promised targets. Persistent high

146. Sandor Peto, "Hungary Fin Min, Cbank Bicker over Convergence Plan," Reuters, June 29, 2004; and "Hungary's Ruling Party Accepts EU Convergence Plan Terms," Dow Jones International News, July 6, 2004.

147. Miklós Blahó, "Járai: Kulturálatlan javaslat [Járai: An uncultured proposal]," Népszabadság, October 29, 2004 and Ben Aris, "Muddling Through Deficit Troubles," Euromoney, March 28, 2005.

148. See "Czech Cbanker Chides Govt for Slow Reform Progress," Reuters, March 28, 2003.

149. "Klaus Says Deflation in Czech Rep Not Good, Blames CNB," CTK Business News, April 22, 2003; "Klaus Calls Adoption of Euro 'Unwise,'" Interfax Czech Republic & Slovakia Weekly Business Report, August 1, 2003.

150. Czech Government and Czech National Bank, "The Czech Republic's Euro-area Accession Strategy," September 2003, https://www.cnb.cz/miranda2/export/sites/www.cnb.cz/en/monetary_policy/strategic_documents/download/en_eurostrategie_09_2003.pdf.

151. "Govt Puts Off Euro Strategy Talks on CNB Governor No-Show," CTK Business News, October 8, 2003.

deficits exacerbated by another spate of pre-election spending in mid-2006 finally forced a complete revision of the strategy in August 2007. Despite the protestations of Tůma and Finance Minister Miroslav Kalousek, the revised strategy did not set a new target date for euro adoption at all. Prime Minister Miroslav Topolanek refused to set a date because his tenuous center-right coalition government—with one hundred ODS deputies plus their smaller coalition partners facing off against one hundred ČSSD opposition deputies—could not ensure long-term compliance with its plans for fiscal reform.[152]

Not only did the CNB lose the political battle over early euro adoption, but domestic opponents undermined its pro-euro stance from within. President Václav Klaus revised the CNB board's membership when the terms of vice governor Dědek and members Pavel Štěpánek and Pavel Racocha ended in February 2005, adding three close allies and fellow Euroskeptics to the board.[153] Klaus did it again in November 2006, when he replaced two more outgoing board members with like-minded economists. Afterward only Governor Tůma and Vice Governor Niedemeyer remained from the seven-member board that had approved the CNB's initial ambitious euro strategy in 2002. Once on the board, the Klaus appointees publicly spoke with great wariness about the euro.[154] Faced with challenges from without and within, Tůma began to state simply that the timing of Czech eurozone entry would be "a political decision."[155] Like the MNB, the CNB suffered a loss of domestic influence and credibility during its failed battle for early euro adoption.

The Slovak Exception

Alone among the inflation-targeting new member states, the National Bank of Slovakia gained and maintained government support for its early euro adoption plan. While this would seem to demonstrate that Central and East European central bankers could win the euro battle without supportive international partners, a closer look reveals that Slovakia is the exception that proves the rule.

---

152. "Czech Euro Strategy Says Public Finances still Hamper Adoption," CTK Business News, August 27, 2007.

153. "Press—Klaus Prepares Shake-Up at CNB," Interfax Czech Republic Business News Service, August 16, 2004. Given that Klaus had led the earlier charge to require governmental approval of presidential nominees to the CNB board, his unilateral use of this power to alter the CNB's euro adoption strategy during his own presidential term appeared somewhat ironic.

154. For example, Mojmír Hampl urged caution and argued that successful euro adoption did not represent a meaningful measure of a country's economic health. "Czech Central Banker Urges Patience in Shift to Euro Zone," Dow Jones International News, October 19, 2007.

155. "Czech Ctrl Bker: Euro-Zone Entry Is Political Decision-Report," Dow Jones International News, November 5, 2007.

NBS governor Marián Jusko and his successor Ivan Šramko promoted an early euro adoption strategy for Slovakia by appealing to the same logic as their colleagues in the Czech Republic and Hungary, and similarly chastised the government when they felt that its fiscal policies did not support this goal.[156] Unlike the Czechs and Hungarians, however, Jusko and Šramko did so under an increasingly unpopular center-right coalition government that expected to lose power in the June 2006 elections. Faced with the likelihood of an incoming leftist coalition, the NBS and the government of fiscally conservative euro supporter Mikuláš Dzurinda effectively tied the hands of the future government by moving Slovakia into ERM II in November 2005, earlier than originally planned. In short, the NBS and the Dzurinda government united to pursue rapid euro adoption *despite* strong domestic opposition and inconsistent international support by entering Slovakia prematurely into ERM II.

By doing so, Dzurinda and the NBS found an alternative way to create the international pressure needed to force the incoming government to maintain conservative policies. ERM II entry locks a country into monetary and fiscal rectitude because it immediately becomes that country's central symbol of economic credibility to the outside world.[157] Entering ERM II provided the otherwise missing international influence necessary to maintain a steady path toward euro adoption, substituting the pressure of international financial markets for that of the transnational central banking community.

The post-election predicament of new Slovak prime minister Robert Fico and his center-left coalition demonstrated the force of the ERM II commitment. The moment Fico implied that Slovakia might consider postponing its euro adoption for fiscal reasons, currency speculators attacked the Slovak koruna, forcing him to reiterate Slovakia's commitment to the 2009 target date. This international pressure made Fico an unwilling supporter of Maastricht, as actually achieving euro-zone membership became the only way for him to regain any fiscal policy flexibility. Recognizing the pro-euro forces' deft maneuver, NBS governor Šramko received *The Banker*'s European Central Banker of the Year award for 2006. The magazine praised the early entry of the Slovak koruna into ERM II, describing it as "a shrewd approach ... to maintaining currency stability."[158] In short, in the Slovak case the unusual combination of a lame duck pro-euro

---

156. "Slovakia Should Join EMU as Soon as Possible—NBS," CTK Business News, June 4, 2003; "NBS Governor Thinks Parliament's Pro-Reform Mood Has Weakened," Slovenska Tlacova Agentura, February 26, 2004; "Euro Introduction No Cause for Concern, Says NBS Governor," Slovenska Tlacova Agentura, March 23, 2006.

157. Frieden 1997.

158. The Banker, "Central Banker of the Year/Europe," January 2, 2006.

governing coalition and the alternative international credibility provided by ERM II ultimately led to Slovakia successfully adopting the euro in January 2009. Only serendipitous circumstances and clever policy allowed the NBS to avoid the fate of the MNB and CNB.

Central Bankers under Pressure

With their old economic paradigm shattered and a desire to regain "European" status, Central and East Europeans turned West for advice and support after the fall of communism. The transnational central banking community, for reasons of its own, answered that call. The transformation campaign integrated the Hungarian, Czech, and Slovak central banks into the community in less than a decade. Not only did these central banks accept international assistance, but they also proudly became assistance providers themselves, with the Czechs leading the way. For example, the CNB hosted the first JVI seminar held outside of Vienna, a seminar on monetary policy that I attended in May–June 2000 featuring a speaker from the IMF, four speakers from West European central banks, and nine speakers from the CNB. Participants came from Poland, the Baltic states, Bulgaria, Hungary, Slovakia, and the CNB itself.[159] In 2002 the CNB started organizing its own technical assistance seminars, inviting other central bankers to the CNB to hear about the Czech approach to monetary policy, statistics, financial stability, and many other topics. As Czech governor Tůma put it, "The Czech National Bank was receiving a lot of help from foreign central banks and international institutions. Today, we are at the level of state-of-art and we do not receive but provide foreign technical assistance. We assist a number of countries directly and our experts are invited to IMF missions around the world."[160]

This assistance provision grew over time. The CNB and Bundesbank jointly worked on an EU twinning project in 2012–13 to help the National Bank of Serbia develop its HR department, for example, while the CNB's chief modeler Tibor Hlédik travelled throughout the region helping other postcommunist

---

159. As a side note, some rivalry among the Baltic central bankers became apparent during the course. At lunch one day the Latvian participants claimed that the Estonians only adopted a currency board because they did not have anyone who understood monetary policy. Later, in a presentation, the Lithuanians said that the only reason Estonia's currency board had not collapsed was because of timely intervention by Swedish owners of Estonian banks. The Estonian central bankers predictably reacted sharply to these charges.

160. Zdeněk Tůma, speech delivered at the CMC Graduate School of Business, December 4, 2004, Prague, www.cnb.cz/www.cnb.cz/en/conferences/speeches/tuma_cmcgraduation04122004.html.

central banks develop their modeling capabilities. Central bankers I spoke with in Albania, Kosovo, and Macedonia in 2014 all lauded Hlédik for his sustained assistance with their models; many said that they now even preferred to work with community members like Hlédik, because colleagues from more advanced postcommunist states better understood their challenges and constraints.[161] MNB modelers worked with these countries as well, and the MNB began offering courses at its own Budapest School for Central Banking Studies in 2009 that brought in noted economists to discuss modeling and macroeconomics.[162] Even the smaller NBS began regularly to provide technical assistance, signing formal bilateral cooperation agreements with the central banks of Ukraine and Belarus, and participating in several ECB-sponsored multilateral assistance efforts. With the gradual transition from assistance recipients to providers, the Central and East European central banks solidified their membership in the transnational central banking community.

Indeed, in a short period of time the community had drawn the Central and East European central bankers into their wormhole network. This process reinforced the postcommunist central bankers' identities as independent promoters of price stability, but without effectively generating more widespread domestic support for these institutions and their guiding principles. As Central and East European governments became increasingly aware of the policy implications of central bank independence as well as secure and self-confident enough to pay less attention to outside advice, relations with their central banks often became more conflictual. The central banks' rapid transformation brought problems of internalization to a head.

As a result, although many Central and East European central bankers gained enormous stature at the international level and became full members of the transnational central banking community, in some respects their domestic policy influence actually began to wane. This uncertain domestic support encouraged central bankers to press for euro adoption faster than many politicians and the

---

161. Focus groups at the Bank of Albania, Central Bank of the Republic of Kosovo, and the National Bank of the Republic of Macedonia, conducted with Leonard Seabrooke, Cornel Ban, and the author in June 2014.

162. In 2014 the MNB bought a 1.3 million euro luxury resort property in Tiszaroff that it planned to use for its training courses and staff retreats. Once this became public the MNB came under fire from the Socialists for engaging in wasteful spending; it was also the topic of a critical *Financial Times* blog post. See Kester Eddy, "Company Resort Makes Its Comeback at Hungary's Central Bank," *Financial Times* Beyond BRICS blog, August 11, 2014, http://blogs.ft.com/beyond-brics/2014/08/11/company-resort-makes-its-comeback-at-hungarys-central-bank/? See also the MNB's entertaining response to the blog post at http://english.mnb.hu/mnben_pressroom/press_releases/mnben_pressreleases_2014/mnben_pressrelease_20140815.

ECB preferred, and faster than was economically advisable. Without consistently effective tools to address inflation and with price stability threatened by increasing budget deficits, they turned to the Maastricht criteria and the euro to attempt to restrain their governments' fiscal policies. Neither the CNB, facing a center-right government, nor the MNB, facing a center-left government, ultimately succeeded in persuading their governments to stay on the early adoption path.

The central banks failed in their early adoption efforts precisely because they could no longer count on the international pressures and support that had enabled them to overcome previous challenges. The CNB and MNB fought on their own, lost, and suffered significant blows to their credibility. The National Bank of Poland and, later, the National Bank of Romania had similar experiences.[163] Alone and exceptionally among the larger Central and East European states, Slovakia managed to enter the euro zone in 2009 by trading the discipline of international financial markets for that of the transnational community. These battles for the euro foreshadowed the even greater difficulties that the central bankers in the new member states would face after 2008, when the global financial crisis and the European sovereign debt crisis hit their domestic economies hard, destabilized the euro zone, and fundamentally challenged the Western central banking model itself. But before turning to the crisis and its aftermath let us move further east to explore the fate of the transplant model in rockier soil: Russia and Kyrgyzstan.

---

163. Epstein and Johnson 2010.

THE TRIALS OF POST-SOVIET CENTRAL BANKERS

"Technical assistance teaches us to speak the language of a market-oriented economy. It fills us with the sense of unity with the international community of central banks."

—Aleksandr Khandruev, Bank of Russia (1994)

The Bank of Russia inspired the book that you are now reading. I spent much of the 1990s researching and writing a book on Russian banking after the Soviet collapse, an era that Russians describe with the telling word *bespredel*—without limits.[1] Fortunes were made and lost, corruption and criminality ran rife, uncertainty reigned, and indeed, everything and anything seemed possible. These years saw the rise of the so-called oligarchs, the band of wealthy commercial bankers who loomed so large over the political system that prominent academics and policy makers spoke of Russia as a captured state.[2] Both wealth and political power became concentrated quickly and jokes about the "New Russians" of Moscow with more money than taste, empathy, or ethics proliferated.

Yet amid the thievery, the venality, the political instability, and the Soviet-era norms and practices that made Russia very nearly the last place one might expect to find Western-style institution building, I noticed something that I could not explain. The Bank of Russia, the massive bureaucratic heir to the Soviet Gosbank, seemed to be changing faster than it had any right to under the circumstances. In less than a decade, an institution rooted in the Soviet command economy had transformed first into a zealous defender of its independence and then into an inflation-averse, technically skilled central bank. Moreover, it had developed a

---

1. Johnson 2000.
2. For example, see Hellman 1998 and Hellman et al. 2003.

reputation as one of the least corrupt and most professional Russian government institutions. One international advisor put it well, saying that, "I trust the Central Bank of Russia much more than any other Russian institution, although this is because everything is relative."[3] The Bank of Russia went from being a thorn in the side of the international community to having, albeit with some exaggeration, "totally bought into the international consensus."[4] When I looked around, it turned out that the same could be said for most other postcommunist central banks, particularly in more politically open states. My search for answers led me to the transnational central banking community.

Although no one will mistake central banks in the former Soviet Union for the Czech National Bank any time soon, the scope of post-Soviet central bank transformation was arguably more dramatic, and certainly more unexpected, than in Central and Eastern Europe. Apart from the tiny, EU-oriented Baltic states, post-Soviet central banks began and remained in a much more difficult position than their former comrades to the west. They faced greater internal obstacles to transformation, such as high turnover in skilled positions, language barriers, and command-era organizational cultures. They had to deal with the legacy of a much older and more deeply embedded command economy, a shared Soviet-era currency, a dual monetary circuit in which cash and credit circulated separately and not interchangeably, extensive dollarization, and scores of parasitic yet influential new "commercial" banks that had proliferated due to botched liberalization policies in the late Soviet era. These central banks had to find their own way in the international system as well, as Russia represented the strongest regional influence and EU membership was not in the cards. In essence, they had far more to do and far less with which to do it. The transnational central banking community stepped in to close this gap with its training and technical assistance programs. Its efforts brought the central banks to which it had access much closer to international norms and practices than other surrounding post-Soviet institutions.

This chapter explores the community's role in the transformations and troubled internalizations of the Bank of Russia and the National Bank of the Kyrgyz Republic (NBKR). As the central bank of the largest, the wealthiest, and the most geopolitically important Soviet successor state, the Bank of Russia received a disproportionate share of international attention and assistance. Although the Bank of Russia itself gradually transformed along Western lines, the slow pace of complementary institution building, advising mistakes in the 1990s, and an

---

3. Author's interview with a senior international technical assistance provider, November 2001.
4. Author's conversation with a former Bank of Canada official, May 2008.

increasingly authoritarian government made its work difficult and often coun-terproductive. As the central bank of a small, resource-poor state in Central Asia, the NBKR presented a fundamental challenge to the transnational central banking community. With early and consistent community access but unstable domestic conditions and few internal resources, the NBKR's experience starkly demonstrated both the possibilities and the limits of internationally driven insti-tutional transplantation.

Heir to Empire: The Bank of Russia

The careers of two long-time Russian central bankers, Viktor Gerashchenko and Andrei Kozlov, epitomize the multi-layered and contradictory transformation of the Bank of Russia. Gerashchenko, a wily Soviet-era operator nicknamed "Ger-akl" (Hercules) for his resilience and seeming ability to do the impossible, first served as head of the Soviet Gosbank before becoming Bank of Russia governor from 1992 through 1994 and again from 1998 through 2002. Battered by chal-lenges from all sides, he fought to maintain the Bank of Russia's political inde-pendence while at the same time initially remaining skeptical that it should con-centrate primarily on fighting inflation. In frustration, US advisor Jeffrey Sachs notoriously and unfairly labeled him the "world's worst central banker."[5] By the time he left office in late 1994, Gerashchenko's experience with Russian mone-tary crises and regular exposure to the transnational central banking community had convinced him that the Bank of Russia should pursue a more conservative monetary policy. He never did come to believe, though, that it should undertake serious banking reform, in great part because he felt that the Bank did not have enough political support to carry it out. Brought back to head the Bank of Russia after the 1998 financial crisis, Gerashchenko was forced out for the final time in 2002 in the midst of a battle with President Vladimir Putin over protecting the Bank's independence.

In contrast to Gerashchenko, Kozlov represented the new generation of Rus-sian central bankers who quickly adopted the twin mantra of independence and price stability. Elevated to a position on the board while only thirty years old, he forged close ties with the transnational central banking community during the development of the Russian treasury bill market in the 1990s and led the Russian division of the Financial Services Volunteer Corps while between posts at the Bank of Russia. Upon returning to the Bank of Russia in 2002 he took

---

5. *The Economist*, "The World's Worst Central Banker," October 16, 1993, 78.

on the immense challenge of overhauling banking supervision in order to bring the unruly Russian commercial banking system to heel. Unfortunately, both of Kozlov's major professional efforts ended badly. The first Russian treasury bill market collapsed in 1998, destroyed by a government that essentially turned the market into a pyramid scheme and by a misplaced effort to maintain the ruble's value in the face of the Asian financial crisis and collapsing commodity prices. Kozlov's banking reform efforts came to an even more devastating conclusion. After successfully fighting to shut down a number of shady banks and to introduce a deposit insurance system in Russia, contract killers gunned Kozlov down outside a Moscow sports stadium in 2006. He was forty-one at the time.

This section thus focuses on two intertwined trends. First, it demonstrates the community's pivotal but also problematic role in the Bank of Russia's embrace of the international central banking model. The Bank of Russia's entrenched culture, immense size, and unusually challenging economic and political environment meant that the community had to work much harder to persuade Russian central bankers and to transform the Bank. The Bank of Russia had inherited its own Soviet-era training centers and certain alternative norms and practices. One consequence was the Bank's initial adoption of a self-serving interpretation of central bank independence divorced from the usually corresponding belief in the primacy of price stability. Advising missteps by the community also undermined its authority in the 1990s, most notably the IMF's initial support for maintaining the ruble zone. The Bank of Russia's embrace of independence, price stability, and banking reform emerged sequentially rather than as a whole, based on both persistent community exposure and adverse experience.

Second, it documents how the Bank of Russia's ideas and practices came into conflict with other Russian domestic forces, most notably the government and commercial bankers. Although most commercial bankers resisted Bank of Russia policy consistently through the post-Soviet era, the government flip-flopped between promoting more orthodox monetary and fiscal policies than the Bank of Russia in the early 1990s to eventual opposition to the Bank's increasingly mainstream international views. The end result was a Bank of Russia better integrated into the transnational central banking community, but less politically independent after President Vladimir Putin consolidated power in Russia.

Transforming the Bank of Russia

The IMF made Russia its top priority in the 1990s and continued regular consultation after its active lending programs ceased in 2001. It prioritized Russian membership in 1992, granting Russia an individual, constituency-free seat on the IMF executive board and an unusually large 3 percent quota given Russia's relatively weak economic position at the time.[6] The IMF set up a full-time staff in Russia, and both the European II Department (after 2003 the European Department) and the Monetary and Exchange Affairs Department were heavily involved in advising. Through 2001 the IMF sent five or six high-level missions to Russia each year—with monthly missions in 1995–96—and provided sixty-three person-years of technical assistance, much of which went directly toward transforming the Bank of Russia.[7] The IMF also worked with the EU's TACIS program to coordinate several major training projects that brought foreign experts to the Bank of Russia and sent Russian central bankers abroad.

The Joint Vienna Institute, the Centre for Central Banking Studies, and the IMF Institute each trained more central bankers from Russia than from any other postcommunist country, with the CCBS leading the way.[8] According to the Bank of Russia, in the late 1990s it was sending at least two hundred to three hundred staff per year for training courses outside Russia; many IMF and national central bank experts came to Russia to give courses at the Bank's own training centers as well.[9] The Bundesbank did its most intensive work with Russia in terms of both training and technical assistance.[10] In fact, the Bank of England and the Bundesbank both enthusiastically started working with Russian central bankers as early as 1990, well before the IMF arrived.[11] The Banque de France had a special relationship with the Bank of Russia as well, sending numerous long-term advisors through the IMF and conducting regular seminars for the Bank, including at the Bank's own training facilities. Many smaller national central banks were involved in training and technical assistance too, as was the Financial Services Volunteer Corps, US Agency for International Development, the World Bank, the European Bank for Reconstruction and Development, and other international agencies.

---

6. Momani 2007.

7. Odling-Smee 2004. He wrote further, "In the four peak years, May 1992 to April 1996, nearly 6 percent of the IMF's worldwide TA effort was devoted to Russia. In the early 1990s, well over half of the technical assistance to Russia was devoted to the development of the [Bank of Russia] as a modern central bank."

8. The JVI trained 552 Bank of Russia staff from 1992–2013, the CCBS 993 from 1990–2005, and the IMF Institute 209 from 1989–2006. Data provided by the JVI, CCBS, and IMF Institute.

9. Manukova 2001.

10. By mid-2001 the Bundesbank had "held 49 seminars in Russia attended by over eleven hundred participants. In addition, 243 Russian specialists have visited the Bundesbank on study trips," Bundesbank president Ernst Welteke, "Speech to the Central Bank of Russia," March 2001, Moscow, Russia. From January 2000 through November 2007, the Bundesbank had conducted 188 separate activities for the Bank of Russia ranging from short-term technical assistance to larger training programs. Data supplied to the author by the Bundesbank TZK.

11. Author's interview with a former senior official in the Bank of Russia, Moscow, Russia, June 2006.

The United States, perhaps naturally given its Cold War history, paid more attention to Russia than to any other postcommunist country, and the Russian government returned the compliment. Even before the Soviet collapse Yeltsin sought out US officials, arranging to meet quietly with US Federal Reserve Board chairman Alan Greenspan, former chairman Paul Volcker, and New York Federal Reserve president Gerald Corrigan at the White House in June 1991 in order to learn more about the Federal Reserve.[12] Yeltsin and Corrigan formed a quick bond, facilitating early cooperation between the two sides. The US Federal Reserve, the FSVC, the US Treasury, and USAID worked closely with the Bank of Russia, especially in the 1990s. In sum, Western central bankers and financial experts came in droves to help transform the Bank of Russia.

The Bank of Russia was not an easy partner for the transnational central banking community, especially in the early years. In interviews many community members referred to the Bank of Russia as an "imperial" central bank; tellingly, with the Bank of Russia they used the phrase technical cooperation instead of technical assistance from the very beginning so as not to offend. Russian authorities saw themselves as the successors to the Soviet superpower and insisted on being treated as equals or better. Bank of Russia leaders often refused to delegate key tasks, creating bottlenecks that made change more difficult even when it was desired. The bank also had a deep-seated hierarchical, bureaucratic, and secretive culture, the so-called Gosbank mentality. Reflecting upon his start at Gosbank in 1989, Andrei Kozlov remembered internalizing the Gosbank mind-set and how hard it had been afterward to change it, despite his relative youth.[13] Some staffers, especially older ones, resisted that change. The bank also experienced extensive turnover in the late 1980s and early 1990s as many of the best-qualified staff left to make their fortunes in the newly lucrative commercial banking system. This had a short-term negative effect as the most knowledgeable officials abandoned the Bank; however, it also gave more open-minded central bankers in their twenties and early thirties the chance to rise quickly to important positions.

Beyond Russia's own imperial history, the Bank of Russia was an empire unto itself. The largest central bank in the world, it had between 60,000 and 80,000 employees, over 80 assorted regional offices, and nearly 500 cash settlement centers during the two decades after the Soviet collapse.[14] This unwieldy, immense

---

12. Author's interview with a senior official of the Federal Reserve Bank of New York, New York City, December 2001.

13. Author's interview with Andrei Kozlov of the FSVC and Bank of Russia, Moscow, Russia, March 2002.

14. See www.cbr.ru/today/Default.aspx?PrtId=tubr. In 2014 the Bank of Russia opened two additional branches in Crimea. For staff and branch numbers, see the Bank of Russia annual reports.

structure resulted in a status and cultural division between the Bank's headquarters and branches. The headquarters on Neglinnaya street in Moscow had only 2,000–4,000 employees in total, much closer to the size of a typical postcommunist central bank. The regional branches, however, had many thousands of employees dispersed across the vast Russian expanse who were responsible for banking supervision and cash operations in their territories. The Bank of Russia also had its own central personnel training center, a network of fourteen banking schools, an interregional training center in Tula, and three regional centers providing training to branch staff. While many Bank of Russia staff at headquarters had economics degrees, most regional staff did not. Few in either headquarters or regional branches read or spoke English, either, as Russian had been the dominant language of Soviet finance and key specialist journals such as the Bank's own *Deng'i i kredit* (Money and credit) and the domestic academic journal *Voprosy ekonomiki* (Questions of economics) were published in Russian.

Moreover, as discussed in chapter three, in the late Soviet era both the Soviet and Russian governments had increased the legal independence of their central banks during their tug of war over Russia's financial resources. This political battle for sovereignty provided few incentives (and indeed, some significant disincentives) for the central bankers to increase their technical capabilities or to stop funneling cheap credits to state enterprises. Instead, Gosbank and the Bank of Russia competed to offer easier registration and lighter regulation to the rapidly proliferating commercial banks. As a result, when the Soviet Union collapsed and the Bank of Russia swallowed Gosbank, Russia had a relatively independent central bank but one whose institutional framework, internal culture, and technical capabilities had otherwise changed little.

The Bank of Russia jealously defended its independence and regularly invoked international practice in doing so. Yet it was independence with two unusual characteristics. First, the post-Soviet Bank of Russia leadership initially acted in the service of its traditional mission, financing enterprise and bank activity. Western advisors like Jeffrey Sachs mistook such policies as indications of political subordination because they assumed that independent central banks would be natural inflation hawks. But as liberal economist and former prime minister Yegor Gaidar pointed out in his memoir, the Bank of Russia's behavior accurately reflected its own institutional preferences.[15] Second, the Bank of Russia sought to protect its autonomy both domestically and internationally in ways that did not follow the Western playbook. Its wariness regarding transparency and advice, its embrace of capital controls during the 1998 Russian financial crisis, and its use

---

15. Gaidar 1999. For a more detailed account, see Johnson 1999.

of a Jersey-based bank called FIMACO to hide Russian hard-currency reserves from foreign creditors in the 1990s reflected the Bank of Russia's willingness to defy international actors as well as domestic ones. It wanted to be part of the transnational central banking community, but on its own terms.

These characteristics colored the relationship between the community and the Bank of Russia, making the bank's transformation and community integration lengthier and more complicated than in Central and Eastern Europe. Although he kept a certain personal distance from the community, Gerashchenko himself was usually not a barrier to international training or technical assistance, and he often spoke positively of international experience and models. As early as 1989, in response to a question criticizing his frequent reference to foreign examples, he said that "Indeed, I am not bound by the experience and habits of working in the environment of the administrative-command system . . . how is it bad if we want to create an efficient banking system corresponding to economic restructuring in our country on the basis of world experience?"[16] Top Bank of Russia officials recognized early on that the bank needed to take "serious action to strengthen the professional staff."[17] Nevertheless, the Bank of Russia had its internal fiefdoms, with certain areas and departments more open to community advice than others. As one experienced donor put it, "there are people there who are not our friends."[18] The Bank of Russia's institutional culture and strong sense of independence also meant that it had better relationships with other national central banks than with the IMF, upon which it was dependent for money and whose approach often rankled as coercive, prescriptive, and insensitive to Russian conditions. Russia's own importance to the IMF and to the United States also meant that the IMF could not credibly threaten the Bank of Russia with strict conditionality, and so had to rely even more than usual on persuasion and socialization.[19]

The Bank of Russia's size, needs, assertiveness, and internal divisions encouraged it to make unfocused, overlapping, numerous, and ongoing demands for training and technical assistance programs from multiple sources. The Bank of Russia staff took little the community said on faith; donors repeatedly told me that Russians needed to see and experience practices concretely before they were willing to adopt them. The Bank of Russia could engage in bricolage as well,

---

16. *Izvestiia* interview with Viktor Gerashchenko, "Gosbank Head Sees Need for Central Bank," October 5, 1989, printed and translated in FBIS-SOV-89-201, October 19, 1989, 97.

17. Interview with Vladimir Rassakov, deputy chairman of the Bank of Russia, on the *Parliamentary Herald* television program, December 3, 1991, printed and translated in FBIS-SOV 91-235, December 6, 1991, 60–62.

18. Interview with a senior official of a European national central bank, April 2006.

19. See Stone 2002 for a fuller discussion of the IMF's coercive limitations in Russia.

borrowing slightly different technical practices from various central banks and putting them together to create a "Russian" version, often to ill effect. Several interviewees mentioned the evolving payment system as a key example of this phenomenon. At times the Bank of Russia made seemingly tangential requests, such as when it asked the ECB to send trainers to Moscow to give staff a one-week course on euro adoption. Russia's perceived importance encouraged the transnational central banking community to accede to these demands when possible but also to create organizational tools through which to channel and manage them.

The Bank of Russia staff's initially weak English meant that training programs and materials had to be translated for many years, while the Bank's importance meant that community members often did provide this service. Still, many courses and networking opportunities took place in English and thus excluded non-English-speaking Bank of Russia officials. Central and East European central bankers reported that when staff from the Bank of Russia and other post-Soviet central banks took courses at the JVI, CCBS, and elsewhere they sometimes socialized primarily with each other in Russian rather than mixing more broadly. This language barrier made integrating Russian central bankers into the community a slower and more limited process, as the younger and better-educated staff at headquarters gradually learned English while the older and regionally based staff generally did not. The Bank of Russia's size exacerbated the effect, as headquarters staff could regularly take advantage of community programs abroad while the more numerous and far-flung regional officials could not. Over time this solidified the Bank of Russia as two central banks in one—a transformed headquarters integrated into the community network and its more distanced regional affiliates.

Nevertheless, despite these barriers, energetic Bank of Russia officials and the intensive, persistent, and consistent efforts of the community eventually did substantially reform the Bank along international lines. As one knowledgeable insider observed, "There is a quiet revolution going on [in the Bank of Russia]. Russian professionals [in the Bank] are discovering how institutions in what they quaintly call the civilized countries—i.e. mature market economies—work. This discovery is no accident. Western governments, institutions, and individuals have all leapt to help. The building blocks of a proper central bank are being put into place"[20] Andrei Kozlov concurred, telling me in 2002 that the Bank of Russia had become "one of the most developed and advanced institutions in the country," albeit with some distance still to go. On the donor side, the IMF's John Odling-Smee lauded the "transfer of knowledge" that took place, saying that "what came

---

20. Special correspondent 1994/5.

out of it were . . . a large number of officials and experts with a fine understanding of macroeconomic policy issues . . . This has ensured that the [Bank of Russia] and the government as a whole now design and manage macroeconomic policies in ways recognizably similar to those in western industrial countries."[21] Other community members with whom I talked agreed, saying that despite the challenges and the frustrations, in the end the Bank of Russia earned a strong international reputation as a technically skilled central bank that took inflation fighting seriously. Yet as always with Russia, the story is more complicated than initial analysis might make it seem. To see why, I turn to the transformation of monetary policy making and banking supervision in the Bank of Russia.

The Bank of Russia and Monetary Policy

The Bank of Russia's advisors in the 1990s concentrated on convincing its leadership to focus on inflation reduction and on helping the bank to develop new tools to conduct monetary policy. Both of these efforts succeeded. However, community members at the time, particularly in the IMF, did not fully appreciate the bank's limited control over the money supply, the weakness of monetary policy transmission mechanisms, or the implications of the poor coordination between the Bank of Russia and the government. This led to advice on the ruble zone that would make it impossible for the bank to fight inflation, to the development of a securities market that turned into a government pyramid scheme rather than a tool of monetary policy, and to the introduction of an exchange rate regime that cost the Bank of Russia billions to attempt to defend. More than anywhere else in the postcommunist world, early community advice had unexpected and adverse consequences in Russia.

From the IMF's perspective, its main success from 1992 through 1995 was persuading the Bank of Russia to take inflation seriously. In January 1992 the Russian government of President Boris Yeltsin and Prime Minister Gaidar liberalized prices, unleashing a predictable wave of hyperinflation. People quickly spent down the monetary overhang accrued in Soviet times when scarcity rather than price had rationed consumption, and a cash and liquidity shortage developed. Russian companies raised prices and granted each other increasingly larger, unrepayable credits, creating what became known as the inter-enterprise debt crisis.[22] Achieving macroeconomic stabilization would have required Russia to

---

21. Odling-Smee 2004.
22. Ickes and Ryterman 1992.

starkly limit new government spending and money creation. Two barriers to this plan became immediately apparent: Bank of Russia governor Viktor Gerashchenko did not agree with the strategy and the bank could not fully control the flow of money.

Even though Gaidar himself had nominated Gerashchenko to succeed Grigorii Matiukhin in mid-1992, Gerashchenko and Gaidar were at loggerheads over policy almost immediately. As Gaidar explained:

> Once confirmed by the Supreme Soviet, Gerashchenko promptly showed himself to be a highly qualified manager and a forceful organizer ... But a single negative factor canceled all this out, and this was that Viktor Vladimirovich was unable to comprehend what should have been axiomatic for bank management during an inflationary crisis. He sincerely believed that accelerating the growth of the money supply by issuing more currency would straighten out the economy ... Changing the mind of someone with deeply rooted, firmly fixed notions about the interconnections within a free market economy is not easy ... Pursuing a stabilization policy when the head of the country's chief bank does not accept the very essence of that policy is a remarkably unproductive business.[23]

For his part, Gerashchenko argued that the "young reformers" substituted book knowledge for a substantive understanding of the Russian economy, saying "I considered the liberalization of prices—[a policy] that Gaidar lifted from Poland—to be fundamentally wrong ... Poland is not Russia. They could carry out the process much more easily. In our country ... leaving enterprises without credit in conditions of ever-increasing prices was suicidal."[24] The government and Bank of Russia traded accusations of sabotage as government spending began to increase after an initial pause and after Gerashchenko in effect created 1.2 trillion rubles of new state credit in July 1992 by wiping out the inter-enterprise debts that had accrued.[25] The inter-enterprise debt crisis had brought the economy to its knees, illustrating that the Bank of Russia could not yet control the domestic money supply. After canceling the debt the Bank of Russia eliminated

23. Gaidar 1999.

24. Interview with Viktor Gerashchenko, "Viktor Gerashchenko: Iz-za togo, chto ia postoianno rugal Kudrina, mne ne dali personal'nuiu pensiiu [Viktor Gerashchenko: Because I constantly berated Kudrin, I was not given a personal pension]," *Odnako*, March 21, 2011, www.odnako.org/almanac/material/viktor-gerashchenko-iz-za-togo-chto-ya-postoyanno-rugal-kudrina-mne-ne-dali-personalnuyu-pensiyu-1/.

25. See Johnson 2000 for a more detailed discussion of Bank of Russia policy making in the 1990s.

the Soviet-era accounting mechanism that had allowed it to build up in the first place, but continued to use its autonomy to issue credits faster than the IMF or government preferred. Gerashchenko defended his actions by declaring that a cash shortage did in fact exist and that enterprises needed to be financially supported during the transition.

Just as significantly, the existence of the ruble zone made it impossible for the Bank of Russia to bring inflation down rapidly even if it had wanted to do so. At the time of the Soviet breakup other newly independent post-Soviet states still used the ruble, and they were not brought on board with Russia's liberalization and macrostabilization plan. Even though the Bank of Russia controlled the printing presses, the other central banks could—and many did—increase the money supply by granting ruble credits to their state-owned enterprises. They could—and many did—also issue parallel currencies to circulate with the ruble. The Bank of Russia supported retaining the ruble zone, but only if Russia could gain sole authority over the money supply. The IMF initially not only wanted to maintain the ruble zone, but to do so in a way that would grant ruble-zone members shared decision-making power over emissions. Put bluntly, this made little sense, and the IMF was criticized for its recommendation.[26]

As with euro adoption in Central and Eastern Europe, the transnational central banking community's model did not include whether or how to maintain a currency union; this issue fell outside the script and generated no international consensus. Only once the Bank of Russia began to assert its monetary sovereignty in November 1992 by refusing to accept non-Russian credit rubles to settle Russian accounts did the IMF's position move in favor of independent currencies.[27] The Bank of Russia unilaterally dealt the final blow to the ruble zone in July 1993 by circulating new ruble notes within Russia while invalidating the old ones. The ruble-zone break up would likely have been earlier, less costly, and more coordinated if the IMF had assisted rather than delayed the process in Russia. The IMF's reputation suffered in Russia because of this mistake.

Between 1993 and 1995 a potent combination of community socialization, IMF conditionality, and policy learning through adverse experience eventually led to macroeconomic stabilization in Russia. As Bank of Russia official Aleksandr Khandruev noted at a conference:

> [one key] example of productive cooperation between the Central Bank of the Russian Federation and the IMF in the area of monetary control

---

26. Granville 2002, Aslund 2002.
27. Odling-Smee and Pastor 2002.

is the Central Bank of the Russian Federation's gradual increase in the refinancing rate to market levels in mid-1993. This move was preceded by thorough preliminary work and a series of intensive consultations between the top leadership of the Central Bank and the Moscow office of the IMF.[28]

Bank of Russia officials such as Dmitrii Tulin, Andrei Kozlov, and Tat'iana Paramonova, influenced by Western economic theories and community advisors, began to express more inflation-averse views. Even Gerashchenko himself gradually moved in that direction as well. Successive emission-related economic shocks, in particular "Black Tuesday" when the ruble's value fell almost 30 percent on October 11, 1994, solidified opinion within the central bank that too-loose monetary policy did at that point have a negative impact on the economy. Gerashchenko acknowledged his responsibility for Black Tuesday by tendering his resignation in November 1994, to be replaced as acting director by his protégée Paramonova. Donors reported a significant transformation in the Bank of Russia through 1994–95 under Paramonova and then under new governor Sergei Dubinin, as its staff began to understand open market operations, grasped the role of monetary policy committees, and learned to read Bloomberg data screens. Kozlov, remembering this time, remarked that the IMF and other community advisors pushed the Bank of Russia to analyze monetary policy in "Western ways." For example, the IMF asked the Bank of Russia staff to draft Russia's monetary policy memoranda themselves, but insisted that it be done using Western standards and methods. In sum, Bank of Russia officials both began to accept the community's principles and to learn its technical practices.

At the same time, the IMF, the FSVC, the Federal Reserve Bank of New York, and USAID consultants worked with the Bank of Russia and other Russian officials to create new short-term treasury instruments known as GKOs (short for *gosudarstvennye kratkosrochnye obligatsii*). Kozlov's team visited New York and Chicago to learn how to create the technical infrastructure for a securities market and then applied these lessons in Russia. First introduced in 1993, GKOs allowed the government to raise revenue without tapping the Bank of Russia and gave the bank a new instrument for open-market operations. By 1995 the government was financing the lion's share of the budget deficit through GKOs and inflation had stabilized at moderate levels. With the IMF's encouragement the Bank of Russia then introduced a "ruble corridor" in July 1995 that promised to lock the ruble-dollar exchange rate within a tight band. The Bank of Russia's credibility

---

28. Khandruyev 1994.

rose and it was better able to hire strong economists. As one community member observed, by 1997 the Bank of Russia had "caught up with the times," was eager to learn how to do things, and was not surprised by change.[29]

However, the initial success of the GKO market and ruble could not be sustained. Russian government spending vastly outstripped tax revenue, and Yeltsin's team began to rely on ever-increasing sales volumes of high-yielding GKOs to fill the gap. For their part, the leading Russian commercial banks enjoyed preferential access to the GKO market and came to rely on it for profits, resulting in GKOs crowding out enterprise lending and stifling financial deepening while the noncash economy (barter and corporate IOUs called *veksels*) increasingly dominated Russian economic activity outside the financial sector.[30] Once the government opened the GKO market to foreigners in 1996, speculative capital rushed in as well. Scandal then shook the GKO market in spring 1997 when USAID admitted that its securities-market consultants from the Harvard Institute for International Development had improperly used their insider positions for personal financial gain.[31]

The Asian financial crisis and falling world oil prices finally brought the GKO pyramid and the ruble corridor crashing down together. In November 1997 about $5 billion fled the GKO market in the wake of the Asian crisis; the GKO and stock markets both continued to tumble in subsequent months.[32] The Bank of Russia attempted to restore confidence by guaranteeing the ruble corridor through at least the year 2000. For the Russian government, the flight from GKOs threatened its solvency and raised the yields it had to offer, while the drop in commodities prices cut into its already meager tax revenue. Meanwhile, the Bank of Russia introduced capital controls and hemorrhaged billions in US dollar reserves trying to maintain the ruble's value. An emergency IMF stabilization loan in July 1998 could not stem the tide. In August, the ruble corridor collapsed and the government defaulted on its GKOs. Russia had lost the GKO market, its foreign exchange reserves, and its ruble corridor all at once.

As Gerashchenko complained later, "It was unreasonable and unrealistic to announce a three-year trading band in late 1997. This decision was sheer stupidity."[33] The IMF later admitted the folly of the fixed exchange rate regime and may

---

29. Author's interview with a senior official in the transnational central banking community, November 2001.

30. Woodruff 1999.

31. Wedel 1998.

32. Dmitry Zaks, "Russia's Biggest Stories of 1997," *Moscow Times*, December 30, 1997.

33. Interview with Viktor Gerashchenko, "Vokrug rublia [Regarding the ruble]," *Argumenty i fakty* 39, 1999.

even have been advocating its loosening by late 1997. Nevertheless, the regime had originally been introduced based on IMF advice and the resulting ruble stability in 1995–97 shaped market behavior and expectations such that the Bank of Russia would have incurred significant costs even if it had abandoned the corridor earlier instead of doubling down. The crisis experience in Russia and elsewhere also forced the IMF to rethink its previously strong line against capital controls.[34] Far from causing trouble, capital controls had shielded countries like Russia and Malaysia from experiencing even worse damage from the financial crisis.

Finally, as the IMF's Martin Gilman noted in retrospect, "the whole opening of the GKO market to nonresidents in 1996 was intended to provide the government with a deep and broad financial capital market to lower the yield so that it could have access to less expensive capital. But it was all predicated on the idea that the budget was going to be brought under control."[35] On this point Gerashchenko agreed with the IMF, writing after his post-crisis return to the Bank of Russia that "the fundamental problem" with the GKO market had been the government's exploitation of GKOs to avoid solving its budgetary dilemmas.[36] They were absolutely right, but given Russia's underdeveloped tax collection infrastructure, barely restructured enterprises, parasitic commercial banks, endemic corruption, political infighting, and social services commitments, serious budget reductions were not in the cards in the 1990s. Moreover, earlier reforms had done little to address the Russian state's heavy reliance on oil and gas revenues, leaving Russia vulnerable to budget catastrophe when world oil prices fell. In sum, while the IMF and the rest of the transnational central banking community did much to transform the Bank of Russia along Western lines and get inflation under control in the 1990s, certain core policy prescriptions proved misguided, premature, or inappropriate for Russian conditions.

Nevertheless, the Bank of Russia bounced back from the crisis to reaffirm its commitment to the transnational central banking community. It ramped up its demands for training and technical assistance in the monetary policy realm less than a year after the crisis occurred and re-declared its allegiance to the twin principles of independence and price stability. Through successive training

---

34. Abdelal 2007, Chwieroth 2009.

35. Martin Gilman, "Russia's Challenges in the 1990s: An Interview with Martin Gilman of the IMF," Washington Profile News Agency, December 3, 2002. Martin Gilman was the IMF senior resident advisor in Moscow from 1997 to 2002. For Gilman's interesting book-length dissection of the 1998 crisis, see Gilman 2010. On the crisis of 1998, see also Illarionov 1999, Sapir 1999, Slay 1999, Dmitriev and Vasiliev 2001.

36. Gerashchenko 1999.

programs with multiple community members, Bank of Russia staff became highly skilled in modeling and inflation forecasting.[37] The Bank of Russia also adopted a range of measures to increase its transparency, including better and more regular publications as well as moving toward international financial reporting standards. Comparing Bank of Russia publications from the mid-1990s and the mid-2000s is like comparing a single AMC Gremlin to a fleet of Toyota Corollas. The difference in quantity and quality is simply astonishing, and reflected systematic modeling of techniques and styles (even, in some cases, fonts) from IMF and other central bank publications. Bank of Russia statements and actions also came more and more to resemble those of the transnational central banking community. Meanwhile, the 1998 crisis and Vladimir Putin's rise to power in 1999 had tamed the oligarchs, rebounding world oil prices filled the government's coffers, and Gerashchenko's contested departure in 2002 led to less central bank independence but better coordination among the Bank of Russia, the Finance Ministry, and the Putin government.

Between the 1998 and 2008 crises, the Bank of Russia's main challenge was to balance its increasingly orthodox desire to fight inflation with the government's insistence that it maintain a stable ruble. High oil prices and US dollar depreciation began to put upward pressure on the ruble, threatening Russian exporters. Following the government's orders, the Bank of Russia began to buy dollars and print rubles, running its foreign exchange reserves up to record levels and spurring moderate annual inflations of 10–12 percent. From 2002 on the IMF complained regularly about the Bank of Russia's attention to ruble stability and blamed the government for pressuring the Bank. The Bank of Russia indeed would have preferred to focus more on inflation and less on the exchange rate, but direct requests from President Putin, the absence of meaningful domestic support, and the government's disinterest in listening to IMF advice once it had no need for loans forced the Bank of Russia to compromise. Oleg Vyugin revealed the Bank's frustration with its incompatible inflation and exchange rate mandates as soon as he left to head the Federal Financial Markets Service in March 2004, immediately denouncing the "protectionist" monetary policy that he himself had so recently been in charge of carrying out.[38]

The Bank of Russia had few tools with which to square the circle of lowering inflation and maintaining exchange-rate stability. Its refinancing rates had little impact as they were well above interbank rates, commercial banks already

---

37. Author's interview with a senior Bank of Russia official responsible for monetary policy, June 2006.

38. Alex Fak, "Vyugin Raps Central Bank's Ruble Policy," *St. Petersburg Times*, April 16, 2004.

complained about its high reserve requirements, and significant ruble appreciation might attract more outside capital to Russia and exacerbate the inflation
problem. In addition, the government itself boosted inflation on a regular basis
through its spending, through raising administered prices, through trade protec-
tionism, and through monetizing benefits, meaning than even moderate ruble
appreciation might not lower inflation. Dollar depreciation in the run up to the
global financial crisis put pressure on the ruble as well, making the situation even
more complicated for the Bank of Russia.

Under these conditions, throughout the decade the Bank of Russia regularly
declared its intention to pull inflation down to the single digits and then failed to
do so. This increased its interest in moving toward a formal inflation-targeting
regime, with director Sergei Ignatiev declaring as early as 2005 that the Bank
of Russia had already introduced elements of the policy.[39] In pursuing inflation
targeting the Bank of Russia worked closely with IMF economists and with the
Bank of England, and translated CCBS director Gill Hammond's 2006 handbook
on inflation targeting into Russian to help guide its transformation. By the time
the global financial crisis hit Russia in 2008, the Bank of Russia had finally raised
reserve requirements and declared its intention to allow greater ruble volatility
in the first official steps toward inflation targeting.[40]

The Bank of Russia and Banking Supervision

Although nearly everything that could go wrong did go wrong with banking
supervision in Russia, any discussion must first acknowledge the enormity of the
Bank of Russia's post-Soviet challenge. The Soviet breakup left Russia with 1,360
commercial "banks" of various sizes, shapes, and solvency, a number that grew
to nearly two thousand in the next few years. These banks made their money
primarily through political patronage, connected lending, currency trading, and
other speculative and downright illicit activities. The introduction of national,
regional, and local elections allowed Russia's bankers to enter the political system
as campaign financiers, lobbyists, and even candidates. Institutional deficiencies,
such as the lack of a treasury system, encouraged state agencies to place their
funds in commercial banks in a process that became heavily politicized. The cash-
strapped Yeltsin government turned regularly to the banking system for funds.
The government could even justify these policies by arguing that its support for
(and dependence on) the banks contributed to the development of capitalism in

---

39. *Kommersant,* "Central Bank Sees a Drop in Inflation," October 15, 2005.
40. Catrina Stewart, "Inflation Threatens an Era of Growth," *Moscow Times,* May 30, 2008.

Russia. Russia's commercial banks thus enriched themselves in the 1990s while simultaneously becoming estranged from both enterprises and households.

Supervising such a banking system would test central bank officials even in an advanced market economy. In Russia, the Bank of Russia's numerous regional offices bore the primary supervisory burden. Bank of Russia leadership and banking supervisors on the ground inherited a Soviet-era attitude toward supervision, insisting on paperwork, formalities, and deference while turning a blind or ignorant eye toward the banks' rapidly evolving, creative, and financially risky activities. At the same time, before the 1997 Asian crisis the transnational central banking community did not make supervision a top priority. This mutual lack of interest and the inherent difficulty of reform made the Bank of Russia supervisory structure slow to evolve. USAID stepped in to offer a supervisory training program from 1994 through 1996, but as a contractor hired to carry it out admitted, "it was not designed the way it should have been designed, but it was what the Russians were willing to accept."[41] He further elaborated that:

> In Russia, we were limited to the outside of the central bank, and that wasn't even in the same building, to do training out of a textbook. Ordinary, generic training about supervision to a large mass of people who would run through month after month after month. So at the end of this training, you could add up the numbers and have retrained two thousand bank examiners. [But] they were retrained in the classroom. In every one of the other countries, we might have done classroom training for a week followed by four weeks of on-the-job training and a bank examination, showing them how to use those same tools. In Russia we never did that. I wanted to, but the Russians didn't accept that.

Beginning in 1996 the Bank of Russia became more open toward having international advisors work with supervisors on the ground, so at that point the US Federal Reserve and FSVC started sending short-term advisors to consult on specific aspects of banking regulation and supervision. The EU sponsored a TACIS program for banking supervisors in the 1990s as well, with a similar model to the unsuccessful USAID one. Program evaluations noted the mismatch between the Western concepts taught and the reality of Russian conditions.[42]

These years saw the Bank of Russia step up its regulatory efforts, but often in ham-handed ways. To give just one example, the IMF suggested that the Bank of Russia reduce the banks' lending limit for single borrowers, and it did so. But the

---

41. Author's interview with a senior consultant, Washington, DC, November 2001.
42. For example, see US General Accounting Office 2000.

implementation made unnecessary enemies. As one FSVC veteran told me, "The handling of existing loans had not been discussed with the IMF. If it had been, IMF advisors would have had no problem making accommodation for loans already on the books. However, the central bank went ahead forcing banks to cancel loans already made, with serious consequences to the borrowers and the banks' credibility with their customer base."[43] In 1995 Bank of Russia officials began to pull licenses from troubled banks, but considered that the end rather than the beginning of the resolution process. A long-time Russian auditor concurred that the Bank of Russia "took its regulations from international textbooks, but without any real understanding," and pointed out that its directives from 1997 through 1998 included text translated directly from the Basel accords.[44]

This approach encouraged commercial bankers to evade and undercut the central bank. When I asked commercial bankers in the 1990s about their attitudes toward the Bank of Russia, many just shrugged their shoulders and gestured toward impressive mounds of CBR directives piling up on their desks. For their part, Bank of Russia supervisors often became cynical in the face of endemic Russian corruption and political pressures. Community members mentioned Russian supervisors who were educated and knew all of the Basel principles, yet felt powerless to do anything in their country. By the 1998 Russian financial crisis, the Bank of Russia had promulgated many and overlapping regulations in its efforts to mimic international practice, but had yet to develop a cadre of effective supervisors and received little political support for sanctioning troubled yet well-connected banks.

The August 1998 crisis forced the Bank of Russia, the Russian government, and the transnational central banking community to focus more serious attention on bank regulation and supervision. This crisis hit Russia's commercial banks hard. Between July 1998 and December 1998, the list of the top fifty Russian banks by assets changed by one-third. By threatening the political power of the largest banks, shaking up the financial system, and boosting the competitiveness of domestic enterprises through ruble devaluation, the crisis provided an opportunity to restructure the commercial banking system. It also brought Russia full circle as the banking system once again came predominantly under state control at both the regional and national levels. Not only did the Bank of Russia put several banks under its own administration, but Sberbank also resumed its earlier position as Russia's near-monopoly savings bank. International and

43. Author's correspondence with an FSVC volunteer and former Federal Reserve official, August 2001.

44. Author's interview with a Russian audit firm director, Moscow, Russia, June 2006.

domestic pressures eventually led the Bank of Russia to gradually divest itself of most commercial bank ownership. It retained control over Sberbank, though, both because Sberbank represented an immense asset (its nickname was the Ministry of Cash) and because a botched privatization or restructuring could destabilize the Russian financial system.[45] This is an instance in which the Bank of Russia acknowledged the international norm—central banks owning commercial ones is a conflict of interest—and simply defied it as not appropriate for Russia at the time.

Initial reform efforts after the 1998 crisis seemed unpromising, as the Bank of Russia and Russian government failed to prevent commercial bankers from inappropriately shifting assets and spent millions bailing some out. In November 1998 the Bank of Russia and the Yeltsin government created ARKO (the Agency for the Reconstruction of Credit Organizations) to handle bank restructuring. Despite the appearance of action, ARKO had insufficient power to deal with the banking crisis. The Bank of Russia and ARKO quickly got into disputes over which banks to rescue, and in general neither stood in the way of the post-crisis redistribution of funds. Vladimir Putin's rise to power in 1999 and subsequent taming of the remaining defiant oligarchs, however, completed what the crisis had started and for the first time lent the Bank of Russia political support for undertaking banking reform. Realizing the massive, unresolved problems in the Russian banking system, in December 2001 the Bank of Russia and the Putin government adopted, after much disagreement and political maneuvering, a joint five-year strategy for banking sector development.[46] The departure of Viktor Gerashchenko (again) in March 2002 ushered in a new leadership team and brought Andrei Kozlov back to the Bank of Russia. With Kozlov put in charge of reforming the commercial banking system, things started moving more quickly. Kozlov arrived determined to introduce a deposit insurance system, force banks to switch to International Financial Reporting Standards (IFRS), and to consolidate the banking system by cracking down on problem banks.

Kozlov drew on his international connections and two major transnational community assistance projects in conducting his campaign. First, at Russia's invitation the IMF conducted a Financial System Stability Assessment in 2002–3. The IMF-led team included advisors from the South African Financial Supervisory Authority, the Bundesbank, the Bank of Finland, the World Bank, the Hungarian Financial Supervisory Authority, and the Bank of England. The report backed

---

45. Tompson 1998b.
46. "O strategii razvitiia bankovskogo sektora Rossiiskoi Federatsii [On the strategy for the development of the banking sector of the Russian Federation]," *Kommersant daily*, January 14, 2002.

Kozlov's plans to create a deposit insurance system, to introduce IFRS, to tighten capital requirements, and to move toward risk-based supervision. On the latter issue, the report delicately but pointedly stated that, "although the [Bank of Russia] has developed an early warning system, the analytical work done by the off-site supervisors still concentrates on the completeness of the reports and the compliance with the prudential standards (rule and ratio-based), but not on the underlying risk reflected in the reviews."[47] The Bank of Russia and the FSAP team jointly devised a stress testing methodology for Russian banks during work on the assessment, and the team's recommendations helped Kozlov finally push through a deposit insurance law in December 2003. Its passage had been preceded by lengthy hearings during which the FSVC brought in top officials from the US Federal Deposit Insurance Corporation and the Hungarian Deposit Insurance Fund to give testimony to Russia's parliamentary banking subcommittee and to visit various government agencies to answer questions.[48]

Second, the EU's TACIS program funded a two-year, ECB-coordinated banking supervision training program for Russia that ran from November 2003 through October 2005.[49] Nine European central banks and three European supervisory authorities officially partnered on the project and officials from twelve European central banks, two supervisory authorities, the EU, the IMF, and the Bank of Russia sat on the project steering committee led by Andrei Kozlov. The project trained roughly eight hundred Russian banking supervisors through thirty-three one-week overview courses and another twenty-nine specialized courses, in addition to eight European study visits for supervisory managers and four high-level seminars in Moscow. The project partners gave the courses at the Bank of Russia's training centers. The Bundesbank took on the largest role, offering the basic course fourteen times. In light of the European banking crisis that arose a few years later it is somewhat ironic that the Banca d'Italia led the specialized courses on "credit, country, and transfer risk" and that the UK Financial Services Authority taught on "market, liquidity, and operational risks." The project also produced a book designed to disseminate the core training materials and messages more broadly throughout the Bank of Russia.

While the ECB insisted that the project intended to share ideas and not tell the Bank of Russia what to do, the content and tone of the book (complete with

47. "Russian Federation: Financial Stability System Assessment," IMF Country Report No. 03/147, May 2003, prepared by the Monetary and Exchange Affairs and the European II Departments.

48. Author's interview with Andrei Kozlov of the FSVC and Bank of Russia, Moscow, Russia, March 2002.

49. Olsen 2005.

quizzes at the end to test readers' comprehension) indicated otherwise. Kozlov and the Bank of Russia contributed their own chapter at the book's end, one that emphasized the Bank's plans to develop risk-based supervision and acknowledged that the "corrective actions" that its branches applied to noncompliant banks "are often untimely and inadequate." The chapter also noted several times that Russian law did not give supervisors enough or the right powers to act in key situations. This kind of complaint had been a bone of contention with the Bank of Russia's community advisors, who saw the legal framework as largely acceptable and politely accused the Bank of using it as an excuse not to act. Underlying tensions also appeared when the Russians' chapter noted that although the Bank of Russia intended to implement Basel II and considered it "authoritative," successfully doing so would require an improved legal framework, better data, economic stability, and "a highly developed general economic and banking culture" in Russia.

Indeed, backlash from commercial banks and the difficulties involved in transforming the Bank of Russia's immense supervisory apparatus made progress slow and uneven despite Kozlov's leadership and the community's attention. For example, commercial bankers and auditors I talked with in Moscow in May 2006 claimed that the Bank of Russia had botched the introduction of IFRS, delegating the task to PriceWaterhouseCoopers and producing an instruction sheet that inaccurately explained how to convert Russian Accounting Standards (RAS) into IFRS.[50] As they pointed out, it is impossible to "convert" accounts from one system to the other; because IFRS are so conceptually different, they cannot be applied by going through RAS first. They also criticized the ECB-supported introduction of "dedicated supervision," which assigned each bank a dedicated coordinating supervisor with whom to work. They accurately observed that while the system might have advantages elsewhere, in Russia's regions having each bank answer to a single lead supervisor opened the door to corruption.

These critiques came from within the small circle of Western-oriented financial professionals in Moscow, ones that otherwise wished the Bank of Russia well in its efforts to improve supervision and regulation. Such complaints paled beside the antagonism that the more numerous and questionable commercial banks directed toward Kozlov's efforts to clean up the banking system. The Bank of Russia had intended to use its new deposit insurance law as a tool of consolidation, protecting the strongest banks while weeding out others. In the

---

50. Author's interviews with the deputy director of a leading Moscow audit firm and with two high-ranking Moscow commercial bank officials, Moscow, Russia, May 2006. For an exhaustive account of the initial transition to IFRS in Russia, see McGee and Preobragenskaya 2005.

end, however, the bank admitted nearly 75 percent of applicants into the system, and even this meager cull spawned vicious press and lawsuits from those left out.[51] The same problems occurred when the Bank of Russia tried to invoke its new anti-money laundering law to crack down on criminal banks. In May 2004 Kozlov announced that the Bank of Russia had revoked its first license under the law, sanctioning Sodbiznesbank for engaging in illicit activities. The bank fought back, barring the Bank of Russia from its premises, organizing demonstrations, and ultimately sparking multiple bank runs when its media campaign implied that many other banks would be sanctioned in the near future. Although the Bank of Russia leadership and the Russian government stood by Kozlov, his public reputation took a beating.

He nevertheless pressed forward, and the government introduced its second, upgraded Strategy for the Development of the Russian Banking Sector in the same month.[52] Among other internationally inspired reforms, the four-year strategy promised to liquidate banks with less than 5 million euros in capital. The Bank of Russia continued to withdraw banking licenses and tighten conditions for commercial banks. Kozlov repeatedly told commercial bankers that the bank was determined to introduce Basel II norms and that "in order to understand what we do and how we are viewed, it is necessary to examine ourselves from the point of view of international practice."[53] Unfortunately, he paid for this persistence with his life. Kozlov's murder in September 2006 shocked the Russian financial community. Investigations revealed that Aleksei Frenkel, the disgruntled owner of Sodbiznesbank, VIP-Bank, and two others whose licenses the Bank of Russia had withdrawn, had ordered the contract killing.[54] Banking reform continued to limp along after Kozlov's death, but only just. While the 2007–8 global financial crisis sparked a brief round of banking consolidation, the Russian system remained dominated by a handful of state-owned banks, was plagued with

---

51. E.g., see Guy Chazan, "Blood Money: Murdered Regulator in Russia Made Plenty of Enemies Targeting Illegal Cash Flows," *Wall Street Journal*, September 22, 2006.

52. "Strategiia razvitiia bankovskogo sektora Rossiiskoi Federatsii [Strategy for the development of the banking sector of the Russian Federation]," interview with first deputy governor of the Bank of Russia A.A. Kozlov, *Garant*, May 7, 2004, www.cbr.ru/today/publications_reports/print. asp?file=kozlov_garant.htm.

53. Andrei Kozlov, remarks to the XIII Congress of the Association of Russian Banks in St. Petersburg, June 3, 2005, www.cbr.ru/today/publications_reports/print.asp?file=kozlov_XIII_mbk.htm.

54. For details on the crime and the sentencing, see Francesca Mereu, "Frenkel Gets 19 Years In Kozlov's Murder," *Moscow Times*, November 14, 2008; Alexandra Odynova, "Frenkel Convicted in Kozlov Murder," *Moscow Times*, October 29, 2008; Nikolai Sergeev, "Andrei Kozlov's Murder Cost Too Little to Keep His Killers from Talking," *Kommersant*, January 15, 2007; Vladimir Barinov, Maria Lokotetskaya, Rustam Taktashev, and Yevgeny Mazin, "A VIP Contract: An Update on the Andrei Kozlov murder investigation," *Gazeta*, January 12, 2007.

over nine hundred smaller banks, and struggled to keep up with international regulatory and supervisory standards.

Central Bank Independence in Russia

As we have seen, the Bank of Russia and the Russian government clashed for years over a wide range of issues, with the defiant Bank of Russia regularly under fire, scapegoated, and politically isolated. This situation persisted until the bank's rapprochement with Putin after Viktor Gerashchenko's dismissal in March 2002. Putin's taming of the Bank of Russia reflected his overall economic strategy in his first two presidential terms, aiming to increase state influence over the "commanding heights" of finance and natural resources while further liberalizing the rest of the economy. Reflecting on that episode reveals much about the Bank of Russia's position within the Russian polity and the balance it subsequently tried to strike between asserting its independence and working with the government.

The Bank of Russia had enjoyed a high level of legal independence in the 1990s. The 1993 constitution and the 1995 revised Law on the Central Bank of the Russian Federation enshrined the Bank of Russia's policy and financial independence into law, and gave the central bank governor a four-year term not coinciding with the electoral cycle. However, after a year of acrimonious debate, in July 2002 Putin signed amendments to the Law on the Central Bank of the Russian Federation that gave the National Banking Council (NBC) greater control over Bank of Russia activities. The twelve-member NBC included three representatives from the government, three from the presidential administration, five from the legislature, and only one from the Bank of Russia. The NBC's main responsibilities included approving a common state monetary and credit policy, evaluating the Bank's annual report, and approving Bank of Russia expenditures. While the Bank of Russia had deflected parliamentary efforts to weaken its legal independence even further, the amended law took a great deal of power out of the Bank's hands.

Gerashchenko had strongly and repeatedly denounced the proposed legislation subordinating the Bank of Russia to the redesigned National Banking Council.[55] He condemned the bill as "unconstitutional," reaffirmed the principle of

---

55. For example, see Gerashchenko's letter to the Duma of December 5, 2001, titled "O proekte federal'nogo zakona O vnesenii izmenenii i dopolnenii v Federal'nyi zakon O Tsentral'nom banke Rossisskoi Federatsii (Banke Rossii) [On the draft federal law On inserting changes and additions to the Federal law On the Central bank of the Russian Federation (Bank of Russia)]," published on the Bank of Russia website at www.cbr.ru/today/publications_reports/letter.htm.

central bank independence, and managed to postpone the second reading of the bill, but could not garner enough support to kill it. Tensions between the government and Bank of Russia over this and other issues had become increasingly high after Putin's March 2000 election as president, and Gerashchenko finally left office in March 2002.[56] Using a standard Soviet-era formulation, presidential administration head Aleksandr Voloshin announced that Gerashchenko had resigned for health reasons. The transnational central banking community did not visibly stand up to support Gerashchenko in this fight, as its distaste for Gerashchenko took precedence over its abstract principles.

Putin immediately moved to bring the oft-warring Bank of Russia and Finance Ministry closer together by nominating Deputy Finance Minister Sergei Ignatiev—the primary author of the final bill curbing the Bank of Russia's powers—to replace Gerashchenko. Ignatiev was closely tied both to Putin and to Finance Minister Aleksei Kudrin, and although a consummate professional was not a particularly prominent figure. Ignatiev's first statements as Bank of Russia governor underlined the political nature of Gerashchenko's departure, as he promised to pursue the same "reasonable policies" as his predecessor. Afterward several other Finance Ministry officials (including two first deputy finance ministers) moved into top posts at the Bank of Russia and Kudrin was named to chair the National Banking Council. Illustrating the new relationship, it was Kudrin rather than Ignatiev who first presented the updated strategy for banking sector development to the public in July 2004. Even more telling, despite Bank of Russia protests the Finance Ministry successfully introduced a change in the state budget requiring the bank to turn over 80 percent of its profits to the Finance Ministry, rather than the legally mandated 50 percent (requiring a temporary amendment to the Law on the Central Bank).

By ousting the Bank of Russia's influential governor and, in effect, affiliating it with the Finance Ministry, Putin ensured that the bank would either lose or not fight a series of battles with the government that it might have won in the past. Three examples illustrate the change. First, since the Soviet collapse the Bank of Russia had controlled Vneshtorgbank, the state's profitable foreign trade bank. Although Gerashchenko had earlier agreed in principle to cede control of Vneshtorgbank to the government, he had insisted that the government fairly compensate the Bank of Russia for handing it over. After Ignatiev's takeover, however, the bank agreed to sell its stake in Russia's second-largest bank for the bargain price

---

56. For Gerashchenko's reflections on his departure at that time, see Nikita Kirichenko's interview with Gerashchenko, "V ukreplenii rublia net nichego plokhogo [There is nothing bad in the ruble's strengthening]," *Expert*, March 25, 2002.

of 42 billion rubles'-worth of ten-year government bonds. In January 2003 the Ministry of Finance and the Federal Property Ministry jointly assumed ownership of the bank. Second, the Bank of Russia had long insisted that it should control any deposit insurance system to be introduced in Russia; this position had contributed to scuttling earlier efforts to introduce deposit insurance. However, the law on deposit insurance signed by Putin in December 2003 created a separate state agency for deposit insurance and instructed retail banks to make contributions to a state insurance fund rather than to the Bank of Russia. Finally, as discussed earlier, Putin and the Finance Ministry pushed the Bank of Russia to adopt what many economists considered to be mutually exclusive policy goals: controlling inflation while maintaining a stable ruble-US dollar exchange rate.

To what extent did this matter? The transnational community had told postcommunist governments that central banks needed independence first and foremost to restrain inflation, but also to provide international credibility and to respond properly to the needs of domestic financial markets. However, these arguments did not always hold water in Russia. Central bank independence in postcommunist economies had at best a mixed relationship to inflation and none at all to economic growth. This was certainly true of Russia, especially in the early 1990s when a fairly independent Bank of Russia under Gerashchenko contributed to high inflation. More important, it presumes that price stability should always be the primary goal of the central bank. Yet despite IMF concerns, Putin's preference for preserving exchange rate stability at the expense of moderate inflation was defensible at the time, especially given the macroeconomic pressures involved in dealing with high oil and gas prices.

Moreover, central bank independence, so the story goes, sends an important signal to international markets that a country's government is committed to macroeconomic stability, which will lead to increased foreign investment. However, Putin's Russia saw an overall rise in foreign investment and credibility with international financial markets at the same time that central bank independence declined. The reason is simple—for a resource-rich economy like Russia, central bank independence was a less important signal to international markets than budget, tax, and privatization policies. The politically motivated October 2003 arrest and imprisonment of oil baron Mikhail Khodorkovsky did much more damage to Russia's international credibility than clipping the Bank of Russia's wings, especially since the latter involved replacing the unloved Gerashchenko with a member of Kudrin's team of economic liberalizers.

Finally, in theory independent central banks benefit their economies in part because they serve the needs of domestic financial institutions and the public rather than the government. In advanced industrial democracies, commercial bankers are often the strongest supporters of central bank independence. Yet many

Russian commercial banks actively fought the Bank of Russia from its inception, lobbying against greater transparency and accountability, against foreign bank competition, and against effectively dealing with the far-too-numerous problem banks. The public, likewise, had a low opinion of the Bank of Russia in part due to media smear campaigns by unhappy commercial bankers. In earlier years commercial banks also had encouraged the Bank of Russia to stoke inflation because of the profit opportunities it created in the transitional environment. With the powerful Putin government committed to at least some commercial bank reform, the less independent but more politically shielded Bank of Russia for the first time had enough support to attempt to clean up the problematic sector.

In short, a less independent Bank of Russia did not necessarily have the downsides that independence proponents might expect, and it had the added benefit of improving policy coordination between the Bank of Russia and the Finance Ministry, coordination often not evident in the past. As demonstrated by its evolving monetary policy, the Bank of Russia under Putin attempted to balance its more community-oriented preferences with domestic demands. Not fully independent but not (yet) forced to choose between its transnational community and its national government, it walked a careful middle ground in the years leading up to the global financial crisis. In that sense the Bank of Russia proved more fortunate than the NBKR, which faced even greater challenges to its independence.

The Highest Mountain: The National Bank of the Kyrgyz Republic

Independent Kyrgyzstan's first president Askar Akayev famously promised to turn tiny, mountainous Kyrgyzstan into the "Switzerland of Central Asia." Given its difficult starting position and President Akayev's openness to economic liberalism, the NBKR enthusiastically welcomed intensive technical assistance and training from the transnational central banking community. While most analyses focus on the IMF's role in Kyrgyzstan, Kyrgyz central bankers with whom I spoke equally emphasized the importance of bilateral relationships with central banks like the Swiss National Bank, the Bundesbank, and the Bank of Finland, as well as assistance provided by USAID, the World Bank, and the Asian Development Bank. As one NBKR board member remarked, "The organizational structure of the former Gosbank was oriented to a different set of goals and challenges, so it was an antiquated structure in relation to our present demands . . . our present structure is the result of the influence of a variety of experts and the experience of different countries."[57] From the beginning the NBKR leadership adopted without hesitation the view that it must strive to be "maximally independent" in its decision making in order to manage the transitional economic environment.[58]

Near-continuous IMF funding agreements provided the continuity and conditionality under which the NBKR and the Kyrgyz financial system developed. The IMF's May 1993 Stand-By Arrangement, the March 1994 Enhanced Structural Adjustment Facility, the subsequent Poverty Reduction and Growth Facility arrangements (1998, 2001, 2005), and the 2008 Exogenous Shocks Facility all included detailed program compliance criteria in monetary policy and financial sector development. Kyrgyzstan had trouble meeting some program targets in the early years, but as the IMF itself noted in retrospect, "Most of the noncompliance . . . can be traced to over-optimism. This feeling of optimism was shared by the staff and authorities . . . there are examples, especially on the fiscal side, where the program targets were unachievable under any reasonable assumptions."[59] To help Kyrgyzstan attempt to meet the ambitious criteria the IMF organized substantial technical assistance spearheaded by long-term resident representatives and resident advisors, often seconded from national central banks.

The NBKR relied on extensive technical assistance and training for longer than did the other central banks discussed in this study for the simple reason that it had the most ground to make up. Although the IMF made its loans conditional on structural reforms, the NBKR itself did not embrace technical assistance for this reason; rather, it invited scores of advisors to Kyrgyzstan with the hope that community assistance could help to make the economic transition as smooth as possible.[60] In fact, advisors to the Kyrgyz financial system were so thick on the ground that both the NBKR and the in-country advisors had to develop formal and informal local mechanisms for coordinating their efforts to attempt to avoid duplication and contradiction. Continuity and follow up becomes especially important in such circumstances; interviewees in three separate NBKR departments remarked that their departments' development slowed after their dedicated advisors left. By the same token, in contrast to the other cases the relationship

57. Author's interview with an NBKR board member, Bishkek, Kyrgyzstan, June 2001.

58. Taranchieva, M.A. "Rol' tsentral'nykh bankov v uskorenii peremen v ekonomikakh s poet-apnym perekhodom k rynku [Role of the central bank in the acceleration of change in the economy since the market transition]," *Bankovskii vestnik*, November 1995.

59. IMF, *Kyrgyz Republic—Ex Post Assessment of Longer-Term Program Engagement*, February 2005, IMF Country Report 05/32, 7. The World Bank's assessment concurred on the problem of over-optimism: World Bank 2001.

60. "Tekhnicheskoe sodeistvie mezhdunarodnykh organizatsii bankovskomu sektoru Kyrgyzskoi Respubliki [Technical cooperation of international organizations with the banking sector of the Kyrgyz Republic]," *Bankovskii vestnik*, August 1995.

between Kyrgyz central bankers and their advisors retained a strong student-teacher rather than collegial character for at least a decade after independence.

The IMF and the Som

Monetary policy making in the NBKR began literally from nothing. Kyrgyzstan continued to use the ruble as its official currency after the Soviet Union broke up, and in practice had a highly dollarized, informal economy. The new Kyrgyz financial authorities had few tools with which to work: no sovereign national currency, no currency convertibility (so no legal foreign exchange markets), cash circulation occurring primarily outside the financial system, "commercial banks" that engaged almost entirely in connected lending using state credits, and no treasury bills with which to conduct open market operations. Moreover, with Russia's (and then Kyrgyzstan's) price liberalization in early 1992 and the subsequent growth in parallel currencies and noncash government credits to enterprises throughout the ruble zone, Kyrgyzstan suffered hyperinflation along with other ruble zone members.

In parallel, the NBKR staff had no experience conducting monetary policy; until 1992 the NBKR did not even control Kyrgyzstan's foreign exchange reserves. One former advisor noted with dismay that NBKR staff at the time did not even know how to draft a telex to exchange currencies. One of the first NBKR employees to learn to send telexes in 1992 said that "The experience was very interesting . . . I was like a typist . . . yes, when I started to work here we had nothing."[61] Another high-ranking NBKR staffer reflected that she had never touched US dollars until the first foreign currency auctions in 1993, since exchanging hard currency had formerly been a crime. A Bundesbank official remarked that, "I visited them in 1994 or 1995. At the central bank I looked into the open vault and one woman sat there by herself counting money, with no security."[62] The first technical assistance meetings thus covered extremely basic issues.

Creating a national currency was the first prerequisite for conducting independent monetary policy. In early 1992 the IMF and Kyrgyz officials believed that Kyrgyzstan would be better off remaining in the ruble zone. By fall 1992, however, official sentiment on both sides had begun to swing toward an inde-

---

61. Author's interview with a senior official in the Foreign Exchange Department, National Bank of the Kyrgyz Republic, Bishkek, Kyrgyzstan, May 2001.

62. Author's interview with a senior Bundesbank official, June 2000. NBKR governor Sarbanov remarked that afterward, Bundesbank help was "invaluable" in establishing a treasury at the NBKR. Baktygul Aliev, interview with Ulan Sarbanov, Bishkek, Kyrgyzstan, August 2007.

pendent Kyrgyz currency.[63] This kicked off an intense public debate over the wisdom of leaving the ruble zone. President Akayev and top NBKR officials, with IMF support, led the charge for introducing the som. The NBKR argued that the ruble zone left Kyrgyzstan dependent on Russia's policy and printing press, and vulnerable to volatility in other post-Soviet countries.[64] Russian policies had already contributed to hyperinflation and a collapse of the Kyrgyz payment system.[65] NBKR governor Nanaev noted in November 1992 that the NBKR could not influence inflation rates in the ruble zone, and any discussions of creating a re-unified monetary zone would take too long.[66] By April 1993, Nanaev was stressing that the IMF had promised loans if the Kyrgyz introduced the som, and that other countries such as Estonia had successfully left the ruble zone.[67] A few days later President Akayev insisted that the road had been chosen and announced the creation of a committee to introduce the som consisting of the NBKR governor, key officials, and foreign advisors.[68]

Nevertheless, many Kyrgyz argued vigorously against the idea, including economists, members of parliament, businesspeople, and journalists. There was even some dissent within the NBKR itself.[69] Opponents argued that introducing the som would lead to capital flight, a loss of trade, and further inflation.[70] One economist called the proposal "national suicide."[71] In parliament, delegates expressed concern about introducing a new currency given Kyrgyzstan's extreme dependence on imports, with some suggesting a wait-and-see approach while

63. On the IMF, see Odling-Smee and Pastor 2002. On the NBKR, see author's interview with a senior official at the Kyrgyz Agricultural Finance Corporation and former senior official in the NBKR Foreign Exchange Department, Bishkek, Kyrgyzstan, May 2001.

64. E. Avdeeva, E., "Reformy budut. No 'ozdorovitel'nye' [There will be reforms. But healthy ones]," *Vechernii Bishkek,* February 18, 1992; E. Avdeeva, "Rubl' umer. Budem ego khoronit? [The ruble is dead. Should we bury it?]," *Vechernii Bishkek,* October 20, 1992, 3; I. Shafrova, "Den'gi budut. I eto vser'ez [There will be money. And this is serious]," *Vechernii Bishkek,* April 1, 1992, 1.

65. Author's interview with an NBKR board member, May 2001.

66. G. Deviatov, "Vremia vybora: som ili rubl'? [Time to choose: The som or the ruble?]," *Vechernii Bishkek,* November 6, 1992, 2.

67. V. Niksdorf, "Kemelbek Nanaev: My letim v propast'. I etot polet mozhet ostanovit' svoiia valiuta [Kemelbek Nanaev: We are flying into an abyss. And this flight might stop our currency]," *Slovo Kyrgyzstana,* April 24, 1993.

68. "President ubezhden: nastal den' i chas dlia kyrgyzskikh somov [The president is convinced: The day and hour has come for the Kyrgyz som]," *Slovo Kyrgyzstana,* April 29, 1993.

69. Author's interview with a senior official at the Kyrgyz Agricultural Finance Corporation and former senior official in the NBKR Foreign Exchange Department, Bishkek, Kyrgyzstan, May 2001.

70. "Som? Net, poka rubl' ili dazhe dollar [The som? No, for now it's the ruble or even the dollar]," *Slovo Kyrgyzstana,* March 30, 1993.

71. I. Samigullin, "Natsional'naia valiuta: spasatel'nyi krug ili kamen' na shee? [National currency: A life belt or a rock around the neck?]," *Slovo Kyrgyzstana,* March 6, 1993.

others recommended introduction of a parallel currency only.[72] Russia and the other Central Asian states also denounced the move.[73]

In the end, Akayev insisted that it was the only solution and had to be done.[74] He gave a speech lasting over an hour to parliament before the May 5 vote to approve the som's introduction, arguing that national sovereignty, macroeconomic stability, and IMF funding depended on it. He also gave each deputy a flyer outlining the many problems of the current ruble zone.[75] Parliament approved the plan on May 5, Kyrgyzstan introduced the som on May 10, and the IMF approved the Kyrgyz petition for a $62 million SBA on May 12.

An IMF technical assistance team played a pivotal role in facilitating the introduction of the som.[76] The NBKR also brought in experts from Estonia to advise them, given their own recent experience with issuing a new currency.[77] The IMF served as matchmaker as well, setting the NBKR up with long-term advisors from De Nederlandsche Bank for assistance in currency production and with the Swiss National Bank for assistance in foreign exchange. When the NBKR held its first som/dollar foreign exchange auction in May, an IMF representative spoke at the occasion.[78] On IMF advice and in the face of more domestic criticism, the NBKR and the Kyrgyz government adopted a managed float for the som, as well as quickly introducing current and then capital account convertibility.[79] As NBKR first deputy chairman Emil Abdumanapov summed up, the IMF was of "great moral and financial help" in the som's introduction.[80]

72. V. Niksdorf, "Som poluchaet prava grazhdanstva [The som obtains the rights of citizenship]," *Slovo Kyrgyzstana,* May 5, 1993.

73. A. Allakbarov, "Tverdaia pochva pod 'miagkoi' valiutoi [Firm ground under a 'soft' currency]," *Slovo Kyrgyzstana,* September 14, 1993. Interview with NBKR first deputy chairman Emil Abdumanapov, "K dvukhletiu vvedeniia soma [On the second anniversary of the introduction of the som]," *Bankovskii vestnik,* April 1995.

74. Author's interview with an NBKR board member, Bishkek, Kyrgyzstan, May 2001.

75. "Budut reformy—budut den'gi [There will be reforms—there will be money]," *Slovo Kyrgyzstana,* May 4, 1993; V. Niksdorf, "Teper' my sami s somom! [Now we have our som!]," *Slovo Kyrgyzstana,* May 4, 1993.

76. Asel' Otorbaeva, "Diadiushka Som—uchitel' [Grandfather Som—teacher]," *Slovo Kyrgyzstana,* July 28, 1994; see Broome 2010 for a more detailed discussion of the IMF's role in Kyrgyzstan.

77. "President ubezhden: nastal den' i chas dlia kyrgyzskikh somov [The president is convinced: The day and hour has come for the Kyrgyz som]," *Slovo Kyrgyzstana,* April 29, 1993.

78. V. Niksdorf, "Som obretaet dollarovoe priznanie [The som finds the dollar's recognition]," *Slovo Kyrgyzstana,* May 18, 1993.

79. Interview with Ulan Sarbanov, NBKR governor, August 15, 2002, Winne VIP Interviews, www.winne.com/kyrgyzstan/vi04.html. M. Titova and D. Omurbekov, "Kyrgyzskomu somu 5 let [5 years of the Kyrgyz som]," *Bankovskii vestnik,* April 1998.

80. Interview with NBKR first deputy chairman Emil Abdumanapov, "K dvukhletiu vvedeniia soma [On the second anniversary of the introduction of the som]," *Bankovskii vestnik,* April 1995.

Betting on the som turned out to be a smart move, as the Bank of Russia ultimately forced the remaining post-Soviet countries out of the ruble zone. The successful introduction of the som cemented Kyrgyzstan's "star pupil" role with foreign donors and made the IMF unusually (albeit temporarily) popular in the country. One journalist, praising the decision after the fact, argued that Kyrgyzstan was better off charting its own course with the help of the IMF and the international community rather than relying on Russia because the former came with little ideology and was based on sound economic principles.[81] Akayev considered the successful introduction of the som to be a key symbol and achievement of independent Kyrgyzstan.[82]

The NBKR's Post-Som Transformation

Because the NBKR started with rookie staff, it embraced training opportunities vigorously. Post-Soviet countries like Kyrgyzstan that had to create their central banks from Gosbank branches hired most of their staffs in a matter of months. In Kyrgyzstan, the post-1991 exodus of ethnic Russians from government institutions like the NBKR exacerbated the situation. This did provide an opportunity to hire young, open-minded, energetic staff and start fresh. As one international advisor remarked to me a decade later:

> The NBKR is a younger team, quite professional, they understand what we say. Sarbanov was here for six months at Georgetown. I tell Akayev that I see the same in this central bank as I did in [another postcommunist central bank]—they sacked the old guard. I defend the central bank to Akayev, and think it has good prospects. It's quite common to have younger staff who have Western concepts. If you want to reform, it's important to change the team. The central banks have changed their philosophies quickly.[83]

But the more hiring necessary, the less selective postcommunist central banks could be. Under such circumstances they relied even more heavily on international training courses to provide new hires with the basic tools necessary for their jobs. The NBKR also experienced ongoing turnover afterward because

---

81. A. Krainii, "Akaev okazalsia prav: svoi som luchshe chuzhogo rublia [Akaev turned out to be right: our own som is better than a foreign ruble]," *Slovo Kyrgyzstana*, August 11, 1993.

82. Askar Akayev, "My uzhe vspakhali nivu nashei obshchei zhizni [We have already plowed the field of our common lives]," *Slovo Kyrgyzstana*, August 31, 1993, 1.

83. Author's interview with a senior IMF official, Washington, DC, November 2001.

salaries in commercial banks and international financial institutions were higher than in the NBKR. This resulted in the NBKR losing employees it had already trained. As one former NBKR official noted, "in every commercial bank you can find someone from the National Bank," particularly after the 1998 Russian financial crisis created economic and political difficulties in Kyrgyzstan.[84]

Therefore, the NBKR had to engage in intensive, ongoing training. As table 4.2 revealed, from 1996 through 1999 the NBKR sent more central bankers for training abroad than did the Magyar Nemzeti Bank despite being farther away, poorer, and about half the size of the MNB. In 2000 alone, of 425 total central bank employees, 267 received specialized training.[85] Overall, one board member estimated in 2001 that about 85 percent of NBKR employees had received specialized training in Kyrgyzstan and abroad.[86] The NBKR also sent several staff on long-term exchange programs to central banks such as the US Federal Reserve Bank of Kansas City and the Bank of England.

While invaluable in transforming the NBKR, three factors on the Kyrgyz side prevented training programs abroad from having even more impact. First, as with the Bank of Russia, the language barrier limited NBKR participation in many international courses. The problem eased somewhat once the bank began to offer its own after-hours English courses in 1997, but the English-language abilities of NBKR staff remained comparatively weak for many years. Only by 2011 could an IMF representative in Bishkek tell me that the NBKR staff's English abilities were "quite good."[87] Second, training opportunities abroad were sometimes not allocated by ability or need, but by seniority or queue. Mismatches of program and trainee resulted, with trips occasionally becoming more vacation abroad than serious education for participants.

Finally, while many training programs (such as those at the Joint Vienna Institute) were free for participants, others required the NBKR to pay at least a portion of the costs of travel or attendance. Of all the postcommunist central bankers I talked with, only the Kyrgyz and the Kosovars repeatedly mentioned the difficulty of financing training trips for their staff. An NBKR Human Resources director noted that occasionally they could not

---

84. Author's interview with a commercial banker and former NBKR official, Bishkek, Kyrgyzstan, May 2001.

85. Author's interview with a senior official in the Department of Human Resources, National Bank of the Kyrgyz Republic, Bishkek, Kyrgyzstan, May 2001.

86. Author's interview with a senior board member and technical assistance coordinator of the National Bank of the Kyrgyz Republic, Bishkek, Kyrgyzstan, May 2001.

87. Author's interview with the IMF Resident Representative in the Kyrgyz Republic, Bishkek, Kyrgyzstan, June 2011.

send people to important courses, or could do so only after appealing to external sponsors for aid.[88] She mentioned as an example a course on banking supervision at the Federal Reserve Bank of New York for which USAID and the Soros Foundation provided financial support to send two key staff members. As she noted, "Once they had the opportunity to take part in that course, it was very useful. They acquired invaluable materials and use them in their work. But that was just one case, it doesn't always turn out that well . . . our budget is quite small."

For these and other reasons NBKR staff often attended less expensive courses held in the regional training centers of the Russian and Kazakh central banks, and also founded their own bank training center in 1996 with the help of the Bank of Finland and the World Bank. Initially a part of the NBKR, the Bank Training Center (BTC) became a wholly owned subsidiary in 1999. While local staff taught many courses, the BTC also invited specialists from other postcommunist central banks as well as from organizations such as the Bank of England, the Banque de France, and the Asian Development Bank to lead seminars. These latter courses met with varying degrees of success, as especially early on instructors would sometimes lose their audiences with approaches focusing more on theory than practical experience. Nevertheless, the BTC played a significant role in NBKR staff training, with over one hundred staff members per year taking part in BTC courses. Over time the importance of staff exchange programs with other postcommunist central banks, especially the Bank of Russia, grew as well.

This ongoing training went hand-in-hand with active technical assistance programs. After the som's introduction in 1993, central bank advisors helped the NBKR to develop modern monetary policy tools. After acquiescing to government pressure to provide loans to finance agriculture and industry in 1993, IMF influence and adverse experience with the resulting inflation allowed the NBKR to cut back sharply on government financing in 1994 and end it after 1997.[89] With IMF help, the NBKR liberalized interest rates and introduced credit auctions, thus ending directed credits to commercial banks and making a first step toward using market-based tools of monetary policy. The NBKR also raised reserve requirements in 1994 and again in 1997, with all required reserves to be

88. Author's interview with a senior official in the Department of Human Resources, National Bank of the Kyrgyz Republic, Bishkek, Kyrgyzstan, May 2001.

89. "K dvukhletiiu vvedeniia soma [On the second anniversary of the introduction of the som]," *Bankovskii vestnik*, April 1995; Titova and Omurbekov, "Kyrgyzskomu somu 5 let."

held in som.[90] The NBKR began conducting open-market operations with treasury bills in 1995, introduced repos in 1997, and foreign exchange swaps in 2001.[91] At the same time, the NBKR introduced standing facilities such as Lombards.

Throughout this entire, rapid process, the NBKR received extensive advice and prodding from the IMF and Western central banks. As former NBKR governor Ulan Sarbanov noted, the advice of experts from the Bundesbank and Swiss National Bank "was simply incalculable" in the development of indirect instruments of monetary policy.[92] As a result, the NBKR ceased credit auctions in 1997 and foreign currency auctions in 1998, relying entirely on reserve requirements, open market operations, and standing facilities for conducting monetary policy.[93] By the turn of the millennium, the NBKR targeted broad money as its intermediate target (measured monthly) and liquidity (measured weekly as excess reserves) as its operational target.[94] Its *de jure* and *de facto* goal was to maintain price stability, and it set these targets in cooperation with the IMF. In sum, although shallow financial markets, dollarization, and external shocks often meant that the NBKR's policy did not work as planned, internally the NBKR had the key tools and expertise to conduct modern monetary policy in place within a few short years of creating the national currency.[95] As a Bundesbank advisor observed, "The Kyrgyz have changed their central banking system to one that works. They have new instruments of monetary policy like repos and bills. They would not have been able to do this without our help."[96]

90. This was an unpopular policy. Commercial banker Marat Alapaev complained to me that "the som is claimed to be a unified national currency but the actual currency of the Kyrgyz Republic is the dollar." He argued that the som did not function like real money and that banks should be allowed to hold reserves and value capital in dollars, but the NBKR was too proud of its national currency to allow it. Interview with Marat Alapaev, Bakai Bank, Bishkek, Kyrgyzstan, May 2001. Four years later Alapaev became governor of the NBKR, succeeding Sarbanov. He did not change the NBKR's reserves policy. For a similar argument from a banker at Kyrgyzavtobank, see S.A. Kerimbaeva, "Nekotorye problemy bankovskogo sektora [Several problems of the banking sector]," *Bankovskii vestnik*, December 1999.

91. E.g., see "Problemy i perspektivy RTsB [Problems and perspectives of the RTsB]," *Bankovskii vestnik*, March 1997; "Rynok REPO stanovitsia vse bolee privlekatel'nym dlia bankov [The REPO market becomes ever-more profitable for banks]," *Bankovskii vestnik*, March 1997; Sundararajan et al. 1997.

92. Baktygul Aliev, interview with Ulan Sarbanov, Bishkek, Kyrgyzstan, August 2007. See also M. Dzhumalieva, "Zarubezhnyi opyt: podkhod k otsenke kon"iunktury v Shveitsarii [Foreign experience: the path to appraising the state of the market in Switzerland]," *Bankovskii vestnik*, October 1998.

93. "O denezhno-kreditnoi politike vchera, segodnia i zavtra [On monetary-credit policy yesterday, today, and tomorrow]," *Bankir*, April 22, 1998.

94. IMF, *Kyrgyz Republic: Financial System Stability Assessment*. Prepared by the Monetary and Exchange Affairs and the European II Departments. February 2003, IMF country report 03/52.

95. Author's interview with an NBKR Board Member, May 2001. Knight et al. 1999.

96. Author's interview with a senior Bundesbank official, Frankfurt, Germany, May 2000.

The NBKR's internal auditing department represented another typical example of the technical assistance process at work. As a senior NBKR official noted, "when the internal audit department started in 1995, only three people in the bank knew anything about it."[97] A Barents Group consultant and internal audit veteran spent six months in Kyrgyzstan to lay the department's foundations, and the staff referred to him as the "father" of the department. Two key seminars for auditors at the Banque de France, seminars at the Bundesbank and the Bank of England, and regular visits by a short-term advisor from Finland followed. The auditors regarded their advisors with great affection, showing me pictures from their visits preserved in a Lion King photo album. Over time the department became quite competent, if still dependent upon the occasional foreign advisor to suggest and help implement improvements. Kyrgyzstan had a similar experience with its foreign exchange department, which was initially crafted in great part by advisors from the Swiss National Bank.[98]

Even so, the NBKR did not always appreciate the advice it was given when that advice conflicted with its lofty goals. As an NBKR board member told me, one consultant thought that it was too early for the internal auditing department to move to International Accounting Standards and encouraged them to use the less exacting French domestic standards instead. She remarked that, "we, of course, said no. . . . We are not going to make a transition to the intermediate standards of other foreign countries; if we are going to make the change, it should be right away to international standards."[99] As a result, with extensive technical assistance the NBKR converted to IAS (later called IFRS) in 1997.

Similarly, as early as 2004 the NBKR wanted to move toward inflation targeting. The IMF's response managed to reassert the primacy of the international model while also putting on the brakes, telling the NBKR that "this was a reasonable goal, in the staff's view, but the preconditions for such a regime remained distant, given unstable monetary transmission mechanisms and the current macroeconomic modeling capacity."[100] Later the IMF and the Swiss worked intensively with the NBKR and other state agencies to create a national forecasting model based on IMF financial programming guidelines, introduced in October 2012.

97. Author's interview with a senior official in the Department of Internal Audit, National Bank of the Kyrgyz Republic, Bishkek, Kyrgyzstan, May 2001.

98. Author's interviews with a former senior official and a current senior official of the Foreign Exchange Department of the National Bank of the Kyrgyz Republic, Bishkek, Kyrgyzstan, May 2001.

99. Author's interview with a board member of the NBKR, Bishkek, Kyrgyzstan, May 2001.

100. IMF, "Kyrgyz Republic: 2004 Article IV Consultation and Request to Extend the PRGF Arrangement—Staff Report; Staff Supplement; Public Information Notice and Press Release on the Executive Board Discussion; and Statement by the Executive Director for the Kyrgyz Republic," IMF Country Report No. 05/47, February 2005.

The monetary transmission mechanisms, however, could not be helped. As another IMF report from 2013 concluded, the low monetization, shallow financial system, high dollarization, and a primarily cash-based economy meant that NBKR interest-rate policies had almost no discernable effect on monetary aggregates, and that monetary aggregates in turn had no stable relationship with inflation.[101] In short, the NBKR and its advisors had developed a well-designed monetary policy-making infrastructure that could not work under Kyrgyz economic conditions.

Banking Supervision in the NBKR

Although not on the same scale as Russia, Kyrgyzstan too had a troubled commercial banking sector upon independence. Insolvent heirs of Soviet-era specialized banks dominated the landscape, complemented by several tiny "pocket banks" created by state enterprises or government agencies. Banks gave loans to their shareholders at negative real interest rates and without meaningful collateral, all underwritten by the government. The 1992 hyperinflation then made the commercial banks' already small statutory capital bases miniscule in real terms.[102] Not surprisingly, under such conditions most financial activity occurred in the cash economy.

The NBKR did improve its banking supervision capabilities in the 1990s with the assistance of multiple international donors. The World Bank and IMF provided both technical assistance and conditionality beginning in 1992, with the most important being the World Bank-led FINSAC program in 1996.[103] USAID sent multiple consultants, primarily from Barents Group, to aid in banking supervision from 1993 on.[104] The Asian Development Bank undertook two major financial sector assistance programs, the first in 1994 and the second (the FIRM program) in 1999.[105] The EU, through the TACIS program, provided assistance with its Kyrgyz Banking Consulting Center. The EBRD invested in bank

---

101. IMF, "Kyrgyz Republic: Selected Issues," IMF Country Report No. 13/176, June 2013.

102. Kloc 1995.

103. NBKR press service, "Chtob finansy ne peli romansy [Lest finances sing romances]," *Slovo Kyrgyzstana,* August 3, 1995, 2; E. Avdeeva, "Kogda nam dadut milliony, my perevernem bankovskii mir [When they give us millions, we will stun the banking world]," *Vechernii Bishkek,* April 9, 1996, 2; Otdel reorganizatsii finansovoi sistemy NBKR [NBKR Department of Financial System Reorganization], "O khode vypolneniia meropriiatii po programme FINSAC [On the path to fulfilling the activities of the FINSAC program]," *Bankovskii vestnik,* February 3, 1997; "Itogi missii vsemirnogo banka po programme FINSAC [The results of the World Bank's mission regarding the FINSAC program,]" *Bankovskii vestnik,* October 1997.

104. "Razvitie bankovskoi sistemy respubliki [Development of the banking system of the republic]," *Bankovskii vestnik,* March 1995; "Pomoshch' amerikanskogo agentstva po mezhdunarodnomu razvitiu (USAID) v organizatsii bankovskogo nadzora [Help of the US Agency for International Development in organizing banking supervision]," *Bankovskii vestnik,* January 1995.

105. Asian Development Bank 2002.

capital and provided state-guaranteed loans through select Kyrgyz commercial banks.[106] These various donors worked directly with the NBKR and commercial banks to try to pressure problem banks and improve supervision. NBKR banking supervisors underwent training in Kyrgyzstan and abroad, particularly at the Joint Vienna Institute.[107]

With the encouragement of international advisors, the NBKR significantly slowed and then ended direct credit to banks in the early 1990s. Advisors also assisted NBKR staff in its first audit of commercial banks in 1994–95, resulting in the liquidation of several banks.[108] The FINSAC program in 1996 pushed the reforms further. The NBKR, responding to international advice, continued to increase the statutory capital requirements for commercial banks. The initial capital requirement of 1 million som in 1993 rose to 5 million in 1994 and to 25 million in 1996. International assistance and conditionality also facilitated the passage of an updated law "On Banks and Banking Activity" in 1997. Through the FINSAC program the NBKR liquidated three smaller banks and two of the four legacy specialized banks. The corresponding NBKR investigations confirmed their primitive state. A consultant told me, for example, that one liquidated bank had put all of its individual deposits into a single big account called "deposits," without any subledgers.[109] The bank's only rebuttal was that "no law requires us to keep separate accounts for deposits." The NBKR re-formed the good assets and branches of the liquidated specialized banks into the NBKR-owned Savings and Settlement Company (SSC) and created a debt-resolution agency (DEBRA) to manage the bad assets.[110] The NBKR, World Bank, ADB, and TACIS then created the state-owned Kyrgyz Agricultural Finance Corporation (KAFC) to conduct agricultural lending in place of the liquidated agricultural bank.

106. The EBRD successfully invested in the new bank KICB, and less successfully gave state-guaranteed loans through four Kyrgyz commercial banks. L.N. Tsyplakova, "Kreditnaia liniia EBRR dlia malykh i srednikh predpriiatii chastnogo sektora Kyrgyzskoi Respubliki [The EBRD credit line for SMEs of the Kyrgyz private sector]," *Bankovskii vestnik*, March 1995. Three of these commercial banks later went belly up and controversy ensued over what happened to the loan money and who was responsible for paying it back to the EBRD.

107. Author's interview with an NBKR board member responsible for banking supervision, Bishkek, Kyrgyzstan, May 2001.

108. AKB Saturn, a pocket bank created by the Ministry of Internal Affairs, was a typical example. See O. Dziubenko, "Bank v militseiskikh pogonakh," *Slovo Kyrgyzstana*, June 15, 1995, 2.

109. Author's interview with a USAID consultant, Bishkek, Kyrgyzstan, June 2001.

110. "Raschetno-sberegatel'naia kompaniia sokhranit bankovskie uslugi dlia kazhdogo kyrgyzstantsa [Transactions-savings company maintains banking services for every Kyrgyzstani]," *Bankovskii vestnik*, August 1996; "Bankovskaia sistema v tiazhelom, no ne v beznadezhnom polozhenii [The banking system is in difficulty, but not in a hopeless situation]," *Bankovskii vestnik*, June 1996.

Although both the NBKR and its international advisors congratulated themselves on a job reasonably well done, their enthusiasm turned out to be premature. The 1998 Russian financial crisis and the Kyrgyz fallout revealed significant weaknesses in the NBKR's banking supervision. With the crisis-inspired drop in the som's value, many commercial banks could not meet their obligations due to large US dollar-denominated loans to enterprises and over-reliance on bonds from the state natural gas company—bonds on which the state defaulted.[111] On international advice, the NBKR raised capital requirements again in response to the systemic weakness, at first threatening to increase them to 100 million som (a level not actually reached until 2008) and then settling on 50 million, which few banks in the system could meet.[112] The NBKR also attempted to close several more banks in 1999, but met with significant resistance from the banks, the parliament, and the court system (discussed below). It succeeded in withdrawing licenses from four large banks, in great part due to assistance from the ADB's FIRM program.[113] The NBKR also moved more deeply into the banking business itself, forming NBKR-controlled Kairat bank from the assets of three liquidated commercial banks.

With former NBKR staff running SSC, KAFC, and Kairat—all with the blessing of international advisors—the formal line between the NBKR and the commercial banking system it regulated became muddled. It seems ironic that at the same time international advisors were telling the Bank of Russia to divest itself of commercial bank ownership, they simultaneously facilitated the creation of multiple new state-owned banks in Kyrgyzstan. Informally the situation was even more complicated, as NBKR staff regularly left the NBKR for the better-paying commercial banks. Over time, this meant that commercial bankers often had better supervisory training than the new NBKR bank supervisors, meaning that the commercial bankers could manipulate the rules and that many lacked respect for the NBKR supervisory staff. Community advisors also complained that, as in Russia, NBKR supervisors felt more comfortable giving orders than advice to banks, putting supervisors in a no-win adversarial relationship with commercial bankers.

On the donor side, while specialized assistance from the IMF and national central banks predominated in other areas such as monetary policy or payment systems, in banking supervision multiple international financial institutions and

111. IMF, *Kyrgyz Republic—Ex Post Assessment of Longer-Term Program Engagement*, February 2005, IMF Country Report 05/32.

112. Johnson, L., "Budushchee Kyrgyzskoi bankovskoi sistemy [The future of the Kyrgyz banking system]," *Bankovskii vestnik*, January 1999.

113. Baktygul Aliev, interview with Ulan Sarbanov, Bishkek, Kyrgyzstan, August 2007.

government aid agencies (with their typical reliance on consultants) predominated. Much, of course, depended on the individual consultant. While NBKR staff and international advisors agreed, for example, that one experienced, Russian-speaking consultant had "walked on water," many others did not receive such favorable reviews.

The multiplicity of donors and programs, as well as the lack of consensus on best practices in banking supervision, contributed to uneven coordination and contradictory advice to the NBKR.[114] In one case, a US-based advisor asked me not to look at the Kyrgyz banking supervision program as a representative example of his agency's work because of the serious disagreements between the US home office and the Central Asia-based office on how to conduct the program. This was also the area in which advisors from the different organizations most criticized each other's work (for example, one advisor said of others that they "all have textbooks in their heads"). Even formal agency assessments of the assistance programs took on a dark tone after 1998. For example, in 2001 the World Bank identified duplication of technical assistance programs, poor government cooperation, inadequately prepared consultants, problematic relationships with other donors (particularly TACIS) and high staff turnover in target agencies as key problems in its financial sector assistance, and declared that the FINSAC program's initial achievements were unlikely to be sustainable.[115] Although the 1998 financial crisis refocused central bankers' attention on banking supervision, by this time poor patterns and practices had become endemic in Kyrgyzstan. NBKR banking supervision remained nothing short of disastrous, with embattled supervisors lacking the knowledge or authority to handle Kyrgyzstan's commercial banks.

The Martyrdom of the NBKR

The NBKR took great pains to explain its role and policies to journalists, politicians, and the public, trying constantly to bring them into the circle of believers. In 1994 it created a Department of External and Public Relations with the close and continuing cooperation of the Bundesbank.[116] With

---

114. For example, different donors gave radically different advice about when and whether the NBKR should introduce deposit insurance. Though under serious discussion since 1995—including drafts of legislation—deposit insurance was not actually introduced until 2008.

115. World Bank 2001. See also IMF, *Kyrgyz Republic—Ex Post Assessment of Longer-Term Program Engagement,* February 2005, IMF Country Report 05/32.

116. Author's interview with a senior official in the Department of External and Public Relations, National Bank of Kyrgyzstan, Bishkek, Kyrgyzstan, May 2001.

help from the Swiss National Bank and the Bank of England, it produced a series of television shorts on the NBKR.[117] The NBKR published numerous newspaper articles explaining the basics of its work over the years.[118] It even ran special seminars for financial journalists.[119] Nevertheless, despite these efforts the NBKR's reputation took a constant beating among politicians and in the press.

The situation escalated when the NBKR attempted to crack down on problem banks after the 1998 financial crisis. Powerful legislators in parliament—four of whom controlled commercial banks—undermined the NBKR through harassment, stopped the planned sale of the SSC, and attempted to pass legislation weakening the NBKR's independence. Most commercial bankers chafed against the higher capital requirements imposed after the crisis, accusing the NBKR of blindly listening to inappropriate international advice.[120] When the NBKR actually tried to withdraw licenses from some banks a full-scale revolt broke out, with many bankers and members of parliament publicly bashing the NBKR almost daily. Even worse, the NBKR's pre-crisis governor, Marat Sultanov, had since become a member of parliament supported by these commercial bank interests and joined in the fray against the NBKR.[121]

In September 2000 the battle came to a head as parliament considered legislation that would require the NBKR to obtain commercial bank consent for changing prudential norms and would transfer control of monetary policy to

117. Baktygul Aliev, interview with Ulan Sarbanov, Bishkek, Kyrgyzstan, August 2007.

118. L. Tsyplakova, "Dva etazha sistemy [A Two Tier System]," *Slovo Kyrgyzstana*, August 25, 1994; M. Abakirov, "Na perestroechnom puti [On the perestroika path]," *Slovo Kyrgyzstana*, August 11, 1994; "Natsbank kreditov ne vydaet [The National Bank won't issue credit]," *Slovo Kyrgyzstana*, June 12, 1997, 9.

119. "Natsbank obuchit zhurnalistov bankovskomu delu [The National Bank teaches banking to journalists]," AKIpress, February 20, 2004.

120. E.g., author's interview with a Bishkek commercial bank director, Bishkek, Kyrgyzstan, May 2001. His critiques were notable as he formerly ran the NBKR's dealing operations and characterized himself as an NBKR supporter.

121. Sultanov lost credibility and his job after the som plummeted against the dollar, despite his (and local IFI representatives') insistence that the Russian financial crisis could not spread to Kyrgyzstan because of its solid macroeconomic and fiscal management. "Podtverzhdennoe pravo na stabil'nost', blagosostoianie i liderstvo [Confirmation of the right to stability, well-being, and leadership]," *Bankovskii vestnik*, May–June 1998; Insu Kim, "Krizis ne nakroet [The crisis won't catch us]," *Slovo Kyrgyzstana*, September 3, 1998; "Finansovye krizisy v usloviiakh globalizatsii: vzgliad iz Kyrgyzstana [The financial crisis in conditions of globalization: a view from Kyrgyzstan]," *Bankovskii vestnik*, October 1998; O. Pozdniakova, "Chto nedostupno predskazaniiu? [What is unintelligible for prediction?]," *Vechernii Bishkek*, September 1, 1998; O. Pozdniakova and Kabai Karabekov, "Obval [Collapse]," *Vechernii Bishkek*, November 12, 1998.

parliament.[122] Only intervention by international donors prevented the legislation from being adopted, as the IMF, ADB, and EBRD said that they would pull their funding if the law passed.[123] Kyrgyzstan's continuing reliance on this funding served to deter parliament from destroying the legal basis of NBKR independence. Still, as a result of this pressure the NBKR watered down its policies, permitting banks that could not reach the newly required capitalization levels to continue operating with limited licenses.[124]

Furthermore, a weak and compromised judicial system—along with inadequate legislation—allowed commercial banks under threat of liquidation to sue the NBKR and often win, as the courts failed to permit bank supervisors the legal discretion that is customary in more developed financial systems.[125] Commercial banks regularly appealed to Kyrgyz courts over capital requirements, liquidation orders, and many other NBKR policies from the 1990s on.[126] Such court challenges exhausted and demoralized NBKR banking supervisors, as they were forced both to return licenses to problem banks and to defend themselves from public charges of inadequate supervision after banks they had repeatedly tried to close years earlier eventually collapsed.[127] Donor reports mentioning this issue began to sound like a broken record as the government refused to fix the problem. As a 2011 IMF assessment noted, "Continued, rampant litigation against the NBKR has not only strained staff resources but also increased reputational risks

122. "Zaiavlenie Natsional'nogo banka Kyrgyzskoi respubliki [Declaration of the National Bank of the Kyrgyz Republic]," *Bankir,* September 29, 2000; "Vstrechi i vystupleniia predsedatelia NBKR U.K. Sarbanova v noiabre 2000 goda [Meetings and speeches of the governor of the NBKR U.K. Sarbanov in November 2000]," *Bankovskii vestnik,* October 2000; E. Listvennaia, "Razreshite byt' poleznym [Pleased to be of service]," *Slovo Kyrgyzstana,* November 23, 2000, 8; "Ataka na nezavisimost' Natsbanka sviazana s zhestkoi pozitsiei v otnoshenii problemnykh kombankov [Attack on the independence on the National Bank is connected with its strict position in relation to troubled commercial banks]," *Bankir,* December 6, 2000, 1.

123. Author's interview with a senior official of the Asian Development Bank, Bishkek, Kyrgyzstan, May 2001; Author's interview with a West European consultant, Bishkek, Kyrgyzstan, June 2001.

124. D. Glumskov, "Polemika [Polemic]," *Slovo Kyrgyzstana,* February 22, 2001, 7.

125. Both Gary Gegenheimer (a former USAID advisor) and the World Bank's FSSA criticized the donor community for not focusing early enough on the judiciary and on the legislation necessary to protect bank supervisors. Gegenheimer 2006; IMF, *Kyrgyz Republic: Financial System Stability Assessment.* Prepared by the Monetary and Exchange Affairs and the European II Departments. February 2003, IMF country report 03/52.

126. O. Stepanova, "Nekotorye problemy likvidatsii i bankrotstva bankov [Several problems with the liquidation of bankrupt banks]," *Bankovskii vestnik,* September 2002; "Zaiavlenie Natsional'nogo banka Kyrgyzskoi Respubliki v sviazi s resheniem Bishkekskogo gorodskogo suda v otnoshenii OAO 'Ak Bank' [Declaration of the National Bank of the Kyrgyz Republic in connection with the decision of the Bishkek city court in relation to OAO Ak Bank]," *Bankovskii vestnik,* April–May 2005.

127. Valentina Andreeva, "Khochesh' nazhit' vraga—odolzhi den'gi [If you want to make an enemy—lend money]," *Moia Stolitsa—Novosti,* October 2, 2002.

to the NBKR and prevented it from taking decisive actions against the problem banks."[128]

Finally, after the April 2005 Tulip Revolution that ousted Askar Akayev, new president Kurmanbek Bakiyev fired internationally respected but politically isolated NBKR governor Ulan Sarbanov, most likely because Sarbanov's actions threatened the interests of those close to his administration. At first Sarbanov had retained his post despite strong pressures from Bakiyev associates to remove him. But in late 2005 Sarbanov was placed under house arrest, accused of illegally transferring $420,000 to the state treasury on Akayev's behalf in 1999.[129] While Sarbanov waited to stand trial, Bakiyev temporarily discharged him from his NBKR post by decree on March 1, 2006. Although found not guilty of all charges on April 25, Sarbanov had no choice but to step down as NBKR governor. Immediately afterward, Bakiyev named former commercial banker and close political ally Marat Alapaev to the post.

Sarbanov has argued that his fall 2005 investigation of the robbery of the Jalal-Abad NBKR branch during the Tulip Revolution and the NBKR's subsequent February 2006 investigation of alleged money laundering in AsiaUniversalBank (a bank closely allied with Bakiyev's son) ultimately cost him his job.[130] The latter allegation received strong circumstantial corroboration after Bakiyev fell from power in 2010. Back in February 2006, the Bank of Russia had issued a rare warning to Russian banks to break ties with AsiaUniversalBank due to unusual patterns of financial transfers that indicated likely money laundering activity.[131] The NBKR under Sarbanov then began its own investigation of the bank.[132] But once Alapaev became NBKR governor he ended the inquiry, declaring that AsiaUniversalBank had likely engaged in suspicious financial transfers but that under existing Kyrgyz law no sanctions could be laid. During Bakiyev's five-year presidency, AsiaUniversalBank became the largest commercial bank in Kyrgyzstan, holding nearly 36 percent of the banking system's total assets (the next largest bank had 9.3%).[133] When Bakiyev was overthrown in 2010, over three billion som (about $250 million) from AsiaUniversalBank allegedly vanished abroad with

128. Amaglobeli et al., "Kyrgyz Republic: Selected Issues," IMF Country Report, June 2, 2011.

129. Julian Evans, "Kyrgyzstan: Central Banker under House Arrest," *Euromoney*, November 1, 2005.

130. Iren Saakian, Interview with Ulan Sarbanov, *Vechernii Bishkek*, November 26, 2010.

131. "TsB RF obviniaet kirgizskii AziiaUniversalBank v somnitel'nykh operatsiiakh [The CB RF accuses Kyrgyz AsiaUniversalBank of questionable activities]," Reuters (Russian), February 13, 2006.

132. "National Bank of Kyrgyzstan checks JSC AsiaUniversalBank after Letter of Russian Central Bank," Organisation of Asia-Pacific News Agencies, February 14, 2006.

133. Philip Alexander, "Kyrgyzstan's Banks Are under Pressure," *Banker*, August 30, 2010.

him and his associates.[134] NBKR governor Alapaev fled the country as well; he, Baki-yev, and others were charged in absentia with numerous crimes against the state.[135]

In sum, within a decade of its founding and initial transformation, the NBKR became seriously embattled. As Kyrgyzstan's political troubles increased, the NBKR's influence—and particularly its ability to supervise the banking sector effectively—decreased. It managed to retain independence through Sarbanov's term as gover-nor, but under the Bakiyev government the NBKR's independence and prestige (and that of its international advisors as well) fell increasingly in practice, despite the passage of additional legislation formally strengthening its powers. In 2010 the post-Alapaev acting governor of the NBKR, Baktygul Jeenbaeva, publicly lamented the NBKR's lack of independence.[136] While certain structural reform efforts contin-ued, this was due more to impoverished Kyrgyzstan's ongoing need for international financial support than to inherent respect for the central bank and its mission. In the end, the NBKR amassed one of the largest gaps between *de jure* and *de facto* inde-pendence among the postcommunist states. Dincer and Eichengreen's 2013 study singled out the NBKR as the most legally independent central bank in the world, while the NBKR's leadership team at the time boasted close and long-standing ties to the transnational central banking community.[137] Nevertheless, in practice the Kyrgyz government, judiciary, and commercial banks undermined the NBKR with near-impunity and the NBKR's policy making remained broadly ineffective in the Kyrgyz economic environment. Instead of a flourishing transplant well rooted in Kyrgyz soil the community had nourished a container garden, a set of laws, prac-tices, and individuals inspired by and connected to the transnational community but sharply confined in their ability to influence their immediate surroundings.

National Banks, Transnational Bankers

The transnational community's technical cooperation with postcommunist central banks arguably represented the most transformative foreign aid cam-paign conducted after the fall of the Berlin Wall in 1989. As we have seen, even

---

134. "Amangeldy Muraliev: Cronies of Ex-President Bakiev Took Out $250 mln from AsiaUni-versalBank before Introduction of External Administration, Ban of Transactions," AKIpress, October 28, 2010; "Kyrgyz General Prosecutor's Office claims over 3 billion soms stolen from AUB," *Times of Central Asia,* September 2, 2010.

135. The new Kyrgyz government first said that AsiaUniversalBank would be restructured com-mercially and then nationalized it.

136. "My obiazany vosstanovit' nezavisimost' NBKR: interv'iu B. Zheenbaevoi, i. o. Predsedatelia NBKR [We must restore the independence of the NBKR: Interview with B. Jeenbaeva, acting gov-ernor of the NBKR]," *Finansist,* July 2010; Israilov, Erik, "Interv'iu i. o. Predsedatelia NBKR B. Zh. Zheenbaevoi [Interview with acting NBKR governor B.J. Jeenbaeva]," *Obshchestvennyi reiting,* May 5, 2011, www.pr.kg/gazeta/number527/1738/.

137. Dincer and Eichengreen 2013.

central bankers in Russia and Kyrgyzstan often embraced the community's core principles and practices, coming to think like—and when possible act like—central bankers in the advanced industrial democracies. This very result, though, revealed the limitations of internationally driven institutional transformation.

On the one hand, creating technically sophisticated central banks made an important difference in economic management in the postcommunist world. Without the help of the transnational central banking community, postcommunist states' transitions from their command economies would undoubtedly have been much rougher. In that sense, the transnational central banking community played an invaluable role in building state capacity in the postcommunist world. Indeed, the community provided postcommunist central bankers with the knowledge and tools required not only to implement new, internationally inspired policies but also, on occasion, to contest them.

On the other hand, the postcommunist central banks' rapid conversion to the church of central bank independence often meant ongoing battles and coordination failures with other government actors. The adoption of Western central banking practices before the conditions were in place for them to work also led to counterproductive, ineffective, or only partially effective policy making, undermining the central banks' legitimacy. While international conditionality could sometimes restrain postcommunist governments from undermining their central banks de jure, in practice many governments felt freer over time to challenge their central banks and began to succeed more often in those challenges. The end result was usually a central bank reasonably well integrated into the transnational central banking community, but which had limited support from the government, commercial banks, or the public. Those like the Bank of Russia under Putin represented a partial exception, but only because it compromised its policy autonomy for improved coordination with the government.

This raised important questions about how the transnational central banking community's transformation campaign affected national sovereignty in the postcommunist world. While its institution-building strengthened postcommunist state capacity, the community's efforts simultaneously challenged national sovereignty by transforming postcommunist central banks according to a foreign blueprint. The transformed central banks often served as agents of globalization, not only adopting the international community's principles and practices but promoting increased financial interdependence as well. The rapid transformation and international integration of postcommunist central banks as opposed to other domestic institutions often decreased mutual understanding, respect, and cooperation. As a result, many postcommunist central bankers grew to have more in common with central bankers abroad than with other political and economic actors in their own states. For the postcommunist central banks, community membership meant the need to constantly balance and manage the tensions arising from their status as national institutions with their transnational concerns and connections. This challenge deepened with the global financial crisis in 2007–8, when financial meltdown in the community's core revealed fundamental flaws in its central banking model.

PARADISE LOST

> **"Central banks have lost control."**
>
> —George Soros (2008)

In November 2007, former US Federal Reserve economist Marvin Goodfriend published a widely cited report entitled "How the World Achieved Consensus on Monetary Policy." In it, he lauded the process by which central bankers and academic economists worldwide had come to agree on a monetary policy model in the 1990s that reinforced the importance of price stability, inflation targeting, credibility (read independence), and transparency in central banking. Goodfriend concluded that, "the worldwide progress in monetary policy is ... a remarkable success story. Today, academics, central bank economists, and policy makers around the world work together on monetary policy as never before."[1] Central bankers—powerful, respected, and self-assured—were riding high.

The global financial crisis pierced the heart of the central banking community, challenging its very existence as a likeminded, powerful transnational network. Although trouble had been brewing under the surface for some time, the crisis erupted in 2007–8 when the United States' immense asset bubble popped and Lehman Brothers collapsed. The repercussions swept quickly around the world, leading to recession and economic upheaval. Europe was especially hard-hit as an initial, apparently modest European banking crisis had by 2010 turned into a sovereign debt crisis within the euro zone that shook the European Union. Central bankers suddenly found their most trusted monetary policy tools ineffective and their most cherished ideas called into question. In a paper entitled "Paradise Lost,"

---

1. Goodfriend 2007, 32.

former ECB chief economist Otmar Issing dryly admitted that "pre-crisis consensus strategies of monetary policy have been revealed as flawed."[2] Leading central banks were forced to adopt so-called unconventional monetary policies to address the challenges of the crisis and to rethink their basic mandates and operations. Claudio Borio of the BIS summed up the existential nature of the crisis for central bankers:

> Central banking will never be quite the same again after the global financial crisis . . . The crisis has shaken the foundations of the deceptively comfortable central banking world. Pre-crisis, the quintessential task of central banks was seen as quite straightforward: keep inflation within a tight range through control of a short-term interest rate and everything else will take care of itself. Everything was simple, tidy, and cozy. Post-crisis, many certainties have gone.[3]

Indeed, in the wake of the crisis, a paradoxical trend emerged. Although central bankers had lost their mystique, found their fundamental principles criticized, and suffered a deep crisis of legitimacy, governments responded by asking central bankers to do more rather than less. In addition to defending against inflation, central bankers were now to expand their monetary policy toolbox, engage in macroprudential regulation (the pursuit of systemic financial stability), and take a stronger role in micro-level financial sector regulation and supervision. These wider mandates, in turn, undermined the predominant rationale for central bank independence because they demanded increasing cooperation with other government agencies and more overtly engaged political questions of regulation and distribution. In short, the crisis challenged both of the central banking community's core principles: the narrow pursuit of price stability and the independence to do so from a technocratic perspective. This had paradigm-changing implications not just for central bankers, but for the entire international financial system and beyond.

Central Bankers and their Critics

Central banks came under fire from all sides after the crisis. On the right, central bankers took criticism for having allowed too-rapid credit creation through loose monetary policy. In a typical charge, US politician and publisher Steve Forbes wrote that "One point cannot be emphasized enough: If the Federal Reserve, with the connivance of the US Treasury Department, had not debased the dollar,

---

2. Issing 2012, 1.
3. Borio 2011; see also Alexandre Lamfalussy, former president of the European Monetary Institute, keynote address, BIS Ninth Annual Conference, on "The future of central banking under post-crisis mandates," June 24, 2010, Lucerne, Switzerland.

the 'reckless' and egregious excesses could not have happened. Jail bankers? Let's start with the real villains–central bankers and their political masters."[4] Leftist politicians and scholars were even more critical, seeing the crisis and the subsequent bailouts as a confirmation of their worst fears about central bankers and the neoliberal policy paradigm, with "neoliberal" a stand-in term for everything from IMF conditionality to financial deregulation. The right and left differed on the solutions to the problem, but agreed on its cause: central bankers deserved much of the blame for the crisis and its painful aftermath.

Central bankers had long been prime targets for skeptics of the international financial order, but as the crisis evolved, even respected voices from within the mainstream economics profession began to levy serious charges against the central banking community. Critics argued that central bankers had been lulled into complacency by the Great Moderation, the period of relatively stable global inflation and output that began in the 1980s. Believing that their monetary policy-making skills had ushered in a new and sustainable golden era in global finance, central bankers had not only ignored the signs of a potential crisis emerging, but had made the ensuing crisis worse through their narrow focus on price stability.[5]

The global financial crisis struck at the central banking community's weak point: its discomfort with financial regulation and supervision. Although the Asian financial crisis had previously demonstrated the interdependence of monetary policy and financial stability, this time the crisis hit the core states first and so could not be ignored. North American and West European central bankers could no longer blame others' poor choices for bringing on crisis, and instead had to consider to what extent their own ideational limitations and policy frameworks might have been responsible.

The crisis clearly demonstrated the ineffectiveness of the few measures introduced after the Asian crisis to improve financial stability. Czech IMF economist Martin Čihák, for example, found that although over fifty central banks had started to publish Financial Stability Reports (FSRs) by 2006, an astounding 96 percent of them had pronounced their financial systems healthy in the years immediately prior to the crisis. His follow-up post-crisis study found no direct

---

4. Steve Forbes, "Big Government and Central Banks: The Real Criminals," *Forbes*, August 12, 2013, www.forbes.com/sites/steveforbes/2013/07/24/big-government-and-central-banks-the-real-criminals/. For a similar, book-length critique, see Paul 2009. For a detailed analysis of crisis-era US Congressional attacks on the US Federal Reserve and the implications of the crisis for the Fed's independence, see Goodhart 2015.

5. For an excellent overview from the perspective of two well-known mainstream economists, see Davies and Green 2010. For an especially strong statement, see Joseph Stiglitz, "A Revolution in Monetary Policy: Lessons in the Wake of the Global Financial Crisis." Fifteenth C. D. Deshmukh Memorial Lecture, Reserve Bank of India, January 3, 2013.

link between publishing a FSR and actually achieving financial stability.[6] Similarly, in the wake of the global financial crisis the IMF and World Bank had to rework the voluntary Financial Sector Assessment Program launched in 1999, which had generally failed to identify or correct the problems that led to the crisis.[7] The Financial Stability Forum, likewise created in 1999 in response to the Asian crisis, also came under fire and received a name change—to the Financial Stability Board—and an expanded mandate.

Furthermore, a narrow focus on price stability meant that central bankers in both the United States and the United Kingdom had downplayed the domestic financial-sector problems that would eventually spark the crisis.[8] For example, the US Federal Reserve knew that an asset price bubble was building, but did nothing to fend it off. Instead, it kept interest rates at low levels in order to maintain price stability, a policy that may have actually expanded the growing bubble. Why did central bankers sit on their hands as the crisis was brewing? Before the crisis hit most central bankers thought that they had neither the mandate nor the tools to "lean against the wind" and deflate asset bubbles, arguing instead that central banks were better placed simply to clean up after the bubbles popped of their own accord. This preference for cleaning rather than leaning meant that central banks "allowed credit growth to run free and then flooded markets with liquidity after the crash, bailing out financial institutions and bondholders."[9]

The fascination with inflation targeting had exacerbated central bankers' pre-crisis predilection to focus on price stability to the exclusion of financial stability, unemployment, and growth issues. Central bankers' New Keynesian models further supported the pre-crisis prejudice, as the models could not anticipate the effects of financial-sector behavior on the real economy and how that behavior might interact with central bank policy choices.[10] Put simply, the models on which central bankers based their rate-setting decisions inevitably privileged price stability policies and did not take financial-sector developments or the potential international effects of central bank decisions into account. At a basic level, the models and behavior reflected central bankers' underlying beliefs that as long as they maintained price stability, financial stability and economic growth

---

6. Čihák 2006 and Čihák et al. 2012. The second study did, however, find a limited relationship between FSR quality and financial stability for a subset (forty-four cases) of the 80 central banks producing FSRs by 2011. For an even more devastating critique of pre-crisis FSRs, see Davies and Green 2010.

7. Viñals and Brooke 2009.

8. Shigehara and Atkinson 2011.

9. Eichengreen et al. 2011.

10. De Grauwe et al. 2008.

would follow. The prevailing beliefs and practices had thus reinforced each other and led central bankers astray. In short, tinkering around the edges had failed; the system needed a fundamental restructuring and post-crisis central banks needed to take a more hands-on role in promoting systemic financial stability.

Many critics drew a further damning conclusion: that both the central bankers' complicity in the crisis and the need for expanded mandates and tools meant that central bank independence had become an outmoded, inappropriate, or even dangerous concept in the post-crisis world.[11] As former World Bank chief economist Joseph Stiglitz argued, "The crisis has shown that one of the central principles advocated by Western central bankers—the desirability of central bank independence—was questionable at best," pointing out that greater independence had not led to better outcomes in the United States and Europe and had allowed central banks to ignore the distributional consequences of their policies.[12] Echoing these concerns, others pointed out that expanded mandates meant that central banks would more clearly be making political rather than technocratic decisions. Like it or not, therefore, central bank independence as conceived and practiced before the crisis would have to go.

Central Bankers on the Defensive

Central bankers were uncomfortable with proposed new mandates that required them to rethink their models, blurred the lines between monetary and fiscal policy, and challenged their independence. Although they engaged in extensive self-criticism and lesson drawing after the crisis, the community's nature made making a collective paradigm shift from within more difficult. The collapse of communism had played to the transnational central banking community's strengths, as its tightly knit network, relative political autonomy, and shared worldview facilitated the transmission and reinforcement of its received wisdom and practices to the postcommunist world. But these same qualities complicated the community's ability to deal with the global financial crisis. After the crisis, the same community leaders used the same community forums and consultation processes to talk in the same language about the extent to which they should consider abandoning their hard-won beliefs and practices. As a result, while central bankers collectively recognized the need for an increased focus on financial stability, many core community members also circled the wagons to reaffirm

---

11. For example, see Artus 2007, Allen and Carletti 2010, Palley 2013, Pixley et al. 2013.

12. Joseph Stiglitz, "A Revolution in Monetary Policy: Lessons in the Wake of the Global Financial Crisis"; see also Griffith-Jones et al. 2010.

their existing principles and practices at the same time, sowing dissent within the community.[13]

The first defense was to reframe the critical narrative about the causes and aftermath of the financial crisis. Many central bankers argued that if anything they had done their jobs too well during the Great Moderation, because the long period of macroeconomic stability had lulled markets into a false sense of security and contributed to excessive risk-taking in the financial sector.[14] Monetary policy did not cause the crisis; at worst, it failed to prevent it or was a minor contributing factor (and that only because the Fed should have taken its price stability mandate even *more* seriously than it did).[15] Community members similarly congratulated themselves for their responsiveness after the crisis. Most notably, IMF managing director Christine Lagarde dubbed central banks the "heroes" of the financial crisis. One central banker stated that "in [Lagarde's] view, one which is widely held, the extraordinary actions undertaken by central banks, particularly in the advanced economies, probably saved the global economy from a far worse fate than we are currently experiencing."[16] Another said that central bankers were "rightly hailed as saviors of the global financial system."[17] If central bankers had done their jobs well both before and after the crisis, why should they now make fundamental changes?

---

13. I base this section primarily on an analysis of 935 public speeches by central bankers given between 2008 and 2015 that discuss the lessons of the financial crisis. I used the BIS database at www.bis.org/list/cbspeeches/index.htm to identify speeches to analyze (all speeches quoted in this chapter can be accessed through the BIS database). Speeches by central bankers from Western Europe and North America represented nearly 60 percent of the total; other countries appearing most often included India, Japan, Australia, South Africa, Chile, Malaysia, and South Korea, in that order. I supplemented the analysis with IMF and BIS working papers discussing the lessons from the crisis.

14. E.g., Christian Noyer, governor of the Banque de France and chairman of the BIS board of directors, "Monetary Policy—Lessons from the Crisis," speech at the Bank of France/Deutsche Bundesbank Spring Conference on Fiscal and Monetary Policy Challenges in the Short and Long Run, Hamburg, May 19, 2011.

15. For the argument that monetary policy played no role in the crisis, see, e.g., Lars Svensson, deputy governor of the Sveriges Riksbank, "Monetary Policy after the Crisis," speech at the conference Asia's Role in the Post-Crisis Global Economy, held at the Federal Reserve Bank of San Francisco, November 29, 2011. For the view that monetary policy did not play a major role but that the US should have "leaned" against the bubble to properly protect price stability, see, e.g., José De Gregorio, governor of the Central Bank of Chile, "Price and Financial Stability in Modern Central Banking," keynote speech at the joint Latin American and Caribbean Economic Association—Latin American Chapter of the Econometric Society Conference 2011, University Adolfo Ibáñez, Santiago, November 11, 2011.

16. Gill Marcus, governor of the South African Reserve Bank, "The implications of the crisis for monetary policy," speech at the Bureau for Economic Research Annual Conference, Sandton, June 6, 2013.

17. Borio 2011.

The second defense was accordingly to insist that the crisis had actually reinforced the arguments for price stability and central bank independence. As the ECB's Jürgen Stark put it, "we need to reaffirm the principles which have been at the core of modern central banking and have served us well during the crisis, namely the centrality of price stability for monetary policy, and the importance of central bank independence and effective communication in the execution of this goal."[18] Central bankers around the world argued that price stability should remain the primary goal of central banks even if other mandates were added, often defending inflation targeting regimes at the same time.[19] The community's dismissal of IMF research director Olivier Blanchard's proposal to consider even raising inflation targets reflected the narrowness of the post-crisis community debate. In a widely discussed paper, Blanchard and his colleagues argued that low pre-crisis inflation levels had left central banks without the room needed to cut rates enough to revive demand after the crisis hit.[20] Low inflation had led to a liquidity trap, a situation in which central banks trying to stave off recession reached the zero lower bound on the nominal interest rate too quickly and could no longer use conventional rate policy to affect market behavior. The implication was that a higher pre-crisis inflation target—Blanchard suggested 4 percent as a number to explore—might have reduced or prevented the need for central banks to use unconventional monetary policies such as quantitative easing to deal with the crisis. Central bankers took special issue with this call to revise inflation targets upwards, with one dubbing it an idea that had been "universally rejected by the central banking community."[21] In speech after speech, central bankers

---

18. Jürgen Stark, member of the ECB executive board, "The global financial crisis and the role of monetary policy," speech at the 13th Annual Emerging Markets Conference 2011, Washington DC, September 24, 2011. For a similar perspective from another Bundesbank veteran, see Jens Weidemann, who said, "just because something is old, it doesn't necessarily mean that it is also outmoded. That goes for traditional regulatory policy. It also applies to the independence of central banks and price stability as its primary objective . . . The current crisis has . . . above all, shown once again how relevant these guiding economic policy principles continue to be." Jens Weidemann, president of the Deutsche Bundesbank, "Crisis management and regulatory policy," Walter Eucken Lecture at the Walter Eucken Institute, Freiburg, February 11, 2013.

19. For example, when new Bank of England governor Mark Carney suggested the possibility of targeting nominal GDP instead of inflation, there was an immediate backlash from most other central bankers. See, for example, Central Banking Newsdesk, "Nominal GDP dismissed as viable policy target in Central Banking debate," Central Banking, March 21, 2013.

20. Blanchard et al. 2010.

21. John Murray, deputy governor of the Bank of Canada, "Re-examining Canada's Monetary Policy Framework—Recent Research and Outstanding Issues," speech at the Canadian Association for Business Economics, Kingston, Ontario, August 24, 2010. See also the extended criticism of Blanchard and an invocation by name of other leading central bankers who share that criticism in Stefan Gerlach, deputy governor of the Central Bank of Ireland, "Monetary Policy after the Crisis,"

maintained that even with the expansion of their mandates, price stability and independence as previously understood must remain the core values of central banking. The community reinforced these principles through its embrace of "transparency" and "communication."[22] Central bankers adopted transparency measures on the assumption that markets would respond more rationally once given clearer signals such as inflation targets, that governments would support central bank priorities if only they better understood them, and that transparency in terms of *explaining* central bank actions could deflect political desires and attempts to *control* them.

Central bankers' understandable wish to turn the clock back was similarly reflected in their ongoing discussion of "normalization" and "exit strategies" from the "unconventional" monetary policies adopted in the wake of the crisis. This concern with exit strategies had already begun in 2007, in tandem with the introduction of unconventional policies. While it made sense to plan ahead, forward thinking alone cannot explain the intensity, frequency, and immediacy of the exit strategy discussions. The names themselves—exit strategies, normalization, and unconventional policies—were telling. Central bankers are nothing if not lovers of convention. Having had little choice but to engage in policies outside of their comfort zones, many central bankers could not wait to abandon them and restore normality as soon as they deemed it prudent. Indeed, at the extreme the ECB long delayed adopting unconventional policy measures to restore confidence in euro-zone financial institutions, and its eventual decision to do so resulted in the successive resignations of two German representatives from its board.

This desire to right the central banking ship manifested itself most clearly in the central bankers' final defensive strategy, the premature attempt to declare a new consensus around which central bankers could rally. The new consensus would integrate a common approach to financial stability into the existing

address at the 44th Annual Money, Macro and Finance Conference, Trinity College, Dublin, September 8, 2012. For a fascinating declaration that defining price stability as a 2 percent inflation rate has become the core element of the post-crisis central banking consensus, see former ECB president Jean-Claude Trichet's statements in Central Banking Newsdesk, "Trichet Sees 'Conceptual Convergence' among Major Central Banks," Central Banking, October 14, 2013.

22. Transparency refers to central bank openness on policy objectives; data, models, and forecasts; decision-making and operational procedures; and the implications of policy decisions (Eijffinger and Geraats 2006). Communication refers to managing market expectations by releasing central bank voting records and minutes, as well as explaining central bank policy through practices such as issuing "forward guidance" (hints about future central bank policy) (De Haan et al. 2007). Transparency levels and communication efforts rose significantly in the late 1990s and 2000s; see Geraats 2002, Demertzis and Hughes Hallett 2007, Dincer and Eichengreen 2007. For further discussion, see Eijffinger and Cruijsen 2007, Blinder et al. 2008, Crowe and Meade 2008, Dincer and Eichengreen 2013.

consensus on price stability and independence, finding a way to add this third pillar without compromising or contradicting the original two. The transnational central banking community had grown powerful in the 1990s in great part because it spoke with a unified, authoritative voice about its core principles. Deprived of its consensus, central bankers' privileged role on both the international and national stages was at risk. Without such a new consensus defining central bankers' preferred approach to financial stability, central bankers would not only find themselves working at cross purposes, but could lose their ability to act as a community to protect the elements of the old consensus on which they still agreed. Accordingly, time and again central bankers spoke of an "evolving consensus," a "broad consensus coming out of the crisis," the need "to promote a new intellectual consensus," or a post-crisis "convergence" in thinking.

Trouble in Paradise

The language of consensus masked strong disagreements within the community about how to handle the crisis and what to do afterward. The US Federal Reserve had responded to the crisis by rediscovering its dual mandate, letting interest rates hit rock bottom, and engaging in a massive program of quantitative easing that bailed out the domestic financial industry. Meanwhile, the ECB under Jean-Claude Trichet cut interest rates slowly and engaged only timidly in unconventional monetary policy, contributing to the emergence of the sovereign debt crisis in Europe. The ECB began to act more boldly after new president Mario Draghi famously declared in July 2012 that, "the ECB is ready to do whatever it takes to preserve the euro."[23] Nevertheless, the resulting Outright Monetary Transactions program stopped short of a true quantitative easing policy since the ECB insisted that any bond purchases would be fully sterilized; that is, they would not result in additional net liquidity in the financial system. Within the European Union, national central bankers from the north and south argued about the ECB's policy choices. The IMF for its part found itself at odds with the ECB over the ECB's draconian austerity-oriented approach to euro zone recovery, with the two sides having especially sharp words over the Greek bailout program.[24]

---

23. Mario Draghi, president of the European Central Bank, speech at the Global Investment Conference, London, July 26, 2012.

24. "Greece: Ex Post Evaluation of Exceptional Access under the 2010 Stand-By Arrangement," IMF Country Report 13/156, www.imf.org/external/pubs/cat/longres.aspx?sk=40639.0. See also Johnson 2014.

Seeking a way forward, sixteen noted economists and former central bankers comprising the Committee on International and Economic Policy Reform argued for expanding central bank mandates in a comprehensive September 2011 report entitled *Rethinking Central Banking*. The Committee called for central banks to adopt financial stability as a key policy goal and to use macroprudential tools to achieve that end, not as a temporary crisis measure but as a permanent expansion of the central banking toolbox. The report stated bluntly that, "the traditional separation, in which monetary policy targets price stability and regulatory policies target financial stability, and the two sets of policies operate largely independently of each other, is no longer tenable."[25] It recommended that central banks adopt tools such as countercyclical capital buffers, credit controls, and improved resolution regimes (especially for Systematically Important Financial Institutions, or SIFIs), and that central banks more formally coordinate their policies at the international level in order to minimize negative cross-border spillovers. In doing so, the report called simultaneously for an expansion of central banks' mandates, increased central bank coordination and responsibility at the national and international levels, and a strengthening of central bank independence.

Although central bankers reluctantly agreed that they would now need to take financial stability more seriously, they disagreed on how to define, prioritize, and pursue it, and these disagreements mattered now that governments demanded that central bankers expand their mandates to include it. How should central bankers understand financial stability? Should it be a co-equal mandate with price stability? Should the policy toolkits for pursuing price stability and financial stability be separate or not? Should the decision-making bodies for the two be separate or not? How much of the responsibility should reside within the central bank itself? What role should the central bank take in financial-sector supervision and regulation? Should central banks consider international spillover effects in their policy making, and if so, how? Central bankers and their governments hotly debated all of these questions, but years after the crisis were far from collectively resolving any of them, much less birthing a new paradigm for central banking. As Bank of Canada governor Stephen Poloz observed in 2015, "Incorporating financial stability into our monetary policy framework remains a work in progress. As a practitioner, it still feels to me like we are adding various rooms onto a house we love, rather than creating a new, elegant, and coherent structure."[26]

---

25. Eichengreen et al. 2011, 3.

26. Stephen Poloz, governor of the Bank of Canada, "Lessons Old and New: Reinventing Central Banking," Western University President's Lecture, London, Ontario, February 24, 2015.

Central bankers also faced the troubling problem that their favorite modeling tools were wholly inadequate for these new tasks. It became clear that attempting to incorporate financial-sector activities into the models might actually make them less useful than before, and that rational expectations models could not in any case cope with the true Knightian uncertainty that arises from complex, fast-moving, adaptive, and interdependent market behaviors. This fundamental uncertainty, rapid financial market evolution, and information-poor environment confounded regulatory reform as well. In his now famous "the dog and the Frisbee" address to the 2012 central banking conclave at Jackson Hole, the Bank of England's Andrew Haldane broke with tradition and decried the ever-increasing complexity of regulatory approaches, stating that "to ask today's regulators to save us from tomorrow's crisis using yesterday's toolbox is to ask a border collie to catch a Frisbee by first applying Newton's Law of Gravity."[27] Haldane used this metaphor to argue for much simpler, more adaptive and intuitive models and regulation: dogs can catch Frisbees with a combination of instinct and practice, so central bankers should emulate them. Yet embracing greater simplicity would also make the new world of central banking less arcane and technocratic, more a political art open to interpretation than the econometric science it had aspired to be. Paradise lost indeed.

Postcommunist Central Banks and the Crisis

The global financial crisis and ensuing discord in the transnational central banking community unsettled postcommunist central banks. As we have seen, internationally directed and well-timed lobbying, training, and technical assistance efforts in the 1990s led to rapid and surprisingly convergent institutional change in postcommunist central banks. The high levels of legal central bank independence introduced in the 1990s had held steady or increased throughout most of the region in subsequent years despite domestic criticisms and challenges. Dincer and Eichengreen found that by the time of the global financial crisis postcommunist states boasted eight of the ten most legally independent central banks in the world, with Kyrgyzstan, the Baltic states, Romania, and Armenia leading

---

27. Andrew G. Haldane, executive director for Financial Stability and member of the Financial Policy Committee and Vasileios Madouros, economist, Bank of England, "The Dog and the Frisbee," speech at the Federal Reserve Bank of Kansas City's 36th economic policy symposium, "The Changing Policy Landscape," Jackson Hole, Wyoming, August 31, 2012.

the way.[28] Postcommunist states as a group also had higher legal independence than central banks in any other region of the world.[29] In many cases, the pre-crisis central banking consensus demanding independence and a primary price stability mandate had been enshrined not just in law but in new constitutions. Postcommunist central bankers had embraced the pursuit and defense of central bank independence. In the postcommunist context, independence had a deeper meaning than in the established democracies of North America and West Europe. For central bankers in Central and East Europe, the Balkans, and Eurasia, independence meant not simply the freedom to conduct their own policies but insulation from entrenched patterns of government corruption. Independence meant that they could act and be treated as technocratic professionals rather than government bureaucrats, with all the communist-era baggage the latter designation entailed.

Within central banks themselves, training and technical assistance programs had transformed the mindsets and practices of central bank staff, and the central banks and bankers of the region quickly came to resemble those in the core of the transnational central banking community in key respects, especially in regard to monetary policy. Nearly all postcommunist central banks declared price stability to be their key objective, even when legislation provided for other objectives as well. The great majority further subscribed to the community's preference for inflation-targeting regimes, either directly through announcing their own inflation targets or indirectly through adopting the euro and thus the ECB's monetary policy.

Central bankers from the region had, by the time of the crisis, become well embedded in the transnational central banking community. More and more came to work at the IMF, BIS, or ECB, as well as to participate in training and technical assistance programs as teachers rather than students. For example,

---

28. Of the nineteen post-communist states they examined, eight increased their already high levels of legal central bank independence after 1998, while the level fell in only two countries (Bulgaria and Georgia), and very slightly at that. They based their calculations on the central bank laws of 89 countries accessed via central bank websites, the IMF Law Library, and the UC-Berkeley Law Library. In only one of the nineteen post-communist cases (Georgia) did the scores change after 2007, indicating that these rankings overwhelmingly represented legislation enacted before the financial crisis. Dincer and Eichengreen calculated the LVAU and LVAW indices for each state using Cukierman, Webb, and Neyapti's (2002) methodology (see table 3.1) and added two more detailed but highly correlated indices, CBIU and CBIW, that include measures on governor and board reappointment, government representation on boards, and government intervention in exchange rate policy. Dincer and Eichengreen 2013.

29. This includes Europe after recalculating its score to exclude the post-communist European states.

in 2011 the IMF resident representative in Kyrgyzstan was a Georgian central banker who had begun his career in the National Bank of Georgia (NBG) in 1993.[30] He told me that for his first assignment at the NBG in 1993, his boss had given him a pamphlet in Russian called "What is the IMF?" and asked him to summarize it for his fellow central bankers. By the time we spoke in his office in the NBKR, he confirmed the high level of integration, rotation, and knowledge among central bank and IMF staff in the region. Central bankers in the new EU member states became even more closely bound to the community. Once in the euro zone postcommunist central bank governors sat on the ECB governing council; many more central bankers from the new-member states worked within the ECB itself. People like Josef Tošovský, the former Czech National Bank governor who became director of the Financial Stability Institute and a board member of the Financial Services Volunteer Corps, epitomized this integration. Postcommunist central banks were typically among the most internationally respected and least corrupt institutions in their countries. While regularly challenged by domestic politicians and difficult circumstances, especially in Eurasia, they had usually been able to count on the support of the transnational central banking community in their efforts to defend and extend their newly adopted principles and practices.

Then came the global financial crisis. The postcommunist EU members were slammed on four fronts: their West European export markets collapsed, their foreign-owned banks significantly slowed credit provision, their foreign-currency denominated loans became difficult to service, and the contagion effect meant that troubles in the weakest financial markets spread quickly to the others. Hungary, Romania, and Latvia required IMF bailouts, while all experienced rising inflation, falling GDP, and a significant credit crunch. The Baltic states and Bulgaria—non-euro zone members with fixed exchange rates—suffered the most, without either the protection of the euro or the monetary flexibility to devalue. Over the criticism of the ECB, the IMF even suggested that the Baltic states consider unilaterally adopting the euro. The crisis pushed the small Baltic countries and Bulgaria painfully toward the euro, while further encouraging Hungary, the Czech Republic, Poland, and Romania to postpone euro adoption and shore up their inflation-targeting regimes. In much of Eurasia the situation was worse. The states most highly integrated into the international economy were most affected, but even Belarus found itself in need of an IMF program. Armenia, Georgia, Moldova, and Ukraine took IMF programs as well, while Russia spent down its

---

30. Author's interview with the IMF Resident Representative to the Kyrgyz Republic, Bishkek, Kyrgyzstan, June 16, 2011.

vast, oil-fueled supply of foreign-currency reserves to support its economy in the face of a significant GDP decline in 2009. The crisis thus tested central banks across the region as they attempted to restore stability under unexpected and difficult conditions.

Postcommunist central bankers acted quickly with their available tools to confront the evolving situation over which they had only limited control.[31] Despite the challenges of the crisis, their reactions to the ensuing debate over central banking's future revealed just how well integrated into the existing system they had become. Most expressed the same kinds of concerns and defended their principles and practices in the same language as core-state central bankers. As the Czech National Bank's Mojmír Hampl wrote:

> Revolution is not on the cards. We are not turning all existing knowledge on its head. No one is saying, for example, that high or higher inflation would be a good thing. Mercifully, IMF chief economist Olivier Blanchard's suggestion in that direction disappeared as quickly as it appeared. Inflation targeting, it seems, will be modified rather than abandoned. Similarly important questions with no clear answers are arising in the currently fashionable area of so-called financial stability.[32]

Long-time Romanian central bank governor Mugur Isărescu echoed these concerns, observing, "Experience has taught me that inflation is an insidious disease and should not be toyed with. As a matter of fact, one of the first pieces of advice I received as governor [in 1990] from experienced central bankers was that for a governor there is no such thing as too low inflation and too high foreign exchange reserves."[33] Postcommunist central banks continued to pursue inflation-targeting regimes, with key precrisis noninflation targeters like Russia and Kazakhstan confirming their intention to move in that direction. They similarly continued to develop and refine their models along standard New Keynesian lines. For example, the Magyar Nemzeti Bank worked with the IMF to introduce a new monetary policy model "constructed to strictly comply with the modern

---

31. For an especially laudatory review of Central and East European policy making during the crisis, see Åslund 2010.

32. Mojmír Hampl, vice governor of the Czech National Bank, "Central Banks after the Crisis: Many Questions, Few Answers," *Central Banking Journal*, January 20, 2011.

33. Mugur Isărescu, governor of the National Bank of Romania, "Monetary Policy during Transition. How to Manage Paradigm Shifts," presentation at the annual conference of the European Association for Banking and Financial History, June 7–9, 2012.

paradigm of monetary policy" and support the MNB in its inflation-targeting efforts.[34] For their part, the smaller postcommunist countries that had pursued euro zone membership continued to deepen their integration, with three joining the euro zone after the crisis hit and the others maintaining their currency boards or euro pegs—all amid talk of Greece and perhaps others abandoning the euro.

At the same time, the crisis exposed an increasing discomfort with the implicit hierarchy between the established and postcommunist central bankers. The central bankers from postcommunist EU member states in particular criticized the ECB for discriminatory practices. While the ECB had quickly granted euro swap lines to central banks in non-euro states such as Denmark and Sweden once the crisis began, it not only initially refused to do so for the postcommunist central banks, but it tried to hide the existence of the Swedish swap line from them.[35] The postcommunist central bankers also criticized the ECB's moves toward developing single supervisory and resolution mechanisms for the euro zone, calling them overly intrusive tools that could be used to bail out big West European banks to the detriment of East European institutions.[36] Many similarly critiqued the micro-management of Basel III, pointing out that the regulatory rules did not take the different conditions of emerging market economies into account.[37]

Acknowledging the need to better address financial stability issues, postcommunist central banks often more decisively embraced macroprudential tools than did their core-state counterparts. In fact, they pointed out that under the current circumstances core central banks perhaps had something to learn from them, since the postcommunist central bankers had more recent experience dealing with financial-sector instability. The Bank of Russia increased its regulatory responsibilities, the Czech National Bank added a financial stability wing, and the Magyar Nemzeti Bank took over the formerly separate Hungarian Financial Services Agency, while the National Bank of Slovakia and the National Bank of the Kyrgyz Republic shored up their existing macroprudential and regulatory capacities. Overall, postcommunist central bankers reacted to the crisis much like their core-state counterparts, using it as an opportunity to reaffirm key elements

---

34. Szilágyi et al. 2013. The IMF and MNB developed the model in 2010–11 and put it into use in 2011.

35. Thanks to Daniela Gabor for raising this point. See also Shahin Vallee, "Behind Closed Doors at the ECB," *FT Alphaville*, March 30, 2010, http://ftalphaville.ft.com/2010/03/30/191041/behind-closed-doors-at-the-ecb/; EurActiv, "'New Europe' Loses Out in ECB Currency Swaps," March 3, 2010, www.euractiv.com/euro-finance/new-europe-loses-ecb-currency-sw-news-299923.

36. For example, see Lehmann et al. 2011.

37. For example, see Central Banking Newsdesk, "Czech Governor Slams One-Size-Fits-All Regulation," *Central Banking*, August 28, 2013. See also the Bank of Russia's 2013 decision to postpone adoption of Basel III standards and lower the planned capital adequacy requirements.

of the existing consensus while struggling through difficult questions of how to best address new financial stability concerns. Throughout the crisis, postcommunist central bankers for the most part retained and defended their previous networks and views.

The same could not always be said for their governments, however. As we have seen, postcommunist central bankers had become well integrated into the transnational central banking community, but their governments often accepted the central banks' independence and price stability pursuits only when they seemed immediately effective or when constrained to do so by external pressures. By demonstrating the fragility of the international financial system and disrupting the coherence and authority of the transnational central banking community, the global financial crisis opened the door for a fundamental rethinking of government priorities regarding central banking and financial globalization.

Two postcommunist governments stood out in challenging the international status quo: Hungary under Viktor Orbán and Russia under Vladimir Putin. The global financial crisis had hit Hungary and Russia especially hard. Hungary became the first state to request an IMF bailout, while Russia experienced the crisis's largest single-year GDP swing in a major world economy. This painful crisis experience convinced both governments that the international financial order was bankrupt and that a fundamentally new approach was necessary. Both turned to system-defying financial nationalist policies in response.

Financial nationalism is an economic strategy that employs financial levers—including monetary policy, currency interventions, and interactions with local and international financial systems—to promote the nation.[38] It entails state direction of the domestic financial system and of financial flows in order to benefit national insiders, protect national wealth, and promote national sovereignty. Financial nationalists are skeptical of universal economic ideologies and of ceding control over national monies and financial institutions to international actors. As such, financial nationalism in practice involves attempting to reduce the influence of external financial conditionality and constraints on domestic politicians' ability to make and implement economic decisions. All of this is done in the name of the nation, in which state financial activism and national patriotism become conflated.

Elected on a nationalist-populist platform in 2010, Orbán's Fidesz government pursued a financial nationalist policy that flaunted community norms and denounced the IMF, ECB, and the role of foreign banks in Hungary. Putin, for his

---

38. See Johnson and Barnes (2015) and Johnson and Köstem (2015) for more detailed discussions of financial nationalism in Hungary and Russia, respectively.

part, demanded the restructuring of the international financial architecture and monetary systems, championed the BRICS group of emerging-market powers as a counterweight, promoted the Russia-led Eurasian Economic Union as an EU alternative, and sought to "nationalize" the Russian financial system by forcing elites to bring their money home and reducing Russian dependence on the Western-led international financial system. In the process, both governments worked to make their central banks instruments with which to advance these alternative visions. The MNB and Bank of Russia took on significant new roles as demanded by their governments, while at the same time trying to protect price stability in their economies and professionalism in their ranks. Central bankers in the MNB and Bank of Russia were pulled in different directions in attempting to reconcile their training and instincts with their governments' programs, revealing the extent to which a "Westernized" central bank could be turned to alternative ends.

The Magyar Nemzeti Bank and "Orbánomics"

In April 2010, Viktor Orbán and his center-right Fidesz party came to power in Hungary by running on a platform of "economic self-rule." Unlike the classical economic nationalist programs of the 1960s and 1970s, however, Orbánomics emphasized financial nationalist policies rather than achieving greater autonomy in trade and production. In pursuing this strategy, Orbán repeatedly disregarded the IMF and the EU, publicly denounced the IMF and its loan programs, undermined the independence of the MNB, and challenged the role of foreign banks and currencies in Hungary. Campaigning on the successes of Orbánomics, Fidesz again dominated the April 2014 parliamentary elections, emerging with its second parliamentary supermajority. In his 2014 State of the Nation address, Orbán boasted that "we had had enough of the politics that is forever concerned with how we might satisfy the West, the bankers, big capital and the foreign press . . . Over the past four years we have overcome that . . . subservient mentality . . . Hungary will not succumb again!"[39]

The global financial crisis and subsequent European sovereign debt crisis provided fertile ground in Europe for a resurgence of financial nationalism.[40]

---

39. Prime Minister Viktor Orbán's State of the Nation Address, Government of Hungary, February 16, 2014, www.kormany.hu/en/prime-minister-s-office/the-prime-ministers-speeches/prime-minister-viktor-orban-s-state-of-the-nation-address.

40. Indeed, many Western European governments moved quickly to protect their own domestic financial institutions at the expense of other EU member states as the crisis broke (Dabrowski 2010).

In Hungary, the crisis had weakened the forint, undermining the ability of mortgage holders and others to repay their extensive foreign-currency denominated loans. To halt the slide in the forint, the Socialist government in power in 2008 had accepted a loan of 20 billion euro from the IMF, World Bank, and EU, and in exchange pledged to redouble its austerity efforts. Those measures included cuts in wages and pensions, as well as the elimination of the thirteen-month salary for government employees.[41] Nevertheless, the economy shrank another 6.8 percent in 2009, even as central government debt rose from 75 percent to 83 percent of GDP. Hungary's financial and trade openness and its international integration, formerly a point of pride and source of strength, had made it exceptionally vulnerable to contagion from the crisis.[42] Moreover, pro-cyclical austerity policies enforced by the IMF and EU not only failed to improve the economic situation in the short term, but made matters worse politically as Orbán and other opposition leaders blamed the Socialists, austerity-oriented international conditionality, and foreign-owned banks for the economic struggles of ordinary Hungarians. As Mark Blyth provocatively argued in *Austerity: The History of a Dangerous Idea*, "Populism, nationalism, and calls for the return of 'God and gold' are what unequal austerity generates."[43] Viktor Orbán and Fidesz contested the 2010 parliamentary elections on a nationalist-populist platform, vowing to cut taxes, restore economic growth, and support local business. Fidesz and its tiny Christian Democratic coalition partner won in a landslide and secured a two-thirds parliamentary super-majority, enough to enact constitutional change.

Once in power, the Orbán government introduced its own particular kind of center-right financial nationalism, using its supermajority to adopt unorthodox financial policies aimed at increasing Hungary's monetary sovereignty and privileging national insiders, while at the same time achieving deficit and debt control. In its pursuit of economic self-rule, the Orbán government most clearly identified the IMF, the MNB's incumbent leadership, and foreign-owned commercial banks as "outsiders." More than any other European leader at the time, Orbán identified the transnational central banking community as unwanted agents of globalization. To put his vision into practice, Orbán had to reject IMF support and bring the MNB under his control, both of which he accomplished in short order.

41. Cordero 2009; BBC, "Premier Says Hungary Needs IMF Agreement Because of Euro-Zone Crisis," BBC Monitoring European, September 11, 2012.

42. Connolly 2012.

43. Blyth 2013.

Rejecting the IMF

Although the Fidesz government initially sought to negotiate a renewed standby loan with the IMF, Prime Minister Orbán made it clear that he intended to protect Hungarian national sovereignty in the process. As Orbán stated at a news conference in April 2010, "In my view, neither the IMF nor the EU's financial bodies are our bosses. We are not subordinate to them . . . We'll be able to come to an agreement with the IMF about the contents of a package that will take effect already this year but . . . we will not accept diktats."[44] Difficulties emerged almost immediately as the IMF and the EU challenged the Orbán government over its revenue-generating strategies, attacks on the central bank, and proposed budget deficit target. Rather than backing down, the government stuck with the key elements of its policies, and Orbán stepped up his nationalist rhetoric, stating that:

> We interpret our agreement with the IMF—our participation in the IMF's system of cooperation—as a borrowing agreement. The IMF sees it as an economic policy agreement. This is not in our interest . . . The Hungarian interest is that if necessary we should make loan agreements with the IMF on a regular basis. It is not in our interest to sign economic policy agreements with the IMF, as that unnecessarily limits the room to manoeuver of . . . the Hungarian government, Hungarian parliament and lawmakers.[45]

Negotiations broke down in July 2010, at which point Hungary declared that it did not need IMF support. A declining forint coupled with the downgrading of Hungarian bonds to "junk" status brought Hungary back to the table in November 2011. Nevertheless, the fundamental obstacles to agreement between Hungary and the IMF remained. Orbán argued that Hungary should be able to chart its own course, since the real reason the country was even considering outside assistance in the first place was because of the crisis in the EU, not because of mistakes inside the country.[46] In fact, his government went so far as to take out full-page ads in Hungarian newspapers in October 2012 that proclaimed, "We will not give in to the IMF!" and "We will not give up Hungary's independence."[47] In December 2012 the Orbán government once again pointedly broke off talks

---

44. Gergely Szakacs and Krisztina Than, "Hungary's Orban Wants Deal with IMF, Cbank Cuts Rates," Reuters News, April 26, 2010.

45. "Hungary PM: IMF Is Lender, Not Economic Policy Setter," Reuters News, August 30, 2010.

46. "Hungary Needs IMF Because of Problems in Europe, Not at Home—Orban," MTI—EcoNews, September 10, 2012.

47. "Aid-Seeking Hungary Launches Anti-IMF Ad Campaign," Agence France Presse, October 9, 2012.

with the IMF after the IMF refused to sanction Hungary's economic program; Hungary's unexpected ability to tap international bond markets in the absence of such an agreement made this continued defiance possible. As a further demonstration of autonomy and defiance, in July 2013 Matolcsy sent a letter to IMF director Christine Lagarde indicating that the MNB would begin proceedings to shut down the IMF's longstanding representative office in Budapest.[48] The IMF resident representative left Hungary at the end of her term in August; at the same time, the Hungarian government repaid in full its remaining debt to the IMF.

Repurposing the NBH

Even during the 2010 election campaign Orbán had criticized the MNB and its governor András Simor for having allowed foreign-currency loans to proliferate in Hungary, for not cutting interest rates fast enough, and for not adopting unconventional monetary policy measures such as quantitative easing to stimulate the economy. They also considered Simor personally disloyal to Hungary because he had owned the Cyprus-based Trevisol Management Company while leading the MNB. Orbán "dubbed Simor an 'offshore knight' and said that the country wanted 'to be proud of the central bank, including its leaders.'"[49] He also cut Simor's pay by 75 percent in October 2010, along with that of other top central bankers, as part of a program to cap government salaries.

Simor lashed back at Orbán, demanding that the independence of the central bank be enshrined in the constitution during Fidesz's planned constitutional revision process and appealing to the transnational central banking community and to international norms in rejecting governmental pressures. The EU and IMF took Simor's side, but their efforts failed to stem the government's attacks on the MNB. Before the four external rate-setters on the MNB Monetary Council came to the end of their terms in February 2011, the government changed central bank legislation to make all four external members parliamentary appointees, as opposed to the previous system in which the central bank choose two and the government the other two. The government used its new powers to replace the four who stepped down with like-minded allies. The new members subsequently

---

48. Central Banking Newsdesk, "Central Bank of Hungary Moves to Shut IMF's Budapest Office," Central Banking, July 15, 2013.

49. Ramya Jaidev, "Incoming Party Renews Efforts to Topple Hungary's Simor," Central Banking, April 28, 2010.

drove interest rates steadily downwards by overriding the votes of the three internal MNB members (including Simor) at repeated Monetary Council meetings in defiance of IMF warnings about the likely inflationary pressures that would result.

On December 30, 2011, the parliament overwhelmingly passed controversial new central bank legislation that conflicted with international norms on central bank independence and operations, provoking an outcry by the MNB, IMF, and ECB. The government backtracked quickly on the most dramatic measure—a proposal to merge the MNB with the Hungarian Financial Supervisory Agency (HFSA) and subordinate the MNB governor to the head of the unified body. However, it was not persuaded to temper the rest of the legislation until the European Commission initiated legal action against Hungary to prevent the law from taking effect.[50]

Attacks on the MNB increased again in February 2013, as the State Audit Office used powers granted to it through the new legislation to accuse the MNB of having illegally passed state secrets in the form of proprietary financial information to the IMF, another indication of the institution's perceived disloyalty to the Hungarian nation. Most significantly, in March 2013 Orbán replaced Simor—who had reached the end of his term—with economics minister György Matolcsy, an Orbán ally and outspoken proponent of easing monetary policy. Indeed, the MNB lowered the central rate by another twenty-five basis points shortly after Matolcsy took office, and then again at regular intervals. Matolcsy followed up his appointment by conducting a housecleaning at the MNB, firing multiple top long-time MNB staffers (including the bank's chief economist, the head of financial analysis, and the director of the research department) and demoting two vice governors. Many others quit as well, including vice governor and financial stability department director Júlia Király, who publicly denounced Matolcsy's policies on her way out the door.[51] The MNB and the HFSA did merge in October 2013, but with the MNB leadership retaining control; under Matolcsy, this development served the government's interests quite well.

Matolcsy and the government worked hand-in-hand to pursue Orbán's financial nationalist program. Beyond the persistent rate cuts and support for reworking foreign currency loans, in April 2013 the MNB introduced

---

50. Central Banking Newsdesk, "Latest Amendments to Hungarian Central Bank Law Appease IMF," *Central Banking*, June 27, 2012.

51. T. Bowker, "Former Hungarian Deputy Says Police Investigation Is the 'Craziest Thing I Have Ever Seen,'" *Central Banking*, December 9, 2013.

the "Funding for Growth Scheme," a massive monetary stimulus package that provided commercial banks with zero-interest loans (with preference to domestic banks) that would then be channeled to Hungarian small and medium-sized enterprises at a fixed 2.5 percent interest rate. As Matolcsy noted in announcing the program, "Hungarian SMEs get loans, if they can, at interest rates three or four times higher than foreign companies operating in Hungary. We consider this unacceptable."[52] This program was designed to boost GDP, counter the drop in business lending, reduce the proportion of foreign-currency loans in the business sector, and funnel resources to insiders. By late 2013 the program had already led to $3.19 billion in funding, with even larger amounts planned for 2014.[53] Similarly, in an effort to boost government financing and reduce Hungary's dependence on foreign bond investors (and foreign-currency bonds), the MNB leadership announced in May 2014 the conversion of its primary two-week policy instrument from a bond to a less attractive deposit in order to encourage Hungarian banks to invest in domestic government bonds instead of placing their money with the central bank.[54]

All Good Things Go Together?

The MNB and the Orbán government formalized their cooperative relationship in a new MNB statute published in May 2014, intended to clarify the MNB's mission and tasks in post-crisis Hungary.[55] The statute was a masterwork of compromise and optimism. It affirmed the MNB's independence and its primary goal of maintaining price stability through its inflation-targeting framework, while at the same time confirming the new two-week deposit facility as the main instrument of monetary policy and including "lending incentive strategies" (a clear reference to Funding for Growth) as an instrument to "support interest-rate policy." It acknowledged the expanded financial stability mandate of the MNB,

52. K. Eddy, "Hungary Unveils Growth Stimulus Package," *Financial Times*, April 4, 2013.

53. Margit Feher, "Hungary's Central Bank Sees Subsidized Loans Aiding Growth." *Wall Street Journal*, November 20, 2013. According to the MNB, by mid-2015 the Funding for Growth Scheme had led to well over $5 billion in loans.

54. In June 2015 it announced a plan to further encourage government debt purchases by introducing a three-month fixed interest rate deposit as its primary policy instrument. See http://english.mnb. hu/mnben_pressroom/press_releases/mnben_pressreleases_2015/mnben_pressreleases_20150602.

55. "Independence and Responsibility: The Statute of the Magyar Nemzeti Bank," May 2014, http://english.mnb.hu/Root/Dokumentumtar/ENMNB/Sajtoszoba/mnben_sajtokozlemenyek/The_Statute_of_the_Magyar_Nemzeti_Bank.pdf.

giving it explicit roles in macroprudential policy making, as Hungary's financial supervisory authority, and as the national resolution authority. At the same time, the statute included a full section on "Supporting the Government's Economic Policy," noting that:

> Supporting the Government's economic policy is not a choice, but rather a statutory obligation for the Magyar Nemzeti Bank. . . . Accordingly, one of the central bank's strategic goals is to play a more active role in stimulating the economy, without prejudice to its primary objective. This means conducting monetary policy conducive to the support, without prejudice to the achievement of its primary objective, economic growth within the framework of the strategic cooperation between the Government and the central bank.

The statute thus rejected trade-offs between price stability and economic growth; denied potential conflicts among monetary, macroprudential, and microprudential policies; and asserted central bank independence while obligating the MNB to support government policies. It included no mechanism for conflict resolution between the MNB and the government if the sides disagreed on when "strategic cooperation" might jeopardize price stability, as it did not explicitly acknowledge that such disagreements could exist. In essence, it retained the strong language and prejudices of the old central banking consensus while introducing multiple new conflicting elements. This reflected an ongoing high-stakes negotiation among the MNB's new leadership, the MNB staff, and the government to define the MNB's post-crisis role in the Hungarian economy.

For our purposes, perhaps the most interesting section of the statute concerned international relations. This section committed the MNB to "cultivating its professional relationships with peer and counterparty central banks, international economic organizations and financial institutions" through extensive central bank research cooperation, exchange and study programs, and international conferences in Budapest. In doing so, it explicitly mentioned the use of English and the intention to "reinforce the professional relationship" among central banks. In essence, the MNB staff wrote the transnational central banking community into the new statute.

This continuing international cooperation operated in practice as well; Matolcsy may have thrown out the IMF resident representative, but MNB central bankers still participated regularly in central bank conferences, exchanges, technical assistance, and training programs. The MNB Research Department published its working paper series in English only and its job advertisements demanded an "excellent command of English" while "knowledge of Hungarian is not required."[56] The MNB annually hosted the Lamfalussy Lectures and its Workshop on Macroeconomic Policy at which established central bankers from Europe and North America represented the most prominent participants. While the MNB's leadership and policies at the very top had changed, the MNB staff retained their international networks, technocratic preferences, and research practices. As such, rather than simply bringing the MNB and government closer together, Matolcsy's efforts divided the MNB internally, with most MNB staff still closely connected to the transnational central banking community and actively involved in that internal community debate over what central banks should do post-crisis.

My discussions with current and former MNB officials in June 2014 made it clear that Matolcsy viewed his MNB leadership as a platform from which to wage a battle for hearts and minds. He promoted Orbánomics as an alternative, nationalist economic program for the post-crisis world and wanted to convert the MNB staff to his beliefs. Upon arrival he distributed a one-page reading list to MNB staff comprised of books such as Joyce's *The IMF and the Global Financial Crisis*, Marsh's *The New Industrial Revolution*, Sharma's *Breakout Nations*, and Al Gore's *The Future: Six Drivers of Global Change*. He required each MNB employee to read at least one book on the list over the summer and write a book report on it. For their part, the MNB staff that remained worked hard to reconcile their new roles with their previous training. For example, one compared the MNB's controversial, politically motivated Funding for Growth program with the Bank of England's Funding for Lending program, saying that the MNB used the Bank of England model to design its program and that despite operational differences their main goals and outcomes were the same.

In summer 2014 Orbán and Matolcsy upped the ante. Matolcsy announced that the MNB would spend more than the state's entire education budget to fund five Hungarian educational institutions that "do not propagate failed neoliberal doctrines," in the process neatly evading EU restrictions on central banks financing their own governments.[57] For his part, Orbán declared a new age of "illiberal democracy" ushered in by the global financial crisis.[58] In Orbán's speech, he

---

56. The ad also noted that preliminary interviews would take place at the Allied Social Science Associations meetings in Philadelphia; http://english.mnb.hu/Kutatas/research-department/job-openings-submenu.

57. "Hungary C.bank Chief Matolcsy Sheds Light on HUF 200 Bn Plan—It's Edifying," Portfolio.hu, August 28, 2014. In January 2014 the MNB also launched a program to spend over $100 million "repatriating" Hungarian art, resulting in, among other purchases, the acquisition of a Titian painting in July 2015 from a private Hungarian collector for $15.8 million. Margit Feher, "Hungary's Central Bank Buys Titian Painting for $15.8 Million," *Wall Street Journal*, July 17, 2015.

58. Prime Minister Viktor Orbán's Speech at the 25th Bálványos Summer Free University and Student Camp, July 26, 2014, Tusnádfürdő (Băile Tuşnad), Romania, www.miniszterelnok.hu/in_english_article/_prime_minister_viktor_orban_s_speech_at_the_25th_balvanyos_summer_free_university_and_student_camp.

proclaimed that, "while breaking with the dogmas and ideologies that have been adopted by the West . . . we are trying to find the form of community organisation, the new Hungarian state, which is capable of making our community competitive in the great global race for decades to come." While many MNB professionals had earlier hoped simply to wait out Orbán and Matolcsy, it became increasingly clear that they would be forced to choose between the transnational community and the new national mission.

The Bank of Russia and Putin's Challenge to the West

In the decade after Russia's 1998 financial crisis, Russian politicians and financial markets had grown steadily more confident.[59] Oil prices rose and the Bank of Russia conducted restrained monetary policies, leading to several years of 7–8 percent annual GDP growth and moderate but stable 9–15 percent annual inflation. Russia accumulated foreign exchange reserves of nearly $500 billion and created a $225 billion stabilization fund to protect against future oil price volatility. But by late 2008, the global financial crisis had plunged Russia's economy into turmoil once again. Russia faced declining terms of trade, capital flight, and a rapid drop in international oil prices. The ruble's value declined steadily, sparking a domestic rush to convert rubles to US dollars and euros. Russia's stock exchanges repeatedly halted trading during autumn 2008 in the face of collapsing share prices. Russian banks and companies with foreign-currency loans were squeezed, and credit dried up. The crisis deepened through 2009, a year in which Russia's GDP fell by 7.9 percent. The swing from nearly 8.5 percent GDP growth in 2007 to -7.9 percent in 2009 was among the largest in the world.

The Russian government shared Orbán's conviction that the global financial crisis indicated the failure of the existing international economic order. Vladimir Putin called the crisis a "contagion" that had spread from the United States and said that the Russian situation was "due to the . . . irresponsibility of [the US] system."[60] The crisis in the euro zone reinforced both the urgency of reform and the perception that the system's traditional leaders in the United States and Europe were unable to respond constructively to its problems. In response, the Russian government—tentatively under President Dmitrii Medvedev and then

---

59. Certain paragraphs from this section are drawn from Johnson 2013.
60. Richard Boudreux, "Dump 'Parasite' US and the Greenback, Urges Putin," *The Australian*, August 3, 2011.

decisively after Vladimir Putin returned to the presidency in 2012—adopted an expansive financial nationalist policy that envisioned Russia as not only financially sovereign at home, but as the rightful leader of an alternative regional economic order. This program implied a further entrenchment of state dominance in the financial sector, including the central bank.

Russian leaders harshly criticized the international financial architecture and international monetary system. They observed that the IMF quota system should be adjusted so that Russia and China no longer had less formal influence than small European countries like Belgium and Switzerland.[61] Such reforms would then lay the groundwork for more thorough institutional transformation.[62] Russian leaders and influential academics further identified the international monetary system's dollar-dependence as a weakness in need of rectification and promoted ruble internationalization as a means of diversification.[63] Russia increasingly used the BRICS forum to create workarounds to existing international institutions as well. The final statement of the 2012 BRICS summit in New Delhi prominently called for a broad-based international reserve currency system and proposed a BRICS development bank.[64] With strong Russian support, the BRICS launched the New Development Bank in July 2015 "as an alternative to the existing US-dominated World Bank and International Monetary Fund."[65]

The Eurasian Economic Union (EEU) project represented Putin's primary challenge to the international order. Years in the making and explicitly intended as an alternative to the European Union, the Eurasian Economic Union would deepen economic integration among its member states. By its official January 2015 launch Russia, Kazakhstan, Belarus, and Armenia had become members, with Kyrgyzstan joining the following August. The Bank of Russia's own training

---

61. See remarks by then-finance minister Aleksei Kudrin in RIA Novosti, "Rubl' i iuan': kto blizhe k rezervnoi valiute? [The ruble and the yuan: Which is closer to a reserve currency?]," June 6, 2009, http://news.mail.ru/economics/2642989/.

62. President Dmitrii Medvedev, Interview with *Kommersant*, June 4, 2009, http://archive. kremlin.ru/eng/text/speeches/2009/06/04/1312_type82916_217709.shtml.

63. For a brief overview see Sidorova 2011. While the majority of the Russian academic community identified the system's dollar-dependence as a significant problem and agreed upon the need to move to a multicurrency world, views remained divided on the feasibility of retiring the dollar, the means by which this should be pursued, and the most appropriate timeline. E.g., see Vlad Grinkevich, "Is the Curtain Closing on the US Dollar?" *Voice of Russia*, July 31, 2012, http://english.ruvr. ru/_print/83552029.html. See also Viktor Gerashchenko's argument at a major April 2008 conference on ruble internationalization that although no currency seemed poised to replace the US dollar on the world scene, in Eurasia the ruble could indeed become a reserve currency or even the core of a currency union (Bazhan 2008).

64. "China to Offer Renminbi Loans to BRICs Nations," *Financial Times*, March 7, 2012.

65. From the opening statement on the New Development Bank website at http://ndbbrics.org/.

efforts facilitated this integration, as the it took the lead in coordinating joint educational programs for the central banks. Putin presented this Eurasian integration project as a natural post-crisis development, a response to the revealed dangers of being too dependent on Western financial structures and as an emerging economic community that would share the strengths of the EU while avoiding its weaknesses.

Domestically, after the crisis the government initiated a policy referred to as "de-offshorization" of the Russian elite, requiring government officials and encouraging business leaders to keep their personal wealth at home rather than in foreign bank accounts and foreign property. The Russian government enhanced this agenda by issuing primarily ruble-based debt, encouraging banks to convert foreign currency loans into rubles at concessional exchange rates, and embarking on a concerted effort to promote the use of rubles rather than US dollars in export contract quotation and settlement.[66] Monetary sovereignty also involved stockpiling foreign exchange reserves, which rose from their post-1998 crisis low of near zero to over $500 billion in 2013 in order to shield Russia from the effects of oil price volatility and other external economic shocks.

The Bank of Russia Presses Forward

As Russia's politicians proclaimed themselves in the vanguard of a new world financial order, Russian central bankers behaved much like the core members of the transnational central banking community: they uncomfortably adapted to new demands while attempting to maintain independence and price stability to the best of their abilities. The Bank of Russia demonstrated its commitment to the pre-crisis central banking consensus by announcing in October 2008 that it would adopt a formal inflation-targeting regime as of 2014.[67] As with central banks around the world, the financial crisis forced the Bank of Russia to lower interest rates, provide emergency funds and bailouts to domestic banks, and spend down foreign exchange reserves to support the currency. The crisis depleted its reserve funds and increased the already high level of state ownership in the banking system. Nevertheless, the Bank of Russia pursued its inflation-targeting goal

---

66. Aleksandr Suvarov interview with Deputy Finance Minister Moiseev—"Moiseev: ob"em rublevykh raschetov budem uvelichivat' [Moiseev: the volume of ruble transactions will increase]," www.vestifinance.ru/articles/42686, May 13, 2014. Moiseev noted that, "Where there are additional inconveniences that arise from using the national currency, these are not very significant. One definitely needs to put up with these inconveniences because the additional security that arises from this is very significant."

67. For an early critique of this policy choice and its implementation, see Sapir 2010.

persistently in the ensuing years, even after the Russian government asked it to take on new financial regulatory roles and added a growth mandate to its original price stability mandate.

While it may seem strange that the Bank of Russia introduced inflation targeting just as that regime came under fire internationally, from the bank's point of view it made perfect sense. The Bank of Russia, by this time well integrated into the transnational central banking community, had struggled with its previous monetary policy regimes. In an economy heavily dependent on natural resource revenues, with volatile capital flows, and with a high percentage of state ownership and control over the economy, the Bank of Russia had great difficulty reducing inflation to its preferred level. The laser-like focus, discipline, and transparency of an inflation target naturally appealed. As the bank's monetary policy chief Ksenia Yudaeva wrote in defending the decision, inflation targeting "at the start of the 21st century has become one of the most widespread models of monetary-credit policy in the world."[68] She referenced the 2–2.5 percent target as the standard in "developed countries" and said that given Russia's more complicated status as an emerging market the bank had selected 4 percent as its planned target rate. Her article wrapped up by approvingly citing former Bundesbank president Otmar Emminger's quote, famous among central bankers, that "If you flirt with inflation, you'll end up marrying her."

For the Russian government's part, its desire to promote the ruble internationally meant that it had a newfound interest in reducing inflation in order to build confidence in the currency. Establishing a more important role in the postcrisis international financial system ironically could entail adopting key practices of its dominant actors, and at least initially the government did not see inflation targeting as a threat to economic growth. Moreover, the Bank of Russia's early progress toward inflation targeting took place under the presidency of Dmitrii Medvedev in the midst of an economic modernization campaign. Inflation targeting fit the model of a more modern Russian policy focused on economic diversification, transparency, and combating corruption. Once Vladimir Putin returned to the presidency in 2012 and adopted his more nationalist, interventionist economic strategy, the Bank of Russia had already progressed substantially toward its inflation-targeting goal.

The Bank of Russia began building its monetary policy model in 2007, announced its first informal inflation target in 2010, improved its monetary policy tools and communications strategies, and gradually increased exchange

---

68. Yudaeva 2014.

rate flexibility.[69] It established new monetary policy and statistics departments in August 2013. The IMF supported the Bank of Russia's transition, providing technical assistance and applauding its preparations for adopting inflation targeting, as did other community central banks like the Bank of England.[70] In January 2014 the Bank of Russia announced that it would seek to refrain from daily interventions in the forex market, and it seemed well set on the path to adopting its first formal target.[71]

While supported by Putin, the Bank of Russia's increasing focus on price stability had engendered calls from many government officials and business leaders to ease monetary policy because of slow economic growth or sluggish bank lending practices. The Bank of Russia responded by pointing out that easing policy would lead to inflation, not to growth, for two reasons. First, sluggish growth was due to lack of investment, and "it's impossible" that easing monetary policy would stimulate investment growth because "it's a totally different sphere of the economy."[72] Second, commercial banks maintained such a wide spread between the Bank of Russia's rates and their own lending rates that Bank of Russia rate-setting policy could not be causing enterprises' problems with accessing commercial credit. The IMF supported these objections, noting in addition that the Russian economy was already operating at full capacity and so expansionary policies would only lead to higher inflation and exchange-rate volatility.[73] Bank of Russia officials further pointed out that the government itself had compromised monetary policy by hiking prices for commodities controlled by government "natural monopolies."[74]

Pressures on the Bank of Russia increased in 2013 as governor Sergei Ignatiev's term neared its end. Ignatiev had established a good reputation in both

---

69. For a description of the early phases in building the Bank's New Keynesian monetary policy model, see Borodin et al. 2008. For a summary of the model as of early 2015, see "Monetary Policy in the Bank of Russia's Forecast" in the Bank of Russia's March 2015 Monetary Policy Report.

70. "IMF Executive Board Concludes 2012 Article IV Consultation with the Russian Federation," Public Information Notice (PIN) No. 12/90, August 2, 2012, www.imf.org/external/np/sec/pn/2012/pn1290.htm. See the similar language in the 2013 Article VI consultation, https://www.imf.org/external/np/sec/pr/2013/pr13355.htm and www.imf.org/external/pubs/ft/scr/2013/cr13310.pdf.

71. Tom Bowker, "Russia 'Welcomes' Weaker Currency as Central Bank Sticks to Float Plan," Central Banking, January 30, 2014.

72. Bank of Russia deputy chairman Aleksei Uliukaev quoted in ITAR-TASS, "Fighting Inflation Is CBR's Main Contribution to Stimulating Russian Economy-CBR Deputy Head," May 22, 2013.

73. "Russian Federation: 2013 Article IV Consultation," IMF Country Report No. 13/310, October 2013, www.imf.org/external/pubs/ft/scr/2013/cr13310.pdf.

74. "Easing CBR Monetary-Lending Policy More Likely to Produce Inflation Than Economic Growth—Shvetsov," Interfax, March 29, 2013. The Orbán government in Hungary had helped the MNB achieve price stability by lowering consumer electricity rates; the Russian government, on the other hand, increased similar (admittedly below market) prices at rates well above the inflation target. Therefore the Bank of Russia's policy had to be stricter in order to achieve its inflation target.

international and domestic financial circles, and had championed the Bank of Russia's move toward inflation targeting. When Ignatiev stepped down in June 2013, Putin chose his close economic adviser Elvira Nabiullina as the next governor, sparking concerns that the Bank of Russia would become even closer to the government and neglect its price stability mandate. Nabiullina turned out to be a strong defender of the Bank of Russia's policies, though, aided by the continuity of the expert staff (including Ignatiev himself, who stayed on as an advisor). Putin further boosted the Bank of Russia by naming deputy governor Aleksei Uliukaev to head the Ministry of Economic Development, thereby putting an inflation-targeting supporter in charge of the ministry traditionally most likely to demand monetary easing to stimulate growth.

At the same time, the Russian government formally expanded the Bank of Russia's legal mandate to include supporting economic growth and gave it significant new regulatory and supervisory powers. As per legislation passed in July 2013, the Bank of Russia acquired the responsibilities of the former Federal Financial Markets Service in addition to its existing bank supervisory role. Uliukaev admitted during a November 2012 parliamentary hearing on the merger that "the Bank of Russia is completely happy with the responsibility that it has now, and probably my colleagues and I don't really want to expand this sphere of responsibility, because this is difficult, major, additional work," but acknowledged that the proposed merger would address a real regulatory problem.[75] The Bank of Russia had already engaged in a recent upgrade of its supervisory abilities through an ECB cooperation program in 2008–11 focusing on the transition to Basel II standards, and officials expressed confidence that they would be able to take on this expanded role. Bank of Russia deputy governor Sergei Shvetsov pointed out that after the global financial crisis world practice had turned toward establishing consolidated regulators, and that doing so would strengthen Moscow's development as an international financial center.[76] He also acknowledged the potential for conflict of interest issues to arise, but insisted that such conflicts would be manageable. Confirming the post-crisis trend toward consolidated supervision, the IMF praised the move as one that could better monitor systemic risks.[77] Bank of Russia officials deflected concerns about the new growth mandate as well, insisting that it would not interfere with their pursuit of price stability because achieving price stability itself would be the best driver of economic growth.

---

75. Quoted in "CBR Has Enough Responsibility without FFMS, but Reasons for Merger Exist—Ulyukaev," Interfax, November 12, 2012.

76. "CBR Willing to Radically Change Management Structure in 3 Years if FFMS Merges with It," Interfax, November 6, 2012.

77. "Russian Federation: 2013 Article IV Consultation."

The Ukrainian Challenge

So far so good for the Bank of Russia—it had defended its pursuit of inflation targeting as its government simultaneously called for a transformation of the international economic order, and had dealt with its expanded mandate and regulatory powers without further compromising its autonomy. However, the Russian government's takeover of Crimea in March 2014 and the subsequent battle over Ukraine presented a more significant threat. In November 2013 Putin had encouraged Ukrainian president Viktor Yanukovych to refuse to pursue an association agreement with the European Union, suggesting that Ukraine would be better off moving closer to Russia and the nascent Eurasian Economic Union. Demonstrations in Kyiv ensued after Yanukovych rebuffed the EU, leading through a complex series of events to Yanukovych's ouster, the installation of an interim government in Kyiv, and the Russian government's decision to annex Ukraine's Crimean peninsula. This in turn led to Western economic sanctions, a ratcheting up of international tensions to levels not seen since the Cold War, and economic instability in Russia.

The Bank of Russia, which had so recently declared its intention not to intervene in the foreign exchange market, had to sell $11 billion and raise its key rate by 1.5 percent on March 3 in order to stem a rapid decline in the ruble's value. There were also credible rumors that it withdrew over $100 billion in US Treasury bills from the Federal Reserve in the days before the Crimean independence referendum in anticipation of possible sanctions.[78] At the same time, the Bank of Russia provided over $27 million in cash to sanctions-targeted SMP Bank, owned by close associates of President Putin.[79] The Bank of Russia became responsible for introducing the ruble and shutting Ukrainian banks in Crimea, while the ruble made significant advances in war-torn parts of eastern Ukraine as well.[80]

Most consequentially, after Visa and MasterCard briefly denied service in March 2014 to Russian banks under US sanctions, the Russian government passed legislation mandating the creation of a separate national payment system and demanding that Visa and MasterCard deposit millions of dollars with the Bank of Russia in order to continue operations in the country. The Bank

---

78. "Russia May Have Withdrawn 105bn Dollars from USA Ahead of Sanctions—Paper," BBC Monitoring, March 20, 2014.
79. "CBR Injects $27m of Cash in Sanctions-Hit SMP Bank," RosBusinessConsulting, March 24, 2014.
80. For example, see Yulia Surkova and Daryna Krasnolutska, "Forget Tanks. Russia's Ruble Is Conquering Eastern Ukraine," Bloomberg Business, May 4, 2015.

of Russia dutifully established the National Card Payment System in June 2014, an expensive and internationally unusual proposition that was justified in the name of national financial autonomy and security.[81] The Bank of Russia would be responsible for administering this system, which would jeopardize Russia's international financial integration and fly in the face of global trends. Then, when crisis and sanctions led international ratings agencies to downgrade Russia's sovereign credit rating to junk level, the Russian government initiated a move to break ties with international ratings agencies and start its own national ratings agency instead.[82] As further unrest in Ukraine led to an escalation of sanctions, tensions, and accusations, the government adopted legislation in July 2015 charging the Bank of Russia with creating the new Credit Rating Agency of the Russian Federation by year's end.[83]

The Ukrainian crisis disrupted the Bank of Russia's activities as much or more than had the global financial crisis. Former Minister of Economic Development and top presidential economic advisor Andrei Belousov told the May 2014 St. Petersburg International Economic Forum that recent events had demonstrated that Russia was not yet ready to let the ruble float and adopt an inflation-targeting regime.[84] Western partners in the transnational central banking community had to cancel much bilateral cooperation with the Bank of Russia due to sanctions, a development that pained central bankers on both sides. Bank of Russia governor Nabiullina reiterated the bank's commitment to inflation targeting and insisted that, "the implementation of structural reforms should not in any way be tied to sacrificing macroeconomic stability."[85] Yet the Bank of

81. Ruslan Krivobok, "Central Bank of Russia Establishes National Card System Operator," RIA-Novosti, June 19, 2014, http://en.ria.ru/russia/20140619/190617988/Central-Bank-of-Russia-Establishes-National-Card-Payment-System.html. For details on the system's evolution, see the Bank of Russia's dedicated webpage for the National Payments System at www.cbr.ru/PSystem/.

82. See "Russia: Moving away from international rating agencies only 'question of time.'" *Russia Today*, May 14, 2014. Putin has also extended his nationalization efforts to bilateral aid, canceling every US-Russian cooperation agreement that "listed the United States as a donor country and Russia as a recipient of US aid . . . For the Kremlin, government policies funded by foreign money were no longer tolerable." Dmitri Trenin, "Russia's Breakout from the Post-Cold War System: The Drivers of Putin's Course," Carnegie Moscow Center, December 22, 2014.

83. See "Federalnyi zakon ot 13.07.2015 g. No. 222-F3 O deiatel' nosti kreditnykh reitingovykh agenstv v Rossiiskoi Federatsii [Federal law of 13.07.2015 No. 222-F3 On the activities of the credit rating agency of the Russian Federation]," http://kremlin.ru/acts/bank/39943 and Bank of Russia Press Service, "O proekte po sozdaniiu novogo kreditnogo reitingovogo agenstva [On the project of the creation of a new credit rating agency]," July 24, 2015, www.cbr.ru/press/PR.aspx?file=2407201.5_122628if2015-07-24T12_23_34.htm.

84. "Russia Not Yet Ready for Floating Ruble Exchange Rate—Presidential Aide," ITAR-TASS, May 26, 2014.

85. Quoted in Grigory Sisoyev, "Structural Reforms Should Not Sacrifice Economic Stability—Russian Central Bank," RIA Novosti, May 23, 2014.

Russia spent over $125 billion in foreign exchange reserves to slow the ruble's fall in 2014, then hiked its key interest rate to a startling 17 percent after the ruble's value crashed in December 2014 in an effort to staunch the bleeding. Throughout 2015 the Bank of Russia found itself actively intervening to moderate volatility in the ruble-US dollar exchange rate while simultaneously affirming its commitment to its inflation targeting goal. Despite continuing support from Putin and much of the transnational central banking community, significant swaths of the Russian elite, press, and public blamed the Bank of Russia for choking the economy with its high interest rates and with destabilizing the ruble, decrying it as a foreign agent and a feminized puppet of the IMF. The Putin government's alienation from Western Europe and North America, its heightened determination to pursue a financial nationalist path, and the resulting uncertainties put the Bank of Russia, like the MNB, increasingly in a position where its transnational inclinations and national responsibilities clashed.

Cooperation, Competition, and Community

ECB president Jean-Claude Trichet observed in April 2010 that "The crisis has had some paradoxical effects: on the one hand it has unleashed a tendency to reengage in financial nationalism if not mercantilism; on the other hand it has contributed to the recognition that . . . interdependencies between economies called for a much higher level of cooperation. These two opposing forces are presently competing."[86] For postcommunist central banks as well as others around the world, the global financial crisis represented an unwelcome challenge to their established principles and practices. The crisis both demonstrated the surprising interdependence of the international financial system and led to a worldwide political backlash against that system and its architects. The transnational central banking community's pre-crisis policy making came under fire, central banks were asked to take on greater responsibilities for financial stability, and central bankers themselves had difficulty articulating what their roles in the post-crisis system should be. Central banks in the post-crisis world had simultaneously become more powerful, less capable, and less unified than in the past, a situation that the central banking community found dangerous both for its own future and for the stability of the international financial system.

---

86. Keynote address by Jean-Claude Trichet, president of the European Central Bank, at the Council on Foreign Relations, New York, April 26, 2010.

These developments generated calls to strengthen formal and informal coordination mechanisms among central banks. While the community's wormhole network had deepened during the Great Moderation and boasted an extensive transnational infrastructure, the shared principles and practices on which it was based did not call for central banks to cooperate on policy making. As long as similarly minded independent central banks defended price stability in their own backyards, explicit international policy coordination would be unnecessary.[87] After the global financial crisis, this position could no longer be sustained. Former deputy governor of the National Bank of Poland Krzysztof Rybinski suggested that the BIS be transformed into a "body for collegial global decision making," arguing that inflation and financial stability had become global rather than national issues, requiring "global coordination of decisions and consistent communication between the largest central banks."[88] The Committee on International and Economic Policy Reform called for "the creation of an International Monetary Policy Committee composed of representatives of major central banks that will report regularly to world leaders on the aggregate consequences of individual central bank policies" under the auspices of the BIS.[89] Two former *Financial Times* reporters spearheaded the creation of the Official Monetary and Financial Institutions Forum (OMFIF) in 2010, an organization designed to bring together central bankers and other public and private financial officials from around the world for discussion and policy coordination. The Financial Stability Board at the BIS took on increased responsibilities and the IMF saw its role in international policy coordination rise as well. The European Union moved the furthest toward centralization, granting extensive new regulatory and supervisory powers to the ECB, committing member states to more formal coordination of fiscal policy, and institutionalizing the ECB's austerity-oriented preferences into its post-crisis reforms.

To what extent would governments grant unelected central bankers formal powers over not just national but international policy making? In a certain sense, this has already happened in the advanced industrial democracies. Over the past few decades these governments have asked their central banks to do progressively more domestically in order to evade responsibility for the difficult distributional decisions that monetary and financial regulatory policies entail. This policy delegation reached new heights after the global financial crisis, with central banks bailing out private-sector financial institutions and other central banks to the

---

87. James 2013, especially 22–23.

88. Krzysztof Rybinski, "The BIS Must Become the Global Central Bank," Central Banking, March 10, 2008.

89. Eichengreen et al. 2011.

tune of billions, introducing new policy instruments that transformed markets, and adopting extensive new financial stability mandates that required enhanced transnational regulation and coordination in order to succeed. In the process, central bank independence has increasingly become a shield for governments rather than central banks. Western political leaders' aversion to taking ownership of national and international financial decision making has unwittingly turned their central bankers from government appointees into leaders of last resort.

Meanwhile, as Hungary and Russia demonstrate, in the wake of the crisis many governments in emerging-market states not only criticized existing international institutions and practices, but proposed alternative, more statist, and more nationalist visions of a new world order. Such financial nationalist policies raised the possibility that the international monetary system could become less rather than more coordinated in the future. In the European Union, the public backlash against EU economic institutions has been strong, with anti-EU nationalist parties gaining support in the United Kingdom and across the continent, and with the Greek crisis threatening to tear apart the euro zone. In the United States no influential politicians have expressed willingness to consider international contagion effects when making policy for the world's largest economy and issuer of the world's key reserve currency. Central banks are increasingly caught in the crossfire, torn between their allegiance to their transnational community and its principles on the one hand and their increasingly diverse and politicized national roles on the other.

Faced with these pressures, will the transnational central banking community unravel? Earlier experience presents a cautionary tale.[90] In the 1920s, central bankers from the United States and Western Europe had worked to foster the creation and transformation of central banks in their own image around the world. As in the postcommunist era, many policy makers initially welcomed these new central banks as symbols of sovereignty and magnets for foreign capital, but later grew disenchanted. The Great Depression then led to the collapse of the nascent transnational central banking community of the time and the widespread political subordination of central banks. Today's community is far stronger, but arguably also faces greater and more complex challenges.

With its independence in question and its mandates widened, the transnational central banking community must rely more than ever on the power of its ideas and organization. In the best of circumstances, the community would employ its transnational network, its training and technical assistance infrastructure, and the nexus between central banking practice and academic theory

---

90. Thanks to Eric Helleiner for bringing this fascinating parallel to my attention.

to conceptualize truly innovative collective principles and practices for central banking's future and to convince governments that these principles and practices are the right ones. The only way that this will work, in turn, is for the community's core to accept a greater intellectual role for developing and emerging-market economies in this process. These governments will only consider a revitalized central banking paradigm if it takes the interests of all countries into account, and a compelling alternative paradigm able to challenge the financial nationalism of illiberal political leaders is apt to emerge only through engaging the ideas and experiences of embattled central bankers on the community's periphery. This may not be likely, but the existence of the transnational central banking community makes it possible. As Korean central bank governor Choongsoo Kim observed, "A crisis is accompanied by severe strains. But, at the same time, it offers an opportunity to broaden our understanding. If we can come up with a new framework that will last for decades or longer, we will be remembered as [a] generation of economists and central bankers that overcame the previous orthodoxy to turn the crisis into the beginning of a new era."[91]

---

91. Choongsoo Kim, governor of the Bank of Korea, "Monetary and macroprudential policies in the aftermath of the crisis," opening remarks at the Bank of Korea International Conference 2012 "Monetary and Macroprudential Policies in the Aftermath of the Crisis," coorganized with the IMF, Seoul, June 14–15, 2012.

Acknowledgments

This book has had a longer gestation than most—I presented the first paper on this project, enthusiastically entitled "Basel or Bust! The 'Westernization' of Central Banks in Post-Communist Democracies," at the September 1999 meeting of the American Political Science Association. It subsequently grew in scope and ambition far beyond what I had initially imagined, and my debts to others grew with it along the way.

My first and heartfelt thanks go to the central bankers, assistance providers, policy makers, and others from the Magyar Nemzeti Bank, Czech National Bank, National Bank of Slovakia, Bank of Russia, National Bank of the Kyrgyz Republic, Croatian National Bank, Bulgarian National Bank, National Bank of Georgia, National Bank of Azerbaijan, Eesti Pank (Bank of Estonia), Bank of Latvia, Bank of Lithuania, National Bank of Romania, Bank of the Republic of Kosovo, Bank of Albania, National Bank of the Republic of Macedonia, Hungarian Bank Supervisory Authority, European Central Bank, International Monetary Fund, Joint Vienna Institute, Bank for International Settlements, Financial Stability Forum, IMF Institute, Deutsche Bundesbank, Bank of England, Österreichische Nationalbank, Banque de France, US Federal Reserve, National Bank of Belgium, Bank of Finland, Bank of Canada, Financial Services Volunteer Corps, European Bank for Reconstruction and Development, World Bank, Asian Development Bank, US Agency for International Development, Barents Group, KPMG Peat Marwick, plus those in postcommunist commercial banks, accounting agencies, finance ministries, journalism, universities, and government who generously took the time to talk with me and to help me gain greater insight into the world of central banking. With the exception of central bank governors and selected others I have not included their names in the book to protect their privacy, but I hope that they recognize their contributions and their community here. Special thanks to the EBRD office in Bishkek, to Charles University in Prague, and to the Central European University in Budapest for being such gracious hosts during extended research trips to Kyrgyzstan, the Czech Republic, and Hungary. My work is in memory of central banker Andrei Kozlov, with whom I spoke at length on two occasions and share a birthday. Andrei was gunned down by contract killers in 2006 for trying to clean up the Russian banking system. Вечная память.

This book has benefited from the help of many exceptional research assistants along the way, including Baktygul Aliev, Vladimir Bagretsov, Katherine Cinq-Mars, Paul Light, Jessica Fortin, Victor Gomez, Gjakush Kabashi, Péter Karádi, Seçkin Köstem, Emil Medetov, Piotr Paradowski, Dóra Piroska, Vladislav Portniaguine, Maciej Szczepaniak, Izabela Steflja, and Jessica Trisko. It has also benefited from several well-timed grants to make the fieldwork, research assistance, and writing possible. A Title VIII National Research grant from the US National Council for Eurasian and East European Research funded my initial field research in 2000–1. A residential National Fellowship at the Hoover Institution at Stanford University from 2001–2 gave me a year to think and write about this project, during which it expanded in interesting and fruitful ways. After I moved to McGill University, a generous grant from the Social Sciences and Humanities Research Council of Canada funded further fieldwork, research assistance, and writing from 2003–7. A European Commission Framework Seven Programme grant (#266809-GR:EEN) sponsored a final whirlwind fieldwork trip in 2014 with Cornel Ban and Len Seabrooke to Vienna, Bucharest, Pristina, Skopje, Tirana, and Budapest.

Numerous friends and scholars have read and commented on this work over the years in its various iterations and incarnations, including Rawi Abdelal, Hilary Appel, Cornel Ban, Andrew Barnes, Jacquie Best, Pamela Bradley, László Bruszt, Mark Blyth, Doro Bohle, Val Bunce, Jerry Cohen, Alex Cooley, Larry Diamond, Kenneth Dyson, Rachel Epstein, Ben Forest, Steve Fish, Daniela Gabor, Randall Germain, Béla Greskovits, Jana Grittersova, Derek Hall, Steve Hanson, Eric Helleiner, Yoshiko Herrera, Roger Haydon, David Howarth, Barry Ickes, Wade Jacoby, Jonathan Kirshner, Jeff Kopstein, Martin Marcussen, Stan Markus, David Mayes, Gerry McDermott, Bessma Momani, Manuela Moschella, Mitchell Orenstein, David Ost, Louis Pauly, Will Pyle, Lucia Quaglia, Scott Radnitz, Karen Remmer, Sebastien Royo, Ulrike Schaede, Len Seabrooke, Pierre Siklos, Aneta Spendzharova, Ron Suny, Bill Tompson, Eleni Tsingou, Carolyn Warner, David Woodruff, Milada Vachudova, Amy Verdun, anonymous reviewers, and others whose names have been lost to the mists of time. The book is undoubtedly far better for their interventions, for which they bear full responsibility. Special thanks to Peter Rutland, who came up with the title *Priests of Prosperity* during a memorable meal we shared at Morimoto in Philadelphia with the Mad Scot Mark Blyth.

Similarly, I have had the opportunity to present research that appears in this book at conferences of PONARS-Eurasia, ASEEES/AAASS, the American Political Science Association, the Association of American Geographers, the European Union Studies Association, and the Society for the Advancement of Socio-Economics; and in talks at the Davis Center at Harvard University, McGill

University, Copenhagen Business School, University of Warwick, University of Luxembourg, Yale University, the Hong Kong Monetary Authority, the London School of Economics, Syracuse University, Ohio State University, Claremont McKenna College, University of Toronto, Carleton University, Central European University, Concordia University, Middlebury College, Northwestern University, Stanford University, and the Kyrgyz Financial Academy. Throughout this process I have also enjoyed the full support of my colleagues at McGill University and in the transnational academic community of PONARS-Eurasia (not yet as influential as the central bankers' transnational community, but give us time).

Much of the euro adoption section of chapter 5 appeared earlier in Juliet Johnson, "Two-Track Diffusion and Central Bank Embeddedness: The Politics of Euro Adoption in Hungary and the Czech Republic," *Review of International Political Economy* 13, no. 3 (2006): 361–86 (reprinted by permission of the publisher, Taylor & Francis, Ltd.). Selected paragraphs in chapters 3 and 5 are drawn from Rachel Epstein and Juliet Johnson, "Uneven Integration: Economic and Monetary Union in Central and Eastern Europe," *Journal of Common Market Studies* 48, no. 5 (2010): 1235–58 (reprinted by permission of the publisher, John Wiley and Sons). Part of the section on Hungary in chapter 7 appeared earlier in Juliet Johnson and Andrew Barnes, "Financial Nationalism and its International Enablers: The Hungarian Experience," *Review of International Political Economy* 22, no. 3 (2015): 535–69 (reprinted by permission of the publisher, Taylor & Francis, Ltd.).

Finally, and most important:

Roger Haydon at Cornell University Press has supported this project since its inception, patiently acknowledging my annual insistence that "it will be done in a few months" without (usually) rolling his eyes. I could not have asked for a better or sharper editor.

Eric Helleiner and Jonathan Kirshner led a full-day manuscript workshop on the first draft of this book at the University of Waterloo in May 2008. It is an incredible experience to have a room full of smart people politely yet mercilessly dissect your work for eight hours straight. Eric and Jonathan, I apologize for having promised after the workshop to get you the revised manuscript "by the end of the summer."

My nephew Cole, born the year I began my fieldwork, inspired me to finish the book before he learned to drive. My sister Jackie, a professional artist, drew the lovely wormhole diagram in chapter one. My mother Margaret, my brothers and sisters, and my entire extended family have been there for me every step of the way. I know how lucky I am.

My daughter Eleanor, born in December 2008, postponed the completion of this book long enough for me to include a final chapter on the global financial crisis and its ramifications. She does not care about that at all, and would rather we play a game or go skating together.

My wonderful husband Ben Forest has suffered through this book for well over a decade now and cannot wait for it to be done. As I write these acknowledgements, he is chilling the champagne in anticipation. Time to pop the cork!

References

Abalkin, Leonid. 1987. "The New Model of Economic Management." *Soviet Economy* 3, no. 4: 298–312.

Abdelal, Rawi. 2001. *National Purpose in the World Economy: Post-Soviet States in Comparative Perspective.* Ithaca, NY: Cornell University Press.

——. 2007. *Capital Rules: The Construction of Global Finance.* Cambridge: Harvard University Press.

Achleitner, Peter, ed. 1997. *Monetary Policy in Transition in East and West: Strategies, Instruments and Transmission Mechanisms.* Vienna: Öesterreichische Nationalbank.

Adler, Emanuel. 1992. "The Emergence of Cooperation: National Epistemic Communities and the International Evolution of the Idea of Nuclear Arms Control." *International Organization* 46, no. 1: 101–46.

——. 2008. "The Spread of Security Communities: Communities of Practice, Self-Restraint, and NATO's Post–Cold War Transformation." *European Journal of International Relations* 14, no. 2: 195–230.

Adler, Emanuel and Peter Haas. 1992. "Knowledge, Power, and International Policy Coordination." *International Organization* 46, no. 1: 367–90.

Adler, Emanuel, and Vincent Pouliot. 2011. "International Practices." *International Theory* 3, no. 1: 1–36.

Adolph, Christopher. 2004. "The Dilemma of Discretion: Career Ambitions and the Politics of Central Banking." Ph.D. diss., Harvard University.

——. 2013. *Bankers, Bureaucrats, and Central Bank Politics: The Myth of Neutrality.* Cambridge: Cambridge University Press.

Akayev, Askar. 2001. *Kyrgyzstan: An Economy in Transition.* Sydney: Asia Pacific Press.

Albegova, Irina. 2006. *Applied Economic Policy Course: Evaluation and Demand Assessment (Draft Report).* Vienna: Joint Vienna Institute.

Alesina, Alberto, and Lawrence Summers. 1993. "Central Bank Independence and Macroeconomic Performance: Some Comparative Evidence." *Journal of Money, Credit, and Banking* 25, no. 2: 151–62.

Allen, Franklin, and Elena Carletti. 2010. "An Overview of the Crisis: Causes, Consequences, and Solutions." *International Review of Finance* 10, no. 1: 1–26.

Allen, Mark, and Rick Haas. 2001. "The Transition in Central and Eastern Europe: The Experience of Two Resident Representatives." *IMF Staff Papers* 48: 9–28.

Anderson, John. 1999. *Kyrgyzstan: Central Asia's Island of Democracy?* London: Routledge.

Andrews, David. 2003. "The Committee of Central Bank Governors as a Source of Rules." *Journal of European Public Policy* 10, no. 4: 956–73.

Arnone, Marco, Bernard J. Laurens, Jean-François Segalotto, and Martin Sommer. 2007. "Central Bank Autonomy: Lessons from Global Trends." Working Paper 07/88. International Monetary Fund.

Artus, Patrick. 2007. *Les Incendiaires: Les Banques Centrales Dépassées Par La Globalisation.* Paris: Perrin.

Asian Development Bank. 2002. *Program Completion Report on the Financial Intermediation and Resource Mobilization Program and Commercial Bank Audits to the Kyrgyz Republic.* Manila.

Åslund, Anders. 2002. "The IMF and the Ruble Zone." *Comparative Economic Studies* 44, no. 4: 49–57.

——. 2010. *The Last Shall Be the First: The East European Financial Crisis, 2008–10.* Washington, DC: Peterson Institute.

Axilrod, Stephen H. 2011. *Inside the Fed: Monetary Policy and Its Management, Martin through Greenspan to Bernanke.* Cambridge: MIT Press.

Bácskai, Tamás. 1997. "Currency Reform and the Establishment of the National Bank of Hungary." In *Rebuilding the Financial System in Central and Eastern Europe, 1918–1994*, ed. Philip L. Cottrell, 5–16. Aldershot, UK: Ashgate.

Balogh, László. 2005. "Hungary." In *Handbook of Central Banking and Financial Authorities in Europe: New Architectures in the Supervision of Financial Markets*, ed. Donato Masciandaro, 258–87. Cheltenham, UK: Edward Elgar.

Barkovskii, Nikolai Dmitrievich. 1998. *Memuary Bankira, 1930–1990* [Memoirs of a banker, 1930–1990]. Moscow: Finansy i statistika.

Barnes, Andrew. 2006. *Owning Russia: The Struggle over Factories, Farms, and Power.* Ithaca, NY: Cornell University Press.

Barnett, Michael, and Martha Finnemore. 2004. *Rules for the World: International Organizations in Global Politics.* Ithaca, NY: Cornell University Press.

Barro, Robert. 1995. "Inflation and Growth." *Federal Reserve Bank of St. Louis Review* 78, no. 3: 153–69.

Barth, James R., Gerard Caprio Jr., and Ross Levine. 2006. *Rethinking Bank Regulation: Till Angels Govern.* New York: Cambridge University Press.

Bazhan, A.I. 2008. "Rossiiskii rubl'—mirovaia reservnaia valiuta? [The Russian ruble— a world reserve currency?]" *Den'gi i kredit* 57, no. 7: 50–62.

Bean, Charles, Matthias Paustian, Adrian Penalver, and Tim Taylor. 2010. "Monetary Policy after the Fall." Federal Reserve Bank of Kansas City Proceedings.

Bearce, David. 2003. "Societal Principals, Partisan Agents, and Monetary Policy Outcomes." *International Organization* 57, no. 2: 373–410.

Beblavy, Miroslav. 2003. "Central Bankers and Central Bank Independence." *Scottish Journal of Political Economy* 50, no. 1: 61–69.

Begg, Iain. 2006. "Real Convergence and EMU Enlargement: The Time Dimension of Fit with the Euro Area." In *Enlarging the Euro Area: External Empowerment and Domestic Transformation in East Central Europe*, ed. Kenneth Dyson, 71–89. Oxford: Oxford University Press.

Beissinger, Mark. 2007. "Structure and Example in Modular Political Phenomena: The Diffusion of Bulldozer/Rose/Orange/Tulip Revolutions." *Perspectives on Politics* 5, no. 2: 259–76.

Belik, Yurii. 1998. "The Party Learns about the Market." In *The Destruction of the Soviet Economic System: An Insiders' History*, ed. Michael Ellman and Vladimir Kontorovich, 237–38. Armonk, NY: M.E. Sharpe.

Berend, Ivan T. 1990. *The Hungarian Economic Reforms, 1953–1988.* Cambridge, UK: Cambridge University Press.

Berger, Helge, Jakob de Haan, and Sylvester Eijffinger. 2001. "Central Bank Independence: An Update of Theory and Evidence." *Journal of Economic Surveys* 15, no. 1: 3–40.

Bernanke, Ben S., and Frederic S. Mishkin. 1997. "Inflation Targeting: A New Framework for Monetary Policy?" Working Paper No. 5893. National Bureau of Economic Research.

Bernhard, William. 2002. *Banking on Reform: Political Parties and Central Bank Independence in the Industrial Democracies.* Ann Arbor: University of Michigan Press.

Blanchard, Olivier, Giovanni Dell'Ariccia, and Paolo Mauro. 2010. "Rethinking Macroeconomic Policy." *Journal of Money, Credit and Banking* 42, no. s1: 199–215.

Blejer, Mario, and Fabrizio Coricelli. 1995. *The Making of Economic Reform in Eastern Europe: Conversations with Leading Reformers in Poland, Hungary, and the Czech Republic*. Aldershot, UK: Edward Elgar.

Blinder, Alan. 1998. *Central Banking in Theory and Practice*. Cambridge: MIT Press.

———. 1999. "Central Bank Credibility: Why Do We Care? How Do We Build It?" Working Paper No. 7161. National Bureau of Economic Research.

Blinder, Alan, Michael Ehrmann, Marcel Fratzscher, Jakob De Haan, and David-Jan Jansen. 2008. "Central Bank Communication and Monetary Policy: A Survey of Theory and Evidence." Working Paper No. 13932. National Bureau of Economic Research.

Blyth, Mark. 2013. *Austerity: The History of a Dangerous Idea*. New York: Oxford University Press.

Bockman, Johanna, and Gil Eyal. 2002. "Eastern Europe as a Laboratory for Economic Knowledge: The Transnational Roots of Neoliberalism." *American Journal of Sociology* 108, no. 2: 310–52.

Bönker, Frank. 2006. "From Pacesetter to Laggard: The Political Economy of Negotiating Fit in the Czech Republic." In *Enlarging the Euro Area: External Empowerment and Domestic Transformation in East Central Europe*, ed. Kenneth Dyson, 160–77. Oxford: Oxford University Press.

Borio, Claudio. 2011. "Central Banking Post-Crisis: What Compass for Uncharted Waters?" Working Paper No. 353. Bank for International Settlements.

Borio, Claudio, Gianni Toniolo, and Piet Clement, eds. 2008. *The Past and Future of Central Bank Cooperation*. New York: Cambridge University Press.

Borish, Michael S., Wei Ding, and M. Noel. 1996. *On the Road to EU Accession: Financial Sector Development in Central Europe*. Washington, DC: World Bank.

Borodin, Alexandr, Elena Gorbova, Sergey Plotnikov, Yulia Plushchevskaya. 2008. "Estimating Potential Output and Other Unobservable Variables Using Monetary Policy Transmission Model (the Case of Russia)." In National Bank of the Republic of Belarus, *Effective Monetary Policy Options in Transition Economy*, Second International Scientific and Practical Conference, May 19–20, Minsk, Belarus.

Bosin, Yury. 2012. "Supporting Democracy in the Former Soviet Union: Why the Impact of US Assistance Has Been Below Expectations." *International Studies Quarterly* 56, no. 2: 405–12.

Boughton, James. 2001. *Silent Revolution: The International Monetary Fund 1979–1989*. Washington, DC: International Monetary Fund.

———. 2012. *Tearing Down Walls: The International Monetary Fund 1990–1999*. Washington, DC: International Monetary Fund.

Boylan, Delia. 1998. "Preemptive Strike: Central Bank Reform in Chile's Transition from Authoritarian Rule." *Comparative Politics* 30, no. 4: 443–62.

———. 2001. *Defusing Democracy: Central Bank Autonomy and the Transition from Authoritarian Rule*. Ann Arbor: University of Michigan Press.

Brada, Josef, and Ali Kutan. 1999. "The Persistence of Moderate Inflation in the Czech Republic and the Czk Crisis of May 1997." Prague Economic Papers No. 4: 313–26.

———. 2002. "The End of Moderate Inflation in Three Transition Economies?" Working Paper No. 433. William Davidson Institute.

Breuss, Fritz, Gerhard Fink, and Peter Haiss. 2004. "How Well Prepared Are the New Member States for the European Monetary Union?" *Journal of Policy Modeling* 26, no. 7: 769–91.

Broome, Andre. 2010. *The Currency of Power: The IMF and Monetary Reform in Central Asia*. Houndmills: Palgrave Macmillan.

Campillo, Marta, and Jeffrey Miron. 1997. "Why Does Inflation Differ across Countries?" In *Reducing Inflation*, ed. Christina Romer and David Romer, 335–62. Chicago: University of Chicago Press.

Carruthers, Bruce, Sarah Babb, and Terence Halliday. 2001. "Institutionalizing Markets, or the Market for Institutions? Central Banks, Bankruptcy Law, and the Globalization of Financial Markets." In *The Rise of Neoliberalism and Institutional Analysis*, ed. John Campbell and Ove Pedersen, 94–126. Princeton, NJ: Princeton University Press.

Cerna, Silviu, Liliana Donath, and Bogdan Dima. 1999. "Central Banking in the Transition Economies of Eastern Europe: The Case of Romania." In *Central Banking in Transition Economies*, ed. Nigel Healey and Zenon Wisniewski, 193–225. Torun: Torun Business School.

Checkel, Jeffrey. 2001. "Why Comply? Social Learning and European Identity Change." *International Organization* 55, no. 3: 553–88.

Chwieroth, Jeffrey M. 2009. *Capital Ideas: The IMF and the Rise of Financial Liberalization.* Princeton, NJ: Princeton University Press.

Čihák, Martin. 2006. "How Do Central Banks Write on Financial Stability?" Working Paper No. 06/163. International Monetary Fund.

Čihák Martin, Sònia Muñoz, Shakira Teh Sharifuddin, and Kalin Tintchev. 2012. "Financial Stability Reports: What Are They Good For?" Working Paper No. 12/1. International Monetary Fund.

Coats, Warren, and Marko Skreb. 2001. "Banques Centrales En Transition: Vue D'ensemble Des Principaux Problèmes Après Dix Ans." In *Dix Ans De Transition En Europe De L'est: Bilan Et Perspectives,* ed. Antoine Mérieux and Ricardo Lago, 265–85. Paris: Revue d'Économie Financière.

Connolly, R. 2012. "The Determinants of the Economic Crisis in Post-Socialist Europe." *Europe-Asia Studies* 64, no. 1: 35–67.

Cooley, Alexander. 2000. "International Aid to the Former Soviet States: Agent of Change or Guardian of the Status Quo?" *Problems of Post-Communism* 47, no. 4: 34–44.

Cordero, Jose Antonio. 2009. "The IMF's Stand-by Arrangements and the Economic Downturn in Eastern Europe: The Cases of Hungary, Latvia, and Ukraine." Briefing Paper. Center for Economic and Policy Research. September.

Cottarelli, Carlo. 1998. "Comment." In *Moderate Inflation: The Experience of Transition Economies*, ed. Carlo Cottarelli and György Szapáry, 171–75. Washington, DC: International Monetary Fund.

Cottarelli, Carlo, and György Szapáry, eds. 1998. *Moderate Inflation: The Experience of Transition Economies.* Washington, DC: International Monetary Fund.

Cox, Robert. 1983. "Gramsci, Hegemony, and International Relations: An Essay in Method." *Millenium: Journal of International Studies* 12, no. 2: 162–75.

Crockett, Andrew. 1997. "The Role of the BIS in Central Banks' Cooperation." In *The Changing Role of Central Banks in Europe*, ed. Arvydas Gaižaukas and Kristina Kačkuviené, 41–54. Vilnius: Bank of Lithuania.

Crowe, Christopher, and Ellen E. Meade. 2008. "Central Bank Independence and Transparency: Evolution and Effectiveness." *European Journal of Political Economy* 24, no. 4: 763–77.

Csaba, László. 1995. "Hungary and the IMF: The Experience of a Cordial Discord." *Journal of Comparative Economics* 20, no. 2: 211–34.

———. 2002. "Economics—Hungary." In *Three Social Science Disciplines in Central and Eastern Europe: Handbook on Economics, Political Science and Sociology (1989–2001)*, ed. Max Kaase and Vera Sparschuh. Berlin, Bonn, and Budapest: GESIS.

Csajbók, Attila, and Ágnes Csermely. 2002. "Adopting the Euro in Hungary: Expected Costs, Benefits, and Timing." Occasional Paper No. 24. Magyar Nemzeti Bank.

Csermely, Ágnes. 2004. "Convergence Expectations and Convergence Strategies. Lessons from the Hungarian Experiences in the Pre-EU Period." *Comparative Economic Studies* 46, no. 1: 104–26.

Cukierman, Alex, S. B. Webb, and Bilin Neyapti. 1992. "Measuring the Independence of Central Banks and Its Effect on Policy Outcomes." *World Bank Economic Review* 6, no. 3: 353–98.

Cukierman, Alex, Geoffrey P. Miller, and Bilin Neyapti. 2002. "Central Bank Reform, Liberalization and Inflation in Transition Economies—an International Perspective." *Journal of Monetary Economics* 49, no. 2: 237–64.

Czech National Bank. 2003. *Czech National Bank, 1993–2003.* Prague: Czech National Bank.

Dabrowski, Marek. 2010. "The Global Financial Crisis: Lessons for European Integration." *Economic Systems* 34, no. 1: 38–54.

Davies, Howard, and David Green. 2010. *Banking on the Future: The Fall and Rise of Central Banking.* Princeton, NJ: Princeton University Press.

De Grauwe, Paul, Thomas Mayer, and Karel Lannoo. 2008. "Lessons from the Financial Crisis: New Rules for Central Banks and Credit Rating Agencies?" *Intereconomics* 43, no. 5: 256–66.

De Haan, Jakob, Sylvester C.W. Eijffinger, and Krzysztof Rybiński. 2007. "Central Bank Transparency and Central Bank Communication: Editorial Introduction." *European Journal of Political Economy* 23, no. 1: 1–8.

De Smet, Charles. 1998. "Assistance of the Phare Program to the Banking Sector." *BIATEC—Fifth Anniversary Special Issue.*

Deane, Marjorie, and Robert Pringle. 1994. *The Central Banks.* New York: Viking; London: Hamish Hamilton.

Dědek, Oldrich. 1996. *The Break-up of Czechoslovakia: An In-Depth Economic Analysis.* Aldershot, UK: Avebury.

——. 1998. "Echoing the European Monetary Integration in the Czech Republic." *Prague Economic Papers,* no. 3: 195–225.

——. 2002. "The Czech Economy and the Euro." *Politika Ekonomie* 50, no. 3: 361–75.

——. 2004. "Adopting the Euro—Brake on or Engine for True Convergence?" *Eastern European Economics* 42, no. 2: 45–62.

Demertzis, Maria, and Andrew Hughes Hallett. 2007. "Central Bank Transparency in Theory and Practice." *Journal of Macroeconomics* 29, no. 4: 760–89.

Dincer, N. Nergiz, and Barry Eichengreen. 2007. "Central Bank Transparency: Where, Why, and with What Effects?" Working Paper No. 13003. National Bureau of Economic Research.

Dincer, N. Nergiz, and Barry Eichengreen. 2013. "Central Bank Transparency and Independence: Updates and New Measures." Working Paper. Bank of Korea.

Djelic, Marie-Laure, and Sigrid Quack. 2010. *Transnational Communities: Shaping Global Economic Governance.* Cambridge, UK: Cambridge University Press.

Dmitriev, M., and S. Vasiliev, eds. 2001. *Krizis 1998 goda i vosstanovlenie bankovskoi sistemy* [The 1998 crisis and the restoration of the banking system]. Moscow: Moscow Carnegie Center.

Down, Ian. 2004. "Central Bank Independence, Disinflations, and the Sacrifice Ratio." *Comparative Political Studies* 37, no. 4: 399–434.

Drábek, Zdenek. 1995. "IMF and IBRD Policies in the Former Czechoslovakia." *Journal of Comparative Economics* 20, no. 2: 235–64.

Dumke, Rolf, and Heidemarie Sherman. 2000. "Exchange Rate Options for EU Applicant Countries in Central and Eastern Europe." In *Essays on the World Economy and Its Financial System,* ed. Brigitte Granville, 153–95. London: The Royal Institute of International Affairs.

Dvorsky, Sandra. 2000. "Measuring Central Bank Independence in Selected Transition Countries and the Disinflation Process." Discussion Paper No. 13. Bank of Finland Institute for Economies in Transition (BOFIT).

Dyson, Kenneth, and Kevin Featherstone. 1996. "Italy and EMU as a '*Vincolo Esterno*': Empowering the Technocrats, Transforming the State." *South European Society & Politics* 1, no. 2: 272–99.

———. 1999. *The Road to Maastricht: Negotiating Economic and Monetary Union.* Oxford: Oxford University Press.

Dyson, Kenneth, Kevin Featherstone, and George Michalopoulos. 1995. "Strapped to the Mast: EC Central Bankers between Global Financial Markets and Regional Integration." *Journal of European Public Policy* 2, no. 3: 465–87.

Efimova, L.G. 1994. *Bankovskoe pravo* [Banking law]. Moscow: Izdatel'stvo Vek.

Égert, Balázs, Thomas Gruber, and Thomas Reininger. 2003. "Challenges for EU Acceding Countries' Exchange Rate Strategies after EU Accession and Asymmetric Application of the Exchange Rate Criteria." *Focus on Transition,* no. 2: 52–72.

Eichengreen, Barry. 2003. "The Accession Economies' Rocky Road to the Euro." Paper presented at the East-West Conference 2003, Vienna, November 2–4.

Eichengreen, Barry, Mohamed El-Erian, Arminio Fraga, Takatoshi Ito, Jean Pisani-Ferry, Eswar Prasad, Raghuram Rajan, Mara Ramos, Carmen Reinhart, and Dani Rodrik. 2011. "Rethinking Central Banking. Committee on International Economic Policy and Reform." First Annual Report, Committee on International Economic Policy and Reform. Washington, D.C.: Brookings Institution.

Eijffinger, Sylvester C.W., and Carin van der Cruijsen. 2007. "The Economic Impact of Central Bank Transparency: A Survey." Discussion Paper No. 6070. Center for Economic and Policy Research.

Eijffinger, Sylvester C.W., and Petra M. Geraats. 2006. "How Transparent Are Central Banks?" *European Journal of Political Economy* 22, no. 1: 1–21.

Elgie, Robert. 1998. "Democratic Accountability and Central Bank Independence: Historical and Contemporary, National and European Perspectives." *West European Politics* 31, no. 3: 53–76.

Epstein, Rachel. 2008. *In Pursuit of Liberalism: International Institutions in Postcommunist Europe.* Baltimore: Johns Hopkins University Press.

Epstein, Rachel A., and Juliet Johnson. 2009. "The Limits of Europeanization: The Czech Republic, Poland and European Monetary Integration." In *The Changing Power and Politics of European Central Banking: Living with the Euro,* ed. Kenneth Dyson and Martin Marcussen, 221–40. Oxford: Oxford University Press.

———. 2010. "Uneven Integration: Economic and Monetary Union in Central and Eastern Europe." *JCMS: Journal of Common Market Studies* 48, no. 5, 1237–60.

European Central Bank. 2000. "The Eurosystem and the EU Enlargement Process." *ECB Monthly Bulletin.* February, 39–51.

Evangelista, Matthew. 1999. *Unarmed Forces : The Transnational Movement to End the Cold War.* Ithaca, NY: Cornell University Press.

Evans, Peter. 1997. "The Eclipse of the State? Reflections on Stateness in an Era of Globalization." *World Politics* 50, no. 1: 62–87.

Federal Reserve Bank of Kansas City. 1990. *Central Banking Issues in Emerging Market-Oriented Economies: A Symposium.* Kansas City: Federal Reserve Bank of Kansas City.

Fedorov, Boris. 1999. *10 bezumnykh let: Pochemu v Rossii ne sostoialis' reformy* [10 crazy years: Why reform hasn't happened in Russia]. Moscow: Sovershenno sekretno.

Finnemore, Martha. 1996. *National Interests in International Society.* Ithaca, NY: Cornell University Press.

Finnemore, Martha, and Kathryn Sikkink. 1998. "International Norm Dynamics and Political Change." *International Organization* 52, no. 4: 887–917.

Fischer, Stanley. 2004. *IMF Essays from a Time of Crisis: The International Financial System, Stabilization, and Development.* Cambridge: MIT Press.

Fleming, Victoria, and Stuart Cole. 1995. "Evolution of Central Banking in Post-Communist Countries." *Bank of England Quarterly Bulletin* 35, no. 1: 54–59.

Fourcade, Marion. 2006. "The Construction of a Global Profession: The Transnationalization of Economics." *American Journal of Sociology* 112, no. 1: 145–94.

Fratianni, Michel, Juergen von Hagen, and Christopher Waller. 1997. "Central Banking as a Political Principle-Agent Problem." *Economic Inquiry* 35, no. 2: 378–93.

Freeman, John R. 2002. "Competing Commitments: Technocracy and Democracy in the Design of Monetary Institutions." *International Organization* 56, no. 4: 889–910.

Frieden, Jeffrey. 1997. "The Politics of Exchange Rates." In *Mexico 1994: Anatomy of an Emerging-Market Crash*, ed. Sebastian Edwards and Moisés Naím, 81–94. Washington, DC: Carnegie Endowment for World Peace.

Frieden, Jeffrey, and Ronald Rogowski. 1998. "The Impact of the International Economy on National Policies: An Analytical Overview." In *Internationalization and Domestic Politics*, ed. Robert Keohane and Helen Milner, 25–47. Cambridge, UK: Cambridge University Press.

Gabor, Daniela. 2012. "The Road to Financialization in Central and Eastern Europe: The Early Policies and Politics of Stabilizing Transition." *Review of Political Economy* 24, no. 2: 227–49.

Gaidar, Yegor. 1999. *Days of Defeat and Victory.* Seattle: University of Washington Press.

Ganev, Venelin I. 2007. *Preying on the State: The Transformation of Bulgaria after 1989.* Ithaca, NY: Cornell University Press.

Garay, Dušan. 1998. "Rewarding Investment in Human Potential." *BIATEC—Fifth Anniversary Special Issue.*

Gavura, Miroslav, and Branislav Rel'ovský. 2005. "A Simple Model of the Transmission Mechanism of Slovakia's Economy, Its Structure and Properties." *BIATEC* 13, no. 4: 15–23.

Gedeon, Péter. 1997. "Hungary: German and European Influences on the Post-Socialist Transition." In *Mitteleuropa: Between Europe and Germany*, ed. Peter J. Katzenstein, 101–48. Providence: Berghahn Books.

Gegenheimer, Gary A. 2006. "Judicial Review of Bank Supervisory Decisions in the Former Soviet Republics: The Case of Kyrgyzstan." *Annual Review of Banking and Financial Law* 25, no 1: 295–579.

Georgiou, Andreas V. 1998. "Foreword to the Special Issue." *BIATEC—Fifth Anniversary Special Issue.*

Geraats, Petra M. 2002. "Central Bank Transparency." *Economic Journal* 112, no. 483: F532–F565.

Gerashchenko, Viktor. 1994. "Rabota Tsentral'nogo Banka Rossii [the Work of the Central Bank of Russia]." *Rossiiskii ekonomicheskii zhurnal*, no. 9: 9–20.

——. 1999. "Aktual'nye problemy bankovskoi sistemy v 1999 godu [Current Problems of the Banking System in 1999]." *Den'gi i kredit*, no. 1.

Geršl, Adam. 2006. "Political Pressure on Central Banks: The Case of the Czech National Bank." *Finance a úvěr — Czech Journal of Economics and Finance* 56, no. 1–2: 18–39.

Gilardi, Fabrizio. 2012. "Transnational Diffusion: Norms, Ideas, and Policies." In *Handbook of International Relations*, second edition, ed. Walter Carlsnaes, Thomas Risse, Beth A. Simmons, 453–77. Thousand Oaks, CA: Sage.

Gilardi, Fabrizio, Katharina Füglister, and Stéphane Luyet. 2009. "Learning from Others: The Diffusion of Hospital Financing Reforms in OECD Countries." *Comparative Political Studies* 42, no. 4: 549–73.

Gill, Stephen. 1996. "Globalization, Democratization, and the Politics of Indifference." In *Globalization: Critical Reflections*, ed. James Mittleman, 205–28. Boulder, CO: Lynne Rienner.

Gilman, Martin G. 2010. *No Precedent, No Plan: Inside Russia's 1998 Default*. Cambridge: MIT Press.

Golikova, Yulia, and Marina Khokhlenikova. 2000. *Bank Rossii: organizatsiia deiatel'nosti* [The Bank of Russia: organization, activities]. Moscow: DeKA.

Goodfriend, Marvin. 2007. "How the World Achieved Consensus on Monetary Policy." Working Paper No. 13580. National Bureau of Economic Research.

Goodhart, Lucy M. 2015. "Brave New World? Macro-Prudential Policy and the New Political Economy of the Federal Reserve." *Review of International Political Economy* 22, no. 2: 280–310.

Goodman, John. 1989. "Monetary Politics in France, Italy, and Germany: 1973–85." In *The Political Economy of European Integration*, ed. Paulo Guerrieri and Pierre Carlo Padoan. New York: Harvester Wheatsheaf.

Grabel, Ilene. 2003. "Ideology, Power, and the Rise of Independent Monetary Institutions in Emerging Economies." In *Monetary Orders: Ambiguous Economics, Ubiquitous Politics*, ed. Jonathan Kirshner, 25–52. Ithaca, NY: Cornell University Press.

Graham, Erin R., Charles R. Shipan, and Craig Volden. 2013. "The Diffusion of Policy Diffusion Research in Political Science." *British Journal of Political Science* 43, no. 3: 673–701.

Granville, Brigitte. 2002. "The IMF and the Ruble Zone: Response to Odling-Smee and Pastor." *Comparative Economic Studies* 44, no. 4: 59–80.

Gray, Simon Thorburn, and Jacob Nell. 2005. *A New Currency for Iraq*. London: Central Banking Publications.

Greskovits, Béla. 1998. *The Political Economy of Protest and Patience: East European and Latin American Transformations Compared*. Budapest: Central European University Press.

——. 2009. "Estonia, Hungary, and Slovenia: Banking on Identity." In *Central Banks in the Age of the Euro: Europeanization, Convergence and Power*, ed. Kenneth Dyson and Martin Marcussen, 203–21. New York: Oxford University Press.

Griffith-Jones, Stephany, José Antonio Ocampo, and Joseph E. Stiglitz. 2010. *Time for a Visible Hand: Lessons from the 2008 World Financial Crisis*. Oxford: Oxford University Press.

Grilli, V., D. Masciandaro, and G. Tabellini. 1991. "Political and Monetary Institutions and Public Financial Policies in Industrialized Countries." *Economic Policy* 6, no. 13: 341–92.

Haas, Peter. 1992. "Introduction: Epistemic Communities and International Policy Coordination." *International Organization* 46, no. 1: 1–32.

Hall, Peter. 1993. "Policy Paradigms, Social Learning, and the State." *Comparative Politics* 25, no. 3: 275–96.

Hall, Rodney Bruce. 2008. *Central Banking as Global Governance: Constructing Financial Credibility*. Cambridge: Cambridge University Press.

Hammond, Gill. 2012. *State of the Art of Inflation Targeting*. London: Centre for Central Banking Studies.

Havel, Jiří. 1992. "Discontinuity of Czech Economic Thought." *Prague Economic Papers* 4: 359–75.

Hayo, Bernd. 1998. "Inflation Culture, Central Bank Independence, and Price Stability." *European Journal of Political Economy* 14, no. 2: 241–63.

Hayo, Bernd, and Carsten Hefeker. 2002. "Reconsidering Central Bank Independence." *European Journal of Political Economy* 18, no. 4: 653–74.

Healey, Nigel, and Zenon Wisniewski, eds. 1999. *Central Banking in Transition Economies*. Torun, Poland: Torun Business School.

Helleiner, Eric. 1994. *States and the Reemergence of Global Finance: From Bretton Woods to the 1990s*. Ithaca, NY: Cornell University Press.

———. 1997. "Braudelian Reflections on Globalization." In *Innovation and Transformation in International Studies*, ed. Stephen Gill and James Mittleman, 90–104. Cambridge, UK: Cambridge University Press.

———. 2003. *The Making of National Money: Territorial Currencies in Historical Perspective*. Ithaca, NY: Cornell University Press.

Hellman, Joel. 1998. "Winners Take All—the Politics of Partial Reform in Postcommunist Transitions." *World Politics* 50, no. 2: 203–34.

Hellman, Joel, Geraint Jones, and Daniel Kaufmann. 2003. "Seize the State, Seize the Day: State Capture and Influence in Transition Economies." *Journal of Comparative Economics* 31, no. 4: 751–73.

Henderson, Sarah. 2002. "Selling Civil Society—Western Aid and the Nongovernmental Organization Sector in Russia." *Comparative Political Studies* 35, no. 2: 139–67.

Herrera, Yoshiko. 2010. *Mirrors of the Economy: National Accounts and International Norms in Russia and Beyond*. Ithaca, NY: Cornell University Press.

Hirschman, Albert. 1989. "How the Keynesian Revolution Was Exported from the United States, and Other Comments." In *The Political Power of Economic Ideas: Keynesianism across Nations*, ed. Peter Hall, 347–60. Princeton, NJ: Princeton University Press.

Hlavatý, Egon, and Ivan Zelinka. 2003. "The Origin of the National Bank of Slovakia: The Result of a Long Journey to National Sovereignty." *BIATEC* 11, no. 7: 25–30.

Hochreiter, Eduard, and Tadeusz Kowalski. 2000. "Central Banks in European Emerging Market Economies in the 1990s." *Banca Nazionale del Lavoro Quarterly Review* 53, no. 212: 45–70.

Hoggarth, Glenn. 1997. "Monetary Policy in Transition—the Case of Central Europe." *Central Banking Journal* 8, no. 1: 32–43.

Holicka, Peter. 1999. "A Book About Payment Systems in Countries Associated with the European Union." *BIATEC* 7, no. 10: 6.

Holtfrerich, Carl-L., Jaime Reis, and Gianni Toniolo, eds. 1999. *The Emergence of Modern Central Banking from 1918 to the Present*. Aldershot and Burlington: Ashgate.

Hrnčíř, Miroslav. 1992. "Monetary and Credit Policies for Transition to a Market Economy." *Prague Economic Papers*, no. 2: 109–25.

Ickes, Barry W., and Randi Ryterman. 1992. "The Interenterprise Arrears Crisis in Russia." *Post-Soviet Affairs* 8, no. 4: 331–61.

Illarionov, Andrei. 1999. "The Roots of the Economic Crisis." *Journal of Democracy* 10, no. 2: 68–82.

IMF Institute. 1994–95. *IMF Institute Report on Training*. Washington, DC: International Monetary Fund.

Independent Evaluation Office. 2005. *Evaluation of the Technical Assistance Provided by the International Monetary Fund*. Washington, DC: International Monetary Fund.

International Monetary Fund. 2000. *World Economic Outlook*. Washington, DC.

———. 2005. *Guidelines for Foreign Exchange Reserve Management*. Washington, DC.

"Interview: Marián Jusko." 2000. *Central Banking Journal* 11, no. 1: 45–51.

Irwin, Neil. 2013. *The Alchemists: Three Central Bankers and a World on Fire*. New York: Penguin.

Issing, Otmar. 2012. "The Mayekawa Lecture: Central Banks—Paradise Lost." *Monetary and Economic Studies* 30: 55–74.

Jacoby, Wade. 2001. *Imitation and Politics: Redesigning Modern Germany*. Ithaca, NY: Cornell University Press.

——. 2004. *The Enlargement of the European Union and NATO: Ordering from the Menu in Central Europe*. New York: Cambridge University Press.

James, Harold. 2013. "International Cooperation and Central Banks." *CIGI Essays on International Finance* 1: October.

Jancková, Stanislava. 2002. "Eurozone Enlargement: Some Risks for Catching-up Countries." *Politiká Ekonomie* 50, no. 6: 759–79.

Jancková, Stanislava, and Kamil Janácek. 2004. "European Monetary Union and Risks for Real Convergence." *Politiká Ekonomie* 52, no. 4: 435–49.

Johnson, Juliet. 1999. "Misguided Autonomy: Central Bank Independence and the Russian Transition." In *The Self-Restraining State: Power and Accountability in New Democracies*, ed. Andreas Schedler, Larry Diamond, and Marc Plattner, 293–311. Boulder, CO: Lynne Rienner.

——. 2000. *A Fistful of Rubles: The Rise and Fall of the Russian Banking System*. Ithaca, NY: Cornell University Press.

——. 2006. "Two-Track Diffusion and Central Bank Embeddedness: The Politics of Euro Adoption in Hungary and the Czech Republic." *Review of International Political Economy* 13, no. 3: 361–86.

——. 2008a. "Forbidden Fruit: Russia's Uneasy Relationship with the Dollar." *Review of International Political Economy* 15, no. 3: 377–96.

——. 2008b. "The Remains of Conditionality: The Faltering Enlargement of the Euro Zone." *Journal of European Public Policy* 15, no. 6: 826–42.

——. 2013. "Russia: International Monetary Reform and Currency Internationalization." Paper #4, series on *The BRICS and Asia, Currency Internationalization and International Monetary Reform*, Centre for International Governance Innovation, Asian Development Bank, and Hong Kong Institute for Monetary Research, June, 1–27.

——. 2014. "Europe's Monetary Union in Crisis." In *Crisis and Reform: Canada and the International Financial System*, ed. Rohinton Medhora and Dane Rowlands, 177–92. Waterloo, ON: Centre for International Governance Innovation.

Johnson, Juliet, and Andrew Barnes. 2015. "Financial Nationalism and Its International Enablers: The Hungarian Experience." *Review of International Political Economy* 22, no. 3: 535–69.

Johnson, Juliet, and Seçkin Köstem. 2015. "Frustrated Leadership: Russia's Economic Alternative to the West." Symposium on Political Leadership and Economic Crisis, Yale University, February 13–15.

Johnson, Peter. 1998. *The Government of Money: Monetarism in Germany and the United States*. Ithaca, NY: Cornell University Press.

Johnston, Alastair Iain. 2001. "Treating International Institutions as Social Environments." *International Studies Quarterly* 45, no. 4: 487–515.

Jonáš, Jiří. 1993. "Relevance of Economic Analysis to Economic Policy: The Experience of Czechoslovakia." *Prague Economic Papers*, no. 4: 297–311.

Jusko, Marian. 1998. "The Results Achieved Exceed All Expectations." *BIATEC—Fifth Anniversary Special Issue*.

——. 2003. "Slovakia within the Context of European Integration." *BIATEC* 9, no. 11: 2–5.

Kaelberer, Matthias. 2003. "Knowledge, Power and Monetary Bargaining: Central Bankers and the Creation of Monetary Union in Europe." *Journal of European Public Policy* 10, no. 3: 365–79.

Kahler, Miles. 1992. "External Influence, Conditionality, and the Politics of Adjustment." In *The Politics of Economic Adjustment*, ed. Stephen Haggard and Robert Kaufman, 89–133. Princeton, NJ: Princeton University Press.

Kapstein, Ethan. 1992. "Between Power and Purpose: Central Bankers and the Politics of Regulatory Convergence." *International Organization* 46, no. 1: 265–87.

———. 1994. *Governing the Global Economy: International Finance and the State*. Cambridge, MA: Harvard University Press.

———. 1989. "Resolving the Regulator's Dilemma: International Coordination of Banking Regulations." *International Organization* 43, no. 2: 323–47.

Karádi, Péter. 1999. "Central Bank Independence in Hungary (1990–1999) [Jegybankfüggetlenség Magyarországon (1990–1999)]." *Közgazdasági Szemle* XLVI: 969–92.

Keck, Margaret, and Kathryn Sikkink. 1998. *Activists beyond Borders: Advocacy Networks in International Politics*. Ithaca, NY: Cornell University Press.

Kenen, Peter B., and Ellen E. Meade. 2004. "EU Accession and the Euro: Close Together or Far Apart?" In *EU Enlargement and the Future of the Euro*, ed. Robert Pringle and Nick Carver, 79–98. London: Central Banking Publications.

Khandruyev, Aleksandr. 1994. "Statement of the Central Bank of the Russian Federation." In *Central Banking Technical Assistance to Countries in Transition*, ed. J.B. Zulu, Ian McCarthy, Susana Almuina, and Gabriel Sensenbrener, 59–60. Washington, DC: International Monetary Fund.

King, Michael. 2005. "Epistemic Communities and the Diffusion of Ideas: Central Bank Reform in the United Kingdom." *West European Politics* 28, no. 1: 94–123.

Király, Júlia. 1993. "A Short-Run Money Market Model of Hungary." In *Hungary: An Economy in Transition*, ed. István Székely, 137–48. Cambridge: Cambridge University Press.

Kirshner, Jonathan. 2003. "The Inescapable Politics of Money." In *Monetary Orders: Ambiguous Economics, Ubiquitous Politics*, ed. Jonathan Kirshner, 3–24. Ithaca, NY: Cornell University Press.

Kissmer, Friedrich, and Helmut Wagner. 2004. "Central Bank Independence and Macroeconomic Performance: A Survey of the Evidence." In *Central Banking in Eastern Europe*, ed. Nigel Healey and Barry Harrison, 107–40. London and New York: Routledge.

Klaus, Václav. 2000. "Three Years after the Exchange Rate Crisis: Recapitulation of the Events and Their Consequences." *Politiká Ekonomie* 48: 595–604.

Kloc, Kazimierz. 1995. "The Banking System in Kyrgyzstan." *Russian and East European Finance and Trade* 31, no. 6: 73–94.

Knight, Malcolm, Arne Petersen, and Robert Price. 1999. *Transforming Financial Systems in the Baltics, Russia, and Other Countries of the Former Soviet Union*. Washington, DC: International Monetary Fund.

Kohutikova, Elena. 2000. "Monetary Policy Is a Living Mechanism." *BIATEC* 8, no. 4: 2.

Kollar, Jozef. 1998. "Questionnaire—What Do You Think Have Been the Most Significant Monetary Policy Measures Taken by the National Bank of Slovakia over the Last Five Years?" *BIATEC—Fifth Anniversary Special Issue*.

Kopstein, Jeffrey, and David Reilly. 2000. "Geographic Diffusion and the Transformation of the Post-Communist World." *World Politics* 53, no. 1: 1–37.

Kralik, Stefan. 1998. "Executive Division." *BIATEC—Fifth Anniversary Special Issue*.

Kreidl, Vladimír, and Zdeněk Tůma. 1996. "Stará Kotva Opuštěna: Kde Hledat Novou? [The old anchor has been abandoned: where should we look for a new one?]." *Ekonom* no. 17: 19–20.

Krenzler, Horst, and Susan Senior Nello. 1999. "Implications of the Euro for Enlargement: Report of the Working Group on the Eastern Enlargement of the European Union." Robert Schuman Center Policy Paper 99/3. European University Institute.

Krzak, Maciej, and Aurel Schubert. 1997. "The Present State of Monetary Governance in Central and Eastern Europe." *Focus on Transition,* no. 1: 28–56.

Kurtz, Marcus, and Andrew Barnes. 2002. "The Political Foundations of Post-Communist Regimes: Marketization, Agrarian Legacies, or International Influences?" *Comparative Political Studies* 35, no. 5: 524–53.

Lehmann, Alexander, Micol Levi, and Peter Tabak. 2011. "Basel III and Regional Financial Integration in Emerging Europe. An Overview of Key Issues." Working Paper No. 132. European Bank for Reconstruction and Development.

Loriaux, Michael et al., eds. 1997. *Capital Ungoverned: Liberalizing Finance in Interventionist States.* Ithaca, NY: Cornell University Press.

Loungani, Prakash, and Nathan Sheets. 1997. "Central Bank Independence, Inflation, and Growth in Transition Economies." *Journal of Money, Credit, and Banking* 29, no. 3: 381–99.

Lybek, Tonny. 1999. "Legislative Framework." In *Transforming Financial Systems in the Baltics, Russia, and Other Countries of the Former Soviet Union,* ed. Malcolm Knight, Arne B. Petersen, and Robert T. Price, 76–86. Washington, DC: International Monetary Fund.

Mahadeva, Lavan, and Peter Sinclair. 2002. "Introduction: The Transmission Mechanism and Monetary Policy." In *Monetary Transmission in Diverse Economies,* ed. Lavan Mahadeva and Peter Sinclair, 1–27. Cambridge, UK: Cambridge University Press.

Mahadeva, Lavan, and Gabriel Sterne, ed. 2000. *Monetary Policy Frameworks in a Global Context.* London: Routledge.

Maliszewski, Wojciech. 2000. "Central Bank Independence in Transition Economies." *Economics of transition* 8, no. 3: 749–89.

Manukova, L.V. 2001. "Tsentr podgotovki personala v sisteme dopolnitel'nogo professional'nogo obrazovaniia personala Banka Rossii [The center for personnel training in the system of supplementary professional education of the personnel of the Bank of Russia]." *Deng'i i kredit* 10, 41–44.

Marcussen, Martin. 1998. "Central Bankers, the Ideational Life Cycle, and the Social Construction of EMU." Robert Schuman Center Working Paper 98/33. European University Institute.

——. 2000. *Ideas and Elites: The Social Construction of Economic and Monetary Union.* Aalborg: Aalborg University Press.

——. 2005. "Central Banks on the Move." *Journal of European Public Policy* 12, no. 5: 903–23.

Mataj, Jiří, and Petr Vojtíšek. 1992. "Právní a Ekonomické Aspekty Nového Zákona o SBČS [Legal and economic aspects of the new law on the SBCS]." *Finance a úvěr* 42: 109–15.

Matiukhin, Georgii. 1993. *Ia byl glavnym bankirom Rossii* [I was the head banker of Russia]. Moscow: Vysshaia shkola.

Maxfield, Sylvia. 1994. "Financial Incentives and Central Bank Authority in Industrializing Nations." *World Politics* 46, no. 4: 556–88.

——. 1997. *Gatekeepers of Growth: The International Political Economy of Central Banking in Developing Countries.* Princeton, NJ: Princeton University Press.

McGee, Robert W., and Galina G. Preobragenskaya. 2005. *Accounting and Financial System Reform in a Transition Economy: A Case Study of Russia.* Boston: Springer.

McNamara, Kathleen. 1998. *The Currency of Ideas: Monetary Politics in the European Union*. Ithaca, NY: Cornell University Press.

———. 2002. "Rational Fictions: Central Bank Independence and the Social Logic of Delegation." *West European Politics* 25, no. 1: 47–76.

Mendelson, Sarah. 2001. "Democracy Assistance and Political Transition in Russia." *International Security* 25, no. 4: 68–106.

Meyer, John W., John Boli, George M. Thomas, and Francisco O. Ramirez. 1997. "World Society and the Nation–State." *American Journal of Sociology* 103, no. 1: 144–81.

Meyer, Richard Hemmig. 1970. *Bankers' Diplomacy: Monetary Stabilization in the Twenties*. New York and London: Columbia University Press.

Mishkin, Frederic S. 2007. "Will Monetary Policy Become More of a Science?" Working Paper No. 13566. National Bureau of Economic Research.

Mizsei, Kálmán. 1993. "Hungary: Gradualism Needs a Strategy." In *Economic Transformation in Central Europe: A Progress Report*, ed. Richard Portes. Budapest: Centre for Economic Policy Research.

Momani, Bessma 2005. "Recruiting and Diversifying IMF Technocrats." *Global Society* 19, no. 2: 167–87.

———. 2007. "Another Seat at the Board: Russia's IMF Executive Director." *International Journal* 62, no. 4: 916–39.

Monetary and Exchange Affairs and European I Departments. 2002. "Hungary: Financial System Stability Assessment Follow-Up." Washington, DC: International Monetary Fund.

Nell, Mathis. 2004. "Monetary Policy in the Slovak Republic: Implicit Inflation Targeting and the Choice of an Optimal Exchange Rate Regime—Part 1." *BIATEC* 12, no. 9: 16–18.

Neményi, Judit. 1997. "Monetary Policy in Hungary: Strategies, Instruments and Transmission Mechanisms." In *Monetary Policy in Transition in East and West: Strategies, Instruments and Transmission Mechanisms*, ed. Peter Achleitner, 131–61. Vienna: Öesterreichische Nationalbank.

"The New Central Banks in the Republics of the Former U.S.S.R." 1991–92. *Central Banking Journal* 2, no. 3: 12–25.

Neyapti, Bilin. 2001. "Central Bank Independence and Economic Performance in Eastern Europe." *Economic Systems* 25, no. 4: 381–99.

Odling-Smee, John 1993. "IMF Economic Reviews: Kyrgyz Republic." Washington, DC: International Monetary Fund.

———. 2004. "The IMF and Russia in the 1990s." Working Paper 04/155. International Monetary Fund.

Odling-Smee, John, and Gonzalo Pastor. 2002. "The IMF and the Ruble Area, 1991–93." *Comparative Economic Studies* 44, no. 4: 3–29.

OECD. 2000. *Economic Survey of Hungary*. Paris: Organisation for Economic Cooperation and Development.

———. 2004. *Economic Survey of Hungary*. Vol. 2. Paris: Organisation for Economic Cooperation and Development.

Offe, Claus. 1997. *Varieties of Transition: The East European and East German Experience*. Cambridge: MIT Press.

Olcott, Martha Brill. 1996. *Central Asia's New States: Independence, Foreign Policy, and Regional Security*. Washington, DC: United States Institute of Peace Press.

Olsen, Michael, ed. 2005. *Banking Supervision: European Experience and Russian Practice*. Moscow: Delegation of the European Commision to Russia.

Orphanides, Athanasios. 2013. "Is Monetary Policy Overburdened?" Public Policy Discussion Paper 13-8. Federal Reserve Bank of Boston.

Palley, Thomas. 2013. "Europe's Crisis without End: The Consequences of Neoliberalism." *Contributions to Political Economy* 32, no. 1: 29–50.

Paul, Ron. 2009. *End the Fed.* New York: Grand Central.

Pauly, Louis. 1997. *Who Elected the Bankers? Surveillance and Control in the World Economy.* Ithaca, NY: Cornell University Press.

Piroska, Dóra 2004. "Internalization of Global Norms by Post-Socialist States: Institutional Analysis of Banking Sector Regulation in Hungary and Slovenia." Paper presented at the Workshop on Efficiency, Competition and Regulation in Banking: Theory and Evidence, Sulzbach-Rosenberg, June 4–5.

Pixley, Jocelyn, Sam Whimster, and Shaun Wilson. 2013. "Central Bank Independence: A Social Economic and Democratic Critique." *Economic and Labour Relations Review* 24, no. 1: 32–50.

Poenisch, Herbert. 1991. "The New Central Banks of Eastern Europe." *Central Banking Journal* 1, no. 4: 9–20.

Polillo, Simone, and Mauro Guillen. 2005. "Globalization Pressures and the State: The Worldwide Spread of Central Bank Independence." *American Journal of Sociology* 110, no. 6: 1764–802.

"The Politics of Central Banking in East Europe." 1991–92. *Central Banking Journal* 2, no. 3: 8–11.

Pomfret, Richard. 1995. *The Economies of Central Asia.* Princeton, NJ: Princeton University Press.

Posen, Adam. 1995. "Declarations Are Not Enough: Financial Sector Sources of Central Bank Independence." *NBER Macroeconomics Annual.* Cambridge: MIT Press.

Pospíšil, Jiří. 1997. "Inflation and the Independence of a Central Bank—Have We Had Any Experience in the Czech Republic?" *Eastern European Economics* 35, no. 2: 21–28.

Pringle, Robert, ed. 1996. *Morgan Stanley Central Bank Directory.* London: Central Banking Publications.

——. 2004. *Morgan Stanley Central Bank Directory.* London: Central Banking Publications.

Prostiakov, Igor. 1998. "Economic Reform in the Interregnum between Andropov and Gorbachev-Ryzhkov." In *The Destruction of the Soviet Economic System: An Insiders' History,* ed. Michael Ellman and Vladimir Kontorovich, 100–116. Armonk, NY: M.E. Sharpe.

Quaglia, Lucia. 2005. "An Integrative Approach to the Politics of Central Bank Independence: Lessons from Britain, Germany, and Italy." *West European Politics* 28, no. 3: 549–68.

Radzyner, Olga, and Sandra Riesinger. 1997. "Central Bank Independence in Transition." *Focus on Transition,* no. 1: 57–91.

Rel'ovský, Branislav. 2004. "Time Inconsistency in Monetary Policy." *BIATEC* 12, no. 10: 13–19.

Riecke, Werner, and László Antal. 1993. "Hungary: Sound Money, Fiscal Problems." In *Economic Transformation in Central Europe: A Progress Report,* ed. Richard Portes, 107–30. Budapest: Centre for Economic Policy and Research.

Risse-Kappen, Thomas. 1994. "Ideas Do Not Float Freely: Transnational Coalitions, Domestic Structures, and the End of the Cold War." *International Organization* 48, no. 2: 185–214.

Roaf, James, Ruben Atoyan, Bikas Joshi, Krzysztof Krogulski, and an IMF staff team. 2014. *Post-Communist Europe and the IMF: Regional Economic Issues Special Report.* Washington, DC: International Monetary Fund.

Rogers, Everett. 1995. *The Diffusion of Innovation.* New York: Free Press.

Rogoff, Kenneth. 1985. "The Optimal Degree of Commitment to an Intermediate Monetary Target." *Quarterly Journal of Economics* 100, no. 4: 1169–89.

Rose, Richard. 2002. "Ten Steps in Learning Lessons from Abroad." Robert Schuman Centre Working Paper 2002/5. European University Institute.

Sapir, Jacques. 1999. "Russia's Crash of August 1998: Diagnosis and Prescription." *Post-Soviet Affairs* 15, no. 1: 1–36.

———. 2010. "What Should Russian Monetary Policy Be?" *Post-Soviet Affairs* 26, no. 4: 342–72.

Sayers, R.S. 1976. *The Bank of England 1891–1944, Volume 3*. London: Cambridge University Press.

Schadler, Susan, Paulo Drummond, Louis Kuijs, Zuzana Murgasova, and Rachel van Elkan. 2005. *Adopting the Euro in Central Europe: Challenges of the Next Step in European Integration*. Washington, DC: International Monetary Fund.

Schaechter, Andrea, Mark R. Stone, and Mark Zelmer. 2000. "Adopting Inflation Targeting: Practical Issues for Emerging Market Countries." Occasional Paper No. 202. International Monetary Fund.

Schatz, Edward. 2006. "Access by Accident: Legitimacy Claims and Democracy Promotion in Authoritarian Central Asia." *International Political Science Review* 27, no. 3: 263–84.

———. 2009. "The Soft Authoritarian 'Tool Kit': Agenda-Setting Power in Kazakhstan and Kyrgyzstan." *Comparative Politics* 41, no. 2: 203–22.

Schoors, K. 2002. "Should the Central and Eastern European Accession Countries Adopt the Euro before or after Accession?" *Economics of Planning* 35, no. 1: 47–77.

Sheppard, Eric. 2002. "The Spaces and Times of Globalization: Place, Scale, Networks, and Positionality." *Economic Geography* 78, no. 3: 307–30.

Shigehara, Kumiharu, and Paul E. Atkinson. 2011. "Surveillance by International Institutions: Lessons from the Global Financial and Economic Crisis." Working Paper No. 860. Organisation for Economic Cooperation and Development.

Sidorova, E.E. 2011. "Global Currency System: A Road to Stabilization." *Studies on Russian Economic Development* 22, no. 5: 540–43.

Siklos, Pierre. 1994. "Central Bank Independence in the Transitional Economies: A Preliminary Investigation of Hungary, Poland, the Czech and Slovak Republics." In *The Development and Reform of Financial Systems in Central and Eastern Europe*, ed. John Bonin and István P. Székely, 71–98. Brookfield, VT: Edward Elgar.

Simmons, Beth. 2001. "The International Politics of Harmonization: The Case of Capital Market Regulation." *International Organization* 55, no. 3: 589–620.

———. 2006. "The Future of Central Bank Cooperation." Working Paper No. 200. Bank for International Settlements.

Simmons, Beth, and Zachary Elkins. 2004. "The Globalization of Liberalization: Policy Diffusion in the International Political Economy." *American Political Science Review* 98, no. 1: 171–89.

Singleton, John. 2010. *Central Banking in the Twentieth Century*. Cambridge: Cambridge University Press.

Slay, Ben. 1999. "An Interpretation of the Russian Financial Crisis." *Post-Soviet Geography and Economics* 40, no. 3: 206–14.

Šmídková, Kateřina, and Miroslav Hrnčíř. 1998. "Transition to the Inflation Targeting Strategy." *Finance a úvěr* 48, no. 4: 205–22.

Sobek, Otto. 2003. "Ten Years of the National Bank of Slovakia." *BIATEC* 9, no. 1: 8–10.

Special correspondent. 1994/5. "The Russian Central Bank: A Quiet Revolution." *Central Banking Journal* 5, no. 3: 78–84.

Šramko, Ivan. 2008. "Slovakia's Road to the Euro—Lessons Learned and Challenges Ahead." In *Currency and Competitiveness in Europe*, ed. Klaus Liebscher, Josef Christl, Peter Mooslechner, and Doris Ritzberger-Grünwald, 288–95. Cheltenham, UK: Edward Elgar.

Stallings, Barbara. 1992. "International Influences on Economic Policy: Debt, Stabilization, and Structural Reform." In *The Politics of Economic Adjustment*, ed. Stephen Haggard and Robert Kaufman, 41–88. Princeton, NJ: Princeton University Press.

Statistics Department. 2001. "Hungary: Report on the Observance of Standards and Codes (ROSC) Data Module." Washington, DC: International Monetary Fund.

Stiglitz, Joseph. 1998. "Central Banking in a Democratic Society." *De Economist* 146, no. 2: 199–226.

Stoliarenko, Vladimir Mikhailovich. 1999. *Tsentral'nyi Bank kak organ gosudarstvennoi vlasti* [The Central Bank as an organ of state power]. Moscow.

Stone, Diane. 2012. "Transfer and Translation of Policy." *Policy Studies* 33, no. 6: 483–99.

Stone, Randall. 2002. *Lending Credibility: The International Monetary Fund and the Post-Communist Transition*. Princeton, NJ: Princeton University Press.

Strang, David, and Sarah Soule. 1998. "Diffusion in Organizations and Social Movements: From Hybrid Corn to Poison Pills." *Annual Review of Sociology* 24: 265–90.

Strange, Susan. 1986. *Casino Capitalism*. Oxford: Blackwell.

Sundararajan, Vasudevan, Arne B. Petersen, and Gabriel Sensenbrenner. 1997. *Central Bank Reform in the Transition Economies*. Washington, DC: International Monetary Fund.

Surányi, György, and János Vincze. 1998. "Inflation in Hungary, 1990–97." In *Moderate Inflation: The Experience of Transition Economies*, ed. Carlo Cottarelli and György Szapáry, 150–70. Washington, DC: International Monetary Fund.

Szapáry, György. 1997. "The National Bank of Hungary: From Cradle to Adulthood Whilst Striving for Independence." In *Rebuilding the Financial System in Central and Eastern Europe, 1918–1994*, ed. Philip L. Cottrell, 17–27. Aldershot, UK: Ashgate.

——. 2002. "Banking Sector Reform in Hungary: What Have We Learned and What Are the Prospects?" *Comparative Economic Studies* 44, no. 2–3: 103–24.

Szilágyi, Katalin, Dániel Baksa, Jaromir Benes, Ágnes Horváth, Csaba Köber, and Gábor D. Soós. 2013. "The Hungarian Monetary Policy Model." MNB Working Paper no. 2013/01. Magyar Nemzeti Bank.

Tardos, Á. 1991. "Problems of the Financial Information System in Hungary." *Acta Oeconomica* 43, nos. 1–2: 149–66.

Taylor, John B. 2000. "Teaching Modern Macroeconomics at the Principles Level." *American Economic Review* 90, no. 2: 90–94.

——. 2007. *Global Financial Warriors: The Untold Story of International Finance in the Post-9/11 World*. New York: W.W. Norton.

Thelen, Kathleen. 2003. "How Institutions Evolve: Insights from Comparative Historical Analysis." In *Comparative Historical Analysis in the Social Sciences*, ed. James Mahoney and Dietrich Rueschemeyer, 208–40. Cambridge, UK: Cambridge University Press.

Thornton, Daniel L. 2012. "The Dual Mandate: Has the Fed Changed Its Objective?" *Federal Reserve Bank of St. Louis Review* 94, no. 2: 117–34.

Tognato, Carlo. 2012. *Central Bank Independence: Cultural Codes and Symbolic Performance*. New York: Palgrave Macmillan.

Tompson, William. 1998a. "The Politics of Central Bank Independence in Russia." *Europe-Asia Studies* 50, no. 7: 1157–82.

——. 1998b. "Russia's 'Ministry of Cash': Sberbank in Transition." *Communist Economies and Economic Transformation* 10, no. 2: 133–55.

Tosunian, Garegin. 1995. *Bankovskoe delo i bankovskoe zakonodatel'stvo v Rossii: Opyt, problemy, perspektivy* [Banking affairs and banking law in Russia: Experience, problems, and perspectives]. Moscow: Akademiia narodnogo khoziaistva.

True, Jacqui, and Michael Mintrom. 2001. "Transnational Networks and Policy Diffusion: The Case of Gender Mainstreaming." *International Studies Quarterly* 45, no. 1: 27–57.

Tsingou, Eleni, Andrew Baker, and Leonard Seabrooke. 2015. "Jackson Hole and Expert Networks in Economic Governance." Paper presented at the International Studies Association annual meeting, New Orleans, February.

Turnovec, František. 2002. "Economics—Czech Republic." In *Three Social Science Disciplines in Central and Eastern Europe: Handbook on Economics, Political Science and Sociology (1989–2001)*, ed. Max Kaase and Vera Sparschuh. Berlin, Bonn, and Budapest: GESIS.

US General Accounting Office. 2000. *Foreign Assistance: International Efforts to Aid Russia's Transition Have Had Mixed Results*. Washington, DC: GAO.

Vachudova, Milada. 2005. *Europe Undivided: Democracy, Leverage, and Integration after Communism*. Oxford: Oxford University Press.

Valach, Vladimír. 2004. "44 Years in Banking, Part 3." *BIATEC* 12, no. 4: 19–22.

———. 2005. "44 Years in Banking, Part 4." *BIATEC* 13, no. 3: 22–24.

Várhegyi, Éva. 1996. "The Selection of Bank Managers in Hungary in the 80s and 90s." *Szociológiai Szemle*, vols. 3–4.

Velek, Jan. 1996. "An Evaluation of the Post-War Activities of the Czechoslovak State Bank (from 1950 to 1989)." In *A Collection of Lectures from the Conference in Honour of the 70th Anniversary of Central Banking in the Czech Republic*, 15–27. Prague: Czech National Bank.

Verdun, Amy. 1998. "The Increased Influence of EU Monetary Institutions in Determining National Policies: A Transnational Monetary Elite at Work." In *Autonomous Policy Making by International Organizations*, ed. Bob Reinalda and Bertjan Verbeek, 178–94. London and New York: Routledge.

Viñals, José, and Penelope Brooke. 2009. *The Financial Sector Assessment Program after Ten Years: Experience and Reforms for the Next Decade*. Washington, DC: International Monetary Fund.

Vintrová, Růžena. 2004. "The CEE Countries on the Way into the EU—Adjustment Problems: Institutional Adjustment, Real and Nominal Convergence." *Europe-Asia Studies* 56, no. 4: 521–41.

Wagner, Helmut. 1998. "Central Banking in Transition Countries." Working Paper 98/126. International Monetary Fund.

Walter, Andrew. 2008. *Governing Finance: East Asia's Adoption of International Standards*. Ithaca, NY: Cornell University Press.

Watson, Max. 2004. "Challenges for Central Banks in the New Member States." In *EU Enlargement and the Future of the Euro*, ed. Robert Pringle and Nick Carver, 53–63. London: Central Banking Publications.

Wedel, Janine. 1998. *Collision and Collusion: The Strange Case of Western Aid to Eastern Europe, 1989–1998*. New York: St. Martin's Press.

Weyland, Kurt. 2006. *Bounded Rationality and Policy Diffusion: Social Sector Reform in Latin America*. Princeton, NJ: Princeton University Press.

Woodruff, David. 1999. *Money Unmade: Barter and the Fate of Russian Capitalism*. Ithaca, NY: Cornell University Press.

Woods, Ngaire. 2006. *The Globalizers: The IMF, the World Bank, and Their Borrowers*. Ithaca, NY: Cornell University Press.

World Bank. 1993. *Kyrgyzstan: The Transition to a Market Economy*. Washington, DC: World Bank.

——. 2001. *Kyrgyz Republic: Country Assistance Evaluation*. Washington, DC: World Bank.

Wriston, Walter. 1992. *The Twilight of Sovereignty: How the Information Revolution Is Transforming Our World*. New York: Scribner.

Yasin, Yevgenii. 1998a. "Getting the Details Wrong." In *The Destruction of the Soviet Economic System: An Insiders' History*, ed. Michael Ellman and Vladimir Kontorovich, 143–53. Armonk, NY: M.E. Sharpe.

——. 1998b. "The Parade of Market Transformation Programs." In *The Destruction of the Soviet Economic System: An Insiders' History*, ed. Michael Ellman and Vladimir Kontorovich, 228–37. Armonk, NY: M.E. Sharpe.

Yudaeva, Ksenia. 2014. "O vozmozhnostiakh, tseliakh i mekhahizmakh denezhno-kreditnoi politiki v tekushchei situatsii [On the Opportunities, Targets and Mechanisms of Monetary Policy under the Current Conditions]. *Voprosii ekonomiki*, no. 9: 1–9.

Zulu, J.B., Ian McCarthy, Susana Almuina, and Gabriel Sensenbrener, eds. 1994. *Central Banking Technical Assistance to Countries in Transition*. Washington, DC: International Monetary Fund.

Index